D1760674

The Law and Ethics of Medicine

THE LAW AND ETHICS OF MEDICINE

Essays on the Inviolability of Human Life

John Keown MA DPhil PhD

Rose F Kennedy Professor of Christian Ethics
Kennedy Institute of Ethics
Georgetown University

OXFORD
UNIVERSITY PRESS

OXFORD
UNIVERSITY PRESS

Great Clarendon Street, Oxford, OX2 6DP,
United Kingdom

Oxford University Press is a department of the University of Oxford.
It furthers the University's objective of excellence in research, scholarship,
and education by publishing worldwide. Oxford is a registered trade mark of
Oxford University Press in the UK and in certain other countries

© J Keown, 2012

The moral rights of the author have been asserted

First Edition published in 2012

Impression: 1

All rights reserved. No part of this publication may be reproduced, stored in
a retrieval system, or transmitted, in any form or by any means, without the
prior permission in writing of Oxford University Press, or as expressly permitted
by law, by licence or under terms agreed with the appropriate reprographics
rights organization. Enquiries concerning reproduction outside the scope of the
above should be sent to the Rights Department, Oxford University Press, at the
address above

You must not circulate this work in any other form
and you must impose this same condition on any acquirer

Crown copyright material is reproduced under Class Licence
Number C01P0000148 with the permission of OPSI
and the Queen's Printer for Scotland

British Library Cataloguing in Publication Data
Data available

Library of Congress Cataloging in Publication Data
Library of Congress Control Number: 2012934401

ISBN 978–0–19–958955–5

Printed and bound by CPI Group (UK) Ltd,
Croydon, CR0 4YY

Links to third party websites are provided by Oxford in good faith and
for information only. Oxford disclaims any responsibility for the materials
contained in any third party website referenced in this work.

BLACKBURN COLLEGE
LIBRARY

Acc. No BB46458

Class No. UCL 344.0419 KEO

Date 11 · 10 · 2013

To John Finnis and Luke Gormally

ACKNOWLEDGMENTS

While much of the material in this book is original, a number of chapters were previously published as articles, though all have undergone at least minor revision.

Chapter 2 originally appeared as "Surveying the Foundations of Medical Law: A Reassessment of Glanville Williams's *The Sanctity of Life and the Criminal Law*" (2008) 16(1) Medical Law Review 85; Chapter 4 as "Restoring the Inviolability of Life and Replacing the Caricature: A Reply to David Price" (2006) 26(1) Legal Studies 109; Chapter 5 as "Back to the Future of Abortion Law: *Roe*'s Rejection of America's History and Traditions" (2006) 22(1) Issues in Law & Medicine 3; Chapter 6 as "'Morning after' pills, 'miscarriage' and muddle" (2005) 2 Legal Studies 296; Chapter 7 as "The Scope of the Offence of Child Destruction" (1988) 104 Law Quarterly Review 120; Chapter 10 as "Mr Marty's Muddle: A Selective and Superficial Case for Euthanasia in Europe" (2006) 32(1) Journal of Medical Ethics 29, "Death in Strasbourg: assisted suicide, the *Pretty* case and the European Convention on Human Rights" (2003) 1(4) International Journal of Constitutional Law 722, "In Need of Assistance?" (2009) 159 New Law Journal 1340, and "Dangerous Guidance" (2009) 159 New Law Journal 1718; Chapter 12 as "Restoring Moral and Intellectual Shape to the Law after *Bland*" (1997) 113 Law Quarterly Review 481 and "A Futile Defence of *Bland*: A Reply to Andrew McGee" (2005) 13(3) Medical Law Review 393. Chapter 9 is based on a booklet commissioned by the Carenotkilling Alliance entitled *Considering Physician-Assisted Suicide: An Evaluation of Lord Joffe's Assisted Dying for the Terminally Ill Bill* (2006) which in turn anticipated "Physician-Assisted Suicide: Lord Joffe's Slippery Bill" (2007) 15(1) Medical Law Review 126.

I am grateful to the editors of the above journals and to the publishers of the above material for permission to reproduce it here. Chapter 2 was originally published as an article co-authored with Professor David Albert Jones, Director of the Anscombe Bioethics Centre, Oxford. I am grateful for his permission to use it in this volume.

I should also like to thank the students who assisted me with the reformatting of the articles, particularly Ms Elizabeth Gresk, Ms Laura Guidry-Grimes, and Ms Anne Langhorne. I am also grateful to Mr David

Wills, Squire Law Librarian in the University of Cambridge, for his generous help tracking down legal materials.

Finally, I should like to thank Mr Alex Flach and Mrs Natasha Flemming of Oxford University Press.

CONTENTS

TABLE OF CASES

TABLE OF STATUTES

LIST OF ABBREVIATIONS

ALDU	Association of Lawyers for the Defence of the Unborn
APS	American Pain Society
BMA	British Medical Association
DPP	Director of Public Prosecutions
DWDA	Death with Dignity Act (Oregon)
FGM	female genital mutilation
HFEA 1990	Human Fertilisation and Embryology Act 1990
HMO	health maintenance organization
IOL	inviolability of life
IUD	intrauterine device
IVAE	involuntary, active euthanasia
IVF	in vitro fertilization
KNMG	Royal Dutch Medical Association
MAP	morning after pill
MCS	minimally conscious state
NVAE	non-voluntary, active euthanasia
NYSTF	New York State Task Force
OAPA 1861	Offences Against the Person Act 1861
OBME	Oregon Board of Medical Examiners
OHA	Oregon Health Authority
OMA	Oregon Medical Association
PAS	physician-assisted suicide
PRO	Public Record Office
PVS	persistent vegetative state
QOL	Quality of life
SLCL	GL Williams, *The Sanctity of Life and the Criminal Law*
SPUC	Society for the Protection of Unborn Children
VAE	voluntary, active euthanasia

INTRODUCTION

The Law and Ethics of Medicine seeks to clarify a fundamental legal principle, the "sanctity" or "inviolability" of human life, in the medical context. The book is aimed primarily at academic lawyers specializing in medical or health law and their students, though it should also be of use to legal practitioners who deal with medico-legal cases, and to judges who decide them. It is concerned mainly with the law in England and Wales but, as the inviolability of life is a foundational principle throughout the common law world (and beyond), lawyers in other jurisdictions may also find it of interest. The book may also appeal to legislators and policy makers, health care professionals, moral philosophers, and general readers interested in bioethical questions concerning the value of human life.

The book's focus is modest. It is not a textbook. It does not attempt a comprehensive analysis of the law concerning the inviolability of human life, even in the medical context. It deals only with selected medico-legal aspects of the principle. Still less does the book attempt a comprehensive moral-philosophical articulation and defense of the principle. There is already a rich and accessible literature which explores the principle and gives a thorough account of its application to vexed issues such as research on human embryos in vitro,[1] abortion,[2] and euthanasia.[3] Chapter 1 does, however, offer a basic outline of the principle and sketches the extent to which it has shaped aspects of the law in the medical context, particularly at the end of life. Some key concepts and distinctions are noted, which are revisited at various points in the book.

---

[1] Eg RP George and C Tollefsen, *Embryo: A Defense of Human Life* (2nd edn, The Witherspoon Institute, 2011).

[2] Eg C Kazcor, *The Ethics of Abortion: Women's Rights, Human Life and the Question of Justice* (Routledge, 2010); P Lee, *Abortion and Unborn Human Life* (2nd edn, Catholic University of America Press, 2010); GG Grisez, *Abortion: The Myths, The Realities and the Arguments* (Corpus Books, 1970).

[3] Eg L Gormally (ed), *Euthanasia, Clinical Practice and the Law* (St Augustine Press, 1994); G Grisez and J Boyle, *Life and Death with Liberty and Justice* (University of Notre Dame Press, 1979); FJ Fitzpatrick, *Ethics in Nursing Practice* (The Linacre Centre, 1988). For a combined theological and philosophical discussion of the principle see A Fisher, *Catholic Bioethics for a New Millennium* (Cambridge University Press, 2011). For the case that the principle, outside the medical context, also prohibits the possession of nuclear weapons see J Finnis et al, *Nuclear Deterrence, Morality and Realism* (Clarendon Press, 1988).

The central theme of the book is that, although the inviolability of life has long been a foundational principle of the law, it remains widely misunderstood by lawyers and judges and that, in no small measure as a result, the law has become, in several important respects, "morally and intellectually misshapen."[4] The book seeks to identify some of the main misunderstandings and thereby help restore the law's shape. For example, it points out that while the principle is opposed to intentionally taking the lives of patients, it does not require (as is often supposed) that their lives be preserved at all costs. The principle is not, then, "vitalist." Nor is it "religious" (by which its critics mean that it can only be defended as a matter of religious faith and not secular reason.) Nor is it "speciesist": it does not exclude rational beings with free will (if any) who are not members of our species.[5] In short, the main goal of *The Law and Ethics of Medicine* is elucidation of the fundamental legal principle of the inviolability of human life in the medical context. It should be of interest to any reader seeking a better understanding of the principle, whether or not he or she subscribes to its ethical basis.

The book is divided into three parts. Part I outlines the ethical principle and its influence on the law and illustrates the misunderstanding of the principle in the work of academic medical lawyers, incuding two of the founding figures of the discipline.

Part II addresses aspects of the beginning of life. It considers the instantiation of the principle by Anglo-American law in its historic prohibition of abortion, first by the common law, and then by nineteenth-century statutes. As we shall see, these statutes were passed at the instigation of physicians who pressed for their enactment to protect human life from conception and to prohibit what they openly called "murder." Chapter 5 contends that the decision of the United States Supreme Court in *Roe v Wade*, creating a constitutional right to abortion, was gravely flawed by its misreading of that history. Chapter 6 argues that the decision of the English High Court in *Smeaton*, that section 58 of the Offences against the Person Act 1861 does not prohibit the administration of the "morning after" pill with intent to prevent the implantation of an embryo, was another instance of judicial misreading of the nineteenth-century legislation's core purpose. Chapter 7 traces the tightening of the law by the Infant Life (Preservation) Act in 1929 to protect the

---

[4] To borrow an apt phrase used by Lord Mustill in *Airedale NHS Trust v Bland* [1993] AC 789, 887.

[5] The book does not discuss the moral status of non-human life. Suffice it to say here that the principle of the inviolability of human life does not imply that human beings have no moral responsibilities in respect of animals.

unborn "child capable of being born alive" and offers an interpretation of that phrase drawing largely on relevant historical materials. All three chapters show the extent to which an understanding of the law's historic purpose of protecting human life from its beginning can valuably inform our contemporary understanding and interpretation of the law. One contemporary issue concerns the legal status of the human embryo in vitro. Chapter 8 addresses the question whether the embryo in vitro should be classified in law as a person or as property. It contends that the case advanced by most commentators and courts for classifying the embryo outside the womb as property, a case based largely on the fact that the civil law does not regard the child in the womb as a person, is unconvincing, not least because it is again difficult to square with the criminal law's traditional goal of protecting all human beings from attack, before as well as after birth.

Part III deals with a number of issues at the end of life. Probably no legislative body worldwide has done more to contribute to the ongoing debate about the decriminalization of euthanasia than the House of Lords. The focus of Chapter 9 is the evidence it has gathered about the practice of euthanasia in the Netherlands and physician-assisted suicide in Oregon. Chapter 10 turns to the euthanasia debate in Europe. It critically analyzes a report of a committee of the Council of Europe which unsuccessfully argued for reversal of the Council's opposition to euthanasia; the decision of the European Court of Human Rights in the *Pretty* case, affirming English law's blanket ban on assisting suicide; and the decision of the Law Lords in the *Purdy* case which, remarkably, undermined that ban. Chapter 11 argues that the euthanasia debate has proved a regrettable distraction from the pressing need to improve the availability of palliative care, and considers whether there is not both an ethical and legal duty to provide such care. It shows that, the inviolability of life not being "vitalistic," both sound ethics and good law permit palliative care even in the unlikely event of death being hastened as an unintended side-effect of such care. Chapter 12 analyzes the landmark *Bland* case, concerning the lawfulness of withdrawing tube-feeding from a patient in PVS. *Bland*, in reaffirming the law's prohibition on intentionally killing the patient by an act, but in allowing him or her to be intentionally killed by dehydration, is the paradigm example of a misunderstanding of the inviolability of life leaving the law in a "morally and intellectually misshapen" state. The chapter replies to an academic defense of the decision, a defense which illustrates some of misunderstandings of the inviolability of life encountered in Part I.

In sum, although the inviolability of life is a historic and foundational principle of the law, *The Law and Ethics of Medicine* will contend that its meaning and application in the medical context have been, and remain, seriously misunderstood in the legal academy, at the Bar, on the Bench, and beyond. If this volume provides some measure of clarification, it will have served its purpose.

The views expressed in this book are those of the author and do not necessarily reflect those of Georgetown University.

Part One

(Mis)understanding the Inviolability of Life

CHAPTER 1

THE "SANCTITY OF LIFE," "BEST INTERESTS," AND "AUTONOMY": AN OVERVIEW

I INTRODUCTION

The "sanctity" or "inviolability of life" is, as has been repeatedly judicially affirmed,[1] a fundamental principle of the common law. Since the phrase "sanctity of life," though judicially hallowed, may have distracting theological connotations, "inviolability of life" (IOL) will be used hereafter. The doctrine and the principle of the IOL were originally formulated by theologians, but can stand on purely philosophical grounds. In *Re A*, the "Conjoined Twins" case, Brooke LJ referred to a brief the court had received from the Archbishop of Westminster. The brief referred to a number of "overarching moral considerations," the first of which was: "Human life is sacred, that is inviolable, so one should never aim to cause an innocent person's death by act or omission."[2] Brooke LJ observed:

There can, of course, be no doubt that our common law judges were steeped in the Judaeo-Christian tradition and in the moral principles identified by the Archbishop when they were developing our criminal law over the centuries up to the time when Parliament took over the task. There can also be no doubt that it was these principles, shared as they were by the other founder members of the Council of Europe 50 years ago, which underlay the formulation of article 2 of the European Convention on Human Rights.[3]

---

[1] See text at n 11.
[2] *Re A* [2001] Fam 147, 211. The IOL has historically been formulated in terms of the wrongness of intentionally taking "innocent" life. "Innocent" excludes anyone actively contributing to unjust aggression. The principle has, therefore, traditionally allowed the use of lethal force in self-defense, the prosecution of a just war, and the execution of capital offenders. This has little relevance to doctor-patient context, which is the concern of this book.
[3] Ibid 212.

The principle appears, accordingly, in declarations on human rights as the "right to life." Indeed, a prohibition on intentional killing is central to the pre-Christian fount of Western medical ethics, the Hippocratic Oath[4] (and the modern reaffirmation of that Oath by the Declaration of Geneva[5]), and many non-believers recognize the right of human beings not to be intentionally killed.[6]

Although foundational to the common law, the IOL has rarely if ever been accurately formulated—put in propositional form—either in judicial decisions or in textbooks on medical/health law. Precisely what it involves is, indeed, mired in confusion, in the academy, at the Bar, and on the Bench. This introductory chapter seeks to outline the principle, summarize its relevance to the law governing medical decision-making at the end of life, and sketch its implications for the important concepts of "best interests" and "autonomy."

II THREE COMPETING APPROACHES
TO THE VALUATION OF HUMAN LIFE

There are three main, competing approaches to the valuation of human life.

A Vitalism

Human life is the *supreme* good and one should do everything possible to preserve it. The core principle, therefore, is: "try to maintain the life of each patient at all costs." Whether the life be that of an anencephalic newborn (one lacking the cerebral hemispheres) or a dying centenarian, vitalism prohibits its shortening and requires its preservation. Regardless of the pain, suffering, or expense that life-prolonging treatment entails, it must be administered: human life is to be preserved at all costs. Vitalism is as ethically untenable as its attempt to maintain life indefinitely is physically impossible. Its error lies in isolating the genuine and basic good of human life, and the duty to respect and promote that good, from the network of standards and responsibilities which make up our ethics and

---

[4] "To please no-one will I prescribe a deadly drug, nor give advice which may cause his death. Nor will I give a woman a pessary to procure abortion.": JK Mason and RA McCall Smith, *Law and Medical Ethics* (4th edn, Oxford University Press, 1994) 429.

[5] "I will maintain the utmost respect for human life from the time of conception; even under threat, I will not use my medical knowledge contrary to the laws of humanity.": ibid 430.

[6] A prohibition on killing is not, of course, exclusive to Western ethics. See D Keown, *Buddhism and Bioethics* (Macmillan/St Martins Press, 1995).

law as a whole; and its neglect of concepts and distinctions (such as between intention and foresight) vital to that network.

B "Quality of life" (QOL)

On this approach, there is nothing supremely or even inherently valuable about the life of a human being. The dignity of human life, such as it is, is only as an *instrumental* good, a vehicle or platform for a "worthwhile" life, a life whose value resides in meeting a particular "quality" threshold (howsoever defined). The lives of certain patients fall below this threshold, not least because of disease, injury, or disability. This valuation of human life grounds the principle that, because certain lives are not worth living, it is right intentionally to terminate them, whether by act or omission. A core principle, therefore, is: "one may try to extinguish the life of a patient which is of such poor quality as to be not worth living." (Many of those who adopt this approach also believe that only a sub-set of human beings, those who meet a criterion such as a particular level of intellectual ability, qualify as "persons.")

C The inviolability of life

Human life is a *basic, intrinsic* good. All human beings possess, in virtue of their common humanity, an inherent, inalienable, and ineliminable dignity. The dignity of human beings inheres because of the radical capacities, such as for understanding, rational choice, and free will, inherent in human nature. Some human beings, such as infants, may not yet possess the ability to exercise these radical capacities. But radical capacities must not be confused with abilities. We may have the radical capacity to speak Swahili but not the ability to do so. All human beings possess the capacities inherent in their nature even though, because of infancy, disability, or senility, they may not yet, not now, or no longer have the ability to exercise them.[7]

The right not to be killed is enjoyed regardless of inability or disability. Our dignity does not depend on our having a particular intellectual ability or having it to a particular degree. Any such distinctions are fundamentally arbitrary and inconsistent with a sound concept of justice:

[E]very human being, however immature or mentally impaired, possesses a fundamental worth and dignity which are not lost as long as he or she is alive. Contrary to the view of some, human worth and dignity do not depend on acquiring and retaining some particular level of intellectual ability or capacity

---

[7] L Gormally (ed.), *Euthanasia, Clinical Practice and the Law* (St Augustine Press, 1994) 118–19.

for choice or for communication. On that view of human worth and dignity, it turns out that the relevant level of intellectual ability (or whatever other characteristic is asserted to be morally decisive) always requires to be determined in an arbitrary fashion. In making the possession of human worth and dignity depend on an arbitrary discrimination between individuals, this view destroys the indispensable foundation of justice in society. For basic human rights belong to us precisely because of our worth and dignity, and if our possession of the latter is to be determined arbitrarily so will be our possession of the former. But there cannot be a framework conducive to just relationships in a society if *who are to count as the subjects of justice* is determined in an arbitrary fashion. That is why recognition of the fundamental worth and dignity of *every* human being is the indispensable foundation of justice in society.[8]

Human life is not, then, only an instrumental good, a necessary precondition of thinking or choosing or doing, but a basic good, a fundamental constituent of human flourishing. It is, in other words, not merely good as a means to an end but is, like other integral aspects of a flourishing human life, like friendship and the appreciation of beauty, something worthwhile in itself. Of course some people, like those who are pictures of health in the prime of life, participate in the good of life and health to a greater extent than others, such as the terminally ill, but even the sick and the dying participate in the good to the extent that they are able.

Although life is a basic good it is not an absolute good, a good to which all the other basic goods must be sacrificed in order to ensure its preservation. The IOL doctrine is not vitalistic. The core of the doctrine is the principle prohibiting intentional killing, not an injunction requiring the preservation of life at all costs. The core principle is: "it is always wrong to try to extinguish a patient's life." Although the doctrine denies that human life is an absolute good, the principle that it may never intentionally be taken is an absolute principle, that is, one which has no acceptable exceptions. Although the value of human life is not absolute, the prohibition on taking it is. The core principle prohibits trying to kill, but the IOL also prohibits exposing life to unreasonable risk. It is wrong to take life not only intentionally but also recklessly or negligently.

To sum up, the doctrine of the IOL holds that we all share, in virtue of our common humanity, an ineliminable dignity. This dignity grounds our "right to life." The principle of the IOL holds in essence that it is wrong to try to extinguish life.

---

[8] J Keown and L Gormally, "Human Dignity, Autonomy and Mentally-Incapacitated Patients: A Critique of *Who Decides?*" (1999) 4 Web Journal of Current Legal Issues Part II (emphasis in original) <http://www.wjcli.ncl.ac.uk>.

III MAIN FEATURES OF THE IOL AND THEIR INFLUENCE ON THE COMMON LAW

A *Ineliminable dignity*

The ineliminable equality-in-dignity of human beings has long been recognized by the common law and by international declarations on human rights. As the Preamble to the Universal Declaration of Human Rights proclaims: "recognition of the inherent dignity and of the equal and inalienable rights of all members of the human family is the foundation of freedom, justice and peace in the world."[9] Inherent human dignity is a core value of English law:

The recognition and protection of human dignity is one of the core values—in truth *the* core value—of our society and, indeed, of all the societies which are part of the European family of nations and which have embraced the principles of the Convention. It is a core value of the common law, long pre-dating the Convention and the Charter [of Fundamental Rights of the European Union]. The invocation of the dignity of the patient in the form of declaration habitually used when the court is exercising its inherent declaratory jurisdiction in relation to the gravely ill or dying is not some meaningless incantation designed to comfort the living or to assuage the consciences of those involved in making life and death decisions: it is a solemn affirmation of the law's and of society's recognition of our humanity and of human dignity as something fundamental.[10]

Just as inherent dignity is a core value of English law, so is the principle of the IOL which is grounded in it. As Lord Goff observed in *Airedale NHS Trust v Bland*:

[T]he fundamental principle [in this case] is the principle of the sanctity of human life—a principle long recognised not only in our own society but also in most, if not all, civilised societies throughout the modern world, as is indeed evidenced by its recognition both in article 2 of the European Convention for the Protection of Human Rights and Fundamental Freedoms 1953...and in article 6 of the International Covenant of Civil and Political Rights 1966.[11]

Article 2(1) of the European Convention on Human Rights provides:

Everyone's right to life shall be protected by law. No one shall be deprived of his life intentionally save in the execution of a sentence of a court following his conviction of a crime for which this penalty is provided by law.

---

[9] See <http://www.un.org/en/documents/udhr/>.

[10] *R (A) v East Sussex County Council (No 2)* [2003] EWHC 167 (Admin) para 86, per Munby J (as he then was) (emphasis in original).

[11] [1993] AC 789, 863–4.

The prohibition on intentional killing was aptly described by the House of Lords Select Committee on Medical Ethics in 1994 ("the Walton Committee") as "the cornerstone of law and of social relationships" which "protects each one of us impartially, embodying the belief that all are equal."[12] The prohibition applies even if a patient is suffering, even if the doctor's motive is compassionate, even if the patient is close to death, and even if the patient autonomously requests a lethal injection. In *Bland* Lord Goff observed:

[I]t is not lawful for a doctor to administer a drug to his patient to bring about his death, even though that course is prompted by a humanitarian desire to end his suffering, however great that suffering may be…So to act is to cross the Rubicon which runs between on the one hand the care of the living patient and on the other hand euthanasia—actively causing his death to avoid or to end his suffering. Euthanasia is not lawful at common law.[13]

Nor is the law concerned to prohibit only active intentional killing. Although there is generally no liability for an omission to preserve life, it is well established that it is murder to omit to discharge a duty to preserve life with intent to kill, as by deliberately starving to death a child in one's care.[14] Also reflecting the IOL, the law punishes assisting or encouraging another to commit suicide. Section 2(1) of the Suicide Act 1961 provides a maximum penalty of 14 years' imprisonment for aiding, abetting, counseling, or procuring suicide or an attempt to commit suicide. The prohibition has been updated by section 59(2) of the Coroners and Justice Act 2009 which, replacing section 2(1), provides that a person commits an offence if he does an act capable of encouraging or assisting the suicide or attempted suicide of another person and the act was intended to encourage or assist suicide or an attempt to commit suicide.

B Intention and foresight

The IOL draws an important distinction between intending death and merely foreseeing death as a side-effect of one's conduct. It adopts the principle of "double effect," according to which it is permissible to bring about a foreseen bad consequence if the bad effect is not intended, whether as an end or as a means, and the foreseen or foreseeable causing of the side-effect does not violate other moral norms, especially fairness. It is

---

[12] 'Report of the Select Committee on Medical Ethics' (HL Paper 21-I of 1993–4) para 237.
[13] *Bland* (n 11) 865.
[14] *R v Gibbins and Proctor* (1919) 13 Cr App R 134.

therefore ethical and lawful to, for example, administer palliative drugs to the dying even if they will shorten life.

Foreseen causation should not be conflated with intention.[15] Intention, properly understood, always means purpose, not merely foresight plus causality and, despite occasional digression, the law (like common sense) always returns to this truth. One may intend and foresee a consequence of one's action (as when one deliberately decapitates another person). But one may intend a consequence without foreseeing that it will occur (as when one buys a lottery ticket to win a million-to-one jackpot). Conversely, one may not intend a consequence even though one foresees it as certain to occur (like the hangover after a bottle of port). As Lord Goff helpfully put it:

[T]here can be intention without foresight that the relevant consequence was likely to occur. Conversely, there can be foresight of consequences without intention. [W]hen Field Marshal Montgomery invaded France on D-Day, he foresaw that many of the troops under his command would be killed on that very day. Obviously, however, he did not intend that any of them should be killed. [I] cannot emphasise too strongly that, because foresight of the consequence of death resulting from your act does not necessarily connote an intention on your part to kill, it cannot, in my opinion, be right for a jury to be told that the former will, as a matter of law, *of itself establish* the necessary intent, however overwhelming the probability of the consequence may be—as witness the example of Field Marshal Montgomery and D-Day.[16]

Some jurists, like Professor Glanville Williams, have proposed that "intention" should be stretched to include "oblique" intent (as Bentham called it) so that killers who foresee death as virtually certain but who do not intend it can nevertheless be convicted of murder. Williams instanced the villain who places a bomb on a plane in order to claim the insurance on a parcel but not to kill the pilot. Lord Goff rejected this proposed extension of intention:

Now I have to confess that, as soon as somebody starts using an expression like "oblique intention," I become suspicious; because I suspect that it is only

---

[15] See generally J Finnis, *Intention and Identity* (Oxford University Press, 2011) Part Three.

[16] R Goff, "The Mental Element in the Crime of Murder" (1988) 104 LQR 30, 45 (emphasis in original). The same example, with Eisenhower substituted for Montgomery, was later used by the judgment of the court in the leading US Supreme Court decision on physician-assisted suicide: *Vacco v Quill* 521 US 793 at 802–3 (1997), per Rehnquist CJ: "The law has long used actors' intent or purpose to distinguish between two acts that may have the same result.... Put differently, the law distinguishes actions taken "because of" a given end from actions taken "in spite of" their unintended but foreseen consequences... ('When General Eisenhower ordered American soldiers onto the beaches of Normandy, he knew that he was sending many American soldiers to certain death.... His purpose, though, was to...liberate Europe from the Nazis')."

necessary to use the rather mysterious adjective "oblique" to bring within "intention" something which is not intention at all. And that is exactly what is happening here. For the trouble with this kind of approach is that it has distorted the plain meaning of the word. To the question—did the defendant mean to destroy the parcel? The answer is, of course, yes, he did. But to the question—did the defendant mean to kill the pilot? The answer is, no, he didn't. Indeed, if he saw the pilot safely descending by parachute, he would no doubt be delighted; and so it is absurd to say that he meant to kill him. Of course, if the pilot is killed by the explosion, I share Professor Glanville Williams' *feeling* that the defendant can properly be called a murderer; but I do not think that that result can be achieved by artificially expanding the meaning of the word "intention." Quite apart from anything else, it can only lead to difficulties in directing juries. In a jury system, it is far better, if you can, to use a word in its plain and ordinary meaning. And you do not intend something merely because you know that it is virtually certain to happen; see the example of Field Marshal Montgomery and D-Day.[17]

His Lordship added that the parcel bomber should be convicted of murder not by way of artificially stretching the ordinary meaning of intention but by expanding the *mens rea* of murder to include "indifference to death":

[T]he jurists have become imprisoned within their own favourite concept of intention, to such an extent that they have tried, illegitimately, to expand it to include other cases. By adopting the solution that the mental element of murder consists of either (1) an intention to kill, or (2) indifference to death, we can, I suggest, both satisfy the general sense of justice as evidenced in the cases, and avoid the trap of using words otherwise than in their ordinary meaning—a trap which it is especially important to avoid in systems in which judges have to direct juries.[18]

English law appears to agree with Lord Goff in thus rejecting "oblique intent". As Professor Peter Skegg has observed, English courts have "tended to say that foresight of virtual certainty is something from which intention may be found or inferred, and ... have stopped short of saying that such foresight is itself a form of intent...."[19]

Consistent with the law's rejection of oblique intent is its endorsement of double effect. Lord Goff has referred to:

the established rule that a doctor may, when caring for a patient who is, for example, dying of cancer, lawfully administer painkilling drugs despite the fact

---

[17] R Goff, "The Mental Element in the Crime of Murder" (1988) 104 LQR 30, 46 (emphasis in original).

[18] Ibid 45.

[19] PDG Skegg, "Medical Acts Hastening Death" in PDG Skegg et al (eds), *Medical Law in New Zealand* (Thomson Brookers, 2006) 505, 524.

that he knows that an incidental effect of that application will be to abbreviate the patient's life.[20]

Unfortunately, the law's rejection of oblique intent is by no means as clear as it could and should be. The reasoning or dicta of the single judgment in the House of Lords in *R v Woollin*[21] is ambiguous enough to be read as holding not only that foresight of virtual certainty can be *evidence of* intention but that it *is* intention. It was, indeed, so interpreted by the majority of the Court of Appeal in *Re A*, the "Conjoined Twins" case, where the question was whether it would be lawful to separate the weaker twin (Mary) to save the stronger one (Jodie), even though it was foreseen that Mary would die. The presiding judge stated: "Unpalatable though it may be ... to stigmatise the doctors with 'murderous intent', that is what in law they will have if they perform the operation and Mary dies as a result."[22] The majority's adoption of "oblique intention," though understandable in view of the ambiguity in *Woollin*, deprived them of the most cogent and coherent way of resolving the tragic dilemma before them: the principle of double effect. According to that principle, the separation of conjoined twins is justified where the death of the doomed twin is not intended and is merely foreseen as a side-effect, and the foreseeable causing of that side-effect does not violate the norm of fairness. Given that both Mary and Jodie would have died without separation, and that Mary was doomed with or without separation, it was not unfair to separate her from Jodie who could, and did, survive. The majority explicitly rejected double effect on the ground that the good and bad effects did not affect the same individual, as is the case with the administration of palliative drugs to a dying patient. However, this limitation has never been a requirement of double effect. The principle could, for example, justify the allied bombing of Nazi headquarters even if it were foreseen that innocent civilians nearby would be killed as a side-effect of the raid. Fortunately, the core common-sense meaning of intention asserts itself at points in the judgments of the Court of Appeal in the Conjoined Twins case where *Woollin*'s authority in relation to the crime of murder is no longer in issue, but rather the issue as framed in civil and human rights law. One such point is the following statement by Robert Walker LJ in relation to the "right to life" in Article 2 of the European Convention on Human Rights:

---

[20] *Bland* (n 11) 867. See also *R v Cox* (1992) 12 BMLR 38, 41 (Ognall J).
[21] [1999] 1 AC 82.
[22] *Re A* [2001] Fam 147, 198–9, per Ward LJ. See also ibid 216, per Brooke LJ.

The Convention is to be construed as an autonomous text, without regard to any special rules of English law, and the word "intentionally" in article 2(1) must be given its natural and ordinary meaning. In my judgment the word, construed in that way, applies only to cases where the purpose of the prohibited action is to cause death.[23]

That is the position to which English law, too, gravitates, as many cases—including those discussed in *Woollin*—demonstrate when properly analyzed.

C *Acts and omissions*

The IOL prohibits intentional killing by act or omission. It therefore prohibits withholding/withdrawing treatment with intent to shorten life. But it permits withholding/withdrawing a life-prolonging treatment which is not worthwhile because it is futile or too burdensome. The IOL is, therefore, not vitalist: it does not require doctors to try to preserve life at all costs. Just as the IOL is not vitalist, neither is English law:

[I]t cannot be right that a doctor, who has under his care a patient suffering painfully from terminal cancer, should be under an absolute obligation to perform upon him major surgery to abate another condition which, if unabated, would or might shorten his life still further. The doctor who is caring for such a patient cannot, in my opinion, be under an absolute obligation to prolong his life by any means available to him, regardless of the quality of the patient's life. Common humanity requires otherwise, as do medical ethics and good medical practice accepted in this country and overseas.[24]

D *Worth of treatment v worth of life: "quality of life benefits" v "beneficial Quality of life"*

It is always wrong to withhold/withdraw treatment because it is thought that the patient, rather than the treatment, is not worthwhile—because death is thought to be in the "best interests" of the patient. The IOL distinguishes what we may call "quality of life benefits" (used to judge whether a treatment would be worthwhile, comparing its benefits and burdens) from "beneficial Quality of life" (QOL) (used to judge whether the patient's life is or will be "worthwhile").

1 "quality of life benefits" v "beneficial Quality of life"
Given that the same phrase, "quality of life," is used to refer to these two very different concepts, it is not surprising that judges and academics have

---

[23] Ibid 256.
[24] *Bland* (n 11) 867, per Lord Goff.

sometimes confused the question whether a *treatment* would be worthwhile with the question whether a patient's *life* would be worthwhile. Examples of its usage in the latter, QOL sense (but without advertence to its use in the alternative, former sense), can be found in leading cases on non-treatment of children (such as *Re J*) and of incompetent adults (most notably *Bland*). In *Re J*, where the question was whether it would be in the best interests of a disabled, premature baby with a short life-expectancy to be ventilated, Taylor LJ stated:

I consider the correct approach is for the court to judge the quality of life the child would have to endure if given the treatment and decide whether in all the circumstances *such a life would be so afflicted as to be intolerable to that child*. I say "to that child" because the test should not be whether the life would be tolerable to the decider. The test must be whether the child in question, if capable of exercising sound judgment, would consider the life tolerable.[25]

Similarly, in *Bland* (a case about which we shall have much more to say in Chapter 12), where the question was whether it would be lawful to withdraw tube-feeding from a patient in a persistent vegetative state even though he would die as a result, Lord Keith ruled:

[A] medical practitioner is under no duty to continue to treat such a patient where a large body of informed and responsible medical opinion is to the effect that no benefit at all would be conferred by continuance. *Existence in a vegetative state with no prospect of recovery is by that opinion regarded as not being a benefit*, and that, if not unarguably correct, at least forms a proper basis for the decision to discontinue treatment: *Bolam v. Friern Hospital Management Committee* [1957] 1 W.L.R. 582.[26]

To hold, as in *Re J*, that life-prolonging treatment may be withheld/withdrawn from a child because the child's life would be "intolerable" involves a judgment that the child no longer has a "beneficial Quality of life." This remains so irrespective of the rider that the judgment should be made from the child's perspective. Even if adopting such a perspective were feasible, the judgment of "intolerability" would remain a judgment that the child's life was no longer beneficial. Similarly, to judge that Tony Bland's existence was not beneficial (or, as one learned Lord Justice described it, a "humiliation")[27] is to judge that his life was no longer worth living. Indeed, a majority of the Law Lords judged that it would be lawful to withdraw his tube-feeding even though they thought that the

---

[25] [1991] FLR, 366, 383–4 (emphasis added). For the current status of the "intolerability" test see *W (by her litigation friend B) and M (by her litigation friend, the Official Solicitor) and S and A NHS Primary Care Trust* [2011] EWHC 2443 (Fam), discussed in the postscript to Chapter 12.

[26] *Bland* (n 11) 858–9 (emphasis added).

[27] *Bland* (n 11) 831, per Hoffmann LJ.

doctor's intention was to kill.[28] Once the law endorses the judgment that certain patients have no "beneficial quality of life," and even that patients may lawfully be killed by deliberate withdrawal of treatment or tube-feeding, it forfeits any principled objection to the taking of positive steps to end their lives. Lord Mustill aptly observed that *Bland* left the law in a "morally and intellectually misshapen" state, prohibiting active intentional killing, but permitting intentional killing by omission.[29] The misshapenness resulted from the courts mistakenly thinking that the key moral distinction is between act and omission when, as the IOL holds, it is between intention and foresight.

Some judges appear to believe that the IOL is consistent with the QOL view that some lives are not beneficial. For example, Lord Keith said in *Bland* that although it was the duty of the state, and the judiciary as one of the arms of the state, to uphold the sanctity of life, the principle was not "absolute." While the principle forbade the taking of active measures to cut short life, it did not, for example, "compel the temporary keeping alive of patients who are terminally ill where to do so would merely prolong their suffering."[30] But once the principle is clarified, and clearly distinguished from vitalism, then we should say, with respect, that it *is* absolute. It endorses allowing terminally ill patients to die but never endorses judging that their lives lack worth, and treating oneself or anyone else as free to *try* to hasten their death. Allowing the terminally ill to die is not an exception to the principle but an application of it. In short, although the value of human life is not absolute, the prohibition on trying to extinguish it, by act or omission, is.

Bland raised ethical and legal issues scarcely less complex and profound than the Conjoined Twins case. But just as the principle of double effect offered a sound way through the thicket of questions raised by separating conjoined twins, it also offered a sound resolution to the question of withdrawing tube-feeding from a patient in a persistent vegetative state. Had their Lordships in *Bland* held that the tube-feeding could be withdrawn on the ground that it was a futile medical treatment, because it could do nothing to improve Tony Bland's medical condition (or quality of life), their reasoning would have left the law in much more reasonable moral and intellectual shape. As the IOL is not vitalist it does not require life to be preserved at all costs. It regards the core purposes of medicine as the restoration to health and well-functioning and, if that cannot be

---

[28] Ibid 876 (Lord Browne-Wilkinson); 877 (Lord Lowry); 887 (Lord Mustill).
[29] Ibid 887.
[30] Ibid 859.

achieved, the alleviation of symptoms. As Sir Thomas Bingham MR (as he then was) noted in the Court of Appeal in *Bland*, the objects of medical care have traditionally been understood as:

(1) to prevent the occurrence of illness, injury or deformity ... before they occur; (2) to cure illness when it does occur; (3) where illness cannot be cured, to prevent or retard deterioration of the patient's condition; (4) to relieve pain and suffering in body and mind.[31]

As the tube-feeding could do nothing to restore Tony Bland to health and well-functioning, its removal could (at least arguably) have been justified on the ground that it was a futile medical treatment. This was in essence the approach taken by Lord Goff, who drew an analogy between the tube-feeding and a ventilator.[32]

In the Conjoined Twins case, the presiding Lord Justice delivered a welcome reaffirmation of the key distinction between judging that a treatment is not worthwhile and that the patient's life is not worthwhile. His Lordship stated:

Given the international conventions protecting "the right to life" ... I conclude that it is impermissible to deny that every life has an equal inherent value. Life is worthwhile in itself whatever the diminution in one's capacity to enjoy it and however gravely impaired some of one's vital functions of speech, deliberation and choice may be.[33]

Moreover, it appears that Parliament has restored the prohibition on intentionally withholding/withdrawing treatment or tube-feeding with intent to kill. In relation to the determination of the "best interests" of a mentally incapacitated adult, section 4(5) of the Mental Capacity Act 2005 provides that where the determination relates to life-sustaining treatment the person making the determination must not "be motivated by a desire to bring about his death." As Professor Finnis has pointed out, this should be interpreted as prohibiting any intent that death be brought about, either as an end or as a means:

The phrase "motivated by a desire" has been used in the courts ... as equivalent to the phrase "influenced by a desire", which is found in the Insolvency Act 1986, s 239(5). These judgments show that the courts treat the motivating desire ... as including ... all purposes which affect the decision-maker's deliberations and

---

[31] *Bland* (n 11) 809.
[32] Bland (n 11) 870. Whether tube-feeding *is* a medical treatment, as opposed to basic care which should be provided to all patients, is a matter for reasonable ethical debate, but at least an approach which considers whether a treatment is beneficial involves no judgment that the patient's life is no longer beneficial.
[33] *Re A* (n 2) 187–8, per Ward LJ.

shape or enter into its conclusions—that is, all the kinds of purpose which are referred to when one says that in carrying out one's decision one has an intent to ... or a purpose of.... And all this is reinforced by the way courts have spoken of intent and motivating desire in the context of Art.81 of the EC Treaty.[34]

Moreover, the alternative interpretation, which would allow a carer to withdraw treatment as a means of bringing about death provided he or she was motivated by a desire to achieve some other end, would gut the obvious protective function of the provision. Such an interpretation would allow a doctor to shorten life if motivated by a desire to get away early for the weekend.

2 "Best interests": subjective or objective?

Though section 4(5) of the Mental Capacity Act 2005 is welcome, the definition of "best interests" in section 4(6) and (7) is less so, for they define "best interests" largely in terms of subjective opinions rather than objective criteria. Section 4(6) provides that the person making the determination must take into account, so far as is reasonably ascertainable:

(a) the person's past and present *wishes and feelings* (and, in particular, any relevant written statement made by him when he had capacity),
(b) the *beliefs and values* that would be likely to influence his decision if he had capacity, and
(c) the *other factors that he would be likely to consider* if he were able to do so.[35]

Section 4(7) adds that the person making the determination must take into account, if it is practicable and appropriate to consult them, the *views* of:

(a) anyone named by the person as someone to be consulted on the matter in question or on matters of that kind,
(b) anyone engaged in caring for the person or interested in his welfare,
(c) any donee of a lasting power of attorney granted by the person, and
(d) any deputy appointed for the person by the court,
   as to what would be in the person's best interests and, in particular, as to the matters mentioned in subsection (6).[36]

As Finnis comments:

This appearance of unrooted subjectivity remains a deep weakness in the Act's treatment of best interests, and it is important that commentaries on the Act

---

[34] J Finnis, "The Mental Capacity Act 2005: some ethical and legal issues" in H Watt (ed), *Incapacity and Care* (The Linacre Centre, 2009) 95, 101–2 (footnotes omitted), citing *Re MC Bacon Ltd* [1990] BCC 78, 86; *Re Hawkes Hill Publishing* [2007] BCC 937, para 33 and, in another context, *R v Greenwich LBC* [1991] 1 WLR 506, 508.
[35] Emphases added.
[36] Emphases added.

encourage carers to feel confident that they have the right, indeed the duty, to consider the *real* true interests of the person and not *simply* the wishes and feelings of someone who may be incapable of sound judgment, or be in the grip of wrong-headed views about his or her own worth, or human worth in general; nor *simply* the views of others involved in the case.[37]

One way of denying worth to incompetent patients is to adopt the judgment that the value of life depends wholly on the value people *give* to their life through their choices, and that the loss of one's capacity to choose means that the only value in one's continued existence depends on the value one had chosen to attach to one's life when competent. Such an approach is inconsistent with the ineliminable dignity which we all share whether or not we are competent:

[E]xercises of autonomy . . . are *not* the fundamental source of worth and value in a person's life. Human beings possess an ineradicable value prior and subsequent to the possibility of exercising autonomy. Autonomy itself as a capacity is to be valued *precisely in so far as its exercise makes for the well-being and flourishing of the human beings who possess it.* But it is plain that many exercises of the capacity, that is, many self-determining choices, are destructive of human well-being—both in the life of the chooser and in the lives of others affected by his or her choices. The mere fact that someone has *chosen* to act or to be treated in a certain way establishes no title to moral respect for what has been chosen. The character of the choice must satisfy certain criteria in order to warrant our respect. The most basic criterion is that a choice should be consistent with respect for the fundamental dignity both of the chooser and of others.[38]

In the leading case on the treatment of mentally incapacitated adults at common law, Lord Brandon observed: "The operation or other treatment will be in their best interests if, but only if, it is carried out in order either to save their lives, or to ensure improvement or prevent deterioration in their physical or mental health."[39] In relation to health care, "best interests" should be understood to include the standard objectives of health care practice:

the restoration and maintenance of health, or of whatever degree of well-functioning can be achieved; the prolongation of life; and the control of symptoms when cure cannot be achieved. It is in serving these ends that doctors serve the good—and, therefore, the best interests—of their patients. And, in the absence of these criteria, how can the courts hope to resolve disputes? If the understanding

---

[37] Finnis (n 34) 100 (emphases in original).
[38] J Keown and L Gormally, "Human Dignity, Autonomy and Mentally-Incapacitated Patients: A Critique of *Who Decides?*" (1999) 4 Web Journal of Current Legal Issues Part II (emphases in original).
[39] *Re F* [1990] 2 AC 1, 55.

of "best interests" fails to include objective, substantive requirements there will be no non-arbitrary way of judging whether the testimony of relatives and others about a patient's "preferences" is self-serving; no non-arbitrary way of settling differences of opinion; and no objective criteria for determining whether a regulatory system is in fact operating to protect patients.[40]

In short, just as doctors and relatives can lose sight of the inherent dignity of a mentally incapacitated patient, so can the patient himself or herself. Misguided subjective views about the patient's worth should never be allowed to obscure what is truly and objectively in the best interests of the patient.

Further, section 4's vaguely defined criterion of "best interests," which guides those making decisions in relation to incompetent adults, does not apply to "advance decisions" made by adults themselves while still competent. There is a real risk, therefore, that some patients will make advance refusals of treatment based on a misguided opinion that in such-and-such a condition their life would not be worth living, and perhaps refuse treatment in advance of incompetence with intent to put an end to their life. It will now be suggested that the courts should make it clear that, while there is a right to refuse treatment, there is no right to commit suicide such as could impose a duty on others to facilitate death for that purpose, even by omission.

E Autonomy

Autonomy is a valuable capacity, and part of human dignity, but its contribution to dignity is conditional, not absolute. Exercising one's autonomy to destroy one's (or another's) life is always wrong because it is always disrespectful of human dignity. So: it is always wrong intentionally to assist/encourage a patient to commit suicide and, equally, there is no "right to commit suicide," let alone a right to be assisted to commit suicide, either by act or omission.

The principle of "respect for autonomy" has in recent years become for many a core if not dominant principle of biomedical ethics and law. It is not, however, unproblematic. Its advocates often fail to agree on precisely what constitutes an "autonomous" choice or to offer any convincing account of why respect for someone else's choice as such should be regarded as a moral principle at all, let alone a core or dominant moral principle.[41] Our

---

[40] Keown and Gormally (n 38).

[41] For valuable contributions to the growing debate about the proper role of autonomy see A McCall Smith, "Beyond Autonomy" (1997) 14 Journal of Contemporary Health Law and Policy 23; O O'Neill, *Autonomy and Trust in Bioethics* (Cambridge University Press, 2002); C Foster, *Choosing Life, Choosing Death: The Tyranny of Autonomy in Medical Ethics and Law* (Hart Publishing, 2009).

capacity for choice is undoubtedly very important, for it is through our choices that we shape our lives and influence the lives of those around us, for good or for ill. But we should exercise our autonomy responsibly, choosing for good, not ill. Neither the common law nor professional medical ethics has ever held that the mere fact *that* I have chosen justifies *what* I have chosen. Consequently, the law refuses to respect various choices, however autonomous. It disallows choices to be owned, eaten, or executed, to be the victim of actual bodily harm,[42] to possess illicit drugs, or to drive while not wearing a seatbelt. In the medical context patients have no right to demand whatever treatment or drugs they may want. A doctor may not amputate a healthy limb even on request, and female genital mutilation is prohibited by section 1 of the Female Genital Mutilation Act 2003, regardless of the woman's consent. The Mental Health Act 1983 allows treatment for mental disorder to be imposed on even a competent patient who chooses not to have it.[43] None of these autonomous choices need involve a risk of harm to anyone but the person making them but they are, nevertheless, disallowed by the law. Other autonomous choices do involve a risk of harm to others, which helps explain why they, too, are rejected by the law even when, as with duelling, the risk of harm may be entirely consensual. Choices which undermine human flourishing or well-being, such as choices to kill or mutilate (whether oneself or another), simply lack moral justification.

It is occasionally suggested that the decriminalization of suicide by the Suicide Act 1961 recognized a right to commit suicide.[44] However, the legislative history of the Suicide Act demonstrates that it was not the intention of Parliament to condone suicide, let alone establish a "right to suicide."[45] Far from it. The government made clear its hope that decriminalization would not give the impression that it regarded what it described as "self-murder" at all lightly.[46] As Lord Bingham explained in *R (Pretty) v Director of Public Prosecutions*:

The law confers no right to commit suicide.... Suicide itself (and with it attempted suicide) was decriminalised because recognition of the common law offence was not thought to act as a deterrent, because it cast an unwarranted stigma on innocent members of the suicide's family and because it led to the distasteful result that patients recovering in hospital from a failed suicide attempt were prosecuted, in effect, for their lack of success. But while the 1961 Act

---

[42] *R v Brown* [1994] 1 AC 212.
[43] Section 62.
[44] Eg *Bland* (n 11) 826–7, per Hoffmann LJ.
[45] *Hansard*, HC vol 645, cols 822–3 (1960–61).
[46] *Hansard*, HC vol 644, cols 1425–6 (1960–61).

abrogated the rule of law whereby it was a crime for a person to commit (or attempt to commit) suicide, it conferred no right on anyone to do so. Had that been its object there would have been no justification for penalising by a potentially very long term of imprisonment one who aided, abetted, counselled or procured the exercise or attempted exercise by another of that right. The policy of the law remained firmly adverse to suicide, as section 2(1) makes clear.[47]

Further, as Professor Skegg has observed, even since the Suicide Act 1961 "it has continued to be accepted that doctors are sometimes free—sometimes, indeed, under a duty—to prevent patients from committing suicide."[48] In *Reeves v Commissioner of Police of the Metropolis*[49] the House of Lords held that police and prison authorities owe even competent prisoners a duty to take care to prevent them from committing suicide. Suicide may, moreover, be committed by omission, such as a refusal to eat, just as it may be committed by an act. In *R v Collins and Ashworth Hospital Authority, ex p Brady* Maurice Kay J (as he then was) observed that there should be circumstances in which public interests such as the preservation of life, the prevention of suicide, the maintenance of the integrity of the medical profession, and the preservation of institutional discipline "would properly prevail over a self-determined hunger strike so as to enable, even if not to require, intervention." His Lordship observed:

It would be somewhat odd if there is a duty to prevent suicide by an act (for example, the use of a knife left in the cell) but not even a power to intervene to prevent self-destruction by starvation. I can see no moral justification for the law indulging its fascination with the difference between acts and omissions in a context such as this and no logical need for it to do so.[50]

In *Bland* Lord Goff said that when a patient refuses life-saving treatment "there is no question of the patient having committed suicide, nor therefore of the doctor having aided or abetted him in doing so": it was simply that the patient had declined to consent to treatment which might or would have the effect of prolonging his life, and the doctor had, in accordance with his duty, complied with his patient's wishes.[51] While this is no doubt generally the case, his Lordship did not appear to have considered the scenario where a patient's refusal of treatment is clearly designed to kill himself and where he demands that doctors assist him to

---

[47] *R v DPP* [2001] UKHL 61 at [35].
[48] PDG Skegg, *Law, Ethics and Medicine* (Clarendon Press, revised edn, 1988) 111 and authorities there cited.
[49] [2000] 1 AC 360.
[50] [2000] 8 Lloyd's Rep Med 355, 367.
[51] *Bland* (n 11) 864.

carry out his suicidal enterprise. Imagine an otherwise healthy diabetic who refuses his regular insulin shot in order to end his life and who demands to be kept comfortable in hospital while he dies, perhaps as part of a campaign to undermine the law against assisting suicide. If the courts were to hold that doctors were under a duty to comply with his demands (and could not for example discharge him), then the law against assisted suicide would indeed be undermined. If the law were to require, or even permit, doctors *intentionally* to help him kill himself by withholding treatment, how could the law, without inconsistency, prohibit doctors from providing him with active assistance? The courts need to be wary of the right to refuse treatment being manipulated to undermine the law against assisting suicide. It is one thing for doctors to withhold/withdraw treatment with the intention of respecting the patient's legal right to refuse treatment (even if they feel sure that the patient's refusal is suicidal). It is quite another for doctors *intentionally to assist*—try to assist—suicidal refusals and for the courts to endorse such intentional assistance.

Surprisingly, the European Court indicated in *Pretty*,[52] albeit cryptically, that the United Kingdom's blanket ban on assisting suicide engaged the respect for "private and family life" guaranteed by Article 8(1) of the Convention, although the ban was saved by Article 8(2). The Court's interpretation of Article 8(1) was (as we shall suggest in Chapter 10) mistaken. The Court should have followed Lord Bingham's opinion in that case that Article 8(1) sought to protect certain choices while people are living their lives, not the choice to live no longer.

Unfortunately (as we shall also see in Chapter 10), the Law Lords in the *Purdy* case went even further than the European Court when they ordered the Director of Public Prosecutions (DPP) to issue guidance spelling out the factors he would take into account in deciding whether to prosecute Debbie Purdy's husband should he assist her to commit suicide.[53] As the Lord Chief Justice rightly observed in that case, delivering the judgment of the Court of Appeal, such an order would in effect create exceptions to the crime, exceptions which Parliament had not chosen to enact.

IV CONCLUSIONS

The IOL has long been a foundational principle of the common law. This has not saved it from being widely misunderstood, in the academy, at the Bar, and on the Bench. The root cause of the misunderstanding is the

---

[52] *Pretty v United Kingdom* (2002) 35 EHRR 1.
[53] *R (Purdy) v Director of Public Prosecutions* [2009] UKHL 45.

tendency to confuse it with one (and sometimes both) of the two alternative approaches to the value of life: "vitalism" and "QOL." The confusion has, inevitably, impaired the law's moral and intellectual coherence. The law would regain its coherence if it:

- clearly denied that "oblique intent" is intent;
- clearly distinguished between "quality of life benefits" and "beneficial Quality of life";
- adopted a definition of "best interests" tied to the objective good of the patient, not least to the patient's life and health;
- clearly ruled out any intent to shorten life, whether by act or by omission, and as a means or as an end;
- recognized that the exercise of autonomy is to be valued to the extent that it serves the good of the patient, and that choices which are inconsistent with that good, not least choices to extinguish life, have no right to be endorsed;
- clearly denied that the right to refuse treatment involves a right to commit suicide and to be intentionally assisted to commit suicide.

CHAPTER 2

SURVEYING THE FOUNDATIONS OF MEDICAL LAW: A REASSESSMENT OF GLANVILLE WILLIAMS' *THE SANCTITY OF LIFE AND THE CRIMINAL LAW*

I INTRODUCTION

Medical law is now an established and thriving academic discipline. Over half a century ago what is widely regarded as its foundation stone (at least in the United Kingdom) was laid by the late Professor Glanville Williams: *The Sanctity of Life and the Criminal Law.*[1] The book dealt mainly with abortion, infanticide, suicide, and euthanasia, but also with contraception, sterilization, and artificial insemination. Its central theme was "the extent to which human life, actual or potential, is or ought to be protected under the criminal law of the English-speaking peoples."[2] To the extent that the criminal law, instantiating the inviolability of life (IOL), opposed abortion, infanticide, suicide, and euthanasia,[3] Williams subjected it to a wholesale assault. The book was based on the Carpentier lectures delivered by Dr Williams (as he then was) in 1956 at Columbia Law School. His lectures sparked a debate within Anglo-American legal circles on abortion law reform, and their publication in book form also had a marked influence. The book prompted the American Law Institute to address abortion in its Model Penal Code.[4] Williams served as a consultant to the project and the Code followed his proposals.[5] In 1967 the American Medical

---

[1] GL Williams, *The Sanctity of Life and the Criminal Law* (revised edn, Faber and Faber, 1958) ("SLCL").

[2] SLCL 11.

[3] This chapter is not concerned with contraception or artificial insemination.

[4] JW Dellapenna, *Dispelling the Myths of Abortion History* (Carolina Academic Press, 2006) 587 ("Dellapenna").

[5] Ibid 595.

Association adopted the Code's approach and only six years later the Supreme Court went even further by creating a constitutional right to abortion.[6] Justice Blackmun, in his judgment for the majority, cited Williams' book.[7] In England, Williams influenced, as President of the Abortion Law Reform Association, the enactment of the Abortion Act 1967.[8] His book's continuing significance was reflected in its citation by Brooke LJ in the "Conjoined Twins" case.[9] The SLCL proved no less influential in the academic world. It attracted laudatory reviews in law journals on both sides of the Atlantic[10] and it has exercised a profound influence on the discipline. The year after his death in 1997,[11] the *Medical Law Review* devoted a commemorative issue to Glanville Williams.[12] It contained a fulsome "personal appreciation" by the then editor, Professor Andrew Grubb, attesting to the inspirational influence Williams had upon him.[13] Grubb commented that if the "fathers" of medical law in England were Ian Kennedy and Peter Skegg, then Williams was its "grandfather," which was why Kennedy and Grubb, as founding editors of the journal, had invited him to contribute its very first article.[14] Grubb concluded: "Medical lawyers of my generation owe him a tremendous debt for founding a subject and through the force of his legal persona giving respectability to a new area of legal investigation. . . ."[15] Of the SLCL, Grubb opined: "It is full of erudition and combines painstaking archival

---

[6] *Roe v Wade* 410 US 113 (1973) (*"Roe"*). The court's misunderstanding of abortion law history will be considered in Ch 5.

[7] *Roe* nn 9, 21.

[8] M Simms and K Owen, *Abortion Law Reformed* (Peter Owen, 1971); Dellapenna 576–89.

[9] *Re A* [2001] Fam 147, 213.

[10] B Russell (1958) 10 Stanford Law Review 382; RC Donnelly (1958) 67 Yale Law Journal 753; JL Edwards (1958) Crim LR 413; HA Hammelmann (1959) 22 MLR 343; JD Morton (1959) 37 Canadian Bar Review 241; ATH Smith (1998) 6(2) Med L Rev 262. Sir Robert Megarry wrote: "The whole book is a triumphant demonstration of the extent to which the verbal accuracy and intellectual clarity of a lawyer make it possible to master a number of fields of knowledge outside the law and synthesize them into a lucid yet penetrating study.": RE Megarry (1959) 75 LQR 111, 112.

[11] There is an account of his life by Professor JR Spencer in the *Oxford Dictionary of National Biography* <http://www.oxforddnb.com/view/article/66017>. The account states that Williams' fame as a criminal lawyer rests on four books, of which the SLCL is one.

[12] (1998) 6(2) Med L Rev.

[13] A Grubb, "Glanville Williams: A Personal Appreciation": ibid 133, 134. The extent of the adulation is reflected by Grubb's comment that anyone who had read Williams' doctoral thesis "would immediately abstain from writing a Ph.D. thesis because of the sheer futility in attempting to match its depth and richness of research and analysis.": ibid 133.

[14] GL Williams, "Controlling the Repetitive Dangerous Offender" (1993) 1 Med L Rev 1. A new intellectual father of the discipline, for whom philosophical inquiry involves no "risky trespass" (see text to n 18), will be proposed in J Keown, "A New Father for Medical Law" in RP George and J Keown (eds), *Reason, Morality and Law: The Philosophy of John Finnis* (Oxford University Press, forthcoming).

[15] (1998) 6 Med L Rev 137.

research and scholarship with insight and vision on issues that continue to perplex medical lawyers."[16]

Given the book's enduring influence on the discipline of medical law and the increasing academic and social importance of that subject, a reassessment of the book's merits will not be of solely historical interest. This reassessment swims against the stream of opinion. The status of Professor Williams as one of the foremost British legal scholars of his time is beyond dispute. But expertise in law does not imply expertise in other fields, and the SLCL was not a law book. As its author noted in the preface, it included "moral, religious, medical, social, eugenic, demographic and penological"[17] dimensions. He realized that this involved "many risky trespasses outside the lawyer's proper sphere."[18] Perhaps he did not realize how risky. The book's reviewers (almost all lawyers) largely overlooked the book's grave deficiencies, particularly in moral philosophy and theology. The philosopher Elizabeth Anscombe penned a scathing review of the book.[19] Theologian Dr (later Cardinal) Cahal Daly observed, in his book-length response to the SLCL: "One feels driven to place it definitely outside the category of scholarly writing."[20] Though the SLCL is by no means devoid of academic interest or scholarly merit, it does betray several grave flaws which have hitherto been overlooked (with rare exceptions[21]) by lawyers. Its central flaw, which reflects Williams' lack of expertise in philosophy and theology, is its misunderstanding of the IOL and its tendency to assume rather than argue for the alternative position it advocates. The central flaw is fed by at least four tributary weaknesses:

[16] Ibid.

[17] SLCL 11.

[18] Ibid.

[19] The review began: "'This is not a work of academic interest. Indeed it is mysterious how an academic lawyer came to write it.": GEM Anscombe, "Glanville Williams' *The Sanctity of Life and the Criminal Law*: A Review" in M Geach and L Gormally (eds), *Human Life, Action and Ethics: Essays by GEM Anscombe* (Imprint Academic, 2005) 243.

[20] CB Daly, *Morals, Law and Life* (Scepter, 1966) 8. Sadly, the fates conspired to prevent the opinions of Anscombe and Daly reaching a wider audience, not least in legal circles. Anscombe's review, though commissioned by a law journal in 1958, was not published by it. Dr Daly's critique originally appeared in the Irish Theological Quarterly, hardly the staple reading of legal academics and practitioners, and his penetrating book-length critique never received the attention it deserved.

[21] Eg WJ Curran, Professor of Legal Medicine at Boston University School of Law, who wrote that "the author does not himself offer any generalizations, any theory or philosophy of his own in regard to the total subject. There is not a single page of synthesis in the book.": WJ Curran (1958) 71 Harvard Law Review 585, 586. Again, Professor Skegg expressed his "frustration" with the book: PDG Skegg, "Criminal Prosecutions of Negligent Health Professionals: The New Zealand Experience" (1998) 6 Med L Rev 220. For reasons which will become apparent, the SLCL does not bear comparison with Skegg's excellent Law, *Ethics and Medicine: Studies in Medical Law* (Clarendon Press, 1984).

- its mischaracterization of the IOL as essentially theological;
- its misunderstanding of theology;
- its evasion of the philosophical basis of the IOL;
- the vagueness of Williams' own position and the fragility of the arguments he deployed in its defense.

The first three weaknesses, which establish the contours of a "straw man" Professor Williams set up, will be addressed in Part II; the fourth, sketching a "hollow man" he erected in its place, in Part III.

II WILLIAMS' STRAW MAN

A Misrepresenting the IOL

The SLCL repeatedly misrepresented the IOL as essentially theological. As Professor ATH Smith aptly observed in his review: "It is a tactic throughout to show that, very frequently, our practices have their origins in a Judeo-Christian tradition to whose tenets not all subscribe."[22] The book's identification of the Judeo-Christian origins of the IOL in Anglo-American law was, by and large, accurate. But the book went much further, implying that the law depended for its justification on theology and could not be independently supported on philosophical grounds.[23]

1 Baptism

In his discussion of infanticide ("the killing of a new-born child committed by the parents or with their consent"[24]) Williams observed that it was condoned by both the Greeks and the Romans and that its condemnation was "very largely, if not entirely, the work of the church."[25] As for the basis of the Christian Church's opposition, he asserted: "The historical reason for the Catholic objection to abortion is the same as for the Christian church's historical opposition to infanticide: the horror of bringing about the death of an unbaptized child."[26] Indeed, if it were not for the need for baptism in order to gain salvation "infanticide might have been regarded as a positive benefit to the child. . . . "[27] Williams argued that such theological notions were "no longer regarded with the assurance that makes them an

---

[22] Smith (n 10) 263.
[23] For example, Williams asserted in the preface that the legal prohibitions on abortion, infanticide, and suicide could be justified, if at all, only on "ethico-religious or racial" grounds: SLCL 12.
[24] Ibid 26.
[25] Ibid 27.
[26] Ibid 178. Dellapenna points out that the argument was repeated in the American Law Institute's *Model Penal Code*: Dellapenna 587, n 133.
[27] SLCL 27.

acceptable support for a rule of the criminal law" adding: "Criminal prohibitions cannot, at the present day, be founded upon supernaturalism of any kind."[28] As we shall see, Williams' assertion about the basis of the Christian Church's opposition to infanticide was but one of several theological errors he committed.

2 Ensoulment

Williams wrote that the laws against abortion owed their origins to "metaphysical notions concerning life and the soul, combined with the interpretation of the Sixth Commandment."[29] Abortion was "in essence a religious offence."[30] He observed that although we still clung to the religious belief in the soul, "we have given up asking when this soul begins, because the question has become evidently insoluble."[31] Perhaps the soul was a miraculous addition to the conceptus but then what of spontaneous abortion? "It would seem, on this theory, that the naturally aborted embryo perishes possessed of a soul."[32] He concluded:

There are other difficulties in the orthodox doctrine of the soul which need not detain us. For the legislator, it seems sufficient to say that theological speculations and controversies should have no place in the formation of rules of law, least of all rules of the criminal law which are imposed upon believers and non-believers alike. If we protect the foetus by law, it should be for reasons relating to the well-being of existing human beings. Can it be said, with any degree of reality, that the week- or month-old embryo is an existing human being?[33]

As we shall see, Williams omitted to consider an obvious answer to the question he posed. This omission illustrates his failure to engage with the IOL's core moral-philosophical argument against abortion and infanticide.

3 Suicide and euthanasia

Williams asserted that there was little condemnation of suicide among the early Christians, that many Christians committed suicide out of fear of

---

[28] Ibid 29. He noted that even the "modern infidel" tended to agree that all human life was sacred and surmised that the basis for such secular thinking "may sometimes be in fact a legacy of their religious heritage.": ibid 30–1.

[29] He mentioned three secular arguments against relaxation of the law: Ibid 202. As we shall see (n 181) his consideration of these arguments was far from rigorous.

[30] SLCL 204.

[31] Ibid 208. His assertion that we have given up asking the question was unsubstantiated. The closely related question of when an individual human being comes into existence continues to occupy a significant place in contemporary bioethical discussion, both secular and religious.

[32] Ibid. He did not consider a response along the following lines: "Why is this morally significant? We all die sooner or later. And do the high rates of infant mortality which exist in certain parts of the world, and have existed in developed countries in times past, mean that newborn children are not human beings?"

[33] Ibid.

falling into temptation, and that although it was "especially good" for a believer to provoke unbelievers to martyr him "in the last resort he might do away with himself directly."[34] Members of one sect, he added, killed themselves in their hundreds by leaping from cliffs and it was by way of reaction to these excesses that St Augustine (354–430 AD) was led to condemn suicide, thereby becoming the chief architect of the Christian position.[35] Williams wrote that since Augustine held that if suicide were permissible to avoid sin it would be the logical course for all those freshly baptized, he could deny this logic only "by postulating a divine prohibition of suicide."[36] Williams concluded: "The interdiction of suicide, as an inflexible principle, is, then, part of a particular system of religious belief, and need not be accepted by the positivist, or indeed by anyone who does not accept the traditional eschatology."[37] Turning to euthanasia (the intentional termination of a patient's life because it is thought that death would benefit the patient), Williams' discussion of the ethics of voluntary euthanasia again suggested that the basis of moral opposition was theological. He concluded: "If it is true that euthanasia can be condemned only according to a religious opinion, this should be sufficient at the present day to remove the prohibition from the criminal law."[38]

The laws against killing which Williams criticized were undoubtedly informed by the Judeo-Christian tradition. However, his implication that those laws could not be defended by moral philosophy as well as by moral theology was, as we shall see, without foundation. In short, Williams set up a straw man. He did so, moreover, in atypically unscholarly language. As Professor Smith noted, the book frequently subjected the Catholic Church to "scarcely disguised sarcasm."[39] Williams described traditional Christian opposition to birth control as "irrational and obscurantist"[40] and Catholic opposition as "extremely primitive if not blasphemous."[41] He even went so far as to allege, having discussed the incidence of maternal mortality from illegal abortion, that the Christian Church was concerned about the "statistics of abortion and post-morbidity merely to the extent that these indicate the existence of a certain volume of

[34] Ibid 229 (footnote omitted).
[35] Ibid 229–30.
[36] Ibid 231.
[37] Ibid. He considered three further arguments against suicide as posited by Aquinas (1225–1274 AD), two of which were not theological: ibid 237–44.
[38] Ibid 278.
[39] Smith (n 10) 263.
[40] SLCL 57.
[41] Ibid 65; "morbid, guilt-ridden": ibid 58; "mischievous dogma": Ibid 67; "fundamentalist": ibid 127; "dogmatic and authoritarian": ibid.

feminine sin."[42] Before illustrating how his preoccupation with theology distracted him from the philosophical basis of the IOL, it is worth illustrating the extent of his theological misunderstanding.

B Misunderstanding theology

Williams wrote expansively on theology. This was as risky as a theologian writing expansively about criminal law. It is not surprising, therefore, that Williams committed a litany of theological errors and that legal reviewers failed to notice.[43] A particularly egregious error, given the heavy reliance Williams placed on it, was his assertion that the main reason for the Christian Church's opposition to abortion and infanticide was its teaching on baptism. The reality is that the Church's primary reason for opposing infanticide has never been concern about the fate of unbaptized souls. As Williams recognized,[44] if this had been the case the Church would have had little objection to the killing of infants after baptism. Williams cited no theologians to support his proposition. This was not surprising: there were none. The source he cited was Finnish sociologist Edward Westermarck's *The Origin and Development of Moral Ideas*.[45] Westermarck in turn cited William Lecky's *History of European Morals*.[46] Lecky did indeed propose that concern for the fate of unbaptized infants "powerfully sustained" the Church's opposition to infanticide. However, he was clear that the primary reason that Christians denounced infanticide was because they considered it "as definitely murder."[47] As early as the first century, Church teaching on abortion and infanticide was unequivocal: "you shall not murder a child by abortion nor kill it after it is born."[48] This Christian opposition to infanticide was inherited from Judaism,[49] which had no doctrine requiring baptism for salvation. Jews and Christians alike were concerned first with the preciousness of the life of each child. Anxiety about the fate of unbaptized infants was a later

---

[42] Ibid 197.

[43] One, for example, simply praised Williams' "masterly" knowledge of the Bible: Smith (n 10) 263.

[44] SLCL 27. He also cited contemporary Catholic moralists who wrote that abortion could not be performed even to baptize the child: ibid 186.

[45] (Macmillan, 1906), cited in SLCL 26, n 2.

[46] (1869). Williams' citation of Lecky is confused. He referred (SLCL 28, n 2) to the 1911 edition of Lecky but his page reference was incorrect. The reference seems to have been lifted from Westermarck, who cited the 1869 edition where the pagination is slightly different. It is therefore doubtful whether Williams read Lecky.

[47] Lecky (n 46) (1911 edn) 10.

[48] *Didache* 2.2

[49] Eg Philo, *Special Laws* 3.117–118; Josephus, *Against Apion* 2:25 and various passages from the Talmud including *Babylonian Talmud Sanhedrin* 72b.

phenomenon within Christianity, in part generated by the doctrine of original sin in the form expressed by Augustine in the early fifth century. This concern had moderated by the time of Aquinas and the subsequent tradition approximated the earlier attitude.[50] Speculation about the damnation of infants played no part in forming the early Christian attitude against infanticide and abortion. Furthermore, even when this concern was at its apogee in the post-fifth century Latin West, it was a secondary consideration. The prohibition on killing the innocent[51] was always the core of Church teaching. Williams was therefore closer to the mark when he identified as the basis of Christian teaching the "belief that it is our duty to regard all human life as sacred, however disabled or worthless or even repellent the individual may be."[52] Yet, as Williams acknowledged,[53] this moral doctrine tended to be held even by the "modern infidel" and could not easily be dismissed as "supernaturalism." Certainly such respect for human life need have nothing to do with theological reflection about the eternal fate of unbaptized infants.

Williams' discussion of the development of the Church's thinking on suicide was also flawed. First, many Christians prior to Augustine denounced suicide.[54] Furthermore, when Williams identified martyrdom with suicide (in a way reminiscent of Durkheim, whose expansive definition he quoted[55]), he conflated categories which would have been regarded as distinct by early Christians.[56] Although there was a debate among early Christians about what conduct constituted suicide, which they understood to mean intentional self-destruction, and what conduct was martyrdom, which they understood to mean death foreseeably resulting from adherence to one's faith (a debate to which Augustine brought clarity), there were no early Christians who defended intentional self-destruction. What informed Augustine's account of suicide, and his account of infanticide, was an appreciation of the good of this life. Far from resting on "supernaturalism," as Williams had it, Augustine

---

[50] PJ Toner, "Limbo" in *The Catholic Encyclopedia* (1913) vol 9, 256.
[51] *Exodus* 20:13.
[52] SLCL 30–1.
[53] Ibid. See n 28.
[54] See Justin Martyr, *Apology* 2.4; Clement Of Alexandria, *Stromata* 6.9; Lactantius, *Divine Institutes* 3.18; Basil, *Letters* 188.2; Jerome, *Letters* 39.3; Ambrose, *Concerning Virgins* 3.7.32; John Chrysostom, *Commentary On Galatians* 1:4.
[55] SLCL 242, n 2: "any cause of death which results directly or indirectly from the positive or negative act of the victim who knew that it was bound to produce this result." The definition presumably included those who persisted in an unhealthy lifestyle foreseeing it would cause earlier death; patients who refused life-prolonging treatments because they were unbearably painful, etc.
[56] See DW Amundsen, "Suicide and Early Christian Values" in BA Brody (ed), *Suicide and Euthanasia* (Kluwer Academic Publishers, 1989) 77.

strenuously denied the Platonic teaching that the soul is better off without the body and that we are all, therefore, better off dead. Augustine argued that life is good, that physical death brings an end to life, and that killing is therefore wrong as an injustice to the victim and as an offense against God who gives life.

Williams committed other theological errors. For example, he claimed:

- that Augustine taught that "Adam's sin was sexual lust,"[57] a notion which was explicitly rejected by Augustine in *The City of God*;[58]
- that Augustine equated the *embryo informatus* with the *embryo inanimatus*.[59] Augustine in fact strenuously resisted this identification, claiming that the early embryo was animated but in an unformed way;[60]
- that "the immaculate conception" refers to conception without sexual intercourse.[61] Williams here confused the Immaculate Conception (the belief that Mary was sinless from her conception) with the Virgin Birth (the belief that Jesus was conceived without sexual intercourse);
- that "the religious opinion illegitimately assumes that we should always legislate morality."[62] The Christian Church has never made such an assumption, as even a basic familiarity with Aquinas indicates;[63]
- that Catholics objected to the use of anesthetics for surgery and childbirth and were indeed among the last to maintain this objection.[64] This claim was based on the fact that in 1956 Pope Pius XII declared that use of anesthetics for surgery and childbirth was a positive good. Williams drew the illegitimate inference that before this pronouncement Catholics must have been opposed to it.

In sum, not only did Williams' focus on the theological aspect of the IOL distract him from its distinct philosophical aspect, but his theological critique was vitiated by error.[65]

---

[57] SLCL 179.

[58] XIV at 13. Williams was aware of this book because he mentioned it (albeit, as was often the case in the SLCL, without a supporting reference): SLCL 230.

[59] SLCL 142.

[60] *Questions on Exodus* 80. Williams also thought that the Latin for soul or life is "animus" (SLCL 143). It is "anima."

[61] SLCL 132.

[62] Ibid 211.

[63] "Human law is enacted for the community in general, and in the community the majority are not perfected in virtue. Therefore human law does not prohibit all the vices which those of special virtue avoid, but only the more serious vices, which the majority of people, with ordinary virtue, can avoid; and especially those vices which injure the common good and whose prohibition is necessary for the preservation of society.": *Summa Theologiae* 1–2, 92, 2. See also ibid ad. 2.

[64] SLCL 66; 278–9.

[65] In the preface he referred to his "heavy indebtedness to the specialists in other disciplines from whom I have drawn" (SLCL 11), by which he evidently meant written sources. However, his citation of theological sources was sparse. Moreover, Williams appears not to have sought the benefit of theological expertise (which would hardly have been lacking in Cambridge University) or even the advice of an educated Christian: there is certainly no acknowledgment of such in the book. At one

C Evasion and misrepresentation of the IOL

As Lord Goff observed in the *Bland* case, a belief in the sanctity or inviolability of human life has long been recognized in most, if not all, civilized societies throughout the modern world.[66] Indeed, a philosophical notion of the IOL stretches back around two-and-a-half millennia from the Universal Declaration of Human Rights (1948) through Immanuel Kant to the Hippocratic Oath (c400 BC). Yet Professor Williams somehow contrived to overlook this long philosophical tradition. The only philosophical approach he considered was the natural law tradition, the philosophical tradition favored by the Catholic Church. Even then, he tended either to evade it by characterizing it as theological or to misrepresent it. This is well illustrated by his discussion of abortion, a topic to which he devoted much space.

1 Evasion of the core natural law argument against abortion

It will be recalled that Williams asked whether the early embryo could be said to be a human being.[67] He posed this as a rhetorical question, but for the philosopher it is a question which must be answered. Williams failed to consider an obvious answer along the following lines:

Yes: it is entirely reasonable to regard the early embryo as a human being. The science of embryology shows that we each began when our father's sperm fertilized our mother's egg.[68] For example, "test-tube baby" pioneers Dr Robert Edwards and Mr Patrick Steptoe described the embryo after in vitro fertilization as a "microscopic human being".[69]

Williams himself recognized, in the very paragraph before posing his question, that "the individual...has his origin in the fusion of two cells."[70] He seemed unaware of the significance of this recognition to the question he posed. He gave no reason to question the teaching of embryological science, since the nineteenth century, that human life begins at fertilization. Moreover, he provided no answer to the philosophical argument that it is wrong intentionally to kill human embryos because doing so breaches the right to life which is enjoyed by all innocent human

---

point he wrote: "the pretension of the moral theologian, sitting in the calm of his study, to dictatorial powers of moral interpretation must be rejected.": ibid 282. So: the moral theologian writing about morality was criticized by the lawyer pronouncing on theology.

[66] *Airedale NHS Trust v Bland* [1993] AC 789, 863–4.

[67] See text at n 33.

[68] With the possible exception of monozygotic twins and clones.

[69] R Edwards and P Steptoe, *A Matter of Life* (Sphere Books, 1981) 83.

[70] SLCL 208. See also ibid 17. He also, appropriately, used the words "human being": ibid 19; "infants" and "child": ibid 24; and "baby": ibid 145 in a prenatal context.

beings. He did note that this was the philosophical basis of the Catholic Church's objection to abortion,[71] but his response was to embark on an irrelevant inquiry into theological reflection on the timing of ensoulment.[72] Had Williams mentioned the proscription of abortion in the Hippocratic Oath[73] he might have realized that opposition to abortion need have nothing to do with Christian reflection about ensoulment.

His failure squarely to confront the argument that abortion is wrong because it involves the killing of an innocent human being was a serious omission, not least because this was precisely the moral argument which explained the nineteenth-century anti-abortion legislation he was criticizing and which was still in force. In the nineteenth century, in both the United States and England, the common law's prohibition of abortion from quickening (the time when the mother first perceives foetal movement) was overtaken by the statutory prohibition of abortion from fertilization.[74] Williams accurately noted that the purpose of the legislation was the protection of the unborn child from fertilization:

At present English law and the law of the great majority of the United States regard any interference with pregnancy, however early it may take place, as criminal, unless for therapeutic reasons. The foetus is a human life to be protected by the criminal law from the moment when the ovum is fertilized.[75]

Again, commenting on the first English statutory prohibition of abortion, by Lord Ellenborough's Act (1803), he wrote that Parliament: "made not merely a legal pronouncement but an ethical or metaphysical one, namely that human life has a value from the moment of impregnation."[76]

The legislation did indeed adopt the ethical position that it is wrong to take life from conception. It is therefore surprising that Williams elected not to engage with that ethical position. Was this, perhaps, because he thought that the law's "ethical" position was "metaphysical" and rooted in belief about when human beings come into existence, or was it because he thought that "Every moral position is dogmatic and ultimately unprovable—if you will, a matter of faith."[77] If the latter, why did he think *his* faith should be preferred to the IOL? He also claimed that the extension of

---

[71] Ibid 180–1.

[72] Ibid 181.

[73] The only reference to Hippocrates in the book concerned his dating of ensoulment: ibid 141. It is odd that Williams, who devoted so much space to ancient history, and who cited Hippocrates, omitted to mention either the Oath's prohibition of abortion or its condemnation of physician-assisted suicide.

[74] Dellapenna chs 3–5.

[75] SLCL 141.

[76] Ibid 206.

[77] Ibid 182.

the law in 1803 was effected by both Church and state,[78] but he cited no evidence either that theological opinion about ensoulment or that the Church as a political institution influenced the legislation. Remarkably, he did not explore the legislative history of the nineteenth-century legislation (an omission which was doubly strange given the substantial space his book devoted to *ancient* history). Had he done so, he would have discovered that the engine behind that legislation, especially in the United States, was not theologians preaching that ensoulment occurred at fertilization but physicians teaching that human life began at fertilization. We shall consider the historical development to the law in detail in Chapter 5, but it is worth sketching it here because of its direct relevance to our present discussion.

As Professor James Mohr relates in his study of the enactment of the United States anti-abortion statutes of the nineteenth century, in 1859 the American Medical Association launched a campaign to restrict the law to protect human life from conception.[79] State medical societies supported this crusade. For example, in 1867 the New York Medical Society called for the state law to be tightened, noting that from "the first moment of conception" there was "a living creature in process of development to full maturity" whose destruction was "murder."[80] The legislature, Mohr, writes, "gave the physicians almost exactly what they wanted."[81] He comments that it was apparent to physicians "that the only way to deal with this question of basic morality was to see that their position was embodied in explicit statutes of their own design"[82] and he adds that the "vigorous efforts of America's regular physicians would prove in the long run to be the single most important factor in altering the legal policies toward abortion...."[83] Similarly, in England, it was doctors rather than theologians who pressed for the restriction of the common law prohibition on abortion.[84] Like their American colleagues, English doctors condemned abortion from conception as "murder" and called for the law to

[78] Ibid 196.

[79] JC Mohr, *Abortion in America. The Origins and Evolution of National Policy* (Oxford University Press, 1978) 157. For a more recent account of the restriction of the law, see Dellapenna Ch 7. Dellapenna's account is more reliable than Mohr's. Both agree on the pivotal role of the medical profession in securing restriction of the law in the US but Dellapenna persuasively criticizes Mohr's contention that the medical profession was largely motivated by a desire to suppress irregular practice. Dellapenna's book confirms the accuracy of Williams' insight that the Anglo-American legislation was "passed for the protection of the unborn child and not as a form of control of unregistered medical practitioners.": SLCL 176.

[80] Mohr (n 79) 216; Dellapenna 323.

[81] Mohr (n 79) 217.

[82] Ibid 166.

[83] Ibid 157.

[84] J Keown, *Abortion, Doctors and the Law* (Cambridge University Press, 1988) Ch 2.

prohibit it from that point.[85] Williams appears to have been unaware not only of the crucial role of medical practitioners in tightening the law but also of the marginal influence of religious bodies. Mohr writes that in the United States doctors "bitterly resented the avoidance of their special issue by the nation's religious spokesmen."[86] Williams' preoccupation with Catholic teaching was particularly inapt. As Dellapenna[87] observes in his treatise on abortion law history in the United States and England, the Catholic Church remained largely silent on abortion in the nineteenth century and Catholics generally were not involved in legislative efforts to tighten the abortion laws. For example, he points out that New Hampshire passed its first anti-abortion statute in 1848 but that Catholics were barred by the state's constitution from sitting in the legislature until 1877.[88] He could have added that in England, Catholics were prohibited from sitting in Parliament when the first statutory prohibition of abortion was enacted in 1803 and when it was amended in 1828 by Lord Lansdowne's Act.[89] It was not until 1829 that the Catholic Relief Act largely put an end to centuries of legal oppression of Catholics. Dellapenna concludes: "While the Catholic Church as an institution was always opposed to abortion, it played at best a negligible role in tightening the laws against abortion in England or the United States in the later years of the nineteenth century."[90]

2 Misrepresentation of the natural law argument against abortion

To the extent that Williams addressed the philosophical basis of the IOL, he exhibited muddled thinking. For example, of the natural law opposition to killing the unborn child to save the mother, he wrote: "The Catholic preference of doing nothing to assist the mother amounts in fact to a preference for the foetus over its mother. . . ."[91] The allegation of a preference for "doing nothing" to assist the mother was doubly inaccurate. First, the Catholic Church strongly commended efforts to save the mother, even efforts which posed a serious and foreseen risk to the unborn child. Second, it forbade not only killing the unborn child to save the mother but also killing the mother to save the child (as by Caesarean section in the era when this was fatal to the mother). A refusal to kill A to save B or vice versa does not amount to a "preference" for either A or B but treats both equally. Williams continued: "The

---

[85] Eg C Severn, *First Lines on the Practice of Midwifery* (S Highley, 1831) 134.
[86] Mohr (n 79) 184.
[87] Dellapenna ix.
[88] Ibid 416–17.
[89] Keown (n 84) 26–9.
[90] Dellapenna 419.
[91] SLCL 182.

proposition that a sinful act cannot be justified by a good end is in itself tautologous, since to describe the act as sinful when its intention is good begs the question."[92] Not so. The road to hell is, as the saying goes, paved with good intentions. There is nothing tautologous (in ethics or law) in holding that it is always wrong intentionally to perform certain acts (such as, say, rape) however good one's motive may be. Williams even claimed that the Catholic philosophical tradition maintained "the absolute irrelevance of ends to means" while preserving a "verbal form of escape for difficult situations" and he cited as examples killing in self-defense or in a just war.[93] He was, again, on shaky ground. The IOL does not hold that it is wrong to kill subject to verbal escape clauses in "difficult situations." It holds that it is wrong to kill *unjustly* and its core principle is that it is wrong intentionally to kill the innocent. Consequently, it permits the use of even deadly force with the intention of defending oneself (or another) against an unjust aggressor. Intending a good end (protecting the innocent from unjust attack) can justify what would, absent such an intention, be impermissible (the use of deadly force). Moreover, applying the principle of "double effect" it can be right to act for a good end even if, as an unintended side-effect of one's conduct, the life of an *innocent* person is shortened. Williams' understanding of the principle of double effect was, however, scarcely more reliable than his understanding of the IOL. He claimed, inaccurately, that "double effect" admitted a choice of the lesser evil. The reality is that the principle never permits an agent to choose an evil, lesser or otherwise, but only a good, even though the good chosen may foreseeably be accompanied by a bad consequence. Conduct which intentionally brings about a bad consequence is wrong; conduct which foreseeably brings about a bad consequence may not be. Williams went on: "To the eye of common sense, a result that is foreseen as certain, as a consequence of what is done, is in exactly the same position as a result that is intended."[94] Let us test this assertion (not one of his most precisely expressed) against couple of everyday scenarios. A doctor administers morphine to ease a dying patient's pain knowing that, as an unintended side-effect, the drug will hasten the patient's death. Is this "exactly the

---

[92] Ibid.

[93] Ibid. Williams claimed that the Church's teaching on the just war was "a concession made by the Church to procure partnership with the state.": ibid n 1. He cited no authority to support this assertion. Indeed, if partnership with the state had been the Church's motivation, why were the requirements for a just war so restrictive? On those criteria, see J Finnis, J Boyle, and G Grisez, *Nuclear Deterrence, Morality and Realism* (Clarendon Press, 1987) 87–9, 233–6, 315–16.

[94] SLCL 186.

same" to "the eye of common sense" as administering arsenic in order to kill the patient? Again, an oncologist administers powerful drugs to cure a child's leukaemia, foreseeing that the drugs will have serious side-effects. Is this "exactly the same" to "the eye of common sense" as administering the drugs intending that the child should suffer the side-effects? How many parents would entrust their child to a doctor who intended, rather than merely foresaw, the harmful side-effects? The moral difference in such everyday situations between trying to produce a bad consequence and merely foreseeing a bad consequence is obvious to the person in the street. The difference was elided by Williams, whose utilitarian lens shifted his focus from the agent's state of mind to the consequence the agent produced.[95]

In sum, Williams' analysis of the philosophical arguments informing the IOL was unsatisfactory. He set up a straw man. What of the arguments he advanced in support of his own position?

III WILLIAMS' HOLLOW MAN

Professor Williams' focus on theology served to distract him not only from the force of the moral arguments informing the IOL, but also from the weakness of his own. Having set up a straw man to knock down he replaced it with a hollow man of his own creation. His position on the value of life, which approximated a crude utilitarianism, was largely undeveloped and undefended. Nowhere did he recount, let alone respond to, standard objections to utilitarianism.[96] Moreover, his application of utilitarianism to the issues he addressed was generally cursory and question-begging. He regularly overlooked even utilitarian counter-arguments. To illustrate the inchoate exposition of his own approach, the nearest Williams got to a sustained account of the wrongness of murder was a short passage in the preface:

Much of the law of murder rests upon pragmatic considerations of the most obvious kind. Law has been called the cement of society and certainly society would fall to pieces if men could murder with impunity. Yet there are forms of

---

[95] For a defence of the distinction between intention and foresight by a doctor-philosopher (and former editor of the *Journal of Medical Ethics*) who does not adopt a natural law ethic, see R Gillon, "Foresight is not necessarily the same as intending" [1999] 318 British Medical Journal 1431. Though our palliative care scenario is familiar in the legal and philosophical literature, it appears that even increasing doses of morphine at the end of life, if properly titrated, do not in fact shorten life. See RG Twycross, "Where there is hope, there is life: a view from the hospice" in J Keown (ed), *Euthanasia Examined: Ethical, Clinical and Legal Perspectives* (Cambridge University Press, 1995) 141, 161–2. We shall return to this point, especially in Ch 11.

[96] Eg J Finnis, *Fundamentals of Ethics* (Oxford University Press, 1983); DS Oderberg and JA Laing (eds), *Human Lives: Critical Essays on Consequentialist Bioethics* (St Martin's Press, 1997).

murder or near-murder, the prohibition of which is rather the expression of a philosophical attitude than the outcome of social necessity. These are infanticide, abortion, and suicide.[97]

However, if "social necessity" were the criterion for the intervention of the criminal law, what would be wrong with allowing a strong majority to oppress a weak minority? The experience of the ancient world, which Williams was so wont to cite, shows that a society can survive not only with abortion and infanticide but also with racism, sexism, slavery, and gladiatorial games. Would he have objected to the intervention of the criminal law to prohibit *these* practices because such laws would be "the expression of a philosophical attitude"? And if he had responded that there were utilitarian reasons for prohibiting such practices (because prohibition would produce "the greatest happiness for the greatest number") would he not have been expressing a "philosophical attitude"? The central question is not whether but which philosophical attitude the law should express. It would have been valuable to have had the benefit of his thoughts on these important issues, issues central to the subject-matter of his book. Unfortunately, he chose not to share them. Moreover, without a concept of *justice* it is difficult to see how he could even begin to give an account of the right to equal protection of all members of society, especially the most vulnerable. Remarkably for a work on the value of life, particularly one written by one of the foremost criminal lawyers of the twentieth century, the concept of justice and the related concept of human rights were notable by their absence. In particular, as we have seen, Williams simply ignored the core moral argument informing the IOL, namely that because all human beings share a fundamental worth in virtue of their common humanity it is unjust to kill anyone on the pretext that their life is not worth living. Let us illustrate the fragility of Williams' own position with reference to his discussion of four of the major issues he addressed (and in the order in which he addressed them): infanticide, sterilization, abortion, and euthanasia.

A Infanticide

Williams' views on the ethics of infanticide were far from clear. Here, as elsewhere, he tended to cite various opinions without identifying which, if any, represented his own.[98] This obscurity did not, however, eclipse his support for infanticide in certain cases. He referred, in expressing his sympathy for infanticide, to the "supreme good" of producing the greatest

---

[97] SLCL 11–12.   [98] Eg Ibid 30.

happiness for the greatest number of human beings.[99] He cited one "courageously expressed" opinion that killing infants caused a minimum of harm because the victim could not feel fear or suffer pain "in appreciable degree," and because the killing of an infant left "no gap in any family circle," deprived no one of a breadwinner and no one of a friend, and caused no sense of social insecurity.[100] Leaving aside the contestable nature of some of these claims (how many mothers would agree that their baby's death left "no gap" in the family circle?) the underlying argument would appear to justify the killing not only of babies but also of older human beings. Imagine the (not fanciful) scenario of a small group of homeless, unproductive people who are a huge drain on public resources and a criminal nuisance to the affluent majority. Would the "supreme good" not permit, indeed require, their elimination (particularly if effected painlessly while they slept)? Though Williams did not point out that a utilitarian ethic might be used to justify killing on a much more extensive scale than he appeared to envisage, he did realize that the principle could be interpreted to *oppose* abortion and infanticide—on the ground that children, born and unborn, are human beings. He refrained from explaining why he did not favor this interpretation.[101] Further, when commenting on an interpretation that would focus not on the child but on the prospect of happiness the child might enjoy, he observed that on this interpretation "severely handicapped infants may rightfully be put to death."[102] He evidently assumed that people with serious disabilities were doomed to lives of such misery that it was right to suppress them at birth. One wonders whether, in later years, he ever consulted his eminent Cambridge colleague, Professor Stephen Hawking, who has lived for many years with motor neurone disease, about this assumption. The assumption was open to the objection of exhibiting the merest prejudice against those with disabilities. Williams observed that he was "not clear in [his] own mind" whether the view that all human life was inviolable "however disabled or worthless or even repellent the individual may be" justified the punishment of a mother who killed her "idiot child" at birth.[103] Toleration was a virtue, and even a moral person could be "flexible in his morality," not looking exclusively to the "rules of a legalistic ethic."[104] He concluded: "Regarded in this spirit, an eugenic killing by a mother, exactly paralleled by the bitch that kills her

[99] Ibid.   [100] Ibid 29.   [101] Ibid 30.
[102] Ibid.   [103] Ibid 31.   [104] Ibid.

mis-shapen puppies, cannot confidently be pronounced immoral."[105] This, then, was at the heart of his defense of infanticide: a question-begging analogy delivered in emotive rhetoric. He assumed the aptness of his analogy between moral agents (mothers) and non-moral agents (dogs). Moreover, he framed the ethical question in the emotive terms of whether it was right to punish the mother rather than whether it was right to kill the child. One may well (depending on the circumstances) sympathize with mothers who kill their children (born or unborn) without thereby condoning their actions. His references to "tolerance" and "flexibility" begged the question whether killing babies was something that *should* be tolerated. And why was an ethic which prohibited the intentional killing of innocent children "legalistic"? Was it because the principle was absolute? If so, why was Williams' (truly inflexible) utilitarian principle any the less "legalistic," not least when utilitarianism imposes a stringent duty always to promote the supreme good of human happiness as opposed to a much more limited duty to avoid wrongful conduct? Finally, if Williams really thought that his analogy was exact, why did he write that he was "not clear" about whether it was right to punish women? Was it perhaps because an open admission that his views justified infanticide and, it appears, in a much wider range of cases than he canvassed, would have alienated his audience? His analogy was revealing. Leaving aside the offense women would reasonably take in being compared to bitches, his equation of puppies and infants disclosed the scant moral worth he attached to the latter. A parent killing an infant who was an "idiot" or "misshapen" was no more objectionable than a bitch killing its deformed puppy. And what could be morally objectionable about a bitch killing its deformed puppy? Williams also appeared to entertain little moral objection to infanticide for financial reasons. He cited the hypothetical case where a mother[106] killed her children to save them from "desperate poverty, perhaps after trying in vain to have them taken off her hands by a children's home."[107] He cited a real case where a Scottish mother of six beat her two-year-old child to death with a broken chair leg. Williams commented that her punishment—six years' imprisonment—was a "terrible" sentence, pointing out that the child, Thomas, was "delicate and sickly, often crying and moaning" and that the "mother's record as to the other children, in care and treatment, was

---

[105] Ibid.
[106] Or, presumably, father or a person acting with the consent of the parents: see n 24.
[107] Ibid 39. Or perhaps not?

good beyond the average."[108] He complained: "Her husband, who had presented the overburdened woman with the six children, was exonerated from complicity!"[109]

Applying the utilitarian calculus advocated by Professor Williams, it is difficult to see what principled objection he might have had to infanticide for reasons other than disability or poverty.[110] But it was disability which commanded his attention and he made little attempt to disguise his disdain for disability. We have already noted his description of some disabled people as "worthless or even repellent."[111] Such pejorative epithets were not uncommon. Children with disabilities were, for example, "defective"[112] and "degenerate."[113] Some were even "monsters." By this he did not mean fictional creatures or pathological results of conception such as hydatidiform moles, but newborn children with disabilities. The medieval language of "monsters," rooted in a mistaken belief that such children were a result of bestiality, was taken up by Williams with gusto. He used the word approvingly on a score of occasions within three pages of text.[114] He even asserted that a monster was not a child, a he or a she, but a thing. He wrote:

On rare occasions such a monster will live. It may belong to the fish stage of development, with vestigial gills, webbed arms and feet, and sightless eyes. The thing is presented to its mother, who struggles to nurture it for a few months, after which she sends it to a home.[115]

This description made no more sense in scientific than it did in moral terms. A syndrome exists in which an excess of fibroblast growth factor during development can prevent the digits from separating and lead to webbed hands and feet,[116] but this has nothing to do with a "fish stage of development." At no stage of development do human beings have "vestigial gills": this is an invention by those who would force foetal development to track

---

[108] Ibid 39–40.
[109] Ibid (footnote omitted). Complicity in what offense? Paternity?
[110] He observed that there would be difficulties in providing by law for the euthanasia of "severely handicapped babies": such a proposal would provoke acute religious conflict and the medical profession might not cooperate. The most practicable course was, therefore, to recognize that the condition of a child killed by the parent may be the strongest mitigation: ibid 31. However, as his discussion of baby Thomas, the "delicate and sickly" two-year-old illustrated, Williams' sympathy for infanticide was by no means limited to "severely handicapped babies."
[111] See text at n 103.
[112] SLCL 34.
[113] Ibid 35.
[114] Ibid 31–3.
[115] Ibid 33.
[116] AM Leroi, *Mutants: On the Form, Varieties and Errors of the Human Body* (Harper Perennial, 2005) 117.

human evolution.[117] Williams' "fish-baby" was a product of his own imagination, derived from a medieval bestiary or a Victorian freak show. Its rhetorical function was simply to obscure the humanity of the disabled child, whom he regarded as a mere object. Williams concluded that it was probably lawful to kill a "monster."[118] He claimed that, while the ancient opinion to this effect by Bracton and others was based on the mistaken belief about bestiality, "the same rule might be approved for a better reason."[119] He did not vouchsafe what this reason might be. He went on to claim that the only objection, apart from the "extreme view" that a "monster" had an immortal spirit, was the difficulty of drawing a line.[120] Williams did not confront the objection that the "monster" is a human being and that human beings enjoy the right not to be intentionally killed even if they are seriously disabled. He concluded his chapter on infanticide with the comment that "a legal inquisition into conduct is not justified on moral or religious grounds if no sufficient social purpose is to be served."[121] He appeared not to consider the purpose of child protection.

B Sterilization

The less than generous attitude to the vulnerable which Williams exhibited in relation to infants, particularly those with disabilities, was also evident in his enthusiastic advocacy of eugenic sterilization. He endorsed the sterilization, both voluntary and compulsory, of potential parents he regarded as "unfit":

The obvious social importance of preventing the birth of children who are congenitally deaf, blind, paralysed, deformed, feeble minded, mentally diseased, or subject to other serious hereditary afflictions, and the inadequacy of contraception for this purpose, has naturally given rise to the proposal to use sterilization of the unfit as a means of racial improvement.[122]

He wrote:

We have evolved by natural selection, but, by keeping alive mentally and physically ill-equipped children, we are opposing natural selection. The logical deduction seems to be that, unless steps are taken to counteract the tendency, we shall as a race become progressively less fit.[123]

Whether or not "genetic decline" had begun, "the fact remains that the community is burdened with an enormous number of unfit members...."[124] There was a striking contrast between "fecklessness" in our own

---

[117] DA Jones, *The Soul of the Embryo* (Continuum, 2004) 170–1.
[118] SLCL 33.   [119] Ibid.   [120] Ibid.
[121] Ibid 42.   [122] Ibid 82.   [123] Ibid 83.   [124] Ibid.

reproduction and the "careful scientific improvement" of other forms of life under man's control: no cattle-breeder would behave as humans did in their own breeding habits.[125] Indeed, if a "human stud farm" produced a "sufficient overplus of good" it could be justified on utilitarian grounds.[126] He quoted Bertrand Russell's lament that "the ideas of eugenics are based on the assumption that men are unequal, while democracy is based on the assumption that they are equal."[127] The moral of the quotation was not, as the reader might innocently have supposed, that there was something morally problematic about eugenics, but rather that eugenicists (like Russell and Williams) should strive to overcome the baleful influence of egalitarian ideas. Williams noted[128] that the United States was the pioneer of sterilization statutes, whose constitutionality had been upheld by Supreme Court in *Buck v Bell*. This was the case in which Justice Holmes' judgment for the majority contained the (in)famous passage:

It is better for all the world, if instead of waiting to execute degenerate offspring for crime, or to let them starve for their imbecility, society can prevent those who are manifestly unfit from continuing their kind. The principle that sustains compulsory vaccination is broad enough to cover cutting the Fallopian tubes.... Three generations of imbeciles are enough.[129]

Williams noted that all of the statutes designated the "feeble-minded," all but one the "insane," and that most included epileptics.[130] Some were voluntary, others compulsory, and around 50,000 sterilizations had been performed by 1949.[131] It was right, he thought, that female "defectives" should submit to sterilization as a condition of leaving an institution. To the criticism that a woman's consent in such circumstances could hardly be said to be free and voluntary, Williams replied: "... few if any choices in life are voluntary, for every choice involves the acceptance of a course that is more preferred in place of one that is less preferred."[132]

---

[125] Ibid. [126] Ibid 134.

[127] Ibid 76. Not surprisingly, Russell thought the SLCL a "wholly admirable" book which was "wise, temperate, learned and kindly." (n 10) 382, 385.

[128] SLCL 84.

[129] *Buck v Bell* 274 US 200 (1927) 207. Cf the later decision of the Canadian Supreme Court that non-therapeutic sterilization of an incompetent person should never be authorized under the *parens patriae* jurisdiction. Delivering the judgment of the Court, La Forest J noted the need to proceed with the utmost caution because of "now discredited eugenic theories" which had encouraged many to regard the mentally handicapped as "somewhat less than human.": *Re Eve* (1986) 31 DLR 4th 1, 78. He concluded: "The grave intrusion on a person's rights and the certain physical damage that ensues from non-therapeutic sterilization without consent, when compared to the highly questionable advantages that can result from it, have persuaded me that it can never safely be determined that such a procedure is for the benefit of that person.": ibid 86.

[130] SLCL 84.

[131] Ibid.

[132] Ibid 88.

To allow such a woman to "run the risk of producing a family" might produce consequences "too tragic for enlightened opinion to tolerate."[133] He commented that states which had given their sterilization laws a fair trial regarded them as "beyond the experimental stage and as a proven means of social betterment."[134] Compulsion had, moreover, been "rarely exercised" and then only in mental institutions.[135] The United States experience had shown, he claimed, how remote from reality was the fear that voluntary sterilization laws might be the thin end of the wedge to widespread violation of human rights as had occurred in Nazi Germany. In the United States the opposite had happened: compulsory sterilization had given way to voluntary sterilization.[136] There was no case for compulsion, in his view, "unless milder methods are inadequate."[137] Finally, the sterilization of habitual criminals and homosexuals had been "restrained and cautious."[138]

Williams' "enlightened" views spoke for themselves. He evidently had no objection to the compulsory sterilization of gays, "habitual" criminals, and people with epilepsy.[139] Nor did he question the validity of consent to sterilization as a condition of release from an institution, regarding it as a choice like any other because all choices involved the preference of one course over another. On this approach there is no difference between one's choice to donate money to Oxfam rather than the Red Cross and one's choice to hand over money to an armed robber. At no point did Williams suggest that any additional burdens in raising a child faced by a woman with mental disabilities should be addressed by providing her with social support, or by offering adoption, rather than surgical sterilization. Was Williams genuinely concerned to help those with disabilities or merely to ensure they did not procreate? It is, moreover, extraordinary that Williams could, without embarrassment, use the language of "racial improvement" of "the unfit" less than ten years after the Nuremberg trials of doctors complicit in Nazi atrocities, acts which stemmed in large part from the decision of some within the medical and legal professions, years before Hitler came to power, to embrace a philosophy according to which certain groups of men, women and children were adjudged to have a "life unworthy of life."[140] The ideology of racial improvement had not been an

---

[133] Ibid.   [134] Ibid 89.   [135] Ibid 90.
[136] Ibid 91.   [137] Ibid 95.   [138] Ibid 91.
[139] He proposed that no person with epilepsy should be allowed to marry unless they had first been sterilized. Ibid 94. He also thought there was a "very strong eugenic reason" for abortion if the child would be diabetic. Ibid 161–2.
[140] A Hoche and K Binding, *Die Freigabe der Vernichtung Lebensunwertem Lebens* (Felix Meiner Verlag, 1920), translated by WE Wright as "Permitting the Destruction of Unworthy Life" in (1992)

accidental feature of Nazism but one of its defining principles. Just as Williams omitted the inconvenient fact of the Hippocratic Oath in his treatment of abortion, the no less inconvenient experience of Nazi eugenics was accorded only a fleeting mention which suggested that his main concern was that the Nazis had brought eugenics into disrepute.[141] Further, other accounts of the United States experience of eugenic sterilization differ from the sanguine picture painted by Williams. These accounts indicate that he was silent about three relevant facts: first, that the Nazis modeled their laws on the United States precedent; second, that the United States laws were also based on the principle of racial improvement; and, third, that compulsory sterilization in the United States was not performed only "rarely." One recent account, commenting on the first six decades of the twentieth century, reads:

Employing a hazy amalgam of guesswork, gossip, falsified information and polysyllabic academic arrogance, the eugenics movement slowly constructed a national bureaucratic and juridical infrastructure to cleanse America of its "unfit". Specious intelligence tests, colloquially known as IQ tests, were invented to justify incarceration of a group labeled "feebleminded". Often the so-called feebleminded were just shy, too good-natured to be taken seriously, or simply spoke the wrong language or were the wrong color. Mandatory sterilization laws were enacted in twenty-seven states to prevent targeted individuals from reproducing more of their kind. Marriage prohibition laws proliferated throughout the country to stop race mixing. Collusive litigation [*Buck v Bell*] was taken to the U.S. Supreme Court, which sanctified eugenics and its tactics.[142]

The account continues:

The goal was immediately to sterilize fourteen million people in the United States and millions more worldwide—the "lower tenth"—and then continuously eradicate the remaining lowest tenth until only a pure Nordic super race remained. Ultimately, some 60,000 Americans were coercively sterilized and the total is probably much higher. No one knows how many marriages were thwarted by state felony statutes. Although much of the persecution was simply racism, ethnic hatred and academic elitism, eugenics wore the mantle of respectable science to mask its true character.[143]

8 Issues in Law and Medicine 231. See M Burleigh, *Death and Deliverance: "Euthanasia" in Nazi Germany c.1900–1935* (Cambridge University Press, 1995).

   [141] SLCL 85.
   [142] E Black, *War Against the Weak* (FourWallsEightWindows, 2003) xv.
   [143] Ibid xvi. See also DJ Kevles, *In the Name of Eugenics* (Harvard University Press, 1995) ix; S Kuhl, *The Nazi Connection: Eugenics, American Racism, and German National Socialism* (Oxford University Press, 1994); Donnelly (n 10) 756.

C Abortion

It will be recalled that instead of answering the key question he posed, namely whether the early embryo could be described as a human being, Williams embarked on a theological discussion about the timing of ensoulment[144] and that, to the extent that he did engage with the philosophical basis of the IOL, he demonstrated an unimpressive grasp of it.[145] These shortcomings inevitably detracted from the case he constructed for relaxation of the law. How cogent could such a case be when it failed to confront the core moral argument that abortion involves the intentional killing of an innocent human being? Williams preferred to focus on alleged "social facts."[146] He sought to show that the law against abortion was a failure; that the effect of the law was "not to eliminate abortion but to drive it into the most undesirable channels."[147] The "social facts" he prayed in aid, chiefly the alleged incidence of illegal abortion, were, however, far from proven. He wrote that in England in 1955 there were 52 prosecutions resulting in 49 convictions out of, as was "agreed by all," some "tens of thousands" illegal abortions.[148] Williams' assertion that "tens of thousands" was an "agreed" figure was unsubstantiated.[149] He cited estimates ranging from 44,000 to 250,000 per year before admitting: "Unfortunately these writers do not state the way in which they arrived at their conclusion."[150] Williams concluded that there were 52,000 cases.[151] Unfortunately, he did not state the way in which he arrived at his conclusion.[152] Professor Dellapenna (who is pro-choice) has concluded, after analysing estimates for the United States and the United Kingdom: "Any estimate of the incidence of illegal abortion must remain largely a

---

[144] See text at n 72.

[145] See text at nn 91–5.

[146] SLCL, Ch 6, in which he advances his case for abortion law reform, is entitled "The Problem of Abortion: Morality and the Social Facts."

[147] Ibid 193.

[148] Ibid 192.

[149] Dr CB Goodhart, Cambridge zoologist and member of the Eugenics Society, concluded on the basis of (the low) maternal mortality statistics that "the true figure could not have exceeded 20,000 and was probably nearer 15,000 criminal abortions a year in Britain before 1967": "Abortion Freedom" <http://www.galtoninstitute.org.uk/Newsletters/GINL9406/abortion_freedom.htm>.

[150] SLCL 192. As Professor Mason has commented of such estimates: "the breadth of the bracket testifies to its lack of authority.": JK Mason, *Medico-Legal Aspects of Reproduction and Parenthood* (2nd edn, Ashgate, 1998) 115.

[151] SLCL 193.

[152] Williams mentioned two sources. The first was second-hand and unreferenced, being a passing mention by one doctor in 1932 of an estimate by another: SLCL 193, n 2 (citing LA Parry, *Criminal Abortion* (John Bale, Sons, and Danielsson Ltd, 1932) at 88). The second source was the Interdepartmental Committee on Abortion (1939) which accepted the suggestion that there were between 110,000 and 150,000 abortions per year of which two-fifths were criminal. But Williams had already included this among those estimates whose basis was unexplained: SLCL 192.

guess."[153] So much, then, for Williams' vanguard "social fact." As for the number of maternal deaths from illegal abortion, Williams admitted that it was "not precisely known."[154] Dellapenna points out that in the United States the figure of 10,000 deaths per year claimed by pro-choice organizations was mere propaganda. He quotes Dr Bernard Nathanson, formerly a leading abortionist, who admitted that his use of the figure had been a deliberate lie aimed at repealing the law against abortion.[155] Dellapenna also quotes Professor John Hart Ely's comment: "it is a strange argument for the unconstitutionality of a law that those who evade it suffer."[156]

By no means all who accepted high estimates of illegal abortion drew the conclusion that the law was ineffective and should therefore be relaxed. To support his own estimate of 52,000 illegal abortions per year, Williams cited the estimate accepted by the Interdepartmental Committee on Abortion (1939), chaired by Norman Birkett KC (as he then was).[157] However, the Committee did not recommend a loosening of the criminal prohibition. It concluded:

The induction of abortion is on ethical, social, and medical grounds essentially an undesirable operation, justifiable only in exceptional circumstances, and the Committee is strongly opposed to any broad relaxation of the law designed to make social, economic, and personal reasons a justification for the operation.... [158]

The Committee's conclusion did not, however, prompt Williams to appreciate that there might be a persuasive secular case against abortion.

---

[153] Dellapenna 557.

[154] SLCL 194. In 1970 John Finnis pointed out that deaths notified as due to abortions induced for reasons other than medical or legal indications numbered no more than 30 per year from 1961–7; that the number of maternal deaths was minute compared to deaths from other avoidable causes such as speeding or smoking; and that no woman whose life was threatened by continuation of her pregnancy need fear that her doctor would decline to terminate her pregnancy for fear of prosecution. He quoted a report by the Royal College of Obstetricians and Gynaecologists which stated that the law "commends itself to most gynaecologists in that it leaves them free to act in what they consider to be the best interests of each individual patient.... We are unaware of any case in which a gynaecologist has refused to terminate pregnancy, when he considered it to be indicated on medical grounds, for fear of legal consequences.": J Finnis, "Abortion and Legal Rationality" (1970) 3 Adelaide Law Review 431, 441; 462, Table B.

[155] Dellapenna 553.

[156] Ibid 557. Dellapenna observes that the US data suggest that there may have been as many maternal deaths from the 30 million legal abortions since *Roe v Wade* 410 US 113 (1973) than from illegal abortions in the years immediately preceding that decision: ibid 702.

[157] See text at n 152.

[158] *Report of the Interdepartmental Committee on Abortion* (1939) 123, para 14. It recommended that the law relating to therapeutic abortion be amended to make it unmistakably clear that a doctor was acting legally when he terminated a pregnancy in the honest belief that continuance of the pregnancy was likely to endanger the woman's life or seriously impair her health: ibid 122 para 13.

Moreover, he accepted that the law *was* effective in preventing registered medical practitioners from performing abortion.[159]

Another argument advanced by Williams in favor of relaxation of the law was that in practice there was no risk of the woman herself being prosecuted and that the "logical next step" would be to exempt doctors.[160] His reasoning was fallacious. It was one thing for the prosecuting authorities to show sympathy to the pregnant woman (not least as they might need her testimony); it would have been quite another for them to have exempted doctors, which would largely have emasculated the prohibition. Williams added that if moral rules were to be enforced, they should be "those that human beings in the mass are able to comply with, without excessive repression and frustration and without over-much need for the actual working of the legal machine. It is evident that this cannot be said of the present law of abortion."[161] He argued that even if his figure of 52,000 were wrong by a factor of 10, it showed "beyond all argument" that the law was ineffective.[162] However, given the difficulties inherent in detecting and prosecuting abortion, a prosecution rate of 1 per 100 might be thought not unreasonable. If 5,200 men each year had beaten their wives, would this have shown that the great mass of people were unable to comply with the law against assault without "excessive repression and frustration" (whatever that meant) or without "over-much need for the actual working of the legal machine" (whatever that meant)? Again, if 5,200 people each year had injected themselves with heroin for recreational purposes (conduct which, like abortion, risks mortality and morbidity but which, unlike abortion, may be entirely "victimless") would that have been a convincing argument for its decriminalization? Further, Williams did not consider the criminal law's educative and symbolic role. As Finnis has observed in his consideration of the effectiveness of the law against abortion, while a main aim of the criminal law is to eliminate undesired conduct, "the criminal law is not futile if it succeeds in doing little more than manifesting society's continuing commitment to its preferred values...."[163]

---

[159] SLCL 193.
[160] Ibid 146. He cited a case in 1932 in which a court held that a woman who had undergone an abortion could not refuse to testify for fear of self-incrimination because there was no substantial risk of her being prosecuted: ibid. Later, however, when illustrating the social problem of illegal abortion, he mentioned the prosecution of a woman in 1952 for attempted self-abortion: ibid 196.
[161] Ibid 211.
[162] Ibid 193.
[163] Finnis (n 154) 436. As examples of laws manifesting such commitment he cited the crimes of speeding and perjury and contrasted them with laws, such as Prohibition, which not only failed to eliminate the undesired conduct but which were "so widely and publicly flouted" by respectable members of society that they "lose even the character of symbolising a real societal commitment to

Williams rejected better enforcement of the law as a solution to the misery caused by illegal abortion.[164] The law against infanticide had succeeded, he wrote, but the law against abortion had failed. This was because the infant after birth, but not the embryo, was *felt* to be a human being and protective feelings were easy to arouse.[165] Miscarriage could happen spontaneously and did not engage our sentiments to any marked degree.[166] The question therefore arose whether the law should fix some lesser measure of protection for the embryo which was "more in accordance with human needs, public opinion, and the possibilities of enforcement."[167] He observed that the line to be drawn should be dictated by "social considerations and human happiness."[168] He rejected quickening (when the mother first perceives foetal movement) because it rested on "a rather obvious superstition" and caused evidential difficulties.[169] He thought viability, which was "conveniently fixed at the twenty-eighth week of pregnancy," was socially satisfactory because illegal abortions did not occur after that time.[170] He made the novel suggestion that in between these two points "one might take the time at which the foetal brain begins to function," which he placed at the seventh month, shortly before viability.[171] If, he added, one were to "compromise" by taking the start of the seventh month, that would virtually eliminate the problem of illegal abortion.[172] He proposed no restriction on abortion until that time.[173]

Williams' arguments were not immune to objection. He did not identify the "human needs" which abortion would meet, let alone those which could not otherwise be met. He had little to say about the state of public opinion, nor did he explain its significance to the question whether the law should be amended. He claimed that laws against abortion had been made by men and implied that there was more support for reform among women. His generalization that women supported repeal rested on a

---

the values they purport to uphold.": ibid. He concluded that the law against abortion was effective in suppressing, if not eliminating, the practice: ibid 437–9. Williams, in his argument to the contrary, seemed to want it both ways: the law should be relaxed if there were few prosecutions or if there were many.

[164] SLCL 196.
[165] Ibid 196–7.
[166] Ibid 206.
[167] Ibid 197.
[168] Ibid 206.
[169] Ibid 209.
[170] Ibid.
[171] Ibid. 210. Dellapenna points out that shortly after Williams wrote it was established that a foetal electroencephalogram could detect activity from the eighth week of pregnancy: Dellapenna 587.
[172] SLCL 210.
[173] He had written earlier, by contrast, that abortion should be "a last-ditch measure where the birth of a child is particularly undesirable.": ibid 201.

single tabloid poll.[174] Having reviewed more polls, Dellapenna has concluded: "Women consistently are less approving than men regardless of the reason for the abortion...."[175] We may add that the Parliament which passed the Abortion Act 1967 was overwhelmingly male and the United States Supreme Court which decided *Roe* was exclusively so.[176]

Williams seemed to assume that the significant question was whether the unborn child was *felt* to be a human being rather than whether it *was* one. As history has all too often shown, however, human sentiment can obscure recognition of our common humanity. Infants have been treated as disposable, women as second-class citizens, and black people as chattels. Williams' point that grief may not be pronounced over an early miscarriage is also unpersuasive. Death, whether of children or adults, may elicit no grief, perhaps because the deceased have no one to grieve for them or because (like serial killers) their passing is widely welcomed. This surely has little bearing on the question whether it is right to kill them. Moreover, the fact that some embryos miscarry naturally gives no warrant for induced abortion. Nature is not a moral agent: we are. Further, it will be recalled that Williams asked whether it could be said that a "week- or month-old embryo" was an "existing human being."[177] But he advocated the decriminalization of abortion up to the twenty-fourth if not the twenty-eighth week. He did not ask whether a child of *that* age could be said to be a human being. It does not follow that someone who replied negatively to the first question would have replied negatively to the second.

Williams' argument for reform purported to be driven by "social considerations and human happiness" but, if this was his criterion, his calculations were incomplete. He omitted to consider the promotion of better education about the humanity of the unborn in order to foster "protective feelings." Moreover, although he instanced being an overburdened mother as a justification for abortion,[178] he failed to consider the option of offering her social assistance. This failure was surprising, not least because the Interdepartmental Committee on Abortion had concluded: "To attempt by social and economic measures to relieve the financial difficulties associated

[174] He wrote that a tabloid poll of 2,000 women had found that 51 per cent of women respondents favored abortion on request and that a substantial proportion favored abortion for health reasons only: ibid 203, n 2.
[175] Dellapenna 956.
[176] *Roe v Wade* 410 US 113 (1973).
[177] See text at n 33.
[178] SLCL 196–8.

with childbirth and parenthood is fundamentally a sound approach to the problem of criminal abortion."[179] The Committee's conclusion made sense.

Such measures would surely provide the overburdened mother with an alternative to abortion. And what of the further alternative of adoption? Either way, there would be the happiness of the parents (biological and/or adoptive) and of the child-teenager-adult to consider. Why did the interests of the "tens of thousands" of unborn children, or at least the adults they would become if allowed to live, not figure in Williams' calculus?[180] By ignoring these relevant factors, he seemed to assume what he needed to prove. Did he genuinely apply the utilitarian ethic he advocated or did he have his elbow on one balance-pan?[181] Finally, his suggested time limit

[179] Williams did mention that if the state denied abortion to the mother of a "considerable family" deserted by her husband it should at least assume responsibility for the unwanted child: ibid 213. This was, however, a passing comment in relation to a specific ground for abortion rather than a serious evaluation of an alternative to relaxing the law.

[180] He subsequently mentioned the risk of emotional disturbance to a woman if an unwanted child was born and the fact of cruelty toward unwanted children: ibid 199. He produced no evidence relating to the risk of emotional disturbance from giving birth to an unwanted child, and he acknowledged the risk of emotional disturbance from abortion (see n 181). Moreover, he implied that an unwanted child resulted from an unwanted pregnancy, which is not necessarily so. A child unwanted during pregnancy may be wanted after birth. Finally, has the incidence of cruelty toward children diminished since the Abortion Act 1967 and *Roe*?

[181] As we noted above (n 29), Williams considered three secular arguments against relaxation of the law. The first was that abortion was medically contra-indicated; the second that it might lead to a decline in population; the third that it might result in a breakdown of sexual restraint: ibid 202. He rejected the first argument on the ground that even if the operation were medically undesirable "it is not for the legislature to pronounce upon this.": ibid 203. In no other branch of medicine, even the performance of lobotomies, did the legislature prescribe what was good for the patient. However, he himself proposed time limits for legal abortion, thereby inviting the legislature to "pronounce" on the permissibility of a medical procedure: ibid 208–10. Indeed, he cited "a leading English authority" who wrote in 1957 that "The hazards of therapeutic abortion in the second trimester are very real: long-term effects such as sterility, habitual abortion, and endocrine shock are as important as the operative risks involved. . . .": ibid 209–10, n2. Williams noted that a psychiatric study of women who had been legally aborted in Sweden showed that at follow-up 14 per cent expressed mild self-reproach and 11 per cent serious self-reproach: ibid 220–1. See also ibid 222, n 1. Moreover, legislation enacted after he wrote would, reasonably, place restrictions on psychosurgery and electro-convulsive therapy: see ss 57 and 58 of the Mental Health Act 1983. Similarly, outside the medical context, the criminal law restricts behavior which may be potentially harmful to life and health, such as driving without seatbelts. Why is a decision to restrict or regulate abortion not similarly within the proper sphere of legislative judgment? The second argument, Williams thought, scarcely merited serious attention, "for if valid it should lead us to penalize not only abortion but celibacy, contraception and emigration." The argument "can hardly apply to unmarried women," he added, and there were administrative means of stimulating fertility such as decreasing the financial cost of raising children: ibid 204. His response involved a non sequitur. Depending on the circumstances, a prohibition on abortion might (whether or not allied with other measures) be a feasible means of promoting sufficient population growth. (It has, indeed, been used, as Williams noted, for precisely this purpose, particularly in totalitarian countries such as the former Soviet Union: ibid 200.) His reference to the non-application of the argument to unmarried women was unexplained. It is noteworthy that Europe, which generally has permissive abortion laws, is now facing a serious fall in population growth. See "Ageing Europe confronts demographic time bomb", *The Times*, 23 June 2007. Williams rejected the third argument because "It seems an odd idea that a woman is to be punished for the sin of sexual intercourse by being forced to bring an unwanted life into the world—odder still when the mother is feeble-minded or psychopathic, so that the child, if only because of the upbringing it will get, is likely to be no asset to

seemed to make little sense, even on his own terms. He rejected quickening as based on an "obvious superstition" as to when life began but suggested others—viability and the start of foetal brain function—which equally bore no relation to the beginning of life. It is not easy to see why, given his apparently utilitarian approach, he did not propose abortion until birth. He certainly gave no principled reason against abortion until birth, which is unsurprising given his sympathy for infanticide.[182] Perhaps, again, he did not wish to alienate his audience. Was his apparently arbitrary line-drawing anything more than window-dressing?

For those who could not accept abortion on request until the seventh month he proposed abortion on a number of specified grounds up to that time. He thought that the strongest case (not surprisingly given his strong eugenic views) was where the child would have a serious disability. He wrote: "To allow the breeding of defectives is a horrible evil, far worse than any that may be found in abortion...."[183] It was an "offence to society."[184] Another ground was rape and other "suggested cases" included incest and women with four children.[185] Strangely, Williams proposed this course of more limited reform even though the "social facts" he cited from countries with experience of such legislation indicated that it did not reduce the number of illegal abortions. He noted the "convincing evidence" that its effect abroad had not been to reduce illegal abortion but to increase the number of legal abortions by creating an "entirely new clientele": women

---

the community.": ibid 204. He added that if the argument were valid it would seem to require a prohibition on contraception and even a ban on curing venereal disease, and it would not justify the whole of the law against abortion because the law was not limited to illegitimate pregnancies: ibid. His response to this third argument was open to the objection of being emotive and superficial. The argument need involve no intention to "punish" any woman for "sin" or to "force" her to bear a child, but need only discourage one form of conduct (sexual promiscuity, whether by the married or unmarried) by denying a means of negating one of its main unwanted effects. If this did help to discourage sexual promiscuity, with its attendant diseases (which are sometimes fatal or incurable) and threats to stable relationships, it is difficult to see why the legislature should be barred from taking these beneficial considerations into account. In relation to sexually transmitted diseases, Dellapenna comments: "there does seem to have been some increase in sexually transmitted diseases as a result of the legalization of abortion." He adds: "The increase seems simply to reflect the greater willingness of persons to engage in sexual relations with multiple partners because of decreased fear of pregnancy.": Dellapenna 706 (footnote omitted). Absent research indicating that the legalization of abortion would not produce adverse consequences to health and/or population, or would not promote sexual promiscuity, it is odd that a professed utilitarian like Williams appears not to have kept an open mind. His conclusion that these three arguments were "fanciful or logically irrelevant ... or both" (Ibid 202) seems wide of the mark.

[182] See Part III.A of this chapter.

[183] SLCL 212.

[184] Ibid.

[185] Ibid 212–3. He considered none of the standard counter-arguments to abortion in these cases. See generally C Kaczor, *The Ethics of Abortion: Women's Rights, Human Life and the Question of Justice* (Routledge, 2011).

who would not otherwise have sought an abortion.[186] The social result had been "to add the total of legal abortions to the total of illegal abortions rather than to reduce the number of illegal abortions...."[187]

D Physician-assisted suicide and euthanasia

Professor Williams made out an uncontroversial case against the criminal prohibition of suicide. He argued that the prohibition could serve to hinder medical treatment and that even if some powers of official restraint were necessary, they need not involve the use of the criminal law.[188] But he then proceeded to argue, controversially, that acceptance of this case equally required acceptance of the decriminalization of both assisted suicide and homicide on request. He began by asserting that the basis of the legal prohibition of suicide was Christian theology.[189] As with his treatment of abortion, Williams omitted to confront the moral philosophical case against suicide. The natural law criticism of suicide was caricatured as an argument from natural instinct.[190] Williams had the argument the wrong way round: human life is not a good because of our instinct to preserve it; it is because it is a basic good that we ought to feel strongly against taking it. It was Williams who committed the naturalistic fallacy when, it will be recalled, he claimed that because nature favored natural selection we ought to prevent the "unfit" from reproducing, and when he implied that because nature aborted embryos, so might we.[191]

He argued that according to "common sense" the rightfulness of suicide depended on the circumstances.[192] He cited approvingly one writer who observed that the greatest happiness of the greatest number may sometimes be attained by personal sacrifice, as the annals of heroism and martyrdom suggested.[193] It does not, however, follow that because heroes or martyrs foresee death, they therefore intend death, but Williams'

---

[186] SLCL 219.
[187] Ibid.
[188] Ibid 259–60.
[189] See nn 37–8. We noted above his misunderstanding of that theology at nn 54–7. He also wrote that Thomas More endorsed assisted suicide in his *Utopia* (SLCL 277) but More appears to have been satirical. See L Gormally, "Walton, Davies, Boyd and the Legalization of Euthanasia" in J Keown (ed), *Euthanasia Examined: Ethical, Clinical and Legal Perspectives* (Cambridge University Press, 1995) 113, 134. Williams also claimed that suicide was made a felony by the courts in order to enrich the royal coffers with property forfeited by suicides: SLCL 245, 248, 234–6. He provided no substantiation for this claim. Nor did he consider whether, if it were true, it accounted for the creation of felonies other than suicide.
[190] SLCL 237. For a classic contemporary exposition of natural law theory see J Finnis, *Natural Law and Natural Rights* (2nd edn, Clarendon Press, 2011). A valuable introduction is A Gómez-Lobo, *Morality and the Human Goods* (Georgetown University Press, 2002).
[191] See nn 123 and 166.   [192] SLCL 241.
[193] Ibid.

conflation of foresight and intention led him to think otherwise. In his world, both Judas and Jesus were suicides.[194]

Williams' argument for decriminalizing suicide was persuasive. He was, however, largely pushing at an open door. He noted that since the First World War, policy had in general shifted to one of non-prosecution of attempted suicides.[195] The decriminalization of suicide by the Suicide Act 1961, only a few years after the publication of his book, can be seen as the culmination of a change in attitude which had dawned long before. Williams did not, however, confine himself to the decriminalization of suicide. The tail of his chapter on suicide contained a sting. Although the bulk of the 50-page chapter was devoted to making an uncontroversial case for the decriminalization of suicide, its final five pages argued, almost as an afterthought, for something much more controversial: the decriminalization of assisting suicide and of homicide on request. His argument ran that if it were no longer illegal to commit suicide then it should no longer be illegal to assist someone to commit suicide.[196] He claimed that it was "universally conceded" that one who incited a young person to suicide was "properly punishable" but that a physician who assisted his dying patient in suicide might well be regarded as beyond "any intelligently conceived prohibition."[197] These "sensible" results could be achieved by punishing only those who acted from "selfish motives."[198] This move, in turn, logically required the endorsement of unselfish homicide by consent for it would be absurd to distinguish between the doctor who supplied a lethal poison to the patient and the doctor who poured it down the patient's throat.[199] Williams submitted, therefore, that the law might well exempt from punishment the unselfish abetment of suicide and the unselfish homicide upon request.[200]

His proposal was, then, far from modest: he urged that the law permit anyone to kill anyone else from "unselfish" motives on request.[201] Motive is, of course, generally irrelevant to criminal liability in the criminal law of English-speaking peoples, and for good reason. What limits would be placed on killing by the notion of "unselfishness"? And if a killer were to claim that his motives had been "unselfish," how could the prosecution prove otherwise? We should also recall the elastic notion of "consent" advocated by Professor Williams: he regarded consent to sterilization as a

---

[194] Ibid 242.
[195] Ibid 249.   [196] Ibid 274 (footnote omitted).
[197] Ibid.   [198] Ibid.
[199] Ibid 275.   [200] Ibid 276.
[201] It seems clear that Williams, who used "request" and "consent" interchangeably, was proposing that an "unselfish" killing be protected provided the victim consented, even if the victim did not request it. This is indicated by a passage in which he stated that his proposal would protect a person who suggested suicide: ibid 274.

condition of discharge from a mental institution as akin to consent to give a penny for the Guy.[202]

Second, it does not follow that the decriminalization of suicide requires, logically or otherwise, the decriminalization of assisted suicide, let alone consensual murder. The decriminalization of suicide need involve no moral condonation of suicide and can be justified on other, prudential, grounds. Indeed, such grounds were at the heart of the case Williams himself advanced for decriminalization.[203] Further, he noted, but did not respond to, the argument that the threat of punishment might not work against a potential suicide but might be effective against a potential abettor.[204] This argument helps to explain the existence of the offense of assisting suicide in the Suicide Act 1961. We noted in Chapter 1 that the government's intention was that the Act should not condone suicide,[205] and that in the *Pretty* case Lord Bingham confirmed that the policy of the law remained firmly adverse to suicide.[206]

Third, even if one thought that suicide were not immoral there would be sound prudential reasons for not following Williams' proposal for decriminalizing "unselfish" assistance in suicide and consensual homicide. Oddly, for an ostensible utilitarian, Williams did not explain why his proposal would produce a surplus of human happiness. Indeed, he had earlier approvingly cited evidence which seemed to undermine his proposal, including one study which indicated that four-fifths of students had said they had sometimes wished for death. Williams had commented: "Common sense suggests the unwisdom of having an institutionalized means of gratifying such a passing fancy promptly and painlessly."[207] Yet would his proposal not have permitted rendering assistance in suicide even though the request was merely a passing fancy? He also seemed to have forgotten his earlier statement that it was "universally conceded" that one who incited a young person to commit suicide was "properly punishable".[208] He noted that besides resulting in the loss of a young life "the suicide of an only son or daughter will almost infallibly destroy the mother's happiness for the rest of her life."[209] Yet his proposal would have permitted "unselfishly" assisting a young person in suicide and thereby helping to destroy not only a young life but also parental happiness. Further, he recognized that suicide was frequently the outcome of a

---

[202] See nn 132–40.   [203] See n 188.
[204] SLCL 274.   [205] Chapter 1, text to nn 44–6.
[206] Chapter 1, text to n 47.   [207] SLCL 240.
[208] See n 197.   [209] SLCL 243. And the father's?

"passing impulse or temporary depression"[210] and that there was an association between committing suicide and being lonely, divorced, or an immigrant.[211] Rather than advocating improved social support and psychiatric help for such vulnerable people, Williams' only proposal was to make it easier to kill them or help them kill themselves. One might have expected that he would at least have required medical evidence that their request was not the result of a "passing impulse or temporary depression" and that their request was free and well-considered,[212] but he did not do so.

We may illustrate the laxity of Williams' proposal with reference to two hypothetical cases mentioned in the Law Commission's discussion of suicide pacts in its consultation paper on the law of homicide. In the first, D and V are involved in a shoot-out with the police. Eventually, they realize that capture is inevitable. D and V agree that D will kill V and then turn the gun on himself. D kills V but is arrested before he can turn the gun on himself as agreed.[213] In the second case, D is the leader of a fringe religious cult. He persuades his followers to meet to commit suicide together. At the meeting, with his followers' consent, he pours a lethal poison down their throats but finds he cannot summon the courage to do the same to himself when the moment comes.[214] The Law Commission observes that in relation to such cases it is "hard to see a reason" for reducing the crime in these cases below first-degree murder.[215] Under the proposal advanced by Professor Williams, however, D would commit no offense whatever. This would be so even if D never intended to commit suicide. Indeed, Williams' proposed reform appears to have been so lax that it would have allowed anyone to tour the country persuading the elderly and disabled to have a plastic bag held over their head to reduce government expenditure on pensions and health care.[216]

---

[210] Ibid 261. On the clear association between suicide, requests for assistance in suicide, and depression, see the statement from the Royal College of Psychiatrists cited in Ch 9, n 26.

[211] SLCL 264.

[212] Earlier he had argued that society should make sure that a determination to commit suicide was "fixed and unalterable.": ibid 262. How his proposal for decriminalization would have ensured this he did not explain. In its recent consultation paper on the law of homicide the Law Commission notes that "Suicide pacts are strongly linked with illness, both mental and physical, in one or both of the participants," that depression is the most frequent mental illness, and that this finding tied in with studies of individual suicide among the elderly in which 50–60 per cent were physically ill and 79 per cent suffered mental disturbance from depression: "A New Homicide Act for England and Wales?," Law Commission Consultation Paper No 177 (2006) para 8.63. The Commission quotes another study which observes that "Homicide-suicides in older people are not acts of love or altruism. They are acts of depression and desperation.": ibid para 8.80.

[213] Ibid para 8.21.

[214] Ibid.

[215] Ibid.

[216] He had observed earlier that society would "fall to pieces if men could murder with impunity.": SLCL 11–12. Would his proposal not have facilitated such killing?

Finally, what of the danger of abuse from purely selfish killing, such as the killing by husbands of wives they wanted to replace as quickly and cheaply as possible, or of children killing elderly parents to accelerate an inheritance? Williams recognized that his proposal might allow relatives to dispatch "invalids" and then plead their consent, safe in the knowledge that their victims could not testify.[217] Not all will find his response to this risk reassuring: "the danger of false evidence is one that the law has to meet in almost all situations, and it is not in itself a sufficient reason for opposing a change that is otherwise desirable."[218]

In arguing that the risk (of murder) was one the law had to meet and that the change in the law was "otherwise desirable" Williams surely begged the question: is not the highest purpose of the criminal law to protect the lives of innocent people? Why was it desirable to expose members of society, not least its most vulnerable members like the "elderly, lonely, sick, or distressed,"[219] those with disabilities, and women,[220] to the risk of being killed with impunity? Because, it appears, Williams thought that it followed logically from the case for decriminalizing suicide.

Williams recognized that his proposal was probably too radical for public opinion and he therefore fashioned a more limited proposal which would have permitted doctors to perform voluntary euthanasia to end severe pain in terminal illness.[221] He rejected the vulnerability of his proposal to the "slippery slope" argument.[222] In fact his proposal made

---

[217] Ibid 275.

[218] Ibid. He added that the killer would, for his own protection, call witnesses to hear the victim's request: ibid 275–6. But if the killer did not, how could the Crown prove beyond reasonable doubt that the request had not been made? It is noteworthy that since voluntary euthanasia and physician-assisted suicide were permitted in the Netherlands in 1984, thousands of cases have been covered up by doctors, despite a legal requirement to report. For an outline of the Dutch experience, see Ch 9, Part III.

[219] *Report of the Select Committee on Medical Ethics* (HL Paper 21-I of 1993–4) para 239. The Committee unanimously rejected the case for legalizing voluntary euthanasia and physician-assisted suicide, in no small measure because it would give rise to "more, and more grave problems than those it sought to address.": ibid, para 238. Similarly, an expert US committee concluded that decriminalization would involve "profound risks to many patients.": New York State Task Force on Life and the Law, *When Death is Sought* (New York State Task Force on Life and the Law, 1994) xiii.

[220] The Law Commission observes that "Gender differences are at work in both suicide pact and homicide–suicide cases.": Law Commission (n 212) para 8.68. It added: "in many cases men remain 'in control' of decision-making within the relationship, which explains the suspicion that, in many suicide pacts cases, men are taking the lead or even using coercion.": ibid para 8.78. There is evidence that even ostensibly voluntary requests by women for hastened death may not in fact be so. Katrina George writes of "a risk that the decisions of some women for assisted death are rooted in oppressive influences inimical to genuine autonomy, such as structural factors, for instance, social and economic disadvantage, and stereotypes that idealize feminine self-sacrifice, passivity and compliance.": K George, "A Woman's Choice? The Gendered Risks of Voluntary Euthanasia and Physician-Assisted Suicide" (2007) 15 Med L Rev 1, 33.

[221] SLCL 303.

[222] Ibid 280–1.

an inviting target for the argument, not least as he admitted that the limiting conditions in his proposal were dictated solely by political expediency. It is not necessary to repeat here Professor Yale Kamisar's classic utilitarian critique of the case advanced by Williams.[223] Suffice it to say that Williams admitted that he had no objection in principle to euthanasia for those unable to consent, whether adults or children.[224] The only reservations he mentioned in respect of non-voluntary euthanasia were pragmatic. These included a concern about trauma to the code of behavior built up by 2000 years of the Christian religion.[225] Given that he had devoted much of his book to trashing traditional Christian attitudes, this concern was peculiar. He concluded his book by quoting without disapproval a writer who had proposed that: "no child shall be admitted into the society of the living who would be certain to suffer any social handicap— for example, any physical or mental defect that would prevent marriage or would make others tolerate his company from a sense of mercy. . . ."[226]

IV CONCLUSION

The Sanctity of Life and the Criminal Law was a groundbreaking attempt to grapple with some of the most profound issues at the interface of law, ethics, and medicine. The book, written with typical flair, stimulated widespread debate and formed the foundation stone of the new discipline of medical law. Half a century after its publication, it is still highly regarded by academic and practicing lawyers around the world. This survey of the foundation stone has, however, detected a serious crack. The book's core critique of the moral tradition which has historically informed Anglo-American criminal law, the IOL ethic, turns out to have been defective. This is largely because of the author's misunderstanding of that tradition. What the author tore down was a straw man of his own making. Further, the ethical alternative he offered was little more than a hollow man, largely a composite of inchoate argument and unsubstantiated assertion.

This chapter has identified four flaws contributing to this central crack in the foundation stone. First, Professor Williams misrepresented the IOL as

---

[223] Y Kamisar, "Some Non-Religious Views Against Proposed 'Mercy-Killing' Legislation" (1958) 42 Minnesota Law Rev 969. For Williams' (unconvincing) reply, see "'Mercy-Killing' Legislation—A Rejoinder" (1958) 43 Minnesota Law Rev 1.

[224] SLCL 310. Any such objection would, moreover, have been difficult to square with his equation of intention and foresight. If he had no objection to palliative treatment of the unconscious which had the foreseeable effect of shortening their lives, how could he object to the purposeful ending of their lives?

[225] Ibid.

[226] Ibid 312, n 1.

essentially theological. He seemed unaware of the long philosophical tradition against intentional killing of the innocent stretching from the Hippocratic Oath through Kant to the Universal Declaration of Human Rights.[227]
Even had the origin of the idea of the IOL been exclusively theological,
criticizing laws reflecting that ethic because of the ethic's religious origin
was akin to criticizing the statute abolishing the slave trade because William
Wilberforce was a Christian.[228] Second, Williams' analysis of theology was
no stranger to error. Third, to the limited extent that he engaged with the
natural law philosophical tradition informing the IOL ethic, he demonstrated that he did not understand it. Fourth, the arguments he advanced
to support his own position, whether based on ethics or social science,
tended toward the tenuous and tendentious. Although he purported to
adopt a utilitarian approach his book was light on utilitarian calculus. His
positions were often more asserted than argued and the promotion of human
happiness seemed to serve more as rationalization than reason. The book did
not even offer a sustained analysis of its central theme: the value of human
life and the proper role of the criminal law in protecting it.[229]

The discipline of medical law is not based on the thinking of a single jurist,
let alone a single book. But Glanville Williams' *The Sanctity of Life and the
Criminal Law* has not unreasonably been described as the foundation stone
of that discipline. To the extent that the discipline has been based upon it,
and continues to rest upon it, the discipline stands on a shaky foundation.

---

[227] There is a bare mention of Kant, in a quotation by another writer: Ibid 240.

[228] Williams' argument exhibited the genetic fallacy: focusing on the historical origins of a theory
at the expense of contemporary arguments in its favor. On this approach, modern Western democracy
and modern science could equally be discredited, for these are distinctive features of Western society
which are heavily indebted to its Judeo-Christian culture. The historical origins of an idea neither
validate nor invalidate it.

[229] One reason for at least some of the book's uncharacteristic deficiencies may well have been its
origin in a series of lectures, and in hastily prepared lectures at that. Williams mentioned to Professor
Skegg that he largely wrote the lectures in the space of five weeks before he delivered them at
Columbia (personal communication from Professor Skegg.) One can only assume that Williams spent
little additional time revising them for publication.

CHAPTER 3

SIR IAN KENNEDY AND THE VALUE OF LIFE: BUILDING ON GLANVILLE WILLIAMS' SHAKY FOUNDATIONS?

I INTRODUCTION

As we noted in Chapter 2, Ian Kennedy (now Emeritus Professor Sir Ian Kennedy) has been described, with Professor Peter Skegg, as one of the two "fathers" of medical law in England. The description is apt. If Glanville Williams laid the foundation stone of the rising academic edifice of medical law and ethics, in England and beyond, Kennedy and Skegg largely constructed the ground floor. Whereas Skegg's focus has been the interface of medicine and law,[1] Kennedy has ventured more widely, like Williams before him, into ethics and social policy. Few lawyers have done more than Ian Kennedy to stimulate popular debate on a range of medico-legal issues, not least those concerning the value of life. Indeed, Professor Gostin has described him as "perhaps the best known and most important figure in health law and ethics in the United Kingdom, and probably one of the most significant in Europe and North America."[2] Despite Kennedy's marked influence, his writing on the value of life (and, indeed, on medical ethics in general) has, like that of Williams, largely escaped critical evaluation. This chapter seeks to repair that omission. Much of his output on the value of life has concerned issues at the end of life which will, therefore, be the focus of this chapter. The chapter will

---

[1] PDG Skegg, *Law, Ethics and Medicine: Studies in Medical Law* (Clarendon Press, revised edn, 1988), deservedly his best-known work, deals mainly with criminal law and tort law.

[2] LO Gostin, "Dedicatory Essay: Honoring Ian McColl Kennedy" (1997–98) 14(1) Journal of Contemporary Health Law and Policy v–vi. He suggests that Kennedy "virtually invented the field" in the UK: ibid vi. He comments that Kennedy has had a "profound impact on legal academia" in the UK (ibid x) and that his views are "now embraced by much of established medicine.": ibid xi. It is therefore appropriate to subject those views to some scrutiny.

conclude that his approach to the value of life suffers from three shortcomings:

- his understanding of the principle of the inviolability of life (IOL) is, like that of Williams before him, flawed;
- he omits, again like Williams, adequately to articulate his own ethical framework concerning the value of life or to defend it: assertions too often substitute for arguments;
- what appears to be his ethical and legal framework appears to lack coherence and consistency. On the one hand it endorses positions which are consistent with the IOL; on the other hand it adopts positions which are at variance with it, in particular by accepting that certain lives are not "worth living", by assigning an inflated importance to self-determination, and by adopting Williams' conflation of intention and foresight.

This chapter will, therefore, suggest that not only is the foundation stone of the law and ethics of medicine, which was laid by Williams, defective, but that so too is a vital, load-bearing part of the ground floor which Kennedy has built upon it.

Kennedy has not written a book devoted to the value of human life. We must draw, therefore, on his three books and a major public lecture he delivered in 1994.[3] His first book, *The Unmasking of Medicine*,[4] was a revised version of the BBC Reith Lectures he delivered in 1980. The lectures were critical of the state of health care in the United Kingdom and urged, for example, wider public involvement in decision-making about health care at both the macro and micro levels. This is not a book which will detain us here for it dealt mainly with issues relating to the sociology of health and illness.[5] It had relatively little to say about the value of life.[6] Another possible source is a work Professor Kennedy edited with Professor Andrew Grubb, *Medical Law: Text and Materials*, the first edition of which appeared in 1989.[7] The book was, despite its title, more

---

[3] "The Quality of Mercy: Doctors, Patients and Dying" (The Upjohn Lecture, 1994).

[4] (George Allen & Unwin, 1981).

[5] Though the book provoked a welcome and lively debate on the state of modern health care, not all reviewers were impressed. The eminent medical sociologist, Eliot Friedson, commented: "This is a book that cannot be reviewed on academic grounds, for there is nothing new in it for readers of this journal, neither in its ideas nor in its rather skimpy data.": "Review Essay: Kennedy's Masked Future" (1982) 4 Sociology of Health and Illness 95. He added: "the intellectual qualities of the book are stereotyped and thin no matter how much one might agree—as I do—with the overall message.": ibid 96.

[6] The book comprised seven chapters: the six lectures plus a seventh chapter on legal and ethical issues at the end of life which drew on previously published papers.

[7] I Kennedy and A Grubb (eds), *Medical Law: Text and Materials* (Lexis Law Publishing, 1989) ("KGI"). A second edition appeared in 1994: idem, *Medical Law: Text with Materials* (2nd edn, Lexis Law Publishing, 1994) ("KGII"). A third edition, *Medical Law: Text with Materials* (3rd edn, Butterworths, 2000), was edited solely by Professor Grubb and will not, therefore, concern us.

materials than text, and its textual analysis of the value of life was surprisingly sparse. Despite the fact that the book ran to over 1000 pages, the editors did not disclose the ethical framework they adopted in their analysis of the cases and materials, an omission which rendered much of their ethical analysis more assertion than argument.[8] Moreover, the book raised doubts about the editors' understanding of the IOL.

The book's skimpy three-page section on the "sanctity of life" (under the subheading "Unhelpful arguments") comprised three misleading extracts on the principle. The first, and most extensive, was written by Peter Singer and Helga Kuhse, two of the principle's most prominent critics.[9] Another was an extract from opinions of the Law Lords in the cardinal case of *Airedale NHS Trust v Bland*,[10] a case in which, according to the editors, the principle "received its most careful examination by an English court."[11] However, the extract served merely to illustrate their Lordships' confusion of the IOL with vitalism.[12] Kennedy and Grubb also misstated the important principle of "double effect" which is central to an accurate understanding of the IOL. They wrote: "The theory of 'double effect' . . . seems to say that if an act may have two effects and the actor *desires* only one of them, which is considered a *good* effect, then he should be regarded as blameless even though his act also produces a bad effect."[13] This was doubly mistaken. First, "double effect" is concerned with the agent's intentions, not desires. One may intend to go to the dentist without desiring to or intend to kill without desiring to. Second, the statement omitted the requirement of proportionality. Conduct which one foresees may or will shorten life must be justified by a proportionate reason: it is unethical to take unreasonable risks with patients' lives. It is one thing for a doctor to administer morphine to ease the pain of a dying patient and thereby risk shortening life by hours. It is quite another to administer morphine to a healthy young patient with a migraine and risk

---

[8] The same is true of the second edition, which exceeds 1400 pages, reviewed by the author in (1995) 54(1) CLJ 190. The preface to this edition does claim that medical has a "conceptual unity" and that the "unifying legal theme" is human rights: KGII 3. This promising theme is not, however, developed in the volume.

[9] KGII 1197–9. Similarly, none of the six general works on medical ethics recommended in the first edition defends the IOL. Most are by its leading opponents (KGI 33), and the book's "brief introduction to moral reasoning" (ibid) is an extract from one of those same opponents. Further, the book's only extracts on whether physician-assisted suicide and euthanasia should be decriminalized are by leading advocates of decriminalization: KGII 1282–9 and 1316–24. And while there are extracts criticizing the law against euthanasia, there are none criticizing the law permitting abortion: ibid Ch 12. In such a sizeable collection of materials whose preface claims that the editors have brought together as much as they can "so that the reader has the opportunity to choose what to read and rely on" (ibid v) the IOL is notable by its absence.

[10] [1993] AC 789; analysed in detail in Ch 12.

[11] KGII 1199.

[12] Chapter 1, Part III.D1.

[13] KGII 1205 (emphases in original).

shortening life by years. The IOL prohibits not only the intentional but also the reckless (and negligent) shortening of a patient's life. Kennedy and Grubb's handling of the ethical distinction between "ordinary" and "extra-ordinary" treatments, which is also important to a proper understanding of the IOL, was also problematic. They began that the distinction, which allows for withholding treatment in some cases, could only be advanced "once an absolutist view of the sanctity of life is rejected."[14] This statement betrayed a confusion between the IOL and vitalism. Moreover, they listed the distinc-tion (as they did the "sanctity of life") under "Unhelpful arguments," but for no good reason. Their two extracts on the distinction pointed out that the determination of whether a treatment is "ordinary" or "extraordinary" turns on consideration of a number of factors. The editors concluded: "the distinc-tion is unhelpful in that the words represent a conclusion reached in the light of consideration of a number of factors."[15] But of course they do, as anyone familiar with the distinction is aware. This hardly makes the distinction "unhelpful."[16] Distinguishing between what is "reasonable" and what is "unreasonable" may turn on consideration of various factors, but does that make the distinction "unhelpful"? Finally, the editors appeared to attach an inflated importance to patient autonomy. They wrote that a "particularly important feature" of the doctor's duty to respect the person of the patient was to respect the patient's autonomy. This duty should bind the doctor "unless very strong counter-arguments can be advanced" and the doctor "must ordinarily act in accordance with the wishes of his patient."[17] As for parents, "their primary duty is to bring their child to an enjoyment of autonomy."[18] Such sweeping claims invited significant qualification.

The book which offers the greatest insight into Professor Kennedy's thinking on the value of life, particularly in relation to the end of life, is *Treat Me Right*.[19] Published in 1988, this is a collection of 18 of his essays on the law and ethics of medicine, half of which address the value of life.

[14] Ibid 1199–200.
[15] Ibid 1203.
[16] Both of the extracts rightly criticized the misunderstanding of "ordinary" to mean "usual" and of "extraordinary" to mean "unusual," but both extracts endorsed the distinction properly understood: ibid 1200–3. For example, in the second extract Dr Raanan Gillon observed that Catholic authorities have identified excessive expense, pain, difficulty, or other inconvenience, or lack of reasonable hope of benefit, as criteria for deciding that a proposed treatment would be "extraordinary" (and therefore not morally obligatory) in a particular case, and that this approach was also reflected in Anglican thinking. He continued: "There can be few people involved in making medical-ethical decisions, whether in practice or merely in theory, who would disagree with the general principles of assessment proposed in either the Roman Catholic or Church of England positions as outlined above.": ibid 1203.
[17] KGI 74.
[18] Ibid 75.
[19] I Kennedy, *Treat Me Right: Essays in Medical Law and Ethics* (Clarendon Press, 1988) ("TMR"). Gostin (n 2) viii describes this work as "vintage Kennedy" exhibiting "rigorous logic."

Our focus will be the final three chapters of the book, dealing with the end of life, which contain his most sustained ethical and legal analysis. The chapters, which overlap somewhat, are entitled: "The Law Relating to the Treatment of the Terminally Ill"; "The Legal Effect of Requests by the Terminally Ill and Aged not to Receive Further Treatment from Doctors"; and "Switching Off Life-Support Machines: The Legal Implications."[20] The three chapters, though pioneering attempts to grapple with complex legal and ethical issues at the end of life, illustrate the three weaknesses identified at the beginning of this chapter. The next part will consider the extent to which Kennedy's analysis is consistent with the IOL, the final part the extent to which it is not.

II A CONSISTENT ETHIC OF INVIOLABILITY?

A Against intentional killing

At various points in his discussion of end-of-life issues Kennedy advances positions consistent with the IOL. He writes that those who make the law have a duty to ensure that it:

strike[s] an appropriate balance between the interests of the various parties involved, without putting in jeopardy certain fundamental commitments, such as, for example, the protection of the individual and the absolute prohibition on the taking of another's life.[21]

He notes that "respect for life" is a cardinal principle of English law:

It follows that the taking of a patient's life by some conduct deliberately designed with the primary intention of bringing about his death is unlawful, whether it be at the patient's request or without his knowledge or consent. This is homicide.[22]

He defends the law governing the treatment of the terminally ill from the criticism that it is too vague and encourages "defensive medicine."[23] He submits that the law is not vague and "when properly understood...is sufficiently sensitive to the diverse realities it would seek to regulate...."[24] He adds that although the law sees the distinction between killing and letting die in terms of active versus passive conduct, he finds the distinction unhelpful in this context. The real argument, he writes, is not about how a doctor's conduct can be characterized but whether the doctor has fulfilled his or her duty to care for the patient in good faith. The principles of good

---

[20] TMR Chs 16–18. Chapter 16 is a reprint of materials published in 1980 and 1982; Ch 17 of a paper published in 1976; and Ch 18 of a paper published in 1977: ibid ix.
[21] Ibid 316.   [22] Ibid 321.
[23] Ibid 317.   [24] Ibid.

faith reflect professional ethics and general social morality, neither of which condones euthanasia. Consequently, to cause the patient's death, whether by act or omission, would be a breach of the doctor's duty to care for the patient in good faith, and hence unlawful. On the other hand, both professional ethics and social morality condone permitting a terminally ill patient to die if no treatment apart from treatment for dying was ethically indicated.[25] He continues that many doctors specializing in the care of the dying consider euthanasia "unnecessary, quite apart from its moral repugnance," for the medicines available allow doctors to relieve pain, distress, and agony which could prompt a consideration of euthanasia.[26] While this is so, he adds, by no means all hospitals and doctors are sufficiently educated in palliative care and "large numbers of patients outside hospices and centres of excellence may well, by virtue of their condition, continue to pose the problem of euthanasia."[27] He concludes:

The appropriate response, however, is not to alter the law so as to allow euthanasia, and thereby arguably undermine the respect for life enshrined both in the law and medical training. Rather, attention must be directed to ensuring that doctors who care for the dying understand and use the medicines and techniques now available.[28]

It seems clear that in the above passages Kennedy defends the prevailing law prohibiting the intentional killing of patients, a prohibition instantiating the IOL. Moreover, he also evinces respect for that principle to the extent that his views track its understanding of the limited scope of the doctor's duty to provide life-prolonging treatment to the dying.

B No duty to preserve life at all costs

To Kennedy, a "terminally ill" patient is one who has an illness which has been accurately diagnosed and which seems certain to bring about death within a relatively short time, since the illness is beyond both cure and palliation.[29] The doctor's duty, professional, ethical, and legal is, he writes, "to use all appropriate medical skills to make the time remaining to the patient as comfortable as possible."[30] Treatment other than symptom control or management is, therefore, inappropriate, unethical, and may subject the doctor to legal sanction.[31] But, just as the doctor should not do too much,

---

[25] Ibid 322.   [26] Ibid.
[27] Ibid.   [28] Ibid.
[29] Ibid 318. Why an illness need be beyond palliation to qualify as "terminal" is not explained.
[30] Ibid.
[31] Treatment aimed at extending the patient's life may be unethical and unlawful but it surely need not be. For example, a dying patient might wish life to be extended to afford a loved one living abroad time to travel to the bedside.

nor should the doctor do too little, as by distancing himself or herself from, let alone abandoning, the patient. As Kennedy puts it: "a dying patient is still a living patient. The law recognizes this and demands that care continue, even if its nature changes. This is an example of the English law's affirmation of its fundamental respect for life."[32] He notes that the doctor's duty to make the terminally ill patient comfortable includes easing any pain, and that because the law has incorporated the ethical doctrine of "double effect," a doctor is not in breach of duty if palliative treatment has the secondary effect of accelerating death, provided the doctor's "principal and primary intention is the alleviation of symptoms which are discomforting and irremediable in any less drastic a way."[33]

He addresses the question whether the doctor, "while prohibited from doing anything deliberately aimed at causing the death of his patient" may allow a patient to die, as by refraining from administering antibiotics to a patient with pneumonia or resuscitating a patient with heart failure.[34] Again, he eschews the distinction between acts and omissions, preferring to ask whether the doctor is under a duty to act.[35] The doctor's duty in relation to the terminally ill patient is to make the patient comfortable until death; the patient's death "is not an evil to be avoided at all costs...."[36] He cites Pope Pius XII[37] as the first to advance the view that doctors were not obliged to give, nor patients to accept, extraordinary medical measures, a view which, Kennedy writes, has been consistently understood as meaning "whatever here and now is very costly or very unusual or very painful or

[32] Ibid 319.

[33] Ibid 325. In a footnote he writes that any "reasonable understanding" of intention in law compels the conclusion that if the doctor knows death will probably follow he intends to bring that death about, and that the "better view" is that double effect is a "legal nicety." What the law is really doing, he writes, is allowing intentional killing as a matter of public policy when life is an "intolerable burden," the patient is dying, and "the only humane treatment" left is one with death as a likely consequence: ibid 325, n 7. This invites two objections, one legal, the other moral. First, while some lawyers (whether when Kennedy was writing or today) would agree that English criminal law equates intention and foresight—at least of consequences which are "virtually certain"—others would not. As we noted in Ch 1, Professor Skegg has observed that although English courts have sometimes come close to equating foresight of virtual certainty of consequences with intention, they "have tended to say that foresight of virtual certainty is something from which intention *may* be found or inferred, and (to the frustration of some academic lawyers) have stopped short of saying that such foresight is itself a form of intent...": PDG Skegg, "Medical Acts Hastening Death" in PDG Skegg et al. (eds), *Medical Law in New Zealand* (Thomson Brookers, 2006) 505, 524 (emphasis in original). Second, if the law regarded foreseen death in certain circumstances as intended death, why would it not endorse intended killing in those same circumstances? As we shall see in the next part, Kennedy's legal conflation of intention and foresight lures him into ethical inconsistency.

[34] TMR 322.

[35] Ibid 322–3.

[36] Ibid 323.

[37] Ibid n 2, citing 49 *Acta Apostolicae Sedis* 1027 (1959). Though the statement by Pope Pius XII was important, he was articulating a distinction which was already well-established in Catholic moral philosophy. See DA Cronin, *Ordinary and Extraordinary Means* (St Augustine's Press, 2009).

very difficult or very dangerous, or if the good effects that can be expected from its use are not proportionate to the difficulty and inconvenience that are entailed."[38] Kennedy concludes that this is not only a moral principle but "also the legal principle," adding that a doctor who continued treatment past this point "would be behaving at least unethically, if not unlawfully."[39] He adds that there is strong support for the idea that "excessive pain, expense, and hardship, together with no hope of benefit, may serve as the starting-points" and that the term "extraordinary treatment" (he reasonably prefers the term "ethically not indicated") is a conclusion rather than a starting-point for analysis.[40] The law, he observes, lays down the general principle, and the doctor who acts skillfully, reasonably, and in good faith is protected.[41]

Kennedy's legal and ethical analysis seems hitherto broadly to adopt traditional Western medical ethics, and to run along the crucial lines that life should never be intentionally taken but need not be preserved at all costs.[42] However, he proceeds to jump the rails, without apparently realizing it.

C From the IOL to quality and autonomy

1 From "quality of life" to "Quality of life"

As we noted in Chapter 1, the IOL draws an important distinction between the worth of patients and the worth of treatments, holding that while the lives of all patients are worth living, not all treatments are worth giving. There is no duty to undergo "extraordinary" or "dispropor-tionate" treatments, those which are, in the circumstances, either futile or too burdensome. This is the moral (and legal) principle identified by Kennedy in his citation of Pope Pius XII.[43] However, Kennedy's under-standing of the principle proves deficient. He writes that terms such as "extraordinary treatment" and "quality of life" merely state the problem

---

[38] TMR 323 citing (ibid n 3) the [Anglican] Church Assembly Board for Social Responsibility, *Decisions about Life and Death* (1965). His endorsement of the distinction here contrasts with his description of it as "unhelpful" (see text at n 15) in KGII.

[39] TMR 323. While the application of an "extraordinary" or "disproportionate" treatment might be unlawful and unethical, it need not be. There is nothing necessarily unlawful or unethical in a patient requesting, and the doctor providing, an extremely burdensome treatment or a treatment offering a very slender chance of success. See n 31.

[40] TMR 324.

[41] Ibid 324.

[42] His reliance on "professional ethics and general social morality" (see text at n 25) is potentially problematic. If he is adopting a relativistic ethic, that the morality of a practice depends on prevailing medical and social opinion, his approach is clearly inconsistent with the IOL, which is immune to such vagaries. The IOL holds that social opinion can no more justify killing patients than it can justify genocide.

[43] See text at n 37.

and that what still has to be worked out are the criteria which would not justify intervening aggressively "or, to put it another way, would amount to a quality of life which was not worth having."[44] Here his analysis begins to unravel. This statement, which assumes that certain lives are not worth living, is clearly inconsistent with the IOL. Once he concedes this, he forfeits any principled objection to the intentional abandonment or even killing of such patients. By accepting the concept of the life which is "not worth living," he begins to saw off the branch he is sitting on. He cuts even more deeply when he allows life to be trumped by autonomy.

2 From life to choice

Kennedy notes that the doctor's general duty to the terminally ill patient comprises two fundamental principles. One, which we have already noted, is respect for life. But the other, which he mentions before respect for life and which he seems to regard as even more important, is respect for self-determination. He writes:

Perhaps the most fundamental precept of the common law is respect for the liberty of the individual. In a medical-legal context this means that a person's right to self-determination, to deal with his body as he sees fit, is protected by law. The doctor's first duty is to respect this right.[45]

This, he adds, applies as much to the terminally ill patient as to any other. The patient may not be abandoned, but the care given must change from treating for living to treating for dying. Thus, if a patient who is aware of the nature of his or her condition and competent to make a decision refuses further treatment from his or her doctor, continued treatment constitutes battery. The "principle of self-determination" overrules any notion that "the doctor knows best" or "some vague notion of there being a public policy in favor of preserving life."[46] Although, he continues, "the first duty of a doctor is to listen to and respect the wishes of his patient", the patient's self-determination is not unlimited:

A person's autonomous choices call for respect only as long as they do not seriously impinge on another's enjoyment of his autonomy and that other has not agreed beforehand to give up certain of his choices as a condition of practising medicine in, for example, the National Health Service.[47]

This limitation on patient autonomy yields two consequences. First, if a patient were to refuse nursing care, the hospital's duty to maintain hygiene and protect the health of the other patients would entitle the

---

[44] TMR 324.   [45] Ibid 320.
[46] Ibid.   [47] Ibid 321.

hospital to demand acceptance of such care as a condition of remaining in hospital. Continued refusal would justify discharging those patients fit enough to be moved and with somewhere to go, and forcing the others to submit. This would not, however, extend to feeding, which Kennedy regards "as a form of aggressive treatment."[48] The second consequence is that, although a patient may refuse certain procedures, it is doubtful that the patient can insist on procedures "which the doctor, in the exercise of reasonable medical judgment, in good faith regards as uncalled-for."[49]

There is a reasonable amount in Kennedy's (albeit sketchy) account of the principle of respect for autonomy with which traditional professional medical ethics would agree. In that tradition, the responsibility for safe-guarding the good of the competent patient's life and health attaches primarily to the patient, not the doctor. It is, therefore, the patient who has the right to decide whether to seek and undergo medical treatment. It is for the patient to decide, in the light of appropriate advice from the doctor, whether a treatment would be "extraordinary" or "disproportion-ate" because it would, say, be too burdensome.[50] Traditional ethics would also agree with Kennedy that patient self-determination is not absolute: the patient has no right to request interventions that the doctor in the exercise of reasonable medical judgment concludes are unwarranted, such as the amputation of a healthy limb. It would also agree that the patient's right to refuse treatment does not extend to the refusal of basic care where the refusal would undermine the hygiene of other patients. Traditional medical ethics would, however, go further. As it sees the primary goal of patient self-determination as the promotion of the goods of life and health, refusals which undermine that good, such as refusals of "ordinary" or "proportionate" treatment and basic nursing care, lack moral justification. Diabetic patients, for example, standardly have no moral justification for refusing routine life-saving insulin injections. Again, patients standardly have no moral right to refuse basic care, even if only their own hygiene will suffer. Patients have no more right to soil their sheets than to starve themselves to death. Crucially, however, Kennedy does not tie the right of patient self-determination to the good it serves: the patient's life and health. He seems to regard choice as a free-standing, self-serving, and almost absolute good. He asserts, we will remember, that perhaps "the most fundamental precept" of the common law is "respect for the liberty of

---

[48] Ibid. Why feeding, apparently whether naturally or by tube, should be regarded as "medical treatment," let alone "aggressive treatment," is not explained.

[49] Ibid.

[50] This is not to say that the patient's judgment is necessarily right, simply that it is primarily the patient's judgment to make, not least because patients vary in their sensitivity to burdens such as pain.

the individual" which, in a medico-legal context, means a person's right "to deal with his body as he sees fit" and that the doctor's "first duty" is to respect this right.[51] This controversial inversion of the relationship between respect for autonomy and respect for life risks confusion. We may begin by noting that Kennedy cites no authority to support his sweeping propositions. While traditional medical ethics and law have long recognized the right of a competent patient to refuse treatment, neither has ever recognized a patient's right "to deal with his body as he sees fit." Indeed, much of the law is concerned with constraining individual choices about what we do with, and to, our bodies. Were there such a radical right, the law would surely permit cannibalism, slavery, snorting cocaine, bestiality, incest, and driving without seatbelts, not to mention dueling and bare-knuckle fighting (at least in private). In the medical context, were it a doctor's "first duty" to respect such a right, doctors would be legally and ethically bound (or at least permitted) to perform both voluntary euthanasia and female genital mutilation and to amputate healthy but unwanted limbs. Contrary to Kennedy,[52] there *is*, as the laws prohibiting voluntary euthanasia and assisting suicide plainly illustrate, a public policy in favor of preserving life.[53] Kennedy criticizes the notion as "vague" but does not explain why it is so, and his assertion of the right of a person "to deal with his body as he sees fit" is anything but precise.

In short, Kennedy seems to exaggerate respect for autonomy and to do so because he overlooks its important but instrumental importance in the medical context: the protection of the goods of life and health. Just as it is easy to slide from "quality of life benefits" to "beneficial Quality of life" without even realizing it, so too it is easy unwittingly to inflate the patient's qualified right to refuse treatment[54] into an absolute right "to deal with one's body as one sees fit." But to do so risks contradiction. This is nicely illustrated by Kennedy's argument, to which we shall now turn, that the refusal of treatment or care cannot amount to suicide, and that withholding or withdrawing treatment or care cannot amount to assisting suicide.

3 From refusal of treatment to assisting suicide

Kennedy notes that assisting suicide is a serious crime and that a doctor is under a duty "to refrain from any act which may aid his patient in

---

[51] See text at n 45. See also text at nn 17 and 18.
[52] See text at n 46.
[53] Not, of course, in the vitalistic sense of preserving life at all costs, but rather of protecting patients from being intentionally killed and from being denied "proportionate" treatments and basic care.
[54] And, in limited circumstances (as where the patient is close to death), food and water.

committing suicide."[55] According to Kennedy, if a competent patient refuses life-prolonging treatment, the doctor is obliged to respect the refusal and does not risk liability for assisting suicide. This is because "the patient is not ... committing suicide, but only declining further medical care."[56] Again, he writes: "If 'suicide' is defined as the doing of a positive act with the intention of ending life, then there would be no question of suicide in the case of patients who refuse treatment, but otherwise do no positive act, merely allowing death to occur."[57] It will be recalled that he even argues that a patient has a right to refuse food, and that to feed a refusing patient is "a form of aggressive treatment."[58] As for switching off a ventilator and hastening a patient's death, Kennedy advances three objections to liability for complicity. First, the "admittedly artificial" argument by Glanville Williams that this is an omission, not an act. Second, that the doctor has merely assisted the patient's refusal of further treatment: "The switching-off facilitates the decision, not the suicide."[59] Third, that "mechanical aids such as ventilators are 'extraordinary measures' in so far as they involve excessive pain or other inconvenience."[60] The fact that the patient has indicated that the treatment is a burden absolves the doctor of any duty to continue treatment.[61]

Kennedy's analysis is unconvincing. First, why may suicide not be committed by omission? If one's intention is to put an end to one's life, why does it matter if one effectuates that decision by an omission rather than an act? What is the moral difference between throwing oneself under a bus and deliberately failing to jump out of the way of an oncoming bus, or between eating food one has laced with a deadly poison and starving oneself to death? Similarly, why may assisting suicide not be carried out

---

[55] TMR 326.

[56] Ibid. He comments that there is a "fine line" between assisting suicide and making available drugs to relieve pain which, if taken in a sufficient dose, will cause death. He adds: "A court would, I submit, be slow to find liable a doctor who merely facilitated the self-determination of someone unable through illness to help himself.": ibid. This is ambiguous, but if it refers to the case of a doctor who gives a patient such drugs knowing that the patient intends to use them to commit suicide, and the patient does so, the doctor surely risks liability for assisting suicide, at least if he or she intended to facilitate the patient's suicide. See *A-G v Able* [1984] QB 795.

[57] TMR 341.

[58] See text at n 48.

[59] TMR 343.

[60] Ibid (footnote omitted).

[61] Ibid. He goes on to consider whether liability for assisting suicide may attach in the case of a "mentally unfit" patient who expresses "the wish to die." He concludes that although there is some authority to suggest that a doctor is under a duty to prevent suicide in so far as there is a duty to control the patient, it seems to be limited to cases where the patient "commits some act to achieve his end. ...": ibid. If the duty is indeed so limited, such that a doctor may be required to prevent a mentally unfit patient with diabetes from committing suicide by hanging, but not by failing to take an insulin shot, Kennedy does not explain why it should be so limited.

by omission? Take Nick. Nick is a young man who broke his neck in a diving accident and is now dependent on a ventilator in his motorized wheelchair. His wife, Candy, has just returned from a reckless weekend in a Vegas casino where she blew the family's savings on roulette. Nick asks his physician, Dr Soft, to disconnect him from the ventilator so that Candy will be able to claim on his life insurance policy and thereby restore the family to solvency. Dr Soft enthusiastically endorses Nick's request, expresses his keenness to facilitate it, and disconnects the ventilator so that Nick dies. In the light of this hypothetical, let us consider Kennedy's three arguments against liability for assisting suicide. The first is that disconnecting a ventilator is an omission rather than an act. Kennedy recognizes that this distinction is "artificial": it is widely accepted in both law and ethics that one may incur responsibility by a deliberate omission as well as by a deliberate act. The second is that the disconnection facilitates the refusal of treatment but not the suicide. This seems no less artificial. If the refusal of treatment is made in order to end the patient's life and if the doctor intends to facilitate that suicidal refusal, the doctor surely assists suicide. (If Dr Soft had administered a lethal injection, could he sensibly say that he did not facilitate Nick's death, but merely "respected his request for an injection"?) Kennedy's third argument against liability—that ventilators are "extraordinary" (or "dispro-portionate")—merits closer consideration. As Chief Justice Rehnquist observed in *Vacco v Quill*, neither a patient who refuses a treatment nor a doctor who withdraws it need intend to hasten death.[62] The intention may simply be to end a treatment which is futile or excessively burden-some and the hastening of death a merely foreseen consequence. Equally, however, both doctor and patient *may* intend the death of the patient, as in Nick's case. Each case must be considered on its own facts. It is not always easy to determine what a person's intention is, but neither is it always difficult: it is a task which juries regularly discharge. In any event, proving intention is a distinct issue from recognizing the legal and moral signifi-cance of intention. In short, the degree of importance Kennedy attaches to patient self-determination evidently leads him to condone refusals of treat-ment and care which are plainly suicidal and the intentional facilitation of those refusals by doctors. This clearly contradicts the principle of the IOL which he earlier appeared to endorse. His attempt to avoid the

---

[62] *Vacco v Quill* 521 US 793, 801: "a physician who withdraws, or honors a patient's refusal to begin, life-sustaining medical treatment purposefully intends, or may so intend, only to respect his patient's wishes and 'to cease doing useless and futile or degrading things to the patient when [the patient] no longer stands to benefit from them'."

contradiction by denying that suicide and assisting suicide may be carried out by omission seems to involve precisely the same sort of "semantic sleight of hand" and "logic-chopping" which, as we shall see, he robustly and rightly rejects elsewhere.[63] Had he written that the crucial ethical and legal issue is not whether patient and doctor carry out their intentions by an act or by an omission but what their intentions *are*, his ethical and legal framework would have been sounder. Although he recognized the importance of the distinction between intention and foresight in his (qualified) endorsement of the principle of "double effect,"[64] his elision of the distinction in the context of suicide and assisted suicide creates a problematic tension in his ethical and legal framework. Moreover, this elision, which emerges in his discussion of suicide and assisted suicide in his first and second chapters, comes home to roost when he considers, in his third chapter, whether the disconnection of a life-support machine may involve the offense of homicide.

4 From assisting suicide to homicide by omission

In addressing the question whether disconnection of a life-support machine may involve homicide, Kennedy considers three scenarios: the unconscious, dying patient; the temporarily dependent, emergency patient; and the conscious, chronically dependent patient whose condition is stable.[65]

a The unconscious, dying patient   Kennedy rejects the argument that liability does not attach because switching off the machine is an omission rather than an act and the doctor is under no duty to continue ventilation.[66] Such an approach, he contends, is "logic-chopping" and "semantic sleight of hand."[67] He argues that in none of the three scenarios does switching off the ventilator "have any significance, of itself, from a medico-legal point of view. 'Pulling the plug' is not an event to tax the criminal lawyer."[68] He seeks to show that the critical medico-legal decision is not switching a ventilator off but rather switching it on, either initially or after having turned it off.[69] If the ventilator is switched off and it is determined that the patient is dead, ventilation need not be resumed.[70] If, however, the patient breathes or shows some others sign of life, then the question arises whether ventilation should be resumed. The answer

---

[63] See text at n 67.   [64] See text at n 33.
[65] TMR 349. For the purposes of exposition, the ordering of his second and third scenarios has been reversed.
[66] Ibid 350–1.   [67] Ibid 351.
[68] Ibid 354.   [69] Ibid 351.
[70] Ibid 351–3.

depends on "what prospect the patient has of advancing along the line from hopelessness to improvement to recovery."[71] He adds that "The less the prospect—and most cases which reach this point will be hopeless— the less the obligation to continue treatment, including the use of the ventilator, which is thus seen as only one factor of many which have to be considered."[72] If, however, the patient is able to breathe and to sustain him or herself, the ventilator is otiose and need not be switched on again.[73] There seems little here to offend traditional medical ethics. The tradi- tional approach, as we noted in our discussion of suicide and assisting suicide, is not fazed by spurious distinctions between acts and omissions. It identifies the central ethical and legal issue as the scope of the doctor's duty, not whether discharge of that duty involves switching a machine on or off. The doctor's duty is to consider whether, in the light of the patient's condition, ventilation is "extraordinary" or "disproportionate," that is, whether it is futile or too burdensome. If it is, there is no duty to provide it or, if it has been provided, to continue it.[74] To the extent that Kennedy adopts this approach, he respects the IOL. His contention that the important question is whether to switch the ventilator on (or on again) rather than whether to switch it off seems distracting. Indeed, it is odd that someone who questions the acts/omissions distinction should attach significance to whether a switch is flicked off or is left off, and should deny that switching a life-support machine off raises questions to tax the criminal lawyer. Disconnection may, just like a failure to recon- nect, raise questions of criminal (and civil) liability. Take, for example, the doctor who disconnects a ventilator so as to be able to get away early for the weekend or to prevent the patient cutting the doctor out of his or her will. The crucial question must always be the content of the doctor's duty in the light of the patient's condition, not whether the switch is moved from "on" to "off" or vice versa. Indeed, Kennedy's focus on switching the machine back on (though it may well have been intended to focus atten- tion on the scope of the doctor's duty) is at least potentially as distracting as the focus he rightly criticizes on switching the machine off.

[71] Ibid 353–4.   [72] Ibid 354.   [73] Ibid.
[74] We should add, however (though Kennedy does not) that a doctor may never withhold or withdraw treatment—whether "proportionate" or "disproportionate"—with intent to kill. Just as it would be homicide to administer palliative drugs with intent to shorten life—even if the palliative dose was objectively in accordance with standard palliative practice—so too it would surely be homicide to withdraw a life-preserving treatment with intent to kill, even if withdrawal of the treatment could have been justified as being futile or too burdensome. While a doctor is not always under a duty to treat, he or she is always under a duty never to engage in conduct, whether by act or omission, with intent to shorten life. Yet again Kennedy appears to overlook the legal and moral significance of the doctor's intention. Cf his correct statement of the law: text at n 22. See also now s 4(5) of the Mental Capacity Act 2005, text at Ch 1, n 34.

b The temporarily dependent, emergency patient   In relation to this patient Kennedy concludes that, provided the prognosis is one of improvement or recovery, anyone who disconnects the ventilator "with knowledge that death will result and an intent to bring this about" is guilty of murder.[75] If, by contrast, the prognosis is poor, and treatment is futile, the ventilator may be disconnected. His analysis seems, as far as it goes, to be consistent with the IOL, which holds that while there is a duty not to intentionally hasten death by omission, there is no duty to provide "extraordinary" or "disproportionate" treatment.[76] It is in relation to the third category, the conscious, chronically dependent patient, that Kennedy's analysis appears to jumps the rails, and at the same point that his analysis of assisted suicide left the tracks: patient self-determination.

c The conscious, chronically dependent patient   In relation to this scenario, Kennedy starts by considering the competent patient who refuses further treatment. "What law," he asks, "governs the situation when a lucid adult whose continued existence depends on a ventilator decides that his existence is no longer tolerable and that he wishes to die?"[77] Kennedy accepts that it would be homicide to stab the patient to death. Why, then, would it not equally be homicide to hasten the patient's death by disconnecting the ventilator? Kennedy rightly rejects the answer that whereas stabbing is "killing" or "active," disconnection is an "omission to treat" or "passive."[78] However, he wrongly rejects the answer that whereas the doctor who stabs the patient plainly intends to kill, the doctor who disconnects the ventilator may well not. Kennedy writes that reasons of "motive or intention" cannot be relied upon if "good faith and the best of intentions prevail throughout."[79] He fails to distinguish an intent to kill from an intent to respect a right of refusal. The correct answer is surely that it *could* be homicide for a doctor intentionally to shorten the patient's life by disconnection, even at the patient's request, but that it would not be homicide if the doctor's intention were solely to respect the patient's right to refuse treatment, even if the doctor foresaw that the patient would die as a consequence. While doctors are under an absolute duty never intentionally to kill their patients they are not under an absolute duty to force treatment on them, even if the doctor believes, and believes rightly,

---

[75] TMR 359.
[76] It also indicates, contrary to his argument about disconnecting the unconscious, terminally ill patient, that switching off a machine, and not merely failing to switch it on again, may involve criminal liability.
[77] TMR 355.   [78] Ibid.
[79] Ibid. It is not clear what he means by this.

that the patient's reasons for refusing treatment are misguided, even self-destructive. It seems, first, that Kennedy's conflation of intention and foresight leads him to conclude that the doctor's intention is to kill in both cases and, second, that this conflation deprives him of the correct answer to the important question he poses. He resorts to four alternative answers, all of which are problematic and difficult to square with his earlier apparent endorsement of the IOL.

First, he cites the "libertarian premiss that a person's position should not be *irremediably* worsened by another's conduct."[80] Stabbing offends this principle, whereas disconnection allows a change of mind by the patient. However, if it is thought that the patient could and would be better off dead, why does stabbing worsen his or her position, irredeemably or otherwise? And disconnection would not allow a change of mind if it caused imminent death. Second, he suggests that it is better to have a clear, if crude, rule prohibiting all *acts* of killing rather than a qualified rule which might invite "chaos."[81] But if, as he rightly emphasizes, there is no inherent difference between intentionally killing by stabbing and intentionally killing by disconnection, why should the law prohibit one and not the other? Why is the risk of "chaos" increased by allowing killing by acts in addition to killing by omissions? Would not the best way to avoid chaos be to uphold, rather than undermine, the law's historic "bright line" rule prohibiting *all* intentional killing of patients? He argues, third, that recourse to stabbing is at least potentially more open to abuse. He fails, however, to explain why. It is not at all clear why killing by an act should be any more open to abuse than killing by omission. Indeed, is it not easier to camouflage killing by omission (as by pretending that the treatment had become "extraordinary")? Fourth, he argues that a patient on a machine who requests disconnection is a "comparatively rare phenomenon" whom the criminal law can regard as a "tolerable and justifiable exception to basic criminal law rules developed long before ventilators ever existed."[82] Even if it is the case that patients requesting disconnection is "comparatively rare," can the legitimacy of killing patients by disconnection turn on the number of people who might request to be killed in this manner? And what if an epidemic of polio, or kidney disease, increased the number dependent on machines and the number who requested disconnection? Would he argue that disconnection on request should once again be treated as murder? And if it were a "comparatively rare phenomenon" for patients dependent on a number of life-saving

---

[80]   Ibid 356 (emphasis in original).
[81]   Ibid.   [82]   Ibid.

treatments not administered by machine to request that their treatment be stopped, should it be lawful to withdraw their treatment with intent to kill them? Finally, what if the number of patients on ventilators who wanted to be stabbed rather than disconnected were a "comparatively rare phenomenon"? Would this be an argument for allowing them to be punctured?

Kennedy claims some support for his statement of the law from the California Natural Death Act 1976. While he recognizes the "very limited" scope of the Act, which allows competent patients to make a duly witnessed directive refusing mechanical or other artificial means which would serve only to prolong death where death is imminent,[83] Kennedy contends that the "general principle it enshrines" should be accepted as part of English law.[84] But the California law is far more modest than his apparent endorsement of suicide and assisting suicide by the withdrawal of treatment (and also presumably, as he regards it as a treatment, by withdrawal of feeding).

Kennedy turns briefly to consider the case of disconnection without the consent of the (competent) chronically dependent patient. He concludes that "given the necessary knowledge and intent" disconnection is murder, even if the motive is the good one of putting an end to misery and suffering. He rejects the argument that disconnection is merely an omission which permits death, contending that it is no different from intentionally cutting the high wire on which a tightrope walker is balanced.[85] He is surely right. But if it is murder to cut the tightrope without the walker's consent, why is it not murder to cut it *with* the walker's consent? The law has long been consistent that the consent of the victim is no defense to murder. Kennedy again appears to allow self-determination to trump the IOL, at least in cases of intentional killing by omission.

There appears to be a serious tension in Kennedy's reasoning. On the one hand, it appears to endorse the IOL by opposing active euthanasia and active assistance in suicide. On the other, it seems to endorse suicide, assisting suicide, and euthanasia by deliberate omission. The tension is aggravated by the author's general rejection of a distinction between acts and omissions. The tension, which is neither addressed nor resolved in *Treat Me Right*, played out six years later when, in a prestigious public lecture, Kennedy came out in favor of legalizing active voluntary euthanasia. His argument rested in no small measure on the conflation of intention and foresight that characterized his earlier analysis of the value of life.

---

[83] Ibid 357.   [84] Ibid 357–8.   [85] Ibid 359.

5 From homicide by omission to active killing

a An introductory hypothetical: Dr A and Dr B   In April 1994 Kennedy
delivered the Upjohn Lecture, arguing that the law against active euthanasia should be relaxed.[86] The lecture posits two hypothetical cases, Mr
X and Mrs Z. Their respective doctors, Dr A and Dr B, are caring,
respected doctors with impeccable backgrounds.[87] Mr X is in the final
stage of terminal illness and in great pain. He asks Dr A to "put him out of
his misery."[88] Dr A explains that he cannot do so but that he will "steadily
vary the cocktail of pain-relieving drugs which Mr X receives" and that
the effect will be that over a period of time, perhaps a few days, the dose
prescribed will be such that Mr X will in fact die, albeit "as a consequence
of the attempt to relieve pain."[89] Two days later, Mr X dies. Dr B's
patient, Mrs Z, is in virtually the same situation. In response to her
entreaties Dr B says "he will give her something which will bring her
the relief and release she seeks."[90] Dr B injects Mrs Z with potassium
chloride. She dies within minutes.[91] Kennedy writes that what charac-
terizes the two courses of conduct taken by the doctors:

is that the doctors' intentions were the same—to ease pain and bring about a
peaceful death—, their motives were the same—to be as caring as they can be for
their stricken patients—, their conduct was the same—the active administration
of injections—and the result was the same—the death of their patients, though in
Mr. X's case it took considerably longer to achieve.[92]

However, while it is true that both doctors may have intended to ease
pain, Dr A intended to do so by administering palliative drugs, whereas
Dr B intended to do so by bringing about the patient's death. In other
words, Dr A intended to kill the pain but Dr B intended to kill the patient.
Their intended end (the relief of pain) may have been the same, but their
intended *means* were not. Clare has £100 under her mattress. She donates
half of to the Red Cross. Dick steals the remaining half and donates it to
the Red Cross. Would it be accurate to describe the intentions of Clare
and Dick as the same: "to donate money to the Red Cross"? Moreover,
Kennedy's claim that the conduct of the two doctors was the same
involves an artificially narrow description of their actions which omits

---

[86] Ian Kennedy, "The Quality of Mercy: Patients, Doctors and Dying" (1994) ("QM"). References
will be to a later and also unpublished version of the paper dated May 1994 and delivered at a
workshop on the regulation of bioethics in Siena in June 1994. I am grateful to Professor Ronnie
Mackay for providing me with a copy of this version.

[87] QM 2.   [88] Ibid.
[89] Ibid.   [90] Ibid.
[91] Ibid.   [92] Ibid.

morally relevant facts. There are injections and there are injections. How can one meaningfully describe the actions of the doctors without mentioning what the injections were for? If, for example, Dr Smith vaccinates a child, Timmy, to protect him from measles, and Dr Jones injects Timmy with a lethal poison because he detests little boys called Timmy, are the actions of the two doctors the same: "the active administration of injections"? Again, if Paul, a shopper, summons the store's lift to get to the toy department on the top floor, and Sharon, an Admiral, launches a nuclear missile from the warship she commands, would it be sensible to claim that their conduct was the same: "pressing a button"?

Kennedy notes that the legal rationale which is offered for acquitting Dr A of murder but convicting Dr B is that doctors may bring about the death of patients such as Mr X and Mrs Z, "provided that their first and primary intention in embarking on the course of conduct that ends in death is to relieve pain."[93] He adds:

They can know that death will result, they can want and intend that death results, but as long as they claim otherwise—that "this is for your pain"—they are entirely within the law. If on the other hand they do something designed specifically to end the patient's life, they break the law.[94]

This statement seems contradictory. Kennedy tells us that if a doctor does something "designed specifically to end the patient's life," the doctor breaks the law. But he also tells us that if a doctor does something intending to end life, and claims that the intention was to relieve pain, the doctor is within the law. It is, moreover, misleading to state that so long as a doctor claims that his or her intention was solely to relieve pain, the doctor is entirely within the law: a jury may find on all the evidence that the doctor's intention was in fact to kill. Kennedy proceeds to advance five criticisms of the current legal prohibition on euthanasia, some of which overlap significantly with each other and with the arguments just considered.

b Ambiguity   Kennedy's first argument is that the law should try to be "clear and unambiguous," nowhere more so than when life and death are in the balance and a charge of murder is a consequence of breaking the law.[95] In the treatment of a patient whose life has become an intolerable burden to him, he adds, the law is far from clear:

It relies on there being an agreed list of pharmacological agents or medical interventions which are universally accepted as having a single function. But

---

[93] Ibid 3.   [94] Ibid.   [95] Ibid 4.

all drugs have multiple functions and are appropriate in some circumstances and inappropriate in others.[96]

What, he asks, is to stop a doctor claiming an intention to relieve pain, albeit through unconventional means?[97] Another source of ambiguity, he claims, is that "Everything turns on what the doctor claims he was trying to achieve."[98] As long as he uses "the right verbal formula" and records it in the patient's notes and to be on the safe side does not use too unusual a drug, he will stay within the law.[99] Knowing how to "play the game" becomes the crucial determinant of criminal liability, rather than what is objectively done.[100]

This argument is not free from difficulty. It asserts two sources of ambiguity. The latter source repeats the mistaken assertion that as long as the doctor claims that the intention was to relieve pain, the doctor is entirely within the law. The law, however, is not a matter of the doctor using "the right verbal formula" or of "playing the game." It is ultimately a matter of the jury determining, in the light of all the evidence, whether the doctor intended to kill. One might as well argue that the law against theft is ambiguous and should be relaxed because defendants may claim they honestly believed they had the owner's consent to take the property. Many crimes require proof of intent. It does not follow that those crimes are therefore ambiguous and that the law against them should be relaxed. What, then, of the former source of alleged ambiguity, namely, the absence of an agreed list of pharmacological agents or medical interventions which are universally accepted as having a single function? Kennedy fails to explain why this should create ambiguity. Is it not like saying that the law prohibiting murder but allowing self-defense relies on there being an agreed list of weapons which are universally accepted as having a single function? Just as a weapon may be used to commit murder or may be used in self-defense, so a drug may be used to kill or solely to relieve pain. The crucial question is whether the doctor's intention was to kill. The type and dosage of drug used may provide valuable evidence. It may or may not be difficult for the jury to decide, in the light of the evidence, particularly expert pharmacological and toxicological evidence, what the doctor's intention was. Difficulties of proof are inherent in the prosecution of many offenses, but this does not mean that the elements of those offenses are unclear.

---

[96] Ibid.   [97] Ibid.   [98] Ibid.
[99] Ibid.   [100] Ibid.

c Hypocrisy Kennedy urges that the law endorses hypocrisy: "We all know what you are doing, but use the magic words, 'I'm doing this to relieve your pain' and all will be well."[101] Alternatively, he argues, the law encourages casuistry, as those who are anxious to do right by their patients, as they see it, feel compelled to resort to subterfuge out of fear of prosecution. Fear of prosecution is, he accepts, eminently desirable when designed to deter what is agreed to be wrong. But when it is neither the means nor the end that is regarded as wrong and only "the absence of attendant rhetoric or ritual," such fear is itself wrong.[102]

No evidence is tendered in support of the allegation of hypocrisy. The allegation is, moreover, difficult to square with the prosecution and conviction of doctors who have performed euthanasia, including those who have sought to disguise their crime as palliative care.[103] And the assertion that euthanasia is not regarded as wrong must confront the fact that it is regarded as wrong by many, not least by the medical profession.[104]

d Patients' interests Kennedy argues that the law works against the interests of patients. Obviously, he writes, those patients who fall into the hands of a murderous doctor appear to be protected but such doctors are rare and what they might do should not determine the law.[105] Instead, we should concern ourselves with the everyday, conscientious doctor. Fearful of the law and not really understanding it, this doctor responds to his or her patient's wish for a peaceful end by embarking on a process of increasing dosage until the desired objective is reached.[106] This may take some time, during which the patient is required to suffer, physically and mentally, so that the proper form may be observed.[107] Furthermore, the patient may fall into that relatively small but no less real group of patients whose pain is beyond the reach of drugs. Such a patient "must simply continue to suffer until the proper legal courtesies have been observed and the final dose can bring the intended death."[108] The law asks him to suffer

---

[101] Ibid 4.

[102] Ibid.

[103] *R v Cox* (1992) 12 BMLR 38.

[104] The British Medical Association, the American Medical Association, and the World Medical Association have long opposed euthanasia.

[105] QM 5. He does not explain why protecting patients from murderous doctors, however rare, should not determine the law.

[106] Ibid.

[107] Ibid.

[108] Ibid. He does not substantiate the assertion that some patients are beyond palliation, and does not consider the option of palliative sedation.

so as to protect others even though, if those others are anything like him, it is precisely this "protection" they do not want.[109]

This third argument begs the question about whether the interests of patients *are* served by being killed, rather than receiving palliative care until natural death. Moreover, its account of the practice of the "everyday conscientious" doctor is scarcely less question-begging, not least in its implication that this doctor is "playing the game" of killing the patient by pretending to kill the pain. Relevantly, recent research indicates that the incidence of euthanasia and assisted suicide by doctors in the United Kingdom is "extremely low" and that doctors administering palliative drugs rarely intend to shorten life.[110]

e Trust   Fourth, Kennedy claims that the law "can harm doctors in their ability to maintain a relationship of trust and support when their patients most need it."[111] If, out of fear of the law or uncertainty about what he or she may properly do, the doctor rejects the patient's entreaties, it would be no surprise if the patient felt abandoned. The patient's trust in the doctor, so critical as death approaches, is lost and suffering is compounded.[112] The doctor is forced to deny his or her training and, to satisfy the patient's request, must engage in subterfuge.[113] Alternatively, the doctor must fail the patient by not providing the means to end the patient's pain.[114]

Like the third argument, the fourth begs several questions. Patients trust that doctors will not abuse their power and that doctors will put the interests of patients first. Doctors do not serve patients' interests simply by granting their requests, a truth Kennedy recognized earlier when he agreed that doctors may rightfully refuse autonomous requests for interventions which they do not believe, in the exercise of their clinical judgment, to be justified.[115] The question is, then, whether killing patients truly serves their interests. Doctors have for centuries taken the view that killing patients is an abuse of their medical power and a contradiction of their medical vocation to heal. This does not mean that by refusing to kill their patients they therefore abandon them. On the contrary, is not the killing of patients because their lives are no longer thought "worth living" (which is ultimately the alleged justification for euthanasia) the ultimate abandonment? What price trust if the patients

---

[109]   Ibid.
[110]   C Seale, "End-of-Life Decisions in the UK Involving Medical Practitioners" (2009) 23 Palliative Medicine 198.
[111]   QM 5.   [112]   Ibid.
[113]   Ibid.   [114]   Ibid.
[115]   See text at n 49.

have to wonder whether, as Professor Alexander Capron once memorably put it, the doctor is entering the room wearing the white coat of the healer or the black hood of the executioner?

f The public interest Kennedy's final argument is that the law undermines the public interest. The "hypocrisy" the law engenders brings it into disrepute, and the care and support a patient receives is made to depend on how alert the doctor may be to ways of manipulating the law.[116] This argument seems little more than a reheated version of his earlier argument that the law encourages hypocrisy. And, if by "care and support" Kennedy means killing, then he is right that the law prohibits it. But, as the palliative care experts who devote their professional lives to caring for the dying show through their inspirational work, there are more, and more positive, ways of providing care and support for their patients than by killing them. It is, moreover, surprising that in his discussion of the public interest, Kennedy makes no reference to the landmark report of the House of Lords Select Committee, the Walton Committee, which was published shortly before his lecture.[117] The Committee unanimously recommended that the law should not permit euthanasia. Its conclusion rested on two main pillars. First, that the prohibition on intentional killing is "the cornerstone of law and of social relationships" which "protects each one of us impartially, embodying the belief that all are equal."[118] Second, that it would not be possible to frame adequate safeguards against non-voluntary euthanasia.[119] The Committee was also concerned that the vulnerable, such as the elderly, lonely, sick, or distressed, would feel pressure, real or imagined, to request early death.[120] The Committee's conclusions are hardly irrelevant to the public interest.

In his argument for relaxation of the prohibition, Kennedy proposes a number of "safeguards." Euthanasia should be limited to patients who are competent, suffering intolerably (and beyond palliation) from a terminal illness, who have made a voluntary request after "appropriate counselling," and have obtained judicial permission for their life to be terminated by a physician.[121] He notes that many of these safeguards mirror those in place in the Netherlands.[122] He omits to mention the fact, exposed by a Dutch government survey published prior to his lecture, that those safeguards have been frequently violated. That survey disclosed that in 1990 Dutch doctors terminated the lives of 1000 patients

---

[116] QM 5.
[117] *Report of the Select Committee on Medical Ethics* (HL Paper 21-I of 1993–4).
[118] Ibid para 237. [119] Ibid para 238. [120] Ibid para 239.
[121] QM 17. [122] Ibid 18.

without consent, and that in the majority of cases they failed to comply with the modest requirement (much more modest than Kennedy's proposed requirement of obtaining court permission) of reporting each case to the authorities. His safeguards do little to assuage concern that they would set English law on the same slippery slope down which the Dutch have swiftly slid. He writes that there may be no slope and that, even if there is, not all slopes are slippery.[123] But he accepts that some of his safeguards are "problematical." The requirement of "terminal illness" could, for example, be relaxed in time.[124] And he gives no reason for withholding euthanasia from incompetent patients.[125] Moreover, he proposes that this fundamental change in the law—the dilution of the crime of murder and the framing of "safeguards"—should be effectuated by the judiciary.[126] But is not the proper role of the judges to uphold such a foundational principle of English law as the IOL? Is not the sort of radical change proposed by Kennedy, a change involving highly controversial issues of ethics and social policy, paradigmatically a matter for the legislature? Kennedy's argument[127] is that the courts have already reshaped the law relating to the withholding/withdrawal of treatment, as in cases like *Re J* and *Bland*.[128] But in those cases the courts (whatever the merits of their reasoning) reaffirmed the fundamental prohibition on the active, intentional killing of patients. As Lord Goff stated in *Bland*:

It is of course well known that there are many responsible members of our society who believe that euthanasia should be made lawful; but that result could, I believe, only be achieved by legislation which expresses the democratic will that so fundamental a change should be made in our law, and can, if enacted, ensure that such legalised killing can only be carried out subject to appropriate supervision and control.[129]

---

[123] Ibid.   [124] Ibid.

[125] He writes: "In this paper I am initially concentrating on the situation in which patients ask their doctors for help to achieve relief from pain and release from a life which no longer has any value to them" and that he is "putting aside other forms of euthanasia for the time being.": ibid 6. He asserts that one reason that Parliament is unlikely to change the law for some time to come is the difficulty of getting any thoughtful debate off the ground. Defenders of the "sanctity of life," he laments, represent themselves as fighting in the last ditch against those whose agenda is Nazi eugenics. Their "intimidatory tactics" (which he fails to specify) are a denial of the normal conventions of a society which boasts the Mother of Parliaments and a commitment to free debate. Euthanasia is regarded as a taboo subject, not to be discussed: ibid 6–7. Kennedy makes no attempt to reconcile these emotive claims with the reasoned rejection of euthanasia by the Walton Committee.

[126] Ibid 7. Kennedy argues that if a proper consideration of human rights requires the law to be changed, it is the duty of the court to do so: ibid 9. He makes no reference to the right not to be intentionally killed in Art 2 of the European Convention on Human Rights.

[127] QM 9–11.

[128] *Re J* [1991] Fam 33; *Airedale NHS Trust v Bland* [1993] AC 789. See ch 1, nn 25–30.

[129] *Bland* (n 128) 865. In *C v DPP* [1995] UKHL 15 the House of Lords issued guidelines for judicial law-making. Judges should beware of imposing a remedy where the solution to a problem is

Professor Kennedy seeks to evade the reaffirmation of the prohibition on active, intentional killing in *Re J* and *Bland* by conflating intention and foresight. The courts may well, he argues, condemn active, intentional killing, but they allow the injection of palliative drugs which foreseeably hasten death. As both actions, he claims, amount to intentional killing, and as the courts already allow the latter, they can simply decide to allow the former. All that is required is a "redescription of the doctor's conduct."[130] Despite the considerable weight placed by Kennedy on his assertion that the law's distinction between the two forms of conduct is unclear and ambiguous, he tenders no evidence that doctors, lawyers, judges, or juries find it so. Further, he ignores substantial evidence the other way, much of it contained in the report of the Walton Committee. The report noted that "The World Health Organization sees no difficulty with double effect."[131] No less importantly, the Home Office in its evidence to the Committee observed: "the existing law is, by and large, producing the right outcomes and not causing problems."[132] The Committee, in the light of all the evidence, robustly defended the principle:

Some witnesses suggested that the double effect of some therapeutic drugs when given in large doses was being used as a cloak for what in effect amounted to widespread euthanasia, and suggested that this implied medical hypocrisy. We reject that charge . . .[133]

The Committee continued:

Some may suggest that intention is not readily ascertainable. But juries are asked every day to assess intention in all sorts of cases, and could do so in respect of double effect if in a particular instance there was any reason to suspect that the doctor's primary intention was to kill the patient rather than to relieve pain and suffering. They would no doubt consider the actions of the doctor, how they compared with usual medical practice directed toward the relief of pain and distress, and all the circumstances of the case.[134]

---

doubtful; should be cautious about making changes if Parliament has rejected opportunities of dealing with a known problem or has legislated while leaving the problem untouched; are more suited to dealing with purely legal problems than disputed matters of social policy; and should not change the law unless they can achieve finality and certainty. Finally, fundamental legal doctrines should not lightly be set aside. These guidelines, which remain as prudent after the Human Rights Act 1998 as they were before, clearly militate against Kennedy's proposal that the judges should relax the law against euthanasia.

[130] QM 15.
[131] *Report of the Select Committee on Medical Ethics* (HL Paper 21-I of 1993–4) para 74 (footnote omitted).
[132] Ibid para 75.
[133] Ibid para 243 (footnote omitted).
[134] Ibid para 243.

Again, in a later debate in the House of Lords on the adequacy of the criminal law in relation to palliative care of the terminally ill, the Attorney-General, Lord Williams of Mostyn, told the House that he did not think a doctor would have the "slightest difficulty" with the "plain, simple" distinction between intentionally ending life and foreseeing the shortening of life as an incidental effect of palliative drugs.[135] The doctrine of "double effect" was not a sophistry, nor was the law difficult or obscure.[136] In short, Kennedy's core criticism of the law against euthanasia appears both conceptually flawed and empirically unsupported.

III CONCLUSION

Ian Kennedy is understandably regarded as a "father" of the discipline of the law and ethics of medicine. Like the discipline's "grandfather," Glanville Williams, he has played a signally important role in raising public awareness of a range of important questions at the interface of law, medicine, and ethics and has made a valuable contribution to academic analysis of those questions. Both he and Williams have been trailblazers of the discipline. But, sadly, the trail they have blazed in relation to the value of life leads into an intellectual thicket. In the preface to *Treat Me Right*, Kennedy writes: "My approach, whether in writing or in teaching is to try always to get the moral tackle in order before proceeding to the law."[137] But it is not clear what this "moral tackle" is. Although his ethical reasoning is more thoughtful and balanced than the crude consequentialism of Williams, and is free of Williams' invective against the Christian Church, it is not easy to detect a coherent, articulated framework of ethical principles.

   As we have seen, his analysis of the IOL and its relation with respect for self-determination is neither clear nor coherent. We will recall that Glanville Williams cautioned that for a lawyer to venture into other disciplines like moral philosophy was a risky trespass. This was confirmed by his own misunderstanding of the IOL, a misunderstanding due in no small measure to his conflation of intention and foresight. The very same conflation fogs Kennedy's analysis of the principle. Both the "grandfather" and "father" of the discipline illustrate how even leading lawyers in the

---

[135] *Hansard*, HL vol 583, cols 742–3 (1997–98). Lord McColl, an eminent surgeon, said that there was "no lack of clarity . . . among the thousands of palliative care doctors and nurses.": ibid col 724.
[136] Ibid col 743.
[137] TMR vii.

field have misunderstood one of its foundational moral principles.[138] Given their considerable combined influence, it is not surprising that there remains, to this day, widespread misunderstanding of the IOL in the legal academy, at the Bar and on the Bench.

---

[138] A new intellectual father for medical law, for whom philosophical inquiry involves no trespass, risky or otherwise, will be proposed in J Keown, "A New Father for Medical Law" in RP George and J Keown (eds), *Reason, Morality and Law: The Philosophy of John Finnis* (Oxford University Press, forthcoming).

CHAPTER 4

RESTORING THE INVIOLABILITY
OF LIFE AND REPLACING
THE CARICATURE

The previous chapters have suggested that both the "grandfather" and "father" of medical law have seriously misunderstood the inviolability of life (IOL). Their misunderstanding is shared by many contemporary medical lawyers. This chapter will consider the work of just two: Professors David Price and Emily Jackson. It will suggest that the representation of the IOL by Professor Price as "vitalist," and by Professor Jackson as "religious" and "speciesist," is something of a caricature, and that their alternative ethical approaches are based on vague and arbitrary notions of "Quality of life", notions which endanger the vulnerable.

I PROFESSOR PRICE

The paper on which we shall focus is one Professor Price wrote in reply to my critique of the British Medical Association (BMA) guidance on the withholding and withdrawal of medical treatment and tube feeding.[1] While I welcome Professor Price's acceptance of the force of my criticisms of the BMA guidance,[2] I demur to his criticisms of the IOL. The burden of my critique of the BMA guidance was that it prohibited the intentional killing of patients by an act but, incoherently, appeared to permit the intentional killing of certain patients (such as those in a persistent vegetative state (PVS)) by withholding or withdrawing medical treatment (including tube-feeding). The guidance thereby tracked the decision of the Law Lords in *Airedale NHS Trust v Bland* which, by allowing the

---

[1] D Price, "Fairly Bland: an alternative view of a supposed new 'Death Ethic' and the BMA guidelines" (2001) 21 Legal Studies 618 ("Price"), replying to J Keown "Beyond *Bland*: a critique of the BMA Guidance on withholding and withdrawing treatment" (2000) 20 Legal Studies 66.
[2] Price 619.

intentional killing of a patient by the withdrawal of tube-feeding but not by an act, left the law in a "morally and intellectually misshapen state."[3] Price submits that the "central thrust of *Bland* is entirely appropriate and that the BMA Guidelines constitute a useful step down an admittedly testing path."[4] His reply to my critique discloses several common misunderstandings of the IOL, but this chapter will confine itself to three. All three show his representation of the IOL to be something of a caricature. As Professor Price is but one of many learned contemporary writers on the law and ethics of medicine who appear to entertain this caricatured view of the IOL, it is important to show why it is misleading.

A Vitalism, IOL, and "Quality of life"

Professor Price exhibits probably the most common and fundamental misunderstanding of the IOL: its confusion with vitalism. He seems to think that there are only two ethical alternatives to the valuation of human life: "vitalism"—which espouses the principle that one should preserve life at all costs—and "Quality of life"—which espouses the principle that one should not preserve and may even intentionally terminate lives that are thought not to be "worth living," that lack sufficient "quality." He sees little room for a middle way: the IOL. Unfortunately, because Price conflates the IOL with vitalism he concludes that my standard account of the IOL, which allows life-prolonging treatment to be withheld or withdrawn in certain circumstances, must be a "modified" version of the IOL. He writes:

The softening [of vitalism] engendered by the modified sanctity of life principle however (excluding the need to administer futile or excessively burdensome treatment), is no more than a very minor concession, or sop, to opponents and it remains unacceptably sweeping.[5]

My account of the IOL (the account sketched in Chapter 1) is not a "modified" version of the IOL: it outlines the principle as historically understood by moral philosophers and as it has historically informed the law.

Price rejects[6] the distinction drawn by the IOL between a judgment about the worth of a proposed treatment (which it permits) and a judgment about the worth of a patient's life (which it does not), between, as we expressed it in Chapter 1, "quality of life benefits" and "beneficial Quality

[3] [1993] AC 789, 887, per Lord Mustill. See Ch 1, text to n 29. *Bland* is analyzed in Ch 12.
[4] Price 619.
[5] Ibid 638. See also ibid 618, 621, and 643.
[6] Ibid 621, 643.

of life."[7] Price makes the bold claim that the distinction drawn by the IOL between worth of treatment and worth of life is false. He claims that "it is not feasible to draw any bright line between such notions, either practically or ethically" and that "the logic of the argument turns out to be, wholly contrary to the thesis submitted, supportive of the very vitalist philosophy rejected by it."[8] He also accuses the IOL of "ignoring underlying handicaps in assessing the worthwhileness of treatment options," of "ignoring the patient's anticipated impairment(s) where successful treatment prolongs life," of "divorcing the individual from the condition and/or the treatment,"[9] and of regarding the objects of medicine "as being divorced from the wishes and interests of patients."[10] Were these claims true, they would amount to a damning indictment of the IOL. But they are not, as has been pointed out in several publications which are in fact cited by Professor Price.[11] The reality is that the IOL takes full account of the patient's condition as it is now and as it would be after the treatment in order to decide whether the benefits of the treatment, if any, would outweigh its burdens, if any. It is not a question of *whether* the principle takes physical and mental disabilities into account but of *how* it takes them into account. Such disabilities may well be relevant in assessing the worthwhileness of a proposed treatment, but the principle does not allow their use in an assessment of the supposed worthwhileness of the patient's life. Price denies that a distinction can be drawn between "quality of life benefits" and "Quality of life," but his denial is unconvincing. The hypothetical case I have posited elsewhere[12] of Angela, a baby born with Down's syndrome and an intestinal blockage, illustrates the validity of the distinction. Her intestinal blockage is preventing Angela from digesting her food. Without an operation to remove the blockage she will die. The operation is a simple procedure (and one which would impose no burden on Angela beyond that imposed by routine surgery). There is surely a clear moral distinction between deciding that the treatment would be worthwhile because it would allow Angela to live the normal lifespan of a person with Down's syndrome and would impose no significant burden on

---

[7] Ch 1, Part III.D.1 above.

[8] Price 621.

[9] Ibid 624–5.

[10] Ibid 641.

[11] J Keown, "Restoring Moral and Intellectual Shape to the Law after *Bland*" (1997) 113 LQR 481; J Keown and L Gormally, "Human dignity, Autonomy and Mentally Incapacitated Patients: a Critique of *Who Decides?*" [1999] 4 Web J Current Legal Issues; and J Finnis "*Bland*: Crossing the Rubicon?" [1993] 109 LQR 329, all cited in Price n 3.

[12] Keown (n 11) 485–6.

her, and deciding that the operation is not worthwhile because *life with Down's syndrome* is not worthwhile. If we change the hypothetical so that the surgery would involve enormous pain and expense, with minimal chance of success, there is again a clear moral difference between deciding that the treatment would not be worthwhile because its burdens would outweigh its benefits, and deciding that the operation should not be performed because life with Down's syndrome is not worthwhile. To frame the distinction another way, it is between, on the one hand, those who think that the lives of all patients are worth living but that not all life-saving treatments are worth giving and, on the other, those who think that certain patients are "better off dead." The fact is, pace Price, that, while some doctors adopt the latter position, by no means all do. Nor need they. Nor should they.

Why does Price resist the distinction, which cases like Angela's show to be in accord with both reason and common sense? A clue can be found in his misunderstanding of the reasons why, according to the IOL, a treatment may be not worthwhile. The IOL holds that a treatment may be not be worthwhile because it is either futile or too burdensome. A treatment may be futile because it would offer no reasonable hope of therapeutic benefit and it may be too burdensome because it would involve excessive pain, expense, or inconvenience. Price quotes the following statement of mine that, in relation to a patient in PVS:

Sanctity of life ethicists are agreed that since medical treatment, whether antibiotics or ventilation, can do nothing to restore those in pvs to a state of health or well-functioning, it is futile and need not be provided.[13]

Revealingly, Price then asks:

But how could such ventilation be properly viewed as being "futile" in the proper, non-normative, physiological sense? It would potentially enable him to be restored to his previous state of existence. If that state is perceived as being an unacceptable level of "health and well-functioning" then an implicit judgment is being made as regards the individual's ('Q'uality) of life. In reality, what is being said is that properly diagnosed pvs is such an extreme condition allowing no prospect of sentient existence that the continuance of his *life* could be of no benefit to him.[14]

Price here exhibits two misconceptions about the IOL, which we shall now consider in more detail.

---

[13] Price 626–7, quoting Keown (n 11) 500.   [14] Price 627 (emphasis in original).

1 IOL as vitalist

First, Price confirms the suspicion that he regards the IOL as vitalist. He refers above to "futility" in what he describes as its "proper, non-normative, physiological sense." But this narrow conception of futility is "proper" only to vitalism: it is rejected by the IOL. A treatment that cannot achieve its physiological purpose is clearly futile. However, according to the IOL (as Price's above quotation from a paper of mine makes clear[15]) a treatment may be futile even if it *can* achieve its physiological effect. For example, one may be able to resuscitate a 99-year-old, irreversibly and imminently dying patient who has suffered a massive cardiopulmonary arrest. However, the IOL would regard such resuscitation as futile because, despite the fact that resuscitation may be physiologically feasible, it would offer no reasonable hope of therapeutic benefit to the patient. Unlike vitalism, the IOL does not advocate keeping people alive at all costs by stretching out the natural process of dying. Price argues that the category of "dying patients" is "arbitrary, obscuring of the ethical rationale for any treatment limiting decision and too crude as a class of case where treatment may legitimately be withdrawn or withheld."[16] While we may lack a precise definition of "dying," this surely no more makes the notion "arbitrary" than the absence of a precise definition of "reasonable" renders that concept arbitrary. Moreover, doctors are surely often able to predict with some accuracy that a patient has only hours or days to live. Indeed, Price accepts, at least in some cases, that "a person can properly be said to be 'dying'."[17] He also accepts that, in another hypothetical case, that of Bertha,[18] a moribund young girl, ventilation is properly withheld because it would impose significant burdens on her. He writes that the fact that she has only hours to live is "an overwhelming factor."[19] Is he not, then, conceding that, in the case of the imminently dying (a not inconsiderable category of patients) the withholding of treatment need involve no judgment whatever about the worth of the patient's life? If so, then is he not accepting the validity of the distinction advocated by the IOL? And if he accepts it in this case, why not in others? Imminent death is but one good reason for not trying to prolong the life of the patient by medical treatment because it cannot restore him or her to anything approaching a state of health and well-functioning. Price continues that not everyone who is "dying" can be said to have only hours to live. This is true, but even if a patient has a day or a week to live, this is surely a relevant consideration in deciding whether the benefits of a proposed treatment

---

[15] See text at n 13.   [16] Price 628.   [17] Ibid.
[18] Keown (n 11) at 486.   [19] Price 628.

would outweigh its burdens. The realization that a patient is dying surely clarifies rather than "obscures"[20] the ethical issues at stake and helps ensure that the focus is on palliative care, not curative medicine.

2 Limited purposes of medicine or "Quality of life"?

Professor Price's second misconception is that if the IOL does not require the ventilation of patients in PVS because ventilation cannot restore the patient to condition of health and well-functioning then in reality it is because the patient's life is thought to be of no benefit.[21] This is a non sequitur. According to the IOL, the purpose of medicine is not (as, again, Price's above quotation from my paper makes clear[22]) to preserve life at all costs, but to restore the patient to a condition of health and well-functioning (or to some approximation of it) and, where that is no longer possible, to palliate symptoms.[23] A decision to withhold or withdraw a treatment because it cannot restore the patient to health and well-functioning is not a decision that the patient lacks value. The IOL holds that the lives of those in PVS are still of value and that it is gravely wrong either intentionally to kill them, by act or omission, or abandon them on the ground that their lives lack worth. The good of their lives remains even though they are in a seriously incapacitated condition and are (at least presumptively) no longer able to enjoy the other goods of life (such as knowledge and aesthetic appreciation). However, given the patients' incapacitated condition and the inability of ventilation to restore them to health and well-functioning, ventilation would be futile.

Price goes on to argue that just as judgments of medical futility must involve "Quality of life" judgments, so too must judgments that treatment would be excessively burdensome. He quotes approvingly one commentator who asks: "how are we to know when a treatment becomes *excessively* burdensome—ie excessively risky, painful, costly—in the absence of any reference to the future quality of life that the treatment promises to purchase?"[24] The IOL would broadly agree, provided "quality of life" refers to the patient's future condition, that is "quality of life benefits," and not to a judgment about the supposed worth of the patient's life. It is

---

[20] Ibid.

[21] See text at n 13.

[22] Ibid.

[23] See Ch 1, n 31. Having quoted the IOL's understanding of the primary role of medicine as being the restoration of health, Price comments: "But 'medicine' and 'health' do not exist in a vacuum divorced from the individual to whom they attach. They have no 'end in themselves', but are intended for the benefit of the individual.": Price 642–3. But of course the role of medicine is to benefit the individual patient. Price's implication that the IOL denies this is puzzling.

[24] Price 629 (emphasis in original).

obviously difficult to decide if a treatment is excessively burdensome without a consideration of its anticipated benefits, just as it is difficult to decide if £30 is excessively expensive for dinner if one does not know whether what is going to be served up is lobster thermidor or a bag of greasy chips. But it is clear from Price's discussion of this quotation that he is using "quality of life" to mean "Quality of life," as including an assessment of the supposed worth of the patient's life. His criticism of the IOL is therefore misdirected. According to the IOL, account should indeed be taken of any improvement the treatment would make to the patient's condition, but this is not at all the same as considering whether the patient's life will or will not be "worth living." To illustrate the distinction, a patient could properly judge that even a treatment which promised a complete restoration to health would be too burdensome because its exorbitant cost would reduce his or her dependents to destitution. "I will not exhaust my family's finances by paying for this hugely expensive treatment" does not mean "My life after the treatment would not be worth living."

The non sequitur which lures Price and other critics of the IOL into error is, to be fair, seductively easy. At first blush it might well seem that one would refrain from prolonging a patient's life, when one had the opportunity and means to do so, only on the basis of a judgment that the patient's life was not worth preserving. Why else would one stay one's hand? As we have seen, however, there are, on closer consideration, other reasons, which in no way question the benefit of each patient's life, whatever the patient's condition or disability. These reasons include the particular purposes of medicine ("ventilation may well prolong the life of this patient in PVS but it will not restore the patient to anything even approaching health or well-functioning") or excessive burdens ("this treatment will be excruciatingly painful for a protracted period" or "will exhaust the entire hospital budget"). The doctor who decides to withhold or withdraw life-prolonging treatment need no more do so on the basis that the patient's life lacks benefit, than a law professor in the south of England, who decides not to take the long train journey to attend the opening day of the Society of Legal Scholars conference in Scotland, need do so on the basis that attendance would be of no benefit. The professor may reason that, although attendance would indeed be beneficial, the chances of getting there in time are too slender (because of an impending transport strike), or that attendance would involve considerable expense (the head of department having stingily refused to fund his or her attendance) or inconvenience (the conference conflicts with the expected birth of his or her child). The professor may, of course, decide not to attend on the (surely misguided) judgment that the Society's conferences are worthless, but such a judgment need play no part in a decision not to attend.

Price also criticizes the IOL for regarding the assessment of the PVS patient's condition as "merely a 'preliminary matter' in deciding the worth of a proposed treatment and no more."[25] This criticism (with its mysterious quotation marks) again misrepresents the IOL. Far from being merely a "preliminary matter" and "no more," the IOL holds that an assessment of the patient's condition now, and as it would be after the proposed treatment, is central to the judgment whether the treatment would be worthwhile. Yet another misunderstanding is exhibited by Price's claim that it is a non sequitur to extrapolate from the position that an operation should be performed to remove Angela's intestinal blockage to the position that "*no* underlying condition could ever produce a defensible opinion that life would not be sufficiently advantageous, so that treatment might legitimately be withheld."[26] So it is, but it is a non sequitur that the IOL nowhere commits. The IOL does not reason that because Angela's life with Down's syndrome is worthwhile therefore all lives are worthwhile. It holds that all lives are worthwhile and that therefore judgments about the supposed worth of those with Down's syndrome have no place in the decision whether the operation should be carried out.[27]

3 Intending death and intentionally assisting suicide
A further misapprehension by Professor Price concerns the significance of intention in the IOL's opposition to killing and assisting suicide.

a The Winterton Bill   The "Winterton Bill" was introduced into the House of Commons by Ann Winterton MP in the wake of the *Bland* case.

---

[25] Ibid 630.

[26] Ibid (emphasis in original).

[27] Price's misunderstanding of the IOL also clouds his analysis of the question whether there is a duty to tube-feed those in PVS. He seems to think that because they cannot suffer discomfort from dehydration (which may not in fact be so: see P McCullagh, "Thirst in relation to the withdrawal of hydration" (1996) 46(3) Catholic Medical Quarterly 3), tube-feeding could only be justified on the basis of its symbolic significance for society or to prevent distress to carers or relatives, since feeding cannot benefit the patient: Price 632. But why cannot feeding benefit the patient? Presumably, in Price's view, because life in PVS is not a benefit. But this is merely to assume what needs to be proved. Price nowhere responds to the argument often advanced by IOL ethicists (even though he mentions it: Price 631) that there is a duty to feed those in our care who cannot feed themselves as a (not merely symbolic) "expression of care for and solidarity with a fellow human being." Instead, Price erects a line of straw men. He states that even if tube-feeding were not "medical treatment" this "should not necessarily obligate its administration indefinitely and indiscriminately" (ibid 632); that all human beings have moral worth but "that does not require that we should ignore their underlying condition in assessing whether a particular treatment would further their best interests" (ibid 640); and that while all human beings possess equal worth "this should not be taken to mandate the need for *equal treatment* regardless of their individual circumstances.": ibid 641 (emphasis in original). Of course not, and the IOL would endorse none of these assertions.

It would have made it clearly unlawful for a person responsible for the care of a patient to withhold or withdraw treatment or sustenance, howsoever delivered, with the (or with a) purpose of hastening the patient's death. In other words, it sought, by restoring the prohibition on trying to kill patients by withholding or withdrawing treatment or tube-feeding, to return the law to its morally and intellectually coherent shape pre-*Bland*. Price repeats several of the wayward criticisms leveled at this Bill by its opponents. As I have replied to these at length elsewhere,[28] it will suffice here to respond to a few of his criticisms.

Price claims that the Bill's "crucial emphasis upon the clinician's mental state would threaten a fundamental distortion which should be firmly resisted" because its "framework of analysis deflects one from the central issue, the *justification* for the withholding or withdrawal."[29] He adds that the decision in *Bland* was "generated principally by an assessment of the benefit to be obtained by the patient from further medical support. As there was no duty to act, the issue of the intention of the physicians became peripheral."[30] Their Lordships in *Bland* did indeed reason that there was no duty to continue tube-feeding because it was of no benefit. But a majority (at least) appeared to reason that this was because Tony Bland's *life* lacked benefit, and held that the withdrawal of tube-feeding was lawful even though they thought that the doctor's intention was to kill Tony. Their ruling permitting even intentional killing is significant, not peripheral, and is precisely why the case was widely recognized, by both supporters and opponents[31] of the IOL, as radically undermining the IOL. The Winterton Bill would have repaired the moral and intellectual misshapenness this ruling inflicted on the law. For Price to criticize a Bill to amend the criminal law because it emphasized the defendant's mental state is surprising. *Mens rea* is, of course, generally key to criminal liability. The criminal law here reflects traditional ethics (not, incidentally, "character ethics," as Price would have it[32]) which emphasizes the importance of the agent's mental state in assessing the morality of acts and omissions. Consider the following examples from the point of view of ethical and legal justification. Q picks up a book in R's study. How can we tell whether Q is justified in picking up the book without considering Q's state of mind? Does Q intend to pass the book to R or to purloin it? Again, imagine that a doctor administers morphine to a terminally ill patient who is in pain

[28] J Keown, *Euthanasia, Ethics and Public Policy* (Cambridge University Press, 2002) Ch 21.
[29] Price 635 (emphasis in original).
[30] Ibid.
[31] P Singer, *Rethinking Life and Death: The Collapse of our Traditional Ethics* (St Martin's, Griffin, 1996) 1.
[32] Price 636.

and that the drug hastens death. How can one decide whether the doctor is justified in so doing without first ascertaining the doctor's purpose? Is the doctor intending to hasten the patient's death by injecting the drug or is he or she intending to ease pain, merely foreseeing hastened death as an inevitable side-effect? Intention is no less important in evaluating omissions that hasten death. Is the doctor who switches off a ventilator intending thereby to spare the patient a futile or excessively burdensome intervention, or is the doctor intending to hasten death the sooner to inherit a large bequest the patient has made the doctor? If all that mattered were whether, objectively, continued ventilation would be futile or too burdensome, then what would be wrong with the doctor (or indeed an impatient heir) switching off the machine intentionally to accelerate the inheritance?[33] Purpose is clearly of pivotal importance in ethics and law: Price's understanding of justification seems to put the cart before the horse.

b Assisting suicide   Professor Price accurately notes my objection to any unqualified right, whether in law or ethics, to refuse treatment.[34] I welcome his agreement[35] that a patient's refusal of treatment in order to hasten death should be regarded as suicide.[36] I also welcome his acceptance that: "It is indeed the case that the view that a patient commits suicide in such instances creates potential liability for assisting suicide...."[37] He adds that this is "why courts traditionally shun the concept" and notes the "inherent sophistry" in their reasoning.[38] Price goes on to defend an absolute right to refuse treatment but his ethical case seems more assertion than argument. He implies that there is an "entitlement" to commit suicide and mentions the decriminalization of suicide by the Suicide Act 1961. However, as we noted in Chapter 1,[39] the Act was anything but a condonation of suicide. Price

---

[33] As we saw in Ch 1, s 4(5) of the Mental Capacity Act 2005 now provides that, in deciding whether life-sustaining treatment would be in the best interests of an incompetent patient, the person making the determination "must not ... be motivated by a desire to bring about his death." See Ch 1, text at n 34.

[34] Price 635.

[35] Ibid 636.

[36] His agreement seems odd, given his earlier argument that what matters is objective "justification" rather than the agent's purpose. He also asserts that in the typical case of suicide there is no purpose to die, only to escape "certain conditions attaching to one's continuing life": ibid 636. But even if death is not intended as an end in itself, it is intended as a means of escaping those conditions.

[37] Ibid. He states that I contend that a doctor who respected a suicidal refusal "would be taken to share the individual's suicidal intent" and would incur liability for assisting suicide: ibid 635. My contention is, more accurately, that the doctor should be liable only for intentional (purposeful) assistance in a patient's suicidal enterprise, not simply for omitting to override the patient's refusal and merely foreseeing the hastening of death: Keown (n 1) 80.

[38] Price 636.

[39] Ch 1, text at nn 44–7. And as Professor Gormally and I pointed out in one of the papers Price cites (n 11) Part III.

adds that "[t]he spectre of physicians quizzing patients as to whether they really 'intend to die' or only to avoid a specific futile or disproportionate treatment" is "unthinkable" and that, once again, the significance of the agent's mental state is being exaggerated.[40] But my argument was not that doctors should quiz patients about their reasons for refusing treatment and override those which are thought to be suicidal (although there is surely much to be said for an open, honest discussion of the patient's reasons and concerns). It was, rather, that if the courts hold that there is a right to commit suicide by refusing treatment, they are undermining the law against assisting suicide (and thereby the law against intentional killing). In other words, my argument was about the coherence of legal principle rather than its implications for medical practice, and I welcome Professor Price's agreement with the essence of my argument. In fact, the implications, in practice, of restoring the law's intellectual coherence might prove minimal for the law could, without undercutting its principled opposition to suicide and assisted suicide, allow doctors to yield to all refusals of treatment (perhaps even those that were clearly suicidal), provided the doctor's intention was not to facilitate suicide. What the law cannot do, without laughing at itself, is to prohibit intentionally assisting suicide by an act while endorsing intentionally assisting suicide by omission.

c Article 2 of the European Convention on Human Rights Having perceptively recognized the "inherent sophistry" in those judicial *dicta* that have incautiously referred to a seemingly absolute right to refuse treatment, Price surprisingly fails to comment on the sophistry in another case he mentions. In *NHS Trust A v M* and *NHS Trust B v H*[41] Butler-Sloss P held that *Bland* was consistent with Article 2 of the European Convention for the Protection of Human Rights and Fundamental Freedoms 1950. Article 2(1) provides: "Everyone's right to life shall be protected by law. No one shall be deprived of his life intentionally save in the execution of a sentence of a court following his conviction of a crime for which this penalty is provided by law." Yet Butler-Sloss P held that stopping an incompetent patient's tube-feeding with intent to kill did not breach Article 2. Why? Because, she ruled, one can only deprive another of life by an act. Her Ladyship omitted to explain the basis of this ruling. Would a hospital or nursing home which intentionally starved

[40] Price 636. He claims that "[t]he vetting of individuals' choices is repugnant to the extent that they would cause no direct harm to others in their implementation.": ibid 641. If he intends this as a general ethical proposition that choices are entitled to moral respect provided they do not cause "direct harm" to others, would it not extend to choices to drive without seatbelts, to take hard drugs, or even to be tortured and killed on a television show to boost its ratings?

[41] [2001] Lloyd's Rep Med 28.

its elderly residents to death in order to free up their beds not breach their right to life? Her Ladyship's ruling surely sits uneasily with the clear terms of Article 2 and illustrates, even more clearly than the cases on refusal of treatment, the extent to which the courts have misunderstood the principle which has shaped the law of murder and assisted suicide and also Article 2: the IOL.

B Quality of life's "slippery slope"

Professor Price's critique of the IOL will not, then, convince everyone. And what does he propose in its place but a defense of the "Quality of life" (QOL) ethic which is scarcely more convincing, being both sketchy and, it seems, contradictory. He rightly rejects the idea that only those human beings with consciousness and rationality are entitled to "serious moral concern."[42] He claims, again rightly, that "[a]ll living human beings have moral worth and dignity and (contra Bland) subsisting interests"[43] and that "all human beings indeed possess equal worth and rights."[44] However, when these admirable pronouncements are unpacked, it seems clear that they emerge from a QOL suitcase. For if he thinks it justifiable intentionally to starve certain patients to death because their lives are thought not to be worthwhile, what does his concept of "equal worth and rights" amount to? Yet he claims that it is the IOL that reduces patient protection.[45] On the contrary, it is the IOL that recognizes that all patients have a right not to be intentionally killed. It is Price's approach that invites doctors to deny this right to those patients they think "better off dead." He acknowledges that one must recognize the "sensitivity and dangers" associated with decisions regarding someone's future "Quality of life" and he quotes Professor Gostin to the effect that it is important to distinguish between those "grave and exceptional cases where the neonate irremediably lacks the capacity to live a recognizably human life" from those where the judgment is based on "comparative social worth" and that the same applies to adults, especially the aged.[46] But Price gives no reason why the line should be drawn at the "capacity to live a recognisably human life" (whatever that means). By setting foot on the slippery QOL slope he can provide no principled reason against drawing the line somewhere further down the slope (as do many of its other advocates), whether at the possession of consciousness or at "comparative social worth." Referring to cases of elderly patients being abused by being denied food and drink, Price comments that the abuse resulted not from a judgment

[42] Price 640.   [43] Ibid 632, n 88 (emphasis in original).
[44] Ibid 641.   [45] Ibid 619.   [46] Ibid 640.

that their lives lacked worth, "but out of sub-standard treatment, some-times the product of inadequate available resources."[47] But why the sub-standard treatment and inadequate resources may not have been the result of such a judgment, Professor Price does not say, and he cites no evidence to support his assertion to the contrary. Dreadful abuse and neglect of vulnerable groups, particularly the elderly and those with severe learning disabilities, has become increasingly evident in the years since Professor Price and I engaged in our exchange.[48] These groups are prime candidates for discrimination on the basis of arbitrary QOL judg-ments. The IOL is the only sound ethical foundation for respecting the equality-in-dignity of all patients, whatever their age or disability. This does not mean, pace Price, that we should all receive the same treatment, that our individual circumstances should be ignored, or that our auton-omy should be overridden. It does mean that none of us should be intentionally killed or neglected on the basis of the arbitrary judgment that, because of our mental or physical disability or perceived social worth, or any other arbitrary criterion, our lives lack worth. Referring to the meaning of "dying," Price concludes that "[t]o deprive a person of treatment by virtue of a fuzzy 'label' per se is unacceptable."[49] Why, then, is it acceptable to use a fuzzy label—"Quality of life"—to deprive a person of life itself?

II PROFESSOR JACKSON

Professor Jackson has argued, citing Ronald Dworkin, that "the sanctity principle, with its commitment to the intrinsic value of lives which have ceased to contain anything of value, does not make sense, other than as an article of religious faith."[50] She writes that most of the candidates for distinctively human qualities which make our lives more valuable than animals, such as consciousness, moral reasoning, and self-awareness, are characteristics which are possessed by most but not all humans, such as those in PVS and anencephalic babies. Citing Peter Singer, she contends that to value a patient in PVS higher than a chimpanzee is mere "species-ism."[51] She asks where the "inherent dignity" of all members of the human

---

[47] Ibid.
[48] E.g. M Evans, "One in seven nursing homes breaking the law on feeding patients", *Daily Telegraph*, 16 October 2011.
[49] Price 628.
[50] E Jackson, "Secularism, Sanctity and the Wrongness of Killing" (2008) 2 Biosocieties 125, 126.
[51] Ibid 133.

family, asserted in the Preamble to the Universal Declaration of Human Rights, comes from.[52] She concludes that there are "no rational grounds" for believing that there is an important difference between all humans and all animals, and that a belief in the unique value of humans "can only be a matter of faith."[53] She attaches moral value not to human beings but to "persons," and cites differing criteria for "personhood" which proponents of this approach have advanced, such as Jeff McMahan's requirement of a capacity for self-consciousness, of a "rich and complex mental life, a mental life of a high order of sophistication."[54] On such an approach, she points out, Tony Bland died as a "person" when he fell into PVS and died as an "organism" after his tube-feeding and hydration were withdrawn years later. Professor Jackson then turns to the implications of her approach for the ethics of killing.

Killing is wrong, she contends, when it "harms" a person. Killing is normally a great wrong because it is normally a very great harm: "Killing is wrong instrumentally because it destroys everything that has been invested in the person's life, as well as depriving the person who is killed of all future experiences."[55] However, "where we can be certain that a human being's future contains no experiences at all, or only pain and suffering which has become unbearable, death may no longer be an instrumental harm."[56] She quotes Dan Brock's view that the right to life should be "waivable" when "the person makes a competent decision that continued life is no longer wanted or a good, but is instead worse than no further life at all."[57] Professor Jackson is "not sure" that she would go so far,[58] for a doctor who gave a lethal injection to a "lovesick teenager" would be "ignoring the fundamental duties of a doctor."[59] In the "vast majority of cases," she reasons, death would be a harm because for most people life will contain both good as well as bad experiences and because we would be speculating about the future, making it impossible confidently to conclude that it would be better for someone to die now. She continues that Tony Bland's death was not a harm and notes that some of the judges thought he had an interest in an end being put to "the humiliation of his being and the distress of his family."[60] She concludes that it will "occasionally be possible" to say that the "balance sheet" militates in favor of an earlier death and that the views of the person whose life it is as to whether their life is worth living is evidence of an "overwhelmingly powerful kind."[61]

---

[52] Ibid 135.   [53] Ibid.   [54] Ibid 137.   [55] Ibid 138.   [56] Ibid 139.
[57] Ibid.   [58] Ibid 140.   [59] Ibid.   [60] Ibid 141.   [61] Ibid 142–3.

Professor Jackson rejects the danger of a "slippery slope," of death being forced upon vulnerable and dependent individuals, because "it is only possible to conclude that death is a good thing for a person if we can be certain that it would be better for them if they died now, and that this would be consistent with their wishes and values."[62] If, she adds, we can confidently conclude that death now as opposed to later is preferable for a patient "either by applying the best interests test for an incompetent patient, or by respecting the competent patient's own choice about whether their life is worth living," where death can be achieved by treatment withdrawal, it seems odd that we cannot make the same assessment when a positive act is necessary to achieve death.[63]

Professor Jackson's criticisms of the IOL are wide of the mark. First, the many atheists and agnostics who subscribe to the concept of inherent human dignity which underpins the Universal Declaration of Human Rights will be surprised to discover that they are religious believers after all, and will doubtless be intrigued to discover to which religion they are thought to belong.

Second, as we noted in Chapter 1, the view that human life has an intrinsic value can be amply supported on solely philosophical grounds, the grounds which underpin the "right to life" in international instruments like the Universal Declaration. Philosophers like Professor Christopher Kaczor have refuted the sort of arguments about the instrumental value of life and "personhood" relied on by Professor Jackson.[64] She misapprehends a cardinal reason for the intrinsic value of human life: our radical and distinctive capacity for rationality, conceptual thought, and free will. That we have this valuable capacity does not entail that we are always able to exercise it. We may be asleep, or a baby, or in a coma, or senile. A radical *capacity* must not be confused with a presently exercisable *ability*. A baby has the natural capacity to reason, even though he or she is not yet able to exercise it. I have the capacity to speak German, though I am not able to do so. A person with dementia has the capacity to reason, even though damage to their brain prevents them from exercising it. Because we are all, by our very nature, beings with this radical capacity, we are intrinsically, and not merely instrumentally, valuable. This basis for rights, including the right not to be intentionally killed, is no more "speciesist" than it is "religious." It would extend to *any* creature, earthly

---

[62] Ibid 143.

[63] Ibid.

[64] C Kaczor, *The Ethics of Abortion: Women's Rights, Human Life and the Question of Justice* (Routledge, 2011).

or alien, which possessed the same capacity for rationality, conceptual thought, and free will.

Third, having misapprehended the IOL as "religious" and "speciesist," Professor Jackson proposes an alternative which, like that suggested by Professor Price, is as vague as it is arbitrary. Its discrimination between human beings who are "persons" and "non-persons" is a vivid illustration of the slippery slope which awaits anyone who abandons the firm philosophical platform provided by rights grounded in our common humanity. It is far from clear how "non-persons" are to be identified. This is problematic, given the potentially lethal consequences of being so categorized. She gestures at various criteria which have been proposed by philosophers who adopt this sort of approach, but is hazy about which it thinks decisive, and to what degree. Is it, perhaps, McMahan's "rich and complex mental life, a mental life of a high order of sophistication"? But what does that mean? How "rich" is "rich," how "high" is "high"? Any such approach is, clearly, inherently arbitrary and provides no sound basis for deciding whom we have a duty to treat justly and whom the law should protect. The disturbing implications for babies, the senile, the comatose, those with learning disabilities, and perhaps even those with a low IQ are clear. Professor Jackson rightly criticizes the Nazis for drawing "a morally repugnant line between lives that were of value and lives that were not, based upon membership of racial, religious and other social groups."[65] But does she not propose the same kind of line, albeit in relation to differently defined social groups? And might not some of the groups, perhaps those with severe learning disabilities, turn out to be the same as those targeted by the Nazis? In his classic commentary on the ghastly practices of the Nazi doctors, Dr Leo Alexander, a consultant during the Nuremberg trials, noted:

Whatever proportions these crimes finally assumed, it became evident to all who investigated them that they had started from small beginnings. The beginnings at first were merely a subtle shift in emphasis in the basic attitude of physicians. It started with the acceptance of the attitude, basic in the euthanasia movement, that there is such a thing as a life not worthy to be lived.[66]

Clearly, once one has accepted that certain human beings are "non-persons" or mere "organisms," they become prime candidates for exploitation and elimination. Professor Jackson writes that an important difference between a severely impaired human being and "a non-human animal" is that the human

---

[65] Jackson (n 50) 136.
[66] L Alexander, "Medical Science under Dictatorship" (1949) 241 New England Journal of Medicine 39, 44.

being has relatives and that the relatives might be harmed if someone they loved was, say, treated as a resource for scientific experiments.[67] But this is cold comfort. What if the "severely impaired human being" has no relatives, or has neglectful relatives, or has relatives who would *like* them to be used for research or for spare parts? Emily Jackson candidly accepts that where there are no family or friends, "there is no one who is likely to be harmed if we were to treat her in the same way as an animal."[68] Her approach invites us to step into a world where the most vulnerable members of the human family are not the beneficiaries of human solidarity, and protected by human rights law, but are exposed to the risk of blatant exploitation. No one who subscribes to an adequate conception of basic human rights could entertain such an invitation.

What of those human beings who manage to clear the bar of "person-hood," whichever criterion is selected and however high it is set? We will recall that Professor Jackson concludes that it will "occasionally" be possible to say with certainty that the "balance sheet" militates in favor of an earlier death, and that the views of the person whose life it is as to whether their life is "worth living" are evidence of an "overwhelmingly powerful kind."[69] But if the views of the person are "overwhelmingly powerful" evidence, why will death only "occasionally" be better than life? What, for example, of the many thousands of elderly people who might want to die because they are physically suffering, or are "tired of life," or feel a burden, or are lonely, neglected, or abused[70]? If they think that their lives are no longer "worth living," why should their autono-mous request for euthanasia not be respected? We will recall Professor Jackson's comment that if we can confidently conclude that death now as opposed to later is preferable for a patient "by respecting the competent patient's own choice about whether their life is worth living" where it can be achieved by treatment withdrawal, it seems odd that we cannot make the same assessment when a positive act is necessary to achieve death.[71] We will also recall that Jackson thinks that a doctor who gives a lethal injection to a lovesick teenager would be "ignoring the fundamental duties of a doctor."[72] But if the teenager's request is autonomous, why is it not a fundamental duty of the doctor to respect it just as if the teenager had requested disconnection from a ventilator? Another "right to die" advo-cate, Dr Philip Nitschke, has no such reservations. He thinks that people have a right to dispose of their life whenever they want and that it is ethical to help anyone exercise that right, including "the depressed, the

---

[67] Jackson (n 50) 134.   [68] Ibid.   [69] See text at n 61.
[70] See text at Ch 11, n 67.   [71] See text at n 63.   [72] See text at n 59.

elderly bereaved, [and] the troubled teen."[73] Even Professor Jackson, we recall, is "not sure" that she rejects an entirely subjective approach.[74] Further, why do we need to be "certain"[75] that someone would be better off dead? Do we need to be "certain" that withdrawal of life-support would benefit the patient? And what if we are "certain" that a person's "balance sheet" favors death but the person, inconsiderately, disagrees? Why should we not try to persuade them of their error, especially if their refusal will soak up valuable health care or social resources? If they do not listen to reason, why should we not withdraw those resources or even end their lives? If they are on a ventilator and death would benefit them, what would be wrong with disconnecting the ventilator, even against their will, especially if we could put the machine to better use? Professor Jackson follows Glanville Williams in conflating intention and foresight.[76] She would, therefore, presumably see no moral difference between withdrawing ventilation against their will, and giving them an injection against their will. And if there is no moral distinction, why not administer the injection, at least if the withdrawal does not end their life?

Professor Jackson, unlike some advocates of the "right to die," is commendably frank about two main pillars on which her approach rests: the moral equation of intentionally hastening death and foreseeably doing so, and the belief that the lives of some human beings lack worth. Those pillars justify the euthanasia of competent and of incompetent patients in a wide range of cases.

III CONCLUSION

In the light of the persistent misunderstanding of the IOL, even by leading contemporary medical lawyers like David Price[77] and Emily Jackson,[78] the endorsement by Ward LJ in the "Conjoined Twins" case

---

[73] KJ Lopez, "Euthanasia Sets Sail. An Interview with Philip Nitschke" (5 June 2001) <http://old.nationalreview.com/interrogatory/interrogatory060501.shtml>.

[74] See text at n 58.

[75] See text at n 62.

[76] Eg E Jackson, "Whose Death is it Anyway?: Euthanasia and the Medical Profession" (2004) 57 Current Legal Problems 415, 433. She also shares Williams' misunderstanding of double effect: ibid 435.

[77] For Price's most recent offering, see "What Shape to the Law After Bland? Historical, Contemporary and Futuristic Paradigms" (2009) 125 LQR 142. Nothing in this paper prompts any amendment to the critique of his earlier writing which has been offered by this chapter.

[78] For a much fuller reply to Professor Jackson, see J Keown, "Against Decriminalising Euthanasia; For Improving Care" in E Jackson and J Keown, *Debating Euthanasia* (Hart Publishing, 2012). A recent book by Elizabeth Wicks, *The Right to Life and Conflicting Interests* (Oxford University Press, 2010) is unfortunately flawed by the all-too-common misapprehension that because the sanctity of life does not preclude all conduct which may or will cause death (such as defending oneself against unjust aggression), the principle is not absolute. But, as we have noted at various points in Part I, the

of the distinction between the worthwhileness of treatment and the worthwhileness of life is all the more welcome and timely. We will recall that his Lordship stated:

I conclude that it is impermissible to deny that every life has an equal inherent value. Life is worthwhile in itself whatever the diminution in one's capacity to enjoy it and however gravely impaired some of one's vital functions of speech, deliberation and choice may be.[79]

No less importantly, he added: "The indispensable foundation of justice is the basic equality in worth of every human being."[80] It is to be hoped that his judgment is built upon by other senior judges in the important enterprise of restoring the law's moral and intellectual shape and of reaffirming the fundamental equality of all patients.[81] For their part, academic medical lawyers have an important role to play in critically reassessing the picture of the IOL they have been bequeathed by some of the founders of the discipline in order to ensure that they have not invested in a fake.

---

principle has never precluded all conduct which may or will cause death. As its core prohibition is against intentionally killing the innocent, killing in self-defense is not an "exception" to the principle justified by "conflicting interests". The principle's core prohibition on intentionally killing the innocent *is* absolute. The right of an innocent person not to be intentionally killed may no more be outweighed by "conflicting interests" than his or her right not to be tortured. If the right to life could be trumped by "conflicting interests", why is the law's prohibition on intentionally killing patients absolute, even if they are only minutes from death, they freely request it, and it is their only way of avoiding agony? Had the book appreciated the crucial formative influence of the Judeo-Christian theological and philosophical tradition on the development of the law and on human rights, it might have avoided this common pitfall.

    [79] *Re A* [2001] Fam 147, 187–8, per Ward LJ. See Ch 1, text at n 33.
    [80] Ibid 188.
    [81] In the more recent case of *Burke v General Medical Council* [2004] EWHC 1879 (Admin), Munby J (as he then was) missed an opportunity to do so. The case concerned an application for judicial review of the guidance of the General Medical Council on withholding and withdrawing treatment and tube feeding. The applicant, who had a progressive neurological illness, feared that the guidance would allow the withdrawal of tube-feeding against his wishes toward the end of his life on the ground that his life was not worth living. The judge cited not the valuable endorsement of equality-in-dignity by Ward LJ in the Conjoined Twins case but the controversial judgment of Hoffmann LJ (as he then was) in *Bland*. However, Hoffmann LJ's judgment exaggerated the importance of autonomy and misunderstood the IOL. See Keown (n 28) 227–30. Munby J held that the General Medical Council guidance was unlawful, not least for giving insufficient weight to patient autonomy. The Court of Appeal reversed Munby J. The court observed: "Although we have said that a great deal in the body of the judgment is uncontroversial, we counsel strongly against selective use of Munby J's judgment in future cases": [2005] EWCA Civ 1003 para 24. A valuable brief, drafted by Eleanor Sharpston QC, Professor John Finnis, and Angela Hewitt, which identified a number of concerns about the first instance judgment, is available at <http://www.catholic-ew.org.uk/Catholic-Church/Media-Centre/Press-Releases/press_releases_2005/leslie_burke_case>.

Part Two

The Beginning of Life

CHAPTER 5

BACK TO THE FUTURE OF ABORTION LAW: *ROE*'S REJECTION OF AMERICA'S HISTORY AND LEGAL TRADITIONS

I INTRODUCTION

Constitutional litigation, perhaps more than any other kind of legal determination, should be based on fact not fiction, truth not untruths, reality not myth. For it makes a unique contribution to shaping us as the people, the community, we constitute, and the persons, the individuals, we are.[1]

In 1997, in *Washington v Glucksberg*, the Supreme Court was faced with the question whether legislation prohibiting physician-assisted suicide was unconstitutional. Chief Justice Rehnquist, delivering the opinion of the court, observed: "We begin, as we do in all due-process cases, by examining our Nation's history, legal traditions, and practices."[2] In light of the fact that for over 700 years the Anglo-American common law tradition had punished or otherwise disapproved of suicide and assisted suicide[3] the court went on to reject the claim that the United States Constitution contains a right to assisted suicide. In determining whether the Constitution contains a right to abortion the nation's history and traditions concerning abortion are no less relevant. It is not surprising, therefore, that in *Roe v. Wade*,[4] which established such a right in 1973, much of Justice Blackmun's leading opinion for the court was devoted to the

---

[1] J Finnis, "'Shameless Acts' in Colorado: Abuse of Scholarship in Constitutional Cases" (1994) 7(4) Academic Questions 10.
[2] 521 US 702, 710 (1997).
[3] Ibid 711.
[4] 410 US 113 (1973) ("*Roe*").

history of abortion in Anglo-American criminal law. Blackmun concluded that a right to abortion was consistent with that history. In 1989, in *Webster v Reproductive Health Services*,[5] a case which was widely viewed as providing an opportunity for the court to reconsider its holding in *Roe*, 281 American historians filed an amicus curiae Brief urging that *Roe* was "consistent with the most noble and enduring understanding of our history and traditions."[6] The Brief, which was eventually to attract the signatures of over 400 historians, was drafted by Sylvia Law, Professor of Law at New York University.[7] It proved influential in both academic and non-academic circles. It was, for example, relied upon by Professor Ronald Dworkin in his argument rejecting constitutional personhood for the unborn.[8]

At the heart of the Brief lay three claims:

- "At the time the Federal Constitution was adopted, abortion was known and not illegal."[9]
- "Nineteenth-century abortion restrictions sought to promote objectives that are today plainly either inapplicable or constitutionally impermissible."[10]
- "The moral value attached to the fetus became a central issue in American culture and law only in the late twentieth century, when traditional justifications for restricting access to abortion became culturally anachronistic or constitutionally impermissible."[11]

This chapter challenges each of these claims. It concludes that *Roe* was a radical departure from the law's historical protection of the unborn child[12] and thereby from its adherence to the IOL. The next part of the chapter presents a short history of Anglo-American abortion law. The third part, the main body of the chapter, illustrates the misunderstanding of that history by Justice Blackmun in *Roe* and proceeds to question the above three claims made by the Brief. The final part raises questions about "advocacy scholarship."

---

[5] 492 US 490 (1989).

[6] "Brief of 281 American Historians as Amici Curiae Supporting Appellees" in *Webster v Reproductive Health Services* (n 5) ("Brief"). For contrasting definitions of an amicus curiae brief in US and English law, see n 158.

[7] For a subsequent discussion of the Brief involving Professor Law, see "Roundtable: Historians and the Webster Case" (1990) 12(3) Public Historian 9.

[8] Citing the Brief, Dworkin argued: "The best historical evidence shows...that even anti-abortion laws, which were not prevalent in the United States before the middle of the nineteenth-century, were adopted to protect the health of the mother and the privileges of the medical profession, not out of any recognition of a fetus's rights.": R Dworkin, "The Great Abortion Debate" (1989) 36 (11) New York Review of Books 49, 50. On the extent of the Brief's influence, see JW Dellapenna, *Dispelling the Myths of Abortion History* (Carolina Academic Press, 2006) 1005–7 ("Dellapenna").

[9] Brief 4.

[10] Ibid 11.

[11] Ibid 25.

[12] "Unborn child" and "foetus" will be used interchangeably to refer to the human being from conception to birth.

II ANGLO-AMERICAN LAW AGAINST ABORTION:
A BRIEF HISTORY

As early as the mid-thirteenth century the common law punished abortion after foetal formation as homicide. Foetal formation, the point at which the foetus assumed a recognizably human shape and was believed to be ensouled, was thought to occur some 40 days after conception. By the mid-seventeenth century, abortion was prohibited as a "great misprision" or serious misdemeanor. By the early nineteenth century at the latest the common law appears to have prohibited abortion only after "quickening." Quickening, which occurs between the twelfth and the twentieth week of pregnancy, is the point at which the mother first perceives foetal movement. The later common law may have chosen this point because it was the point at which the life of the unborn child was believed to begin or because it was the point at which it could be legally proved to have begun, or because the judges confused the earlier common law's prohibition of the destruction of a "quick" (formed and ensouled foetus) with the mother's experience of "quickening." In short, the common law consistently prohibited abortion, at least after quickening, and did so, as the crime's focus on the initiation or at least proof of foetal life illustrates, in order to protect the unborn child.[13]

The nineteenth century, both in England and in the United States, witnessed statutory restriction of the prohibition. A main if not exclusive purpose of this legislation, like the common law from which it grew, was the protection of the unborn child. This is evident from the nature and wording of the statutory provisions themselves. It is no less evident from the fact that the enactment and shape of the legislation was influenced in England, and even more dramatically in the United States, by the emerging medical profession, whose discovery that human life began at fertilization exposed the moral irrelevance of quickening. Responding to concerted pressure by the medical profession, legislatures gradually abolished the quickening distinction so as to protect the unborn from fertilization. The rationale of

---

[13] See Dellapenna, Chs 3–5; PA Rafferty, *Roe v. Wade: The Birth Of A Constitutional Right* (University Microfilm International Dissertation Information Service, Ann Arbor, MI 1993); JW Dellapenna, "Brief of the American Academy of Medical Ethics," *Planned Parenthood of Southeastern Pennsylvania v Casey*, 492 US 490 (1992) ("Dellapenna 2"); RM Byrn, "An American Tragedy: The Supreme Court on Abortion" (1973) 41 Fordham Law Review 807, 815–27; DJ Horan, CD Forsythe, and ER Grant, "Two Ships Passing in the Night: An Interpretavist Review of the White-Stevens Colloquy on *Roe v. Wade*" (1987) 6 St Louis University Law Review 229, 272–300; J Keown, *Abortion, Doctors and the Law* (Cambridge University Press, 1988) ch 1. Similarly, as (pro-choice) Professor Bernard Dickens has written: "The protection the Common Law afforded to human life certainly extended to the unborn child.": BM Dickens, *Abortion and the Law* (MacGibbon & Kee, 1966) 20.

the Anglo-American legislation was accurately identified in 1957 by Glanville Williams. He wrote:

At present both English law and the law of the great majority of the United States regard any interference with pregnancy, however early it may take place, as criminal, unless for therapeutic reasons. The foetus is a human life to be protected by the criminal law from the moment when the ovum is fertilized.[14]

Any suggestion that the common law did not prohibit abortion, or was "lenient" on abortion, or that women had a common law "right" or "liberty" to abort, or that the nineteenth-century statutes did not seek to protect the foetus, is mistaken. Which brings us to Justice Blackmun in *Roe* and the 281 historians in *Webster*.

III JUSTICE BLACKMUN IN *ROE* AND THE HISTORIANS' BRIEF IN *WEBSTER*

A Justice Blackmun in Roe

In *Roe* the Supreme Court decided, by a 7–2 majority, that an implied constitutional right to privacy, whether based on the Fourteenth Amendment's concept of personal liberty or in the Ninth Amendment's reservation of rights to the people, was sufficiently broad to encompass a woman's right to terminate her pregnancy. The court summarized its decision as follows:

(a) For the stage prior to approximately the end of the first trimester, the abortion decision and its effectuation must be left to the medical judgment of the pregnant woman's attending physician.
(b) For the stage subsequent to approximately the end of the first trimester, the State, in promoting its interest in the health of the mother, may, if it chooses, regulate the abortion procedure in ways that are reasonably related to maternal health.
(c) For the stage subsequent to viability, the State in promoting its interest in the potentiality of human life may, if it chooses, regulate, and even proscribe, abortion except where it is necessary, in appropriate medical judgment, for the preservation of the life or health of the mother.[15]

Much of Blackmun J's opinion was devoted to the historical development of the law against abortion. He had inquired into and placed "some emphasis" upon "medical and medical-legal history and what that history

---

[14] GL Williams, *The Sanctity of Life and the Criminal Law* (revised edn, Faber and Faber, 1958) ("SLCL") 141. See Ch 1, text at n 75.
[15] *Roe* 164–5.

reveals about man's attitudes toward the abortion procedure over the centuries."[16] Blackmun J continued that before addressing the appellant's claim that the Texan anti-abortion statute infringed her right to abort, the court felt it "desirable briefly to survey, in several aspects, the history of abortion, for such insight as that history may afford us, and then to examine the state purposes and interests behind the criminal abortion laws."[17] He asserted that it was "undisputed" that at common law abortion before quickening was not an offense and added that whether abortion even after quickening was an offense was "still disputed."[18] Although, he continued, Bracton (d. 1268) regarded post-quickening abortion as homicide and the later and predominant view of the great common law scholars such as Coke (1552–1634) and Blackstone (1723–1780) held it to be "at most" a lesser offense, a recent review of the common law authorities by Professor Cyril Means of New York Law School had argued that Coke had intentionally misrepresented the law and that even post-quickening abortion was never established as a common law offense.[19] "This is of some importance," continued the opinion, because American courts had followed Coke's exposition of the law and had stated that abortion after quickening was a common law crime. Blackmun J added that their reliance on Coke was "uncritical" and that it now appeared "doubtful that abortion was ever firmly established as a common-law crime even with respect to the destruction of a quick fetus."[20] Blackmun J then reviewed the development of anti-abortion legislation in England. He began with Lord Ellenborough's Act 1803 which, *inter alia*, made attempted post-quickening abortion a capital offense and which unambiguously criminalized attempted pre-quickening abortion, and ended with the Abortion Act 1967 which relaxed the law substantially. Turning to US law Blackmun J stated:

In this country the law in effect in all but a few States until mid-19th century was the pre-existing English common law.... It was not until after the War Between the States [1861–1865] that legislation began generally to replace the common law. Most of these initial statutes dealt severely with abortion after quickening but were lenient with it before quickening.... Gradually, in the middle and late 19th century the quickening distinction disappeared from the statutory law of most states....[21]

---

[16] Ibid 117.

[17] Ibid 129.

[18] Ibid 132–4.

[19] Ibid 134–5, citing CC Means Jr, "The Phoenix of Abortional Freedom: Is a Penumbral or Ninth Amendment Right About to Arise from the Nineteenth-Century Legislative Ashes of a Fourteenth-Century Common-Law Liberty?" (1971) 17 New York Law Forum 335 ("Means II").

[20] *Roe* 135–6.

[21] Ibid 138–9.

He concluded:

It is thus apparent that at common law, at the time of the adoption of our Constitution, and throughout the major portion of the 19th century abortion was viewed with less disfavor than under most American statutes currently in effect. Phrasing it another way, a woman enjoyed a substantially broader right to terminate a pregnancy than she does in most States today. At least with respect to the early stage of pregnancy, and very possibly without such a limitation, the opportunity to make this choice was present in this country well into the 19th century. Even later, the law continued for some time to treat less punitively an abortion procured in early pregnancy.[22]

Blackmun J noted that the anti-abortion mood in the "late" nineteenth century was shared by the medical profession and that "the attitude of the profession may have played a significant role in the enactment of stringent criminal abortion legislation during that period."[23] He observed that the American Medical Association (AMA) appointed a Committee on Criminal Abortion in 1857. Its report two years later deplored abortion and its frequency, which it felt was due, first, to a widespread belief that the foetus was not alive until quickening; second, to the fact that doctors themselves were often supposed to be careless of foetal life; and, third, to the "grave defects" of both common and statute laws in recognizing the foetus and its inherent rights for civil purposes but in failing to recognize it, and denying it all protection, when "personally and as criminally affected."[24] He added that the AMA adopted the Committee's resolutions, which protested against "such unwarrantable destruction of human life" and which called upon state legislatures to tighten their abortion laws.[25]

What of the purposes of the legislation? Justice Blackmun stated that those challenging the legislation's constitutionality claimed—pointing to "the absence of legislative history" to support foetal protection—that "most" state laws were enacted not to protect foetal life but solely to protect women from the dangers of abortion.[26] Citing two articles by Professor Cyril Means[27] he noted that there was some scholarly support for this view and stated: "The few state courts called upon to interpret

---

[22] Ibid 140–1.
[23] Ibid 141.
[24] Ibid 141–2.
[25] Ibid 142.
[26] Ibid 151.
[27] CC Means Jr, "The Law of New York Concerning Abortion and the Status of the Foetus, 1664–1968: A Case of Cessation of Constitutionality" (1968) 14 New York Law Forum 411 ("Means I"), and Means II (n 19). Dellapenna observes that Blackmun cited Means 7 times, no one else more than once, and no other historian except in relation to a brief consideration of the Hippocratic Oath: Dellapenna, 689; 1005.

their laws in the late nineteenth and early twentieth centuries did focus on the State's interest in protecting the woman's health rather than in preserving the embryo and foetus."[28] Blackmun J added that supporters of this view pointed out that in many states, including Texas, the pregnant woman could not be prosecuted for self-abortion or for cooperating in an abortion performed on her by another[29] and that the quickening distinction not only recognized the greater health hazards inherent in late abortion but also repudiated the notion that life begins at conception.[30] The court concluded that its decision to uphold a constitutional right to abortion and strike down the anti-abortion legislation was consistent with, *inter alia*, "the lessons and examples of medical and legal history" and with "the lenity of the common law."[31] In short, Justice Blackmun appears to have been persuaded that at common law women enjoyed a "right" to abort in early and very possibly later pregnancy and that the legislative restriction of this "right" in the last century was due to concern to protect maternal rather than foetal life.

B *The Historians' Brief in* Webster

The misunderstanding of abortion law history by Justice Blackmun and by the Historians' Brief will become patent when the three central claims made by the Brief in defense of his historiography are scrutinized.

> *1 "At the time the federal constitution was adopted, abortion was known and not illegal."*

The Brief claimed:

As the Court demonstrated in *Roe v. Wade*, abortion was not illegal at common law. Through the nineteenth century American common law decisions uniformly reaffirmed that women committed no offense in seeking abortions. Both common law and popular American understanding drew distinctions depending upon whether the fetus was 'quick,' i.e. whether the *woman* perceived signs of independent life. There was some dispute whether a common law misdemeanour occurred when a third party destroyed a fetus, after quickening, without the woman's consent. But early recognition of this particular crime against pregnant women did not diminish the liberty of the woman herself to end a pregnancy in its early stages.[32]

This outline of the common law tends to mislead the reader into thinking that abortion was not illegal at common law, even after quickening. The

---

[28] *Roe* 151.   [29] Ibid

[30] Ibid 151–2.   [31] Ibid 165.

[32] Brief 4–5 (emphasis in original).

outline stated that the common law "drew distinctions" at quickening, but rather than explaining why it did so, namely to punish abortion after quickening, proceeded to state that there was some dispute whether non-consensual abortion after quickening was illegal. This distracting assertion (which is in any event erroneous[33]) was likely to mislead the unwary reader into thinking that *consensual* abortion after quickening was not illegal. No less misleadingly, the passage conflated two distinct questions: first, whether abortion was an offense at common law and, second, if it was, whether the mother herself was liable. In relation to the first question the Brief asserted that the court in *Roe* "demonstrated" that abortion was not an offense. The court did not. It observed that it was "doubtful" whether abortion was a common law offense even after quickening.[34] This doubt was, moreover, entirely misplaced. The authorities establish that abortion, at least after quickening, was an offense at common law. Indeed, as the *Roe* court itself stated, the "predominant" view, following that of the great common law scholars such as Coke and Blackstone, was to this effect.[35] Chief Justice Coke wrote in his *Institutes*, the first textbook of the modern common law:

If a woman be quick with childe, and by a potion or otherwise killeth it in her wombe; or if a man beat her, whereby the childe dieth in her body, and she is delivered of a dead childe, this is a great misprision, and no murder.[36]

Similarly, Sir William Blackstone wrote in his *Commentaries* that life was a gift from God, a right inherent by nature in every individual which "begins in contemplation of law as soon as an infant is able to stir in the mother's womb."[37] These authorities lend weighty support to the historic proposition that it was illegal at common law for a woman, or a third party, to procure abortion after she was "quick with child."

---

[33] A footnote accompanying this proposition stated: "Even in cases involving brutal beatings of women in the late stages of pregnancy common-law courts refused to recognize abortion as a crime, independent of assault upon the woman, or in one case witchcraft." The footnote cited A McLaren, *Reproductive Rituals* (Methuen, 1984) 119–21. Far from supporting this proposition, McLaren accepted that abortion was a crime at common law: "Seventeenth-century jurists thus recognized that a woman could be charged with procuring her own abortion, but only after the foetus had quickened.": ibid 122. See also Finnis (n 1) 14–15.

[34] See text at n 20.

[35] See text at n 19.

[36] E Coke, *Institutes* (1641) vol 3, 50. The passage continued: "but if the childe be borne alive, and dieth of the potion, battery, or other cause, this is murder: for in law it is accounted a reasonable creature, *in rerum natura*, when it is born alive." (emphasis in original). For an analysis of the "born alive" rule, see CD Forsythe, "Homicide of the Unborn Child: The Born Alive Rule and other Legal Anachronisms" (1987) 21 Valparaiso Law Review 563.

[37] W Blackstone, *Commentaries on the Law of England* (1765–1769) vol 1, 129.

Why did the Supreme Court in *Roe* doubt such high authorities? The answer appears to lie in the court's reliance on Professor Means. His article (which did not disclose that he was counsel to NARAL, a national association seeking the repeal of the anti-abortion legislation) argued that Coke's statement of the criminality of abortion was an "outrageous attempt" to create a new common-law misdemeanor[38] and a "masterpiece of perversion of the common law of abortion."[39] It claimed that subsequent commentators such as Hawkins and Blackstone uncritically accepted Coke's exposition of the law[40] and that there were plenty of *dicta* but no decisions supporting Coke, certainly none holding the woman herself guilty of an offense.[41] As we saw earlier[42] the court in *Roe* regarded Means' thesis as "of some importance" because most US courts had followed Coke and held that post-quickening abortion was a common law offense.

Scholarship since *Roe* has confirmed that the "masterpiece of perversion of the common law of abortion" flowed from the pen of Means, not Coke. For example, research by Philip Rafferty confirms that the early common law prohibited abortion from foetal formation, the later common law from quickening.[43] Examples of precedents unearthed by such scholars, precedents which Means denied existed, include the indictment in 1602 (before Coke's *Institutes*) of one Margaret Webb for taking poison with intent to destroy the infant in her womb.[44] Another is the trial and conviction of one Elizabeth Beare in 1732 (evidently reported verbatim) for procuring the abortion of another woman by the use of an instrument.[45] A more recent trawl of the authorities by Professor Dellapenna, in his treatise dispelling the mythology about abortion history which has

---

[38] Means II 346.
[39] Ibid 359.
[40] Ibid 348–9.
[41] Ibid 355.
[42] See text at n 20.
[43] Rafferty (n 13) Part IV. Similarly, Byrn concluded: "at all times, the common law disapproved of abortion as *malum in se* and sought to protect the child in the womb from the moment his living biological existence could be proved.": Byrn (n 13) 816 (emphasis in original). See also RA Destro, "Abortion and the Constitution: The Need for a Life-Protective Amendment" (1975) 63 California Law Review 1250, 1267–73; Keown (n 13) ch 1.
[44] Keown (n 13) 7–8.
[45] Ibid 8–9. Interestingly, neither of these precedents mentioned quickening. In *R v Turner* (1755) the defendant was indicted for procuring a woman to take arsenic mixed with treacle "in order to kill and destroy a male bastard child by him begotten on her body and which she was then quick with.": ibid 10. As early as 1532 a defendant was indicted for the rape of a woman on 5 September 1531 and a further indictment charged him with procuring her abortion on 1 February 1532. The abortion may well, given the passage of five months since the rape, have been post-quickening though the indictment simply alleges the killing of two living infants. Moreover, their abortion was charged as murder: Norfolk Record Office, Norwich, C/S3/1 m45c (indictment file). I am grateful to Professor Sir John Baker for drawing this indictment to my attention.

been spun by writers such as Means, confirms that abortion was an offense at common law both in England and in its American colonies.[46] He points out that precedents (in Connecticut, Delaware, Maryland, Rhode Island, and Virginia) show that the prohibition on abortion was at least as strict as in England.[47] In short, the authorities support the following propositions:

- The common law consistently prohibited abortion; the early common law from foetal formation, the later common law at least from quickening.
- The prohibition applied to pregnant women themselves.
- The law's main if not exclusive purpose was, as its early focus on foetal formation and later focus on quickening indicated, the protection of the unborn child. Formation and quickening were thought to mark the point at which human life began, not the point at which abortion became dangerous to the woman.

After the paragraph in which the Brief misleadingly outlined the legal status of abortion at common law, the next three paragraphs considered the incidence of abortion (although the relevance of the supposed incidence of conduct to its constitutionality was not made clear). Although this chapter's focus is the Brief's treatment of legal history, its unreliability as social history should not be overlooked. For example, the Brief asserted, citing social historian Angus McLaren,[48] that "Abortion was not uncommon in colonial America."[49] Leaving aside the fact that McLaren was writing about England not America, even a signatory to the Brief, Professor Estelle Freedman, has taken issue with this sweeping assertion: "I find it hard to argue," she later wrote, "that abortion was 'not uncommon,' given the economic and religious motives for childbearing within families."[50] The Brief nowhere acknowledged her concern.[51]

---

[46] Dellapenna Chs 3–5.

[47] Ibid 228. He comments that "Any supposed 'common law liberty of abortion' is as mythical on this side of the Atlantic as on the other side.": ibid 220 (footnote omitted). In the amicus brief he filed in the *Casey* case Dellapenna concluded that "The historical record shows that abortion and other killings of unwanted children were condemned by all respected legal authorities in England from the start of the common law, and those laws were applied with full rigor in the United States during the colonial era.": Dellapenna 2 1. For one of the colonial precedents, see *Commonwealth v Mitchell* 10 *MD Archives* (1652: published 1891) 171–86 (see n 51).

[48] McLaren (n 33) 114.

[49] Brief 5.

[50] EB Freedman, "Historical Interpretation and Legal Advocacy: Rethinking the Webster Amicus Brief" (1990) 12(3) Public Historian 27, 30.

[51] Dellapenna also questions the alleged frequency of abortion, highlighting the absence of safe or effective methods: Dellapenna Ch 1. The Brief went on to claim that cases of midwives prescribing abortifacient remedies were routine and unaccompanied by any particular disapproval, citing as an example the case of a midwife who, in 1789, wrote in her diary that she had prescribed herbs for a

To return to the Brief's treatment of legal history it is evident that
proposition one, that abortion was not an offense at common law, is
insupportable. Let us now consider propositions two and three.

2 *"Nineteenth-century abortion restrictions sought to promote objectives that are today
plainly either inapplicable or constitutionally impermissible."*

A major source relied on for this proposition was Professor James Mohr's
Abortion in America.[52] Since its publication in 1978 this has been widely
regarded as the leading work on the statutory restriction of the abortion
law in nineteenth-century America (though it has, as we shall see later,
been subjected to trenchant criticism in Professor Dellapenna's *Dispelling
the Myths of Abortion History*,[53] which must now be regarded as the leading
treatise on the subject). Quoting Mohr, the Brief stated, accurately, that
between 1850 and 1880 the American Medical Association (AMA) became
the *"single most important factor in altering the legal policies toward abortion in
this country."*[54] It then stated, inaccurately, that the anti-abortion legislation enacted in the nineteenth century did not have foetal protection as
even *one* of its purposes. The four purposes alleged by the Brief were set
out as follows:

- "From 1820–1860, abortion regulation in the states rejected broader
  English restrictions and sought to protect women from particularly dangerous forms of abortion."[55]

---

patient who was suffering from obstructions: Brief 6, fn 13. The Brief provided no evidence that the
herbs were to procure abortion rather than for amenorrhea. It also asserted, without any substantiation, that there was an absence of legal condemnation of abortion in colonial America: ibid. Freedman,
however, states that sermons and court cases in colonial America revealed widespread condemnation
of non-procreative sexual practices and that efforts to destroy the fruits of intercourse were also
condemned: Freedman (n 50) 29. The Brief further asserted that where abortion was noted it was not
the practice itself that was the subject of comment but rather the violation of other social/sexual
norms that gave rise to the perceived need to attempt to abort: Brief 7. In support of this assertion it
cited the seventeenth-century prosecution of Captain William Mitchell who tried to abort his
mistress's child but against whom the first charge was atheism: Brief 7, fn 16. The original (and
published) records of the case show that Mitchell was investigated in June 1651 on only one ground:
suspicion of having attempted to abort his mistress. At his trial, Mitchell specifically argued that he
must be tried only for matters that were criminal offenses. In June 1652 a jury upheld four charges
against him. The first was indeed atheism, but the third was: "[t]hat he hath Murtherously endeav-
ored to destroy or Murder the Child by him begotten in the Womb of the Said Susan Warren.":
Browne (ed), 10 *MD Archives* 183 (cited in Finnis (n 1) 37, fn 24). Mitchell was sentenced by the
Supreme Court of the province not on the charge of atheism but only on the charge of attempted
abortion and two other charges. See also Dellapenna 215–19. In short, the Brief's attempt to show an
absence of legal condemnation or disapproval of abortion was unsuccessful.

[52] JC Mohr, *Abortion in America: The Origins and Evolution of National Policy* (Oxford University
Press, 1978) ("Mohr").
[53] See n 8 and n 198.
[54] Brief 11 (emphasis in original).
[55] Ibid.

- "From the mid-nineteenth century, a central purpose of abortion regulation was to define who should be allowed to control medical practice."[56]
- "Enforcement of sharply-differentiated concepts of the roles and choices of men and women underlay regulation of abortion and contraception in the nineteenth century."[57]
- "Nineteenth-century contraception and abortion regulation also reflected ethnocentric fears about the relative birthrates of immigrants and Yankee Protestants."[58]

This chapter does not seek to show that these were not legislative purposes (though nor does it accept that they were[59]). It maintains, rather, that foetal protection *was*. The evidence in Mohr's book and in other sources, much of which is either omitted or misrepresented by the Brief, shows that protection of the unborn child was indeed the primary if not sole purpose of the legislation or was, at the very least, *a* purpose of the legislation. Scrutiny of the first two of the Brief's alleged legislative purposes will illustrate this point.

1 Protection of women

The Brief claimed that the objective of legislation enacted between 1820 and 1860 (it is strangely silent about later legislation) was to protect the mother. It cited the first anti-abortion statute, enacted in Connecticut in 1821, which prohibited the administration of any noxious substance with intent to procure the miscarriage of any woman "quick with child."[60] It added, citing Mohr, that in the late 1820s three other states followed the Connecticut model in prohibiting the use of "dangerous poisons *after* quickening."[61] It continued (citing Means) that in 1830 New York, "also animated by a concern for patient safety," prohibited surgical abortion. It asserted (citing *Roe*) that "Because nineteenth-century abortion laws were drafted and justified to protect women, they did not punish women as parties to an abortion."[62] The Brief also claimed that none of the abortion legislation from this period restricting "forms of abortion thought to be particularly unsafe" was enforced.[63]

---

[56] Ibid 13.
[57] Ibid 17.
[58] Ibid 20.
[59] The evidence for the alleged four purposes, whether that adduced by the Brief or by Mohr, is much weaker than the evidence supporting the purpose of foetal protection.
[60] Brief 11–12.
[61] Ibid 12 (emphasis in original).
[62] Ibid.
[63] Ibid 13.

While concern to safeguard the life and health of the mother may have been a purpose of the legislation, the Brief's attempt to eclipse the legislative purpose of foetal protection fails. First, as Professor Witherspoon observed in his comprehensive analysis of the nineteenth-century legislation, it does not follow that a statute which omitted to criminalize the woman was unconcerned with foetal protection. The legislature may have felt that the woman would have sought an abortion only out of desperation and that it would be inhumane to punish her.[64] Or the legislature may have wanted, by removing her fear of self-incrimination, to encourage her to testify against the abortionist.[65] In view of such considerations, he commented, "it is surprising that at least seventeen or more than one-third of the state legislatures did enact laws *expressly* incriminating the woman's participation in her own abortion."[66] Second, if the legislation were intended to protect women, why did it prohibit abortion only *after* quickening and require proof of pregnancy as an element of the offense? Attempts would also have been dangerous before quickening and if the woman was not pregnant. The Brief itself stated: "Prior to scientific understanding of germ theory and antisepsis, any surgical intervention was likely to be fatal."[67] Third, the Brief's assertion that three states followed Connecticut in prohibiting abortion "*after* quickening" is contradicted by its source, Mohr, who points out that the relevant statutes (enacted in Missouri in 1825, Illinois in 1827, and New York in 1828) made no mention of quickening.[68] Fourth, the assertion, citing Means,[69] that the New York statute was, like the others, motivated solely by a concern for female safety, is mistaken. Its unsoundness was exposed as early as 1970 by Professor Grisez in his magisterial work on abortion.[70] Means, drawing on the notes of the commission which revised the New York criminal code in 1828, pointed to an unenacted section which would have criminalized the performance of any surgical operation

---

[64] JS Witherspoon, "Reexamining *Roe*: Nineteenth-Century Abortion Statutes and the Fourteenth Amendment" (1985) 17(1) St Mary's Law Journal 29, 58. He noted that those statutes that did penalize women stipulated lesser penalties than for the abortionist: ibid 58–9.

[65] Ibid 59. He observed that statutes that did incriminate women often afforded protection from prosecution if they testified for the prosecution or provided that evidence they gave for the state could not be used against them: ibid. Moreover, it does not follow that if a statute did not expressly incriminate the woman she was not liable. There remain the possibilities of implied incrimination, liability as a secondary party, and continuing liability at common law.

[66] Ibid (emphasis in original).

[67] Brief 12. Mohr concedes that the quickening distinction in the Connecticut statute of 1821 weakened the measure as a poison control statute: Mohr 22.

[68] Mohr 25–7.

[69] Brief 12, fn 39.

[70] GG Grisez, *Abortion: The Myths, the Realities, and the Arguments* (Corpus Books, 1970) 382–97. See also Byrn (n 13) 827–35; Rafferty (n 13) 47–79.

which destroyed or endangered human life unless the operation appeared necessary to preserve life. He maintained that this unenacted section confirmed the legislature's concern for patient safety and supported the view that the anti-abortion sections were intended to protect women.[71] As Grisez pointed out, however, the revisers devoted distinct clauses to abortion and to unnecessary surgery, provided different penalties for each, and justified each with different notes. Moreover, the legislature enacted the proposed abortion clause but not the "unnecessary surgery" clause.[72] Means' suggestion that the legislature thought the surgery clause otiose because in relation to operations other than abortion a combination of patient's caution and professional conscience sufficed to prevent unnecessary surgery is undermined by the very revisers' notes on which he relied.[73] The revisers expressed concern about loss of life from operations *other* than abortion, stating that due to the "rashness of many young practitioners in performing the most important surgical operations for the mere purpose of distinguishing themselves" the loss of life was "alarming."[74] Further, Byrn pointed out that there can be little doubt that section 9 of the statute, which punished attempts to procure abortion after quickening as "manslaughter" if either the foetus or mother died, was intended to protect the life of the foetus.[75] He also noted that the statute's therapeutic exception was limited to abortions "necessary to preserve the life" of the mother: the life of the child could not be sacrificed for anything less.[76] Moreover, the exception was much narrower than the therapeutic exception to the unenacted section that would have prohibited surgical operations. That exception would have permitted operations performed to save life or simply on the advice of two doctors.[77] Means also failed to consider why, if concern for female safety was the or indeed a purpose of the anti-abortion provisions, they punished attempted abortion only when the woman was in fact pregnant: interference would also have been dangerous if she were not pregnant.[78] Fifth, the Brief's assertions that

---

[71] Means II 388–9.
[72] Grisez (n 70) 383.
[73] Means II 389.
[74] Grisez (n 70) 383.
[75] Byrn (n 13) 831.
[76] Ibid.
[77] Ibid.
[78] Means' reasoning has also been criticized by Mohr as being less than convincing on several points: Mohr 29. In particular, Mohr concludes that it is difficult to imagine that the death rate from abortion in 1828 substantially exceeded that from childbirth especially since contemporary writers did not stress the great dangers of an abortion induced by mechanical means. They were, he claims, much more likely to bemoan the ease and impunity with which irregular practitioners and others were able to induce abortion: ibid 30–1. Mohr's argument that abortion was not perceived as particularly dangerous would, if accurate, further undermine Means' argument. Dellapenna argues that Mohr

the early anti-abortion legislation sought to restrict "forms of abortion thought to be particularly unsafe," and that it was not enforced, were not substantiated.[79]

In short, the legislative evidence offers scant support for the Brief's claim that the legislation sought to protect the mother but not the foetus. The quickening distinction in particular makes little sense if the law's purpose was only to protect women. It makes much sense if the purpose of the law was to protect unborn life from the time it was believed to begin.

2 Medical professionalization

The Brief claimed that a core purpose of the anti-abortion legislation "from the mid-nineteenth century" and of physicians in supporting it was to control medical practice in the interests of public safety.[80] It added that "the most significant explanation for the drive by medical doctors for statutes regulating abortion is the fact that these doctors were undergoing the historical process of professionalization."[81] Their campaign to tighten the abortion law "was intimately connected with professional struggles between proponents of 'scientific medicine' and those who practised less conventional modes of healing."[82] The Brief cited Mohr to the effect that educated or "regular" practitioners were worried that their patients were being poached by uneducated or "irregular" practitioners who were willing to perform abortions, a service which the regulars were precluded from performing by their Hippocratic ethics.[83]

Whether or not the emerging medical profession's campaign for stricter abortion laws was partly intended to suppress their unqualified

understates the dangers of abortion. Nevertheless, Dellapenna, like Grisez, convincingly rejects Means thesis that foetal protection was not a purpose of the legislation: Dellapenna ch 6.

[79] For example, the New York statute of 1828 punished the administration of any medicine, drug, substance, or thing whatever and the use of any instrument or other means whatever: Mohr 27. The Brief cited no authority that such statutes permitted either the use of non-poisonous substances or any safely and skillfully performed non-therapeutic abortions. To support its allegation about absence of enforcement the Brief cited Mohr, but he confines his comment that anti-abortion statutes were unenforced and unenforceable to abortion before quickening: ibid 43. Moreover, Mohr's conclusion seems based solely on the difficulty of proving intent. But many crimes require proof of intent and are nevertheless regularly enforced. Mohr produces neither evidence that it was impossible, as opposed to difficult, to prove intent even before quickening, nor statistics to show that there were no prosecutions. Indeed, he mentions several prosecutions and convictions for abortion. For example, he states that there were 32 prosecutions for abortion in Massachusetts alone between 1849 and 1857: ibid 122. This is hardly evidence of a lack of enforcement, though the failure to secure a conviction in these cases does illustrate the real obstacles confronting prosecutors. That, in spite of such difficulties, legislators enacted anti-abortion legislation, and prosecutors sought to enforce it, suggests how seriously abortion was viewed.
[80] Brief 13.
[81] Ibid 13.
[82] Ibid 15.
[83] Ibid 16.

competitors, there is a wealth of evidence that their campaign was intended to suppress abortion. That the Brief omitted this evidence is remarkable since it forms the core of Mohr's book. Mohr's detailed account of the profession's sustained and vigorous campaign for tighter laws indicates that the protection of unborn life was not only a purpose of the campaign but was its defining purpose. Mohr relates that the regulars' opposition to abortion was "partly ideological, partly scientific, partly moral, and partly practical."[84] Ideologically, he notes that one of the features that distinguished the regulars from irregulars was the regulars' adherence to the Hippocratic Oath. He writes:

Hippocrates's creed had become one of the touchstones of regular medicine in the United States by the early nineteenth century, and the oath was considered the basic platform upon which the regulars were attempting to upgrade the ethical standards of their profession in a host of different areas, not just in regard to abortion.[85]

Scientifically, he adds, regulars had realized for some time that conception inaugurated a more or less continuous process of development, which would produce a new human being if uninterrupted. Consequently, they attacked the quickening doctrine on the logical ground that quickening was a step neither more nor less crucial in the process of gestation than any other.[86] From this scientific reasoning flowed their "moral opposition to abortion at any stage in gestation."[87] There was, he continues, more to the regulars' opposition to abortion than scientific logic, for there was also a firm moral opposition to the taking of life: "The nation's regular doctors, probably more than any other identifiable group in American society during the nineteenth century, including the clergy, defended the value of human life per se as an absolute."[88] He adds: "regular physicians felt very strongly indeed on the issue of protecting human life. And once they had decided that human life was present to some extent in a newly fertilized ovum, however limited that extent might be, they became the fierce opponents of any attack upon it."[89] Having identified the above three reasons for the regulars' opposition, all of which are aspects of their fundamental *moral* objection to abortion, Mohr adds that the regulars also supported anti-abortion legislation because it would inhibit their irregular competitors who were not inhibited by moral considerations from procuring abortion and would relieve pressure by patients on regulars to provide abortions.[90] One of the Brief's own chief sources therefore shows

---

[84] Mohr 34–5.   [85] Ibid 35.   [86] Ibid.
[87] Ibid 35–6.   [88] Ibid 36.   [89] Ibid.   [90] Ibid 37.

that protection of foetal life was *the* ostensible purpose driving the regulars' campaign. And even if the regulars *were* partly motivated by professional self-interest, this is in no way inconsistent with their commitment, which Mohr recognizes as genuine,[91] to protect foetal life. The Brief grudgingly observed: "To be sure, some 'regulars' were morally troubled by abortion,"[92] but this is a violent understatement. That the protection of foetal life was, to put it at its lowest, a purpose of the anti-abortion legislation becomes even clearer when the Brief's third proposition is examined in the light of the effectiveness of the regulars' campaign in producing the anti-abortion legislation of the nineteenth century.

> 3 "*The moral value attached to the fetus became a central issue in American culture and law only in the late twentieth century, when traditional justifications for restricting access to abortion became culturally anachronistic or constitutionally impermissible.*"

This claim sits uneasily with abundant evidence of concern for the unborn in the doctors' campaign for tighter laws against abortion, in judicial interpretation of the resulting legislation, and in the wording of that legislation. We shall consider each in turn.

3 Concern for the unborn inspiring the enactment of the legislation

The Brief asserted that the regulars' concern for the foetus was always subsidiary to "more mundane social visions and anxieties."[93] Their "mid-nineteenth century" campaign sought to prohibit irregular practice and "protection of fetal life is plainly not the driving concern of such a movement."[94] Whether the Brief was tacitly acknowledging that protection of unborn life was *a* concern of their campaign is, like so much else in the Brief, obscure. But even if it was, it still understated the regulars' aim to protect the unborn, which flowed from their moral opposition to abortion. The regulars' campaign was a campaign to restrict abortion, which might also serve to restrict irregular practice, not vice versa. This "crusade,"[95] as Mohr describes it, met with striking success. It pushed state legislatures beyond cautious expressions of concern about abortion to "straightforward opposition to the practice."[96] The regulars' "successful campaign of the 1860s and 1870s . . . *produced measures that reflected the regulars' position on the abortion issue throughout most of the United States.*"[97] He writes:

---

[91] Ibid 166.   [92] Brief 16.   [93] Ibid 25.
[94] Ibid.   [95] Mohr 147.   [96] Ibid 147–8.
[97] Ibid 230 (emphasis added).

Between 1860 and 1880 the regular physicians' campaign against abortion in the United States produced the most important burst of anti-abortion legislation in the nation's history. At least 40 anti-abortion statutes of various kinds were placed upon state and territorial lawbooks during that period; over thirty in the years from 1866 through 1877 alone. Some thirteen jurisdictions formally outlawed abortion for the first time, and at least twenty-one states revised their already existing statutes on the subject. More significantly, most of the legislation passed between 1860 and 1880 explicitly accepted the regulars' assertions that the interruption of gestation at any point in a pregnancy should be a crime and that the state itself should try actively to restrict the practice of abortion. The anti-abortion policies sustained in the United States through the first two-thirds of the twentieth century had their formal legislative origins, for the most part, in the wave of tough laws passed in the wake of the doctors' crusade and the public response their campaign evoked. Though these laws were occasionally rephrased in subsequent code revisions, the fundamental legal doctrines they embodied were destined to remain little changed for a hundred years.[98]

Mohr's story of the campaign makes illuminating reading. At its meeting in 1859 the AMA received the recommendations of the committee it had set up two years earlier to draft a report on abortion. The report recommended, first, that the Association should publicly protest against the "unwarrantable destruction of human life" caused by the quickening distinction; second, that it should urge states to revise their abortion laws; and, third, that state medical societies should press this matter on their state legislatures.[99] These recommendations were unanimously adopted by the Association. Mohr comments that for the rest of the century the AMA would remain steadfastly committed to outlawing the practice of abortion and that the vigorous efforts of the regulars "would prove in the long run to be *the single most important factor in altering the legal policies toward abortion*" in the United States. He adds that, with remarkable persistence, regular state and local medical societies sustained the crusade.[100]

An example Mohr gives of the effectiveness of the regulars' crusade to increase the law's protection of the unborn child is the tightening of the abortion law in New York in 1869 when "the legislature responded positively" to the medical society's following request made two years before:

Whereas, from the first moment of conception, there is a living creature in process of development to full maturity; and whereas, any sufficient interruption to this

---

[98] Ibid 200–1.   [99] Ibid 154–7.
[100] Ibid 157 (emphasis added).

living process always results in the destruction of life; and whereas, the intentional arrest of this living process, eventuating in the destruction of life (being an act with intention to kill), is consequently murder; therefore,... *Resolved,* That this society will hail with gratitude and pleasure, the adoption of any measures or influences that will, in part or entirely, arrest this flagrant corruption of morality among women, who ought to be and unquestionably are the conservators of morals and of virtue.[101]

The legislators, comments Mohr, gave the regulars "almost exactly what they wanted" and, in a sweeping anti-abortion statute, replaced the wording "woman with a quick child" with "woman with child" and proscribed as second-degree manslaughter the destruction of a foetus at any stage of gestation.[102] The medical society, he adds, had been "almost totally successful in persuading the legislature to redraft New York's abortion laws along the lines the physicians had initially indicated in 1867."[103] He concludes:

As the combined pressures from regular medical societies and from the shifts in public opinion that regular physicians worked to bring about began to increase, legislators dropped traditional quickening rules, revoked common law immunities for women, and enlisted the peripheral powers of the state, such as control over advertising and the definition of what was obscene, in the great battle against abortion in America.[104]

He adds that some of the laws were unchanged until the 1960s and that others were altered only in phraseology, not in basic philosophy.[105] Further: "The fundamental premises embodied in most of the abortion-related legislation passed by state legislatures between 1860 and 1880 continued to inform most of the anti-abortion laws" enacted from 1880–1900.[106] The final 20 years of the last century witnessed a confirmation in state courts of the attitudes informing the anti-abortion legislation passed in the wake of the regulars' crusade of the 1860s and 1870s.[107] Finally, "[m]ost of the anti-abortion activity and all of the anti-abortion legislation passed during the first two-thirds of the twentieth century reconfirmed and reiterated the policies that regular physicians had persuaded most American state legislators to embrace by 1880."[108]

What part did opposition to irregular practice play in the enactment of this tide of legislation? Any opposition to irregular practice was evident in the context of the regulars' "great battle against abortion," not vice versa. Although Mohr states that the regulars appear to have persisted in their

[101] Ibid 216 (emphasis in original).   [102] Ibid 217.
[103] Ibid.   [104] Ibid 224–5.   [105] Ibid 225.
[106] Ibid 227.   [107] Ibid 237.   [108] Ibid.

campaign for a number of "professional" reasons, such as restricting irregular practice[109] and a desire to "recapture what they considered to be their ancient and rightful place among society's policymakers and servants,"[110] he accepts that they also had compelling "personal" reasons for carrying forward their campaign.[111] The first was what he describes as a "no doubt sincere" belief that abortion was immoral. That this coincided nicely with their professional self-interest is, he recognizes, no reason to accuse physicians of hypocrisy on the issue.[112] He continues that "[m]ost physicians considered abortion a crime because of the inherent difficulties of determining any point at which a steadily developing embryo became somehow more alive than it had been the moment before. Furthermore, they objected strongly to snuffing out life in the making."[113] It was, he adds, apparent to regulars that *the only way to deal with this question of basic morality was to see that their position was embodied in explicit statutes of their own design.*"[114] Mohr shows convincingly how the AMA's crusade did precisely that.[115] By contrast, his evidence that the legislators who enacted the anti-abortion laws were motivated, either wholly or partly, by a desire to suppress irregular practitioners is distinctly lacking. It is one thing to claim that regulars may have been partly motivated by professional self-interest, quite another to show that legislators who enacted anti-abortion legislation shared this motivation. Legislatures were far quicker to proscribe abortion than irregular practice. Whereas the regulars' efforts to restrict the abortion laws were rewarded with stunning success from the first half of the nineteenth century, Mohr points out that their campaign to control medical practice and overcome laissez-faire attitudes to medical practice did not succeed until they gained control of medical education in the 1880s.[116] In short, the claim that the anti-abortion legislation was enacted to protect the profession rather than the unborn seems to rest on little more than assertion. Moreover, some evidence that the regulars were not seeking to restrict abortion merely as a way of restricting irregular practice is the fact that in New York in 1828 the regulars successfully influenced the tightening of the abortion law even though they had already succeeded in having enacted the previous year what Mohr

---

[109] Ibid 160.   [110] Ibid 163.   [111] Ibid 164.
[112] Ibid 165.   [113] Ibid.
[114] Ibid 166 (emphasis added).
[115] Ibid ch 6.
[116] He describes a proposal by South Carolina regulars in 1883 to restrict the abortion law and also to strengthen the board of health which they hoped to dominate. The former passed, the latter did not: ibid 228–9.

describes as "the toughest medical regulation law the state had ever had" which "granted great power to the regular physicians, who were organized as the state medical society, by declaring the unauthorized practice of medicine a misdemeanor."[117] The fact that anti-abortion legislation would impact more on those irregular practitioners who practiced abortion rather than those regulars who did not does not show that professional self-interest was the (or even a) driving force of the regulars' crusade against abortion, as opposed to a presumably welcome consequence. And, as Professor Finnis has asked, if professional self-interest had been the regulars' main concern:

[W]hy were the doctors not willing to compete with the irregulars by simply supplying safer abortions under more congenial conditions and procedures? Without the support of the doctors' respect for fetal life—a respect established on each and all of the first three grounds [identified above by Mohr on which regulars opposed abortion]—their desire for the professionalization of medicine could just as appropriately have led them to petition the legislators for a *legalization* of abortion by licensed physicians (or, in the Brief's utterly imaginary world, for a medicalization of the 'common law liberty' of abortion).[118]

Professor Dellapenna comments that if the regulars' campaign against abortion was really a "conspiracy" to suppress abortion, it was remarkably successful: "No one has ever turned up a smidgen of direct evidence (in a diary; a letter, or any other record) of such a plan or program...."[119] Even assuming such a conspiracy, he adds, does not explain how regulars succeeded in tightening the abortion laws in the face of Jacksonian democracy's intense passion to democratize the professions by eliminating barriers to entry.[120] The nascent medical societies of the early-to-mid-nineteenth century, Dellapenna adds, did not have the influence of organized medicine today and the regulars "could achieve little legislatively unless their arguments were widely accepted as true."[121] He notes that while Mohr cites as evidence of the regulars' conspiracy the fact of irregular opposition to statutes restricting medical practice, Mohr omits

---

[117] Ibid 38.

[118] Finnis (n 1)17 (emphasis in original).

[119] Dellapenna 295.

[120] Ibid 296.

[121] Ibid. See also ibid 244–5, 344–58. He comments that Mohr's "surmise of a power grab by physicians" is not only unnecessary to explain the features of the laws which Mohr asserts support his surmise but also fails to account for the enactment of the anti-abortion statutes: "At the root of Mohr's argument is the utter absence of the larger legal and medical historical context within which those statutes were enacted. The inclusion of the abortion provisions in the nineteenth-century codifications suggests not a desire to evade controversy, but rather a lack of controversy when the common law of abortion was clarified and carried forward as part of the general law of crimes....": ibid 302.

to point out that the irregulars did not attempt to repeal or modify the anti-abortion statutes.[122] Dellapenna concludes that the evidence that the protection of the unborn was the primary purpose of the abortion legislation is "overwhelming."[123] Finally, Ramesh Ponnuru has noted that three books dealing with the professionalization of American medicine, authored by signatories to the Brief, barely mention the physicians' campaign against abortion, let alone ascribe key significance to it. He notes that the Brief "cites all three books in its section on professionalization without mentioning these points."[124]

4 Concern for the unborn in judicial interpretation of the legislation

Having characterized the regulars' crusade as a campaign against irregular practice, the Brief proceeded to claim that "[n]ineteenth-century laws restricting access to abortion were not based on a belief that the fetus is a human being."[125] In support of this assertion it cited the sole case of *Cooper v State*, decided in 1849, and a passage in a book by Professor Michael Grossberg stating that at common law a foetus "enjoyed rights only in property law and then only if successfully born," that it had "no standing in criminal law until quickening, and none at all in tort," and that the law "highly prized children, not fetuses."[126] These sources do not, however, support the proposition that the unborn child was not regarded in nineteenth-century United States law as a human being. *Cooper* is not an authority on the "nineteenth-century laws"[127] and the passage lifted from

---

[122] Ibid 303. He also notes that Mohr ignores the efforts of the regulars to weed out their own members who were performing abortions, efforts which furnish further evidence that the regulars' concern was over abortion itself rather than over who was performing abortion: ibid 355.

[123] Ibid 313.

[124] R Ponnuru, "Aborting History", *National Review*, 23 October 1995 29, 31.

[125] Brief 26.

[126] Ibid.

[127] In *Cooper* 22 NJL (2 Zab) 52 (1849), the Supreme Court of New Jersey merely held that while post-quickening abortion, by the mother or by another, was illegal at common law, pre-quickening abortion was not. The court declined to extend the prohibition, adding that if the good of society required that the "evil" of pre-quickening abortion be suppressed by law it was far better that it should be done by the legislature: ibid 58. Far from supporting the Brief's proposition that the nineteenth-century laws did not regard the foetus as a human being, *Cooper* goes the other way. While, in a passage quoted by the Brief, the court did say that the law did not "have respect to its preservation as a living being," the court was here referring simply to the foetus before quickening. As the headnote to the case accurately stated, the common law did not recognize the child as a living being until it quickened or stirred in the womb. In other words the court was clearly of the view that the criminal law did recognize the child as a living being from quickening onward. Further, the common law authorities discussed by the court focused not on the woman's safety but on the point at which the life of the child began or could be proved to have begun. Having cited Blackstone that life begins in law as soon an infant is able to stir in the mother's womb, the court observed: "*In contemplation of law* life commences at the moment of quickening, at that moment when the embryo gives the first physical proof of life, no matter when it first received it.": ibid 54 (emphasis in original). The case is nothing

Professor Grossberg's book[128] (whose treatment of the history of the abortion law is hardly a model of accuracy[129]) is not one that summarizes the nineteenth-century cases.[130]

more (and nothing less) than authority for the criminality of post-quickening abortion at common law. Far from advancing the Brief's claims about nineteenth-century legislation, the case serves only to undermine its assertions about the common law. *Cooper* also serves to highlight the purpose of foetal protection in the New Jersey legislation that it inspired. A note appended to the report (ibid 58) reveals that the case induced the legislature to amend the criminal code so as to make pre-quickening abortion a crime. Clearly, the gap in the common law which the case exposed and which the legislature promptly closed was the common law's failure to protect the unborn child before quickening.

[128] M Grossberg, *Governing the Hearth: Law and the Family in Nineteenth-Century America* (1985).

[129] His discussion of the common law and the early abortion legislation is, as the following live examples illustrate, flawed. First, he states that Missouri (in 1825) and Illinois (in 1827) passed similar laws to Connecticut's 1821 legislation prohibiting post-quickening abortion: ibid 161. However, as he states later on the same page, the former two Acts made no mention of quickening. (See also Mohr 26.) Second, he claims that this early legislation "used the common law of abortion more to protect women from the ill effects of abortifacients than to restrict access to abortion.": Grossberg (n 128) 161–2. Yet he has already stated that the common law used the quickening distinction to locate the point at which the foetus became a human being, not the point at which abortion became dangerous to women, and that the Connecticut legislation punished post-quickening abortion as murder: ibid 160–1 Third, he asserts that Lord Lansdowne's Act 1828 (the successor to Lord Ellenborough's Act 1803) punished instrumental abortion for the first time: ibid 162. It did not: instrumental abortion before quickening was prohibited by Lord Ellenborough's Act. Fourth, he asserts that under the English anti-abortion provision enacted in 1837, abortion at any time during pregnancy became illegal. Not so: abortion at any time during pregnancy had been unlawful since Lord Ellenborough's Act. Fifth, he claims that the most significant American contribution to abortion law, the New York legislation of 1828, widened rather than reduced access to abortion: ibid. This striking claim turns out to mean merely that this anti-abortion legislation explicitly condoned therapeutic abortion to save the mother's life. Grossberg, who recognizes that such an exception may have been implicit in Lord Ellenborough's Act, misleadingly describes the 1828 legislation as an example of the priority that early abortion statutes gave to protecting the mother's health: ibid. In fact, the New York legislation, far from widening access to abortion, did the opposite by punishing abortion before quickening.

[130] The passage (Grossberg (n 128) 165) refers merely to the status of the unborn child at common law and to the reluctance of the court in *Cooper* to criminalize pre-quickening abortion. Moreover, the passage acknowledges that the foetus enjoyed standing in criminal law after quickening. Further, Grossberg's outline of the development of the common law recognizes that the quickening distinction was a product of the law's attempt to locate the point at which the embryo became a human being, not at which abortion became dangerous to the mother: ibid 160. He adds that "[b]efore animation, according to theological and customary practice, the fetus was not a person and its destruction was not murder.": ibid. And the legal standing that Grossberg concedes to the foetus after quickening was, of course, extended throughout pregnancy by the nineteenth-century legislation that made pre-quickening abortion illegal. The passage from Grossberg cited by the Brief does not comment on any of the cases referred to later (see nn 135–6) holding that the protection of the foetus was at least a purpose of that legislation. The drafters of the Brief did not have far to look for evidence of such cases. The very page facing Grossberg's quotation about foetal standing discusses a case indicating the legislative purpose of foetal protection: the Vermont case of *State v Howard* 32 Vt 380 (1859). In that case, the Chief Justice stated that that it was not easy to determine precisely which was the more important in the statute, to prevent injury to the child or to the mother: Grossberg (n 128) 164. There are other passages from Grossberg's book, also not quoted by the Brief, which would sit no less uneasily with the Brief's assertion of lack of legal concern for the unborn. Such passages would include Grossberg's recognition that the law, while granting the foetus full legal status only upon live birth, nevertheless accorded the unborn a "special legal niche.": ibid 186. Or his mention of the observation by historian Carl Degler (who, like Grossberg, signed the Brief) that, when seen against the broad canvas of humanitarian thought and practice in Western society from the seventeenth to twentieth century, including the reduced use of the death penalty, the peace movement, and the

The Brief omitted relevant case law indicating the legislative purpose of foetal protection even though the authorities were discussed in readily accessible literature on the subject.[131] In ignoring these precedents the Brief followed in the footsteps of Justice Blackmun in *Roe* who, relying on Means and the single case of *State v Murphy*, concluded that "[t]he few state courts called upon to interpret their laws in the late 19th and early 20th centuries did focus on the State's interest in protecting the woman's health rather than in preserving the embryo and fetus."[132] In arriving at this erroneous conclusion the Supreme Court overlooked Professor Grisez's book, which showed that the protection of foetal life was at least *a* purpose of the legislation and that this had been consistently acknowledged by the courts.[133] His work was also ignored by the Brief. So too was the article by Professor Byrn, published soon after *Roe*, detailing the court's historical errors, including its mistake about judicial construction of legislative purpose.[134] More recently, Philip Rafferty, reviewing the case law from the mid-nineteenth century onward, has observed that the Supreme Court in *Roe* "failed to point out that no less than forty-four appellate court decisions, representing some thirty-two states, including Texas, stated in one form or another that protection of conceived, unborn human life was one purpose of the state's statutory criminal abortion scheme."[135] Finally, even *State v Murphy* does not support the proposition that the statute before the court in that case sought to protect only maternal life.[136] Another notable omission from the Brief was any

abolition of torture and whipping as criminal penalties, "the expansion of the definition of life to include the whole career of the fetus rather than the months after quickening is quite consistent.": ibid 186 (quoting C Degler, *At Odds: Women and the Family in America from the Revolution to the Present* (1980) 247). Or the passage in which Grossberg states that the law's more severe treatment of abortion than contraception since the 1830s paralleled social opinion and practice and that even advocates of women's rights and birth control condoned contraception but not abortion: Grossberg (n 128) 194. Or the passage in which he states that in the first half of the twentieth century the focus of dispute over family planning was contraception, not abortion: "A fertilized egg had the right (sic) to join a family, unfertilized eggs had not.": ibid 195.

[131] See Byrn (n 13) 828–9; Destro (n 43) 1274–7.

[132] *Roe* 151; *State v Murphy* (1858) 27 NJL 112.

[133] Grisez (n 70) chs 5, 7.

[134] Byrn (n 13) 827–9. See also Finnis (n 1 11): "The Court's historical proposition in *Roe* is completely wrong: during the century beginning in 1850, there are decisions in ten states highlighting the statutory purpose of protecting the unborn child, and only two or three decisions that either focus only on maternal health or in any way advance the claim made by Means, and insinuated by the Court, that the state laws 'were designed solely to protect the woman.'"

[135] Rafferty (n 13) 76. The cases are cited in his accompanying fn 137. See eg *State v Gedicke* 43 NJL 86, 90 (1881); *State v Siciliano* 21 NJ 249, 258 (1956). See also PB Linton, "*Planned Parenthood v Casey:* The Flight from Reason in the Supreme Court" (1993) 13(1) St Louis University Law Review 15, App A.

[136] In that case the New Jersey Supreme Court affirmed the appellant's conviction under an Act of 1849 which provided that if any person or persons maliciously or without lawful justification, with intent to cause and procure the miscarriage of a woman then pregnant with child, shall administer to

reference to Professor Witherspoon's extensive analysis of the nine-teenth-century legislation, an analysis which confirmed the legislation's purpose of foetal protection.[137]

her, prescribe for her, or advise or direct her to take or swallow any poison, drug, medicine, or noxious thing, they would be liable to punishment: *State v Murphy* (1858) 27 NJL 112, 113. The court rejected the appellant's submission that the prosecution must prove that the substance was in fact taken by the woman. To ascertain the mischief of the statute the court considered the common law. It observed that at common law it was an offense for a third party or the mother herself to procure abortion if she were quick with child. The court added: "It was an offence only against the life of the child. The law was so held by this court in the case of *The State v Cooper*.": ibid 114. The court went on that the mischief designed to be remedied by the statute was the defect of the common law identified in *Cooper*, namely that the procuring of an abortion with the mother's consent was not an offense against her but only against the foetus. The court stated: "The design of the statute was not to prevent the procuring of abortions, so much as to guard the health and life of the mother against the consequences of such attempts.": ibid. The court, then, claimed that the statute sought not to prevent abortion so much as to protect the mother. But prevention of abortion was nevertheless one of its aims. As Grisez pointed out in his analysis of *Murphy*, "Not so much as does not mean the same as not at all. Rather, not so much as means both this and that, but more the one than the other.": Grisez (n 70) 384. This is confirmed by the Chief Justice's discussion of the liability of third parties under the statute. He said that the offence of third parties was "mainly" against her life and health: mainly, not solely: *State v Murphy* (1858) 27 NJL 112, 114. So, even if the court's reasons for the statute's predominant purpose were sound, the court nevertheless indicated that another purpose was the protection of the foetus. That the court did so was later recognized by the same court in *State v Siciliano* (1956) 21 NJ 249, 258 when it stated that the object of the 1849 legislation was, according to *State v Murphy*, not only the protection of the unborn child but also the protection of the life and health of the mother. Similarly, in a concurring opinion of the same court in *Gleitman v Cosgrove* (1967) 49 NJ 22, 41; 227 A 2d 689, 699, Justice Francis rejected the proposition that the legislation sought only to protect the mother: "It seems to me there were two objectives, of at least equal importance. One was to provide greater protection for the child *in utero* than was given under the common law. To accomplish this, the safeguard against abortion was moved backward from the time when the child became quick, to the instant of conception." He also stated that the purpose of foetal protection from conception was obvious, adding: "The immediate response of the Legislature in 1849 to the circumstances of *Cooper* make plain its design that the law should accept the child as in being from the moment of conception.": (1967) 227 A 2d 689, 696. In 1872, the New Jersey legislature made the death of the mother or child an aggravating factor: Grisez (n 70) 385. And in 1881 the New Jersey Supreme Court held that the 1872 legislation extended the law to protect the life of the child also and inflict the same punishment in the event of its death as if the mother should die: *State v Gedicke* (1881) 43 NJL 86, 90. Earlier in its judgment, commenting on the words poison, drug, medicine, or noxious thing introduced into New Jersey law by the 1849 Act, the court observed: "It is dangerous to the life and health of the mother and to the existence of the child to experiment with any drug, medicine, or noxious thing to produce a miscarriage.": ibid 89. Finally, the reasons of the court in *State v Murphy* for concluding that the purpose of the legislation was more to safeguard the mother than the unborn child are, in any event, questionable. Those reasons were that liability under the statute did not depend on the success or failure of the attempt; that it was immaterial whether the foetus was destroyed or had quickened; that the only gradation turned on whether the woman died, and that the statute did not incriminate the woman: (1858) 27 NJL 112, 114–15. But these reasons are consistent with an equal or even predominant legislative intention to protect the unborn. A legislature could to this end sensibly relieve the prosecution of the difficult burden of proving that an abortion had been successfully procured or that the foetus had been destroyed or had quickened; could make the death of the mother an aggravating factor; and could omit to incriminate her. And the court declared: "Her guilt or innocence remains as at common law. Her offence at the common law is against the life of the child.": ibid 114.

[137] Witherspoon (n 64).

5 Concern for the unborn in the wording and substance
of the legislation

It will suffice here to summarize aspects of Professor Witherspoon's
analysis which indicated the legislative purpose of foetal protection.
Witherspoon concluded that the analysis of the objectives of the nineteenth-century legislation by the Supreme Court in *Roe* was "fundamentally erroneous."[138] He pointed out that Justice Blackmun was wrong to
assert that "the law in all but a few States until mid-19th century was the
pre-existing English common law"; that it was "not until after the War
Between the States that legislation began generally to replace the common law"; and that "[m]ost of these initial statutes" treated abortion
before quickening leniently.[139] By the end of 1849, Witherspoon noted,
no fewer than eighteen of the thirty states had enacted anti-abortion
statutes; by the end of 1864, twenty-seven of the thirty-six; by the end
of 1868, thirty of the thirty-seven.[140] Moreover, of those thirty, twenty-
seven punished abortion before and after quickening.[141] In twenty, the
punishment was the same irrespective of quickening. Witherspoon criticized the court's suggestion[142] that where a statute did provide an
increased punishment after quickening this was because of greater health
risks to the woman. He argued that there was no evidence that post-
quickening abortion was more dangerous,[143] quoted a leader of the
regulars' campaign who stated that post-quickening abortion was in fact
less dangerous,[144] and noted that most of those states which did punish
post-quickening abortion more severely only did so if there were proof
that the attempt had killed the unborn child, a factor clearly relating to
foetal rather than maternal well-being.[145] Witherspoon identified several
other statutory indicators of a legislative intention to protect unborn life:

- Most of the statutes enacted by 1870 increased the penalty for abortion if it
  were proved to have caused the unborn child's death and a majority did so
  irrespective of the age of gestation.[146]
- Many statutes punished attempts only if the woman were proved to be
  pregnant,[147] though several states proceeded, in line with the recommendation by the leader of the regulars' campaign, to repeal the need to prove
  pregnancy in order to facilitate enforcement and "provide more complete
  protection to the life of the unborn child and the health of the pregnant
  woman."[148]

---

[138] Ibid 70.   [139] See text at n 21.
[140] Witherspoon (n 64) 33.   [141] Ibid 35.
[142] See text at n 30.   [143] Witherspoon (n 64) 35, fn 20.   [144] Ibid.
[145] Ibid 35.   [146] Ibid 36.   [147] Ibid 56.   [148] Ibid 56–7.

- Every statute required proof of an intent to procure abortion or to "destroy the child."[149]
- At least 17, or more than one-third of the state legislatures, enacted laws expressly incriminating the woman's participation in her own abortion.[150]
- Of the 14 states that by the end of 1868 punished abortion causing the death of the foetus more severely, nine provided the same punishment as if the attempt killed the mother; by the end of 1883, the figures were 20 and 14 respectively.[151]
- Seventeen states and the District of Columbia had at some time legislation classifying causing the death of an unborn child as "manslaughter," "murder," or "assault with intent to murder."[152]
- By the end of 1868, legislation in 23 states and six territories referred to the foetus as a "child."[153]

To this list may be added the fact that the legislation grew out of and sought to remedy any defects in the common law. The legislation sought, by prohibiting abortion before quickening, to promote the common law's purpose of protecting unborn life.[154] Moreover, Witherspoon pointed out that Blackmun was wrong to assume that there was an "absence of legislative history"[155] to support the legislative purpose of foetal protection, and illustrated one such history by examining in some detail the enactment of the anti-abortion statute in Ohio in 1867.[156]

In conclusion, while the abortion law may historically have sought to protect women as well as the unborn, and while the role of the medical profession in influencing the statutory restriction of abortion law in the last century may not have been disinterested, it is beyond doubt that one of the purposes of the common law and the legislation enacted in the last century—indeed, the predominant if not the only purpose—was the protection of the unborn.[157] This part of the chapter has not sought to identify all the errors in the Historians' Brief. It has, however, sought to

---

[149] Ibid 57.   [150] Ibid 59.
[151] Ibid 40.   [152] Ibid 44.
[153] Ibid 48.
[154] Means stated that all the US legislation was derived from Lord Ellenborough's Act 1803: Means II 359. There can be little doubt that protection of the unborn was the main if not sole purpose of that Act's provisions against abortion: Keown (n 13) ch 1.
[155] See text at n 26.
[156] Witherspoon (n 64) 61–9.
[157] The central purpose of the anti-abortion statutes enacted in England from 1803 to 1861 was also the protection of unborn life, though they may also have sought to protect women. The emerging medical profession, perhaps partly motivated by professional self-interest as well as its overt desire to protect the unborn from conception, appears significantly to have influenced the enactment of at least some of the statutes: Keown (n 13) Chs 1–2. The role of the medical profession in the US on the enactment of its nineteenth-century abortion legislation is far more pronounced.

show, by challenging three of the Brief's central claims, that its version of abortion law history is untenable.

IV ADVOCACY SCHOLARSHIP

A Brief "constructed to make an argumentative point rather than to tell the truth"

In United States law an amicus brief is "filed by someone not a party to the case but interested in the legal doctrine to be developed there because of the relevance of that doctrine for their own preferred policy or later litigation" and such briefs "almost invariably align themselves with one of the parties, making them primarily friends of the parties despite the 'friend of the court' label."[158] However, the Historians' Brief claimed to provide the court with a "rich and accurate description of our national history and tradition in relation to abortion."[159] As we have seen, this claim is unsustainable.

At the annual meeting of the American Historical Association in 1989 a panel of lawyers and historians involved in the drafting of the Brief engaged in a roundtable discussion.[160] The published versions of their presentations amounted largely to an unapologetic defense of the Brief. One of the papers was by Professor Law, the Brief's counsel of record.[161] She revealed her involvement in drafting other amicus briefs defending the "pro-choice position"[162] and that it was she who took the initiative in convening a working group of historian friends to produce the Brief.[163] Law stated that the Brief had three objectives: "to preclude the Court from relying on history in a stupid way, to tell the truth, and to support a political mobilization of pro-choice voices."[164] By the first aim she appears to have meant preventing the court from adopting the standard history of abortion law as traced in Part II of this chapter.[165] And was there not an inevitable tension between the second and third aims? Even Law admitted that the Brief fell short of the truth. Two factors "constrained our ability to 'tell the truth'," namely constraints of space and a "tension between truth-telling and advocacy."[166] Illustrating their "most serious

---

[158] SL Wasby, "Amicus Brief" in KL Hall (ed), *The Oxford Companion to the Supreme Court of the United States* (2nd edn, Oxford University Press, 2005) 38. In English law, by contrast, an amicus curiae is a disinterested adviser to the court.
[159] Brief 1.
[160] "Roundtable: Historians and the Webster Case" (1990) 12(3) Public Historian 9.
[161] SA Law, "Conversations Between Historians and the Constitution" (1990) 12(3) Public Historian 11.
[162] Ibid.   [163] Ibid 12.   [164] Ibid.
[165] Ibid 111–2.   [166] Ibid 14.

deficiencies as truth-tellers" she admitted that the Brief failed to grapple with "the fact that most nineteenth-century feminists supported laws restricting access to abortion."[167] This question, she added, was so serious that limits of space did not justify its exclusion and the silence was "distorting."[168] Law identified another distortion, namely the Brief's treatment of the incidence of and attitudes to abortion in colonial America, but explained the distortion on the ground that the Brief was "constructed to make an argumentative point rather than to tell the truth."[169] Nevertheless, Law defended the Brief as having contributed to the development of "more sophisticated public understanding."[170] How the Brief's distortions, only a few of which she acknowledged, were thought to promote more sophisticated understanding, either by the public or by the Supreme Court, is unclear. Despite their scholarly pretensions, the Historians' Brief and the articles by Means which preceded it,[171] are inaccurate and unreliable.[172]

Finally, it should by no means be assumed that all those who signed the Brief either possessed expertise in relation to its subject-matter

---

[167] Ibid 14–15.

[168] Ibid. On the nineteenth-century feminists' strong opposition to abortion, see Dellapenna Ch 8: "Feminist leaders ... were explicit, and uncompromising, and virtually unanimous, in condemning abortion as 'ante-natal murder,' 'child-murder,' or 'ante-natal homicide'.": ibid 374. He notes that "women physicians in the nineteenth century were also outspoken supporters of the criminality of abortion.": ibid 404.

[169] Law (n 161) 16. And as Law's co-counsel admitted in their contribution to the roundtable: "First and foremost, it was a legal argument designed to persuade the Supreme Court that it should decide the abortion rights issues in the *Webster* case in a particular way.": JE Larson and C Spillenger, "That's Not History: The Boundaries of Advocacy and Scholarship" (1990) 12(3) Public Historian 33, 34. They added: "Probably no one, lawyers or historians, considered the brief to be primarily a work of scholarship. It was instead an essay, a view of the field, a summation of existing secondary works rather than an exercise in original research.": ibid 36. Its view of the field was, as we have seen, blinkered. Referring to the Brief's silence about the opposition to abortion by nineteenth-century feminists, they explained that their "preference as legal advocates for assertive rather than tentative argument" led them to omit this inconvenient fact: ibid 39–40. In so doing, they "missed the mark of good scholarly method.": ibid 40.

[170] Law (n 161) 16.

[171] Commenting on Means I, a memorandum from David Tundermann to Roy Lucas (principal counsel to the successful side in *Roe*), during the time when both were developing the argument which was to prevail in *Roe*, stated that Means' conclusions sometimes strained credibility: in the presence of manifest public outcry over foetal deaths just prior to the passage of New York's 1872 abortion law, Means disclaimed any impact upon the legislature of this popular pressure (even though the statute itself copied the language of a pro-foetal group). Tundermann added: "Where the important thing is to win the case no matter how, however, I suppose I agree with Means's technique: begin with a scholarly attempt at historical research; if it doesn't work, fudge it as necessary; write a piece so long that others will read only your introduction and conclusion; then keep citing it until courts begin picking it up. This preserves the guise of impartial scholarship while advancing the proper ideological goals.": DJ Garrow, *Liberty and Sexuality: The Right to Privacy and the Making of* Roe v. Wade (University of California Press, 1994) 853–4.

[172] Means helped draft the Brief: Larson and Spillenger (n 169 above) 34.

(signatories included, for example, historians of architecture[173]) or that they had even read it.[174]

B "Preserving the guise of impartial scholarship while advancing the proper ideological goals"?[175]

1 The historians in the roundtable discussion

To what extent did the historian contributors to the roundtable discussion defend the Brief as consistent with scholarly objectivity? Professor Grossberg did not share Sylvia Law's reservations about its distortions. He claimed that the Brief stood up well to the standard evaluative measures of the discipline.[176] He added that it fulfilled the public responsibilities of historians by being a "well-constructed, professionally legitimate document."[177] In praise of the Brief as history he claimed that its argument was drawn from a "thorough examination of the relevant secondary sources" and "quite fairly synthesizes the judgments of that literature."[178] It is remarkable that Professor Grossberg, described in the introduction to the roundtable discussion as a "specialist in the nineteenth-century legal history of abortion,"[179] did not advert to the sources the Brief either omitted or misrepresented. Moreover, he endorsed the Brief's main claims that abortion has been "tolerated and widely practiced for most of the American past"; that the nineteenth-century legislation "reversed traditional practice"; that the doctors pressed for statutes "framed as protection for women's health";[180] that "[f]etal rights did not figure prominently in the debates that produced anti-abortion legislation"; and that "doctors ... paid little attention to the status and fate of fetuses."[181] As we have seen, these claims are untenable. What is more, they are difficult to square with his own book, which acknowledges that for centuries abortion after quickening was a crime at common law because that was when human life was believed to begin,[182] and that nineteenth-century legislatures tightened the law in response to lobbying by medical societies which condemned abortion from "the first moment of conception" as "murder."[183]

Professor Freedman's endorsement of the Brief was less fulsome. She stated that she would find it hard to argue, given the economic and

---

[173] See Ponnuru (n 124) 32; Dellapenna 841.

[174] Dellapenna comments that one professor disclosed that she had recruited 38 historians to sign it who had not read it, let alone read another brief that presented a contrary view: Dellapenna 841–2.

[175] See n 171.

[176] M Grossberg, "The Webster Brief: History as Advocacy, or Would You Sign It?" (1990) 12(3) Public Historian 45, 48.

[177] Ibid 51.   [178] Ibid 48.   [179] Ibid 10.

[180] Ibid 46.   [181] Ibid 47.   [182] Grossberg (n 128) 160.

[183] Ibid 173.

religious motives for childbearing, that abortion in colonial America was "not uncommon."[184] She added, however, that "for the practical purposes of writing this brief, it was necessary to suspend certain critiques to make common cause and to use the legal and political grounds that are available to us."[185] The goal of the Brief was, she stated, "to make a legal argument that would influence the court (not to provide a long-distance history seminar). . . ."[186]

Professor Mohr's contribution to the discussion was hardly a ringing endorsement of the Brief. He began by comparing a legal brief with a historical argument and observed that lawyers tended to minimize countervailing evidence because they cared less about what the past might teach than about what the past might do to achieve a desired result in the present, since that was the lawyer's purpose in turning to the past.[187] Lawyers "ultimately want that version of the past which serves their desired result in the present to prevail."[188] He added: "Nor do I ultimately consider the brief to be history, as I understand that craft. It was instead legal argument based on historical evidence. Ultimately, it was a political document."[189] Why, then, did he sign the Brief, particularly when it misrepresented his own book? When challenged, he said that where the Brief conflicted with his book, he stood by his book,[190] but that he defended his association with the Brief because it was a "political" rather than an "academic" document.[191] However, as Professor Bradley has remarked, "A document whose professed purpose is to address and validate *historical* analyses cannot take refuge in being a 'political' document. It represented matters of historical fact and put the full weight of its signatories' professional reputations behind those representations."[192] Even Mohr has written that those who signed it signed "as historians" as well as citizens.[193] Interestingly, when Professor Law submitted an almost identical brief to the Supreme Court in a later Supreme Court abortion case, Mohr's signature was notable by its absence.[194]

---

[184] Freedman (n 50) 28–30.
[185] Ibid 32.
[186] Ibid 28.
[187] JC Mohr, "Historically Based Legal Brief: Observations of a Participant in the *Webster* Process" (1990) 12(3) Public Historian 19, 20.
[188] Ibid.
[189] Ibid 25.
[190] GV Bradley, "Academic Integrity Betrayed", First Things, August/September 1990 10.
[191] Ibid 12.
[192] Ibid (emphasis in original).
[193] Mohr (n 187) 25.
[194] "Brief of 250 American Historians as Amici Curiae in Support of Planned Parenthood of Southeastern Pennsylvania, in Planned Parenthood of Southeastern *Penn. v Casey*, 505 US 833

2 Mohr's book

This chapter has argued that the Brief is undermined by one of its major sources, Mohr's book, which shows in impressive detail that the engine behind the nineteenth-century abortion legislation was the medical profession's campaign to extend the legal protection of the unborn. Remarkably, however, in the final chapter of his book, Mohr does advance the argument (having prefaced his remarks with the qualification that "as a work of history" his book ended with the previous chapter[195]) that *Roe* "is not as great a departure of policy in the long view as it might at first have seemed."[196] He writes sympathetically of the *Roe* court's view that the nineteenth-century legislation was a deviation from the norm and claims that its trimester guidelines "returned to American women a virtually unconditional right to terminate a pregnancy" during the first trimester.[197] However, his contention that *Roe* marked a return to an earlier norm is mistaken.[198] First, as Mohr recognizes,[199] *Roe* did not strike down statutes prohibiting only "early" abortion. It struck down statutes prohibiting abortion until viability, and even between viability and birth,

---

(1992)." Dellapenna writes that the reason Mohr has given for declining to sign this virtually identical brief was lack of time and that Mohr declined to discuss the reason with him: Dellapenna 843.

[195] Mohr 247.

[196] Ibid 259.

[197] Ibid 248.

[198] As Dellapenna has pointed out, the claim is scarcely less contentious from the perspective of social history. Dellapenna argues that Mohr's twin theses, that abortion was a generally accepted and common practice in American society at the start of the nineteenth century and that the nineteenth-century anti-abortion legislation was a device used by (usually male) regular medical practitioners to oppress (usually female) irregulars, are erroneous: Dellapenna 1005–6. Dellapenna writes: "neither Cyril Means nor James Mohr considered abundant evidence relevant to their inquiries. Even more troubling are the major methodological errors in their approach to the evidence. Means and Mohr both characteristically project our present knowledge onto persons writing or acting in prior centuries. Thus they riddled their work with contradictions.": ibid 1012. As examples of such contradictions he cites Mohr's insistence that people saw nothing wrong with killing an unborn child while admitting that the people he quoted did not think that a child was present early in pregnancy, and his insistence that safe and effective pharmacological methods were available while acknowledging that they were dangerous and ineffective: ibid 1012, n 106; 303. Dellapenna adds: "Even more troubling is Means' and Mohr's pervasive pattern of dismissing any evidence inconsistent with their theses as a ruse to conceal the person's 'true' motives—motives that support their theses, and for which, peculiarly, no evidence has survived except Means's or Mohr's own surmise.": ibid 1012; 19–22. Dellapenna observes that Mohr sought to avoid scrutiny of his treatment of the history of the law by shifting the focus to "the 'true' social attitudes" about abortion found in non-legal sources, not the least problem with which is its assumption that "the best way to determine the *legal* tradition underlying the Constitution is to examine *non-legal* sources...": ibid 1043 (emphasis in original). Dellapenna also contends: "At the root of Mohr's argument is the utter absence of the larger legal and medical historical context" within which the nineteenth-century anti-abortion statutes were enacted: ibid 302. Dellapenna observes that, far from abortion being socially accepted, a "true social consensus" appears to have existed in support of the anti-abortion statutes, which explains why they were passed unanimously or nearly so: ibid 462. Dellapenna concludes: "In sum, Mohr's book simply does not withstand careful reading even without additional research into his claims.": ibid 22.

[199] Mohr 248–9.

provided the abortion is thought to be in the interests of the woman's "health." Further, in the companion case of *Doe v Bolton*, the court adopted an interpretation of "health" so wide as to allow virtually any unwanted pregnancy to be terminated.[200] In his book[201] Mohr accepts that the common law prohibited abortion after quickening (and, as we saw in Part II of this chapter, at least the early common law prohibited abortion before quickening, from foetal formation). *Roe*, then, allows abortions in the second half (at least) of pregnancy which were illegal at common law. Moreover, over 700 years of consistent prohibition, as homicide or serious misdemeanor, is hardly evidence of tolerance or lenity. Second, Mohr writes that the basis of the quickening distinction was twofold: contemporary belief about ensoulment of the foetus and the need to prove that the woman was indeed pregnant rather than suffering from amenorrhea.[202] He therefore accepts that the common law used quickening to establish when human life began. To suggest that the common law tolerated the destruction of foetal life before quickening is misleading: even on Mohr's own reading, human life was simply not thought to have begun. Third, the restriction of the law in the nineteenth century flowed naturally from the underlying rationale of foetal protection. Once quickening was exploded as an unscientific indicator of the beginning of human life, legislatures accordingly moved to tighten the law in order to protect the unborn from fertilization. Mohr's detailed demonstration of the hugely influential role of regular medical practitioners in this regard serves usefully to confirm that rationale. His speculation about the possible influence of medical professionalization risks confusing alleged, hidden motives of the regulars with the patent purposes of the regulars, the legislators, and the legislation.

3 Mohr's senate testimony

In 1998 Professor Mohr repeated his misinterpretation of *Roe* to a Senate Judiciary Subcommittee which was holding a hearing on *Roe* on the twenty-fifth anniversary of the decision. Far from toning down his argument in the light of Professor Bradley's incisive criticism of his association with the Brief,[203] Mohr went even further, contradicting his own book in the process. He testified that from the beginning of the Republic "through

---

[200] The doctor's medical judgment, ruled Justice Blackmun, may be exercised "in the light of all factors—physical, emotional, psychological, familial, and the woman's age—relevant to the well-being of the patient. All these factors may relate to health.": *Doe v Bolton* 410 US 179, 192 (1973).
[201] Mohr 3–4.
[202] Ibid 4.
[203] See text at n 192.

the Civil War" early abortions were "not illegal" and that "[o]nly in the last third of the 19th century did early abortion become indictable in most American states...."[204] However, his book states that by 1840 five of twenty-six states had proscribed abortion before quickening,[205] and that of some seventeen states or territories to enact anti-abortion legislation between 1840 and 1860, around three-quarters punished abortion before quickening.[206] Mohr also testified: "Even during the period when the practice of abortion was theoretically illegal, it was always the person performing the abortion who was open to indictment, not the pregnant woman."[207] Yet his book discusses a number of statutes that made the woman expressly liable.[208] Further, Mohr testified that *Roe* improved the health and safety of American women, which was "something 19th century legislators had no concern about."[209] But again, his book relates that protecting maternal health "was something many nineteenth-century legislators had been deeply concerned about in the various abortion laws they enacted."[210] Mohr's testimony that *Roe* "resonates with the nation's previous 200-year record of tolerance and sympathy" towards women seeking early abortion and that "every state and every court in the nation implicitly favored a degree of tolerance"[211] is contradicted by the historical record, even as portrayed by his own book. Professor Mohr is of course entitled to change his mind, but it would be interesting to know his reasons.

An analogy will, by way of conclusion, serve to illustrate Mohr's skewed, and the Brief's perverse, interpretation of abortion law history. This analogy also concerns the law's concern to protect human life, but at

---

[204] Constitution, Federalism and Property Rights Subcommittee of the Senate Judiciary Committee, Hearing on the 25th Anniversary of the Supreme Court's Decision in *Roe v Wade*, 105th Congress 13, 21 January 1998, 1998 WL 27127, Federal Document Clearing House ("*Roe* Anniversary Hearing").

[205] Mohr 43.

[206] Ibid Ch 5. The proportion may be higher: Mohr is imprecise about the scope of some of the legislation he discusses. It will be recalled that Witherspoon pointed out that by the end of 1868, 30 out of 37 states had legislated against abortion, and that 27 of those 30 punished pre-quickening abortion. See text at nn 140–1.

[207] *Roe* Anniversary Hearing 14.

[208] For example, his book mentions New Hampshire's first anti-abortion statute enacted in 1849 which "revoked the long-standing immunity from punishment afforded American women who sought their own abortions prior to quickening.": Mohr 134. And, it will be recalled, Witherspoon pointed out that no fewer than 17 states enacted laws expressly incriminating a woman's participation in her own abortion. See text at n 150. Nor, as the authorities cited in Part II and Part III.B.1 of this chapter show, was the woman immune from prosecution at common law.

[209] *Roe* Anniversary Hearing 13.

[210] Mohr 248.

[211] *Roe* Anniversary Hearing 14.

the end of life rather than at its beginning. The common law has historically been concerned to protect human beings from being killed until their
natural death. Imagine that, from the thirteenth century until the nineteenth century, natural death had been thought to occur when respiration,
tested by breath misting a mirror placed close to a patient's mouth, had
ceased. The law, accordingly, punished killing before, but not after, that
time. Indeed, after the point at which the mirror no longer misted there
was no life to be taken, or so it was thought. Imagine also that it was,
moreover, common practice, immediately after the mirror ceased to mist,
for patients to be declared dead and for unqualified dissectors to cut them
up or for relatives to cremate them. The dissectors also practised medicine, but their lack of hygiene sometimes led to their patients contracting
fatal diseases. In the nineteenth century educated medical practitioners
discovered, through greater understanding of human physiology, that,
despite appearances, respiration continued for some time after the patient's breath could no longer mist the mirror, and that integrated organic
functioning did not in fact cease until the brain died some 48 hours after
that point. The medical profession vociferously and repeatedly criticized
the law's historic definition of death as outdated and unscientific. Legislators across the country, in response to a concerted campaign by the
medical profession, enacted legislation extending the reach of the crime of
homicide until 48 hours after the point at which breathing could no longer
mist a mirror. In 1973 euthanasia campaigners petitioned the Supreme
Court. They invited the court to find a constitutional right for those in the
last 48 hours of life to be painlessly euthanized. In support of the petition
281 historians, knowing that the court could be influenced by the nation's
history and traditions, filed an amicus brief. The brief argued that euthanasia in those circumstances, far from being a break with legal tradition,
would return the law to an older tradition. For, the brief argued, the
common law never prohibited *all* killing of human beings: it allowed
patients during the last 48 hours of life to be dissected or cremated.
Granting the right claimed by the petitioners would represent a return
to the common law's "tolerance" of such killing and restore the relatives'
"common law right" to dispose of dying relatives. As for the nineteenth-
century legislation redefining death, the brief continued, it was a "deviation from the norm." It was the result of an exercise in professional self-
interest by a group of qualified medical practitioners whose motivation,
despite appearances, was to suppress competition by unqualified dissectors whose want of hygiene was, moreover, a threat to public health. The
legislation "was really about who should be allowed to practice medicine,"

not about furthering the law's purpose of protecting human beings toward the end of their lives.

V CONCLUSION

From the thirteenth century the common law, seeking to protect human life from the time it was believed to have begun, proscribed abortion, at least from quickening, as a serious offense. The nineteenth century heralded improved understanding of embryological development, which showed that life began not at quickening but at fertilization. Pressed by educated medical practitioners to bring the law up to date with this advanced understanding, legislators across the United States filled the gap by protecting the unborn from that point. In short, the primary purpose of the prohibition on abortion, both at common law and by statute, has been the protection of the unborn.[212] *Roe*'s discovery of a constitutional right to abortion therefore represented a radical break with America's legal history and traditions. To argue otherwise is, frankly, to stand history on its head. The tailoring by the Historians' Brief of a historiography to clothe *Roe*'s new right relies on a patchwork of threadbare materials which leaves it exposed. It is to be hoped that, just as the Supreme Court brought an accurate understanding of the nation's history and traditions to bear on the question of whether the Constitution contains a right to physician-assisted suicide, it will in time do likewise on the no less important question of whether the Constitution contains a right to abortion.

---

[212] Dellapenna 1055.

CHAPTER 6

"MORNING AFTER" PILLS, "MISCARRIAGE," AND MUDDLE

I INTRODUCTION

> [A]bortion techniques have changed since we legislated in 1967.... Nowadays they can be carried out by injection or what is euphemistically called the morning after pill, which is an early abortifacient. There have always been legal doubts about whether the morning after pill can be prescribed within the present abortion law.... [T]he drug...works in the early period of pregnancy.[1]

In *Smeaton*[2] Munby J (as he then was) held that intentionally to prevent the implantation of an embryo in the uterus by administering the "morning after" pill (MAP) is not to procure a "miscarriage" contrary to section 58 of the Offences against the Person Act 1861 (OAPA 1861). His decision may well remain the leading authority in the common law world on the legal status of the MAP. Despite its significance as one of the most important decisions to be handed down by a High Court judge, it has attracted hardly any academic analysis. This chapter respectfully questions the judgment's soundness.

It seems clear that one mode of operation of the MAP is to prevent fertilization. This does not engage section 58. But it appears that another mode of operation may be to prevent the implantation in the lining of the womb of any embryo conceived after intercourse.[3] Does this engage section 58? Section 58 prohibits the use of means with intent to procure

---

[1] Sir David Steel MP, *Hansard*, HC vol 174, col 1142 (1989–90).

[2] *R (Smeaton) v Secretary of State for Health* [2002] EWHC 610 (Admin), [2002] 2 FLR 146 ("*Smeaton*"). In the United States the MAP is also called "Plan B."

[3] See The Westchester Institute, "Emergency Contraceptives and Catholic Healthcare: A New Look at the Science and the Moral Question" (2011) and the colloquy between Yeung et al. and Austriaco in (2008) 8(2) National Catholic Bioethics Quarterly 217. This chapter considers the legality of the administration of the MAP with intent to prevent the implantation of any embryo which may have been conceived.

the "miscarriage" of any woman, and the prohibition applies whether or not she be "with child," that is, pregnant.[4] Section 59 prohibits the procurement or supply of means knowing that they are intended to be used with intent to procure "miscarriage," whether or not the woman is pregnant.[5] The Abortion Act 1967 neutralizes sections 58 and 59 if certain conditions are satisfied, such as the certification by two registered medical practitioners that the balance of risk to the woman's health favors abortion.[6] The novel question confronting Munby J was whether the word "miscarriage" should be given an unrestricted interpretation, which would include the prevention of implantation, or a restricted interpretation, which would not. His Lordship's ruling that it should be given a restricted interpretation echoed an opinion delivered in 1983 by the then Attorney-General, Sir Michael Havers. In response to a Parliamentary Question, Sir Michael stated that "miscarriage" should be interpreted as it was ordinarily understood in 1861, and that it was clear that "the ordinary use of the word 'miscarriage' related to interference at a stage of prenatal development later than implantation."[7] A paper of mine published the following year took issue with the Attorney's opinion. It pointed out that that in 1861 "miscarriage" was ordinarily used in an unrestricted sense to include the prevention of implantation;[8] that the few relevant judicial decisions supported the unrestricted construction; and that section 58's purpose of protecting unborn life from fertilization (and the likely allied purpose of protecting women from potentially dangerous interference) rendered the Attorney's interpretation untenable. The paper also noted the dearth of authority to support Sir Michael's interpretation and that he himself offered none.

From 1984 the MAP was available on prescription. On 1 January 2001 the Prescription Only Medicines (Human Use) Amendment (No 3) Order 2000[9] came into force. It allowed the MAP to be made available by pharmacists without prescription. The Society for the Protection of

---

[4] Section 58 provides: "Every woman, being with child, who, with intent to procure her own miscarriage, shall unlawfully administer to herself any poison or other noxious thing, or shall unlawfully use any instrument or other means whatsoever with the like intent, and whosoever, with intent to procure the miscarriage of any woman, whether she be or be not with child, shall unlawfully administer to her or cause to be taken by her any poison or other noxious thing, or shall unlawfully use any instrument or other means whatsoever with the like intent...." shall be liable to a maximum punishment of life imprisonment. The argument that it is still an offense at common law to destroy an embryo from fertilization was apparently not raised in *Smeaton* and is not considered in this chapter.

[5] The punishment is imprisonment for a maximum of five years.

[6] Abortion Act 1967, s 1(1)(a), amended by the Human Festilisation and Embryology Act 1990, 537.

[7] *Hansard* HC vol 42, cols 238, 239: Written Answers 10 May 1983.

[8] IJ Keown, "'Miscarriage': A Medico-Legal Analysis" [1984] Crim LR 604.

[9] SI 2000/3231.

Unborn Children (SPUC), a pro-life organization, challenged the Order by way of judicial review. Counsel for SPUC argued that the MAP is an abortifacient and that its administration, in the absence of compliance with the Abortion Act 1967, is prohibited by section 58.[10] SPUC's action was opposed by the Secretary of State for Health, by Schering Health Care Limited (the manufacturer of the brand of MAP which had been approved for use by the Order), and by the Family Planning Association.

Munby J rejected SPUC's argument. He doubted whether in 1861 "miscarriage" included the prevention of implantation and held that, in any event, an "updating" construction should be applied to give the word the meaning it bore today. He concluded that the current meaning of the word did not include the prevention of implantation. SPUC's case therefore failed. Few judges can match Sir James Munby's knowledge and experience in matters medico-legal and since *Smeaton* he has, not surprisingly, been elevated to the Court of Appeal. Nevertheless, this chapter respectfully questions the judge's reasoning in *Smeaton*. It offers five criticisms:

- that his doubts about the unrestricted meaning of "miscarriage" in 1861 were misplaced;
- that there is far more room to doubt the restricted meaning he attributed to "miscarriage" today than there is to doubt the unrestricted meaning the word enjoyed in 1861;
- that his analysis of the judicial precedents was questionable;
- that his evaluation of academic opinion was unconvincing; and
- that an "updating" construction, even if appropriate, was misapplied, not least because it served to frustrate the core purpose of section 58: the protection of human life from fertilization.

II FIVE CRITICISMS

A "Miscarriage" in 1861

Munby J did not accept the argument that the ordinary meaning of "miscarriage" in 1861 included the prevention of implantation. He claimed that some of the most authoritative medical works of the time "strongly supported the idea that miscarriage became possible only

---

[10] SPUC sought to quash the 2000 Order and a declaration that it was *ultra vires* the Secretary of State; that a person who administered the MAP with the intention of expelling any embryo which may exist committed an offense under s 58; and that a person supplying the MAP intending it be used for such a purpose committed an offense under section 59.

after implantation."[11] His claim sits uneasily with the nineteenth-century medical and medico-legal sources, a sample of which had been cited in my 1984 paper.[12] That paper, based on a survey believed to include all major obstetrical texts published in England between 1788 and 1910, concluded that "miscarriage" was ordinarily used in the 1800s include a failure to implant, and that those texts were unanimous in either supporting or not contradicting this conclusion. Munby J said that he did not propose to examine the sources in exhaustive detail because his decision in the case turned on what "miscarriage" meant today rather than what it meant in 1861.[13] He did, however, conclude: "the texts, as it seems to me, are very far from unanimous. Some, as I read them, on their face contradict Dr Keown's reading."[14] With respect, the judge's interpretation of the nineteenth-century sources was mistaken. This can be illustrated by his reliance on three leading authorities: Drs James Whitehead, John Burns, and Francis Ramsbotham.

1 James Whitehead

In 1847 Dr Whitehead's text on abortion read:

Miscarriage is the term usually employed to signify the expulsion of the foetus from the womb at any period before the completion of its growth. . . . I shall . . . use the word *abortion* in its widest signification, to denote the untimely arrest of the process of utero-gestation at any period of pregnancy.[15]

Whitehead held that the period of "utero-gestation" ran "from the moment of impregnation, when the ovum . . . receives the fertilising stimulus."[16] He therefore adopted an unrestricted definition of "miscarriage" and "abortion." Munby J, however, concluded that even on a "benevolent

---

[11] *Smeaton* para 19.

[12] The sources were detailed in witness statements I was invited to submit on behalf of the claimant: ibid para 150. Two expert witnesses tendered written evidence about the nineteenth-century sources. One (myself) gave evidence in statements dated 19 October and 14 December 2001. The other, Ms Joan Walsh, a witness for the Department of Health, gave evidence in statements dated 11 July 2001 and 26 January 2002. Her first witness statement described her (at para 1) as "a Researcher at the Clinical Effectiveness Unit at the Faculty of Family Planning and Reproductive Health Care." It added that prior to this position she had spent eight years as a clinical embryologist and five as Research and Policy Officer at the Family Planning Association. It continued: "My professional roles have required in-depth knowledge of relevant areas in the history of bio-medicine, in particular the development and use of fertility control methods in 19th and 20th century Britain." If she had any formal qualifications or relevant publications in medical or legal history she did not disclose them, and her witness statements were flawed.

[13] *Smeaton* para 152.

[14] Ibid.

[15] Ibid para 158 (emphasis in original).

[16] Ibid para 159.

reading" Whitehead "might perhaps be thought to be ambiguous."[17] His Lordship omitted to explain why.

2 John Burns and Francis Ramsbotham

The judge observed that Drs John Burns and Francis Ramsbotham defined "miscarriage" by reference to "detachment" and "expulsion" and that they were therefore "strongly supportive of the idea that miscarriage becomes possible only after implantation."[18] It is hardly surprising that obstetrical texts should have focused on abortions with which physicians would have had to deal in practice, namely those occurring after implantation. Those occurring before implantation would typically have been as undetectable in 1861 as they are today. But for a source to have focused, even exclusively, on post-implantation abortion does not mean that the source thereby denied the possibility of pre-implantation abortion. A nineteenth-century text on obstetrics which defined abortion as involving "detachment" no more contradicted the possibility of pre-implantation abortion than a twenty-first century text on embryology which defines human life as beginning with the fertilization of the egg by the sperm contradicts the possibility of human life beginning by cloning. The implausibility of Munby J's reading of Burns and Ramsbotham is confirmed by two sources. The first is Burns himself. As the expert evidence for SPUC pointed out, Dr Burns, having defined "abortion" as involving "detachment" and expulsion,[19] explained:

The ovum may be thrown off at different stages of its growth; and the symptoms, even at the earliest period, vary in duration and degree. The process of gestation may be checked, even before the foetus or vesicular part of the ovum has descended into the uterus.[20]

Similarly, in 1843 William and Alexander Campbell's *Introduction to the Study and Practice of Midwifery* stated: "Abortions of the early months consist, *first*, in the separation of the ovum; and, *secondly*, in its expulsion."[21] That the authors did not understand their use of the word "separation" to exclude pre-implantation abortion is clear from the fact that the passage continued: "When abortion is excited before the ovum

---

[17] Ibid para 165.
[18] Ibid para 169.
[19] J Burns, *The Principles of Midwifery* (3rd edn, Longman, Rees, Orme, Brown, Green & Longman, 1814) 193.
[20] Ibid 194.
[21] W Campbell and AD Campbell, *Introduction to the Study and Practice of Midwifery* (2nd edn, Longman, Rees, Orme, Brown, Green & Longman, 1843) 651 (emphases in original).

has reached the womb, the only thing visible is a profuse sanguineous discharge."[22]

3 Unanswered questions

The judgment's reading of the historical sources becomes even more problematic in the light of three questions. First, if the restricted interpretation was supported, let alone "strongly" supported, by eminent authorities, why did the judge and the historical witness for the Secretary of State fail to identify a single source denying in terms that a miscarriage could occur from fertilization? (Moreover, the judgment omitted to explain why, if there had been a strong disagreement between the doctors on this point, none evidently alluded to its existence.) Second, why did those experts who explicitly considered the phenomenon of pre-implantation loss describe it without qualification as "abortion" or "miscarriage"? Third, why would any of the experts have denied that miscarriage could occur between fertilization and implantation? What reason would they have had for distinguishing between loss of the embryo before and after implantation?

4 General usage

In any event, even if the judge had been right to conclude that the few experts whom he claimed contradicted the unrestricted usage actually did so, this would not have sufficed, without more, to rebut the statement[23] that "miscarriage" was generally understood in 1861 to include the prevention of implantation. Given that the judge went on to hold that in any event an "updating" construction should be applied, it is perhaps surprising that he should have embarked on an analysis of its meaning in 1861 at all. But, having embarked on that analysis, it should surely have been comprehensive. Was the judge's interpretation of the meaning of "miscarriage" in the twenty-first century any more sure-footed?

B *"Miscarriage" today*

Applying an "updated" construction of "miscarriage," the judge concluded that there was "no substantial dispute" that the current meaning of "miscarriage" was the "termination of... a post-implantation pregnancy."[24] Such was clear, he said, from the evidence of Professor Drife, Professor of Obstetrics and Gynaecology at Leeds University, of a medical expert for

---

[22] Ibid.
[23] Advanced in my second witness statement.
[24] *Smeaton* para 351.

Schering, and of various current medical dictionaries. With respect, the evidence seemed much less clear than the judge claimed. If Professor Drife's evidence as to the current medical usage of "miscarriage" was correct, that usage was confused if not contradictory. Moreover, a preponderance of the current medical dictionaries considered by the judge supported the unrestricted construction.

1 *Professor Drife*

Professor Drife gave evidence that in his opinion "pregnancy" begins "when the pregnancy test is positive, some ten to fourteen days after conception."[25] He went on: "My reasons relate to the large numbers of fertilised oocytes [eggs] which are believed to be lost during the normal menstrual cycle. I do not believe these can be described as 'pregnancies'."[26] He added that "miscarriage" meant "the loss of a clinically recognised pregnancy" and that "Since a pregnancy cannot be recognised until HCG [human chorionic gonadotrophin[27]] can be detected, and HCG is not produced until implantation has been initiated, a miscarriage will not occur prior to implantation."[28] The professor claimed that his definitions were the norm among doctors and women.[29] However, there are questions about their cogency.

Was the reason for his restricted use of "miscarriage" the number of embryos lost before implantation, or the fact that the earliest pregnancy test currently available detects the embryo's presence only after implantation? If the former, why should the percentage of embryos that fails to implant render it inappropriate to describe their loss as "miscarriages"? Further, expert medical evidence tendered by Professor Braude, a medical expert for the Secretary of State, claimed that even after implantation "the failure rate is prodigious."[30] Would Drife therefore claim that these post-implantation losses are not "miscarriages"? If the basis for Drife's restricted definition was the earliest point at which pregnancy can be detected, then his definition seems tautologous. His definition of "miscarriage" as the loss of a "clinically recognised pregnancy" itself implies that there are pregnancies which have not been clinically recognized. Further, why should the definition of "pregnancy" be tied to its detection? If a woman is "pregnant" only when a test has detected the presence of the embryo some days after conception, is a person "HIV +" only when a test

---

[25] Ibid para 133.
[26] Ibid.
[27] He defined HCG as "a hormone produced by the placenta or the cells destined to form the placenta": ibid para 132.
[28] Ibid para 134.
[29] Ibid para 132.
[30] Ibid para 129.

has detected the virus, even if this is some months after the virus has been contracted? Moreover, if pregnancy begins with its detection some "ten to fourteen" days after conception (as Drife claimed), and if implantation usually begins (as the judge noted) about six days after conception (and possibly as early as four to five days[31]), is it Drife's view that the woman is not pregnant, even after implantation, between day six and day ten? Again, if the embryo implants but is then lost (even after day fourteen) without its presence having been detected, has the woman "miscarried"? Drife would presumably hold that, as there has been no loss of a "clinically recognised" pregnancy, she has not. Indeed, he seems to have accepted as much when he stated: "losses of fertilised eggs, whether before or *after* implantation in a cycle ending with normal menstruation, do not involve a clinically recognised pregnancy and are not covered by the term 'miscarriage'."[32]

The judgment addressed none of these questions and endorsed the surely questionable definition advanced by Professor Drife (who has, incidentally, long been a leading advocate of the MAP[33]). The judge also seemed unaware that other scientific experts have expressed a contrary view. For example, Professor Robert Edwards, the pioneer of in vitro fertilization, wrote in 1980: "Pregnancy surely begins at fertilization . . . and discussions on the merits of I.U.D.s or 'morning after' pills will be best served by accepting their role as early abortifacients. . . ."[34] As we shall see later, Edwards is not alone in his view that preventing implantation is procuring abortion.[35]

2 Modern medical dictionaries
Having consulted eight medical dictionaries the judge concluded that they "support the view that pregnancy begins once the blastocyst [the early embryo] has implanted in the endometrium [the lining of the uterus] and, more particularly, that miscarriage is the termination of such a post-implantation pregnancy."[36] Leaving aside the fact that this was not the definition tendered by Professor Drife who, as we have seen, referred to the loss of a "clinically recognised" pregnancy,[37] of the eight dictionaries, a clear majority supported the unrestricted definition.[38]

---

[31] Ibid para 126.
[32] Ibid para 134 (emphasis added).
[33] *The Times*, 5 May 1983, Letters.
[34] RG Edwards, *Conception in the Human Female* (Academic Press, 1980) 1000.
[35] See text at nn 91–6.
[36] *Smeaton* para 148.
[37] See text at n 28.
[38] The eight were: *Taylor's Principles and Practice of Medical Jurisprudence* (ed AK Mant, 13th edn, Churchill Livingstone, 1984); *The International Dictionary of Medicine and Biology* (ed SI Landau et al., Churchill Livingstone, 1986); *Churchill's Illustrated Medical Dictionary* (ed R Koenigsberg, Churchill

To illustrate the judge's misinterpretation of these sources it will suffice to consider one of those he claimed was "unambiguously support-ive" of the restricted interpretation: *Dorland*. Having noted the description of *Dorland* as, in the opinion of many, the world's finest medical dictio-nary, the judge set out its relevant definitions. "Miscarriage" was "loss of the products of conception from the uterus before the fetus is viable; spontaneous abortion"; "conception" was "the onset of pregnancy, marked by fertilisation of an oocyte by a sperm or spermatozoon; formation of a visible zygote"; and "pregnancy" was "the condition of having a devel-oping embryo or fetus in the body after union of an ovum and spermato-zoon."[39] It is not easy to see how *Dorland* was thought to support the restricted construction.

C Precedents

1 Foreign precedents

Munby J considered four cases cited by the claimant in support of the unrestricted construction: from India, Australia, Malaya, and Ireland. In the first, decided in 1886, the Court of Appeal at Madras, interpreting "miscarriage" in the Indian Penal Code, held that it consisted in the expulsion of the "immature product of conception" and that the "stage to which pregnancy has advanced and the form which the ovum or embryo may have assumed are immaterial."[40] The second, a decision of the Full Court of the Supreme Court of Victoria in 1943, interpreted "miscarriage" in the Crimes Act 1928 as the expulsion or removal of "the contents of a gravid uterus" and "the untimely emptying of a uterus which contains the products of a conception."[41] The third, a decision of the Court of Appeal of Malaya in 1958, interpreted "causes a woman with child to

---

Livingstone, 1989); *Butterworth's Medical Dictionary* (2nd edn, Butterworths, 1978, reprinted 1990); *Reproductive Medicine: from A to Z* (ed HE Reiss, Oxford University Press, 1998); *Stedman's Medical Dictionary* (27th edn, Lippincott, Williams & Wilkins, 2000); *Melloni's Illustrated Dictionary of Obstetrics and Gynaecology* (ed IG Dox et al., Informa Healthcare, 2000); and *Dorland's Illustrated Medical Dictionary* (29th edn, Saunders, 2000). Even on the definitions as set out by the judge (*Smeaton* paras 138–48), it is clear that while two (*Stedman* and *Reproductive Medicine*) supported the restricted interpretation, and two (*The International Dictionary* and *Churchill*) seemed ambiguous, four (*Taylor*, *Dorland*, *Butterworths*, and *Melloni*) supported the unrestricted interpretation. Moreover, a closer reading of the two ambiguous texts—which takes account of their definition of "impregnation" as fertilization—discloses that they too should be read as supporting the unrestricted interpretation: *The International Dictionary of Medicine and Biology* (1986) vol II 1412; *Churchill's Illustrated Medical Dictionary* (1989) 926.

[39] *Smeaton* para 147.
[40] *Queen-Empress v Ademma* (1886) ILR 9 Mad 369, 370.
[41] *R v Trim* [1943] VR 109, 116.

miscarry" to mean causing her "to lose from the womb prematurely the products of conception. . . ."[42]

Munby J commented that these cases provided no support for an unrestricted interpretation and that "their uniform references to miscarriage as involving the loss of the contents of the uterus would tend to support the defendants' case."[43] However, all three cases focused on the loss of the product of "conception." Munby J did not question that the standard historical meaning of "conception" (which is probably still predominant today) is fertilization, not implantation. None of these cases attached the slightest significance to implantation and therefore tend to support the unrestricted interpretation. Perhaps Munby J thought otherwise because of their reference to the loss of the product of conception from the "uterus." However, this does not assist a restricted interpretation. The prevention of implantation takes place in the uterus. The consequent expulsion of the embryo is the loss of the contents of the uterus. From where else could the embryo be expelled? Moreover, just as Munby J offered no reason as to why nineteenth-century medical experts should have drawn a definitional line at implantation, he offered no reason as to why the courts in these cases should have done so.

The judge then turned to an Irish case: *Attorney-General (ex rel Society for the Protection of Unborn Children Ireland Ltd) v Open Door Counselling Ltd and Dublin Wellwoman Centre Ltd.*[44] In this case, Hamilton P in the High Court noted that section 58 (which continues in force in Ireland as in England) protects "the foetus in the womb" and that "the right to life of the foetus, the unborn, is afforded statutory protection from the date of its conception."[45] Munby J downplayed this *dictum* with the comment that the issue in *Smeaton* was not raised in that case and that, unless by "conception," Hamilton P was referring to implantation, Hamilton P's words seemed inconsistent, since he referred to statutory protection applying both to "the foetus in the womb" and from "the date of . . . conception." However, although the point before Munby J was not directly in issue, Hamilton P's *dictum* surely remains in point in respect of statutory purpose. Moreover, there is no inconsistency in his *dictum*. The natural meaning of his words is that the aim of section 58 is the protection of the unborn from fertilization. In other words, he used "conception" to refer to fertilization and "foetus" and "womb" in a correspondingly unrestricted

[42] *Munah binti Ali v Public Prosecutor* (1958) 24 MLR 159, 160.
[43] *Smeaton* para 231.
[44] [1987] ILRM 477 (High Court).
[45] Quoted by Munby J in *Smeaton* para 241.

way. This usage of "conception" would be consistent with the standard, historical usage of the word (including its usage in the preceding three cases), with its usage in most modern medical dictionaries, including most of those considered by Munby J, and indeed with the use of the word by Munby J himself in his own judgment.[46] This interpretation is fortified by Hamilton P's reference to "the date of *its* conception,"[47] which far more naturally relates to the origin of the foetus at fertilization than to its implantation in the lining of the womb. Munby J seems to have considered a restricted interpretation of "the date of conception"[48] but not an unrestricted interpretation of "the foetus in the womb."

Moreover, Munby J did not address a line of cases from the United States (of which my 1984 paper cited five[49]) which supports the unrestricted interpretation in respect of the nineteenth-century anti-abortion legislation in that country.

In conclusion, though few in number and not concerned with the precise question raised in *Smeaton*, the foreign precedents do tend to support the unrestricted construction.

2 *Dhingra*

Much of Munby J's consideration of precedents was devoted to *R v Dhingra*, an unreported decision of Wright J at Birmingham Crown Court in 1991. In that case a doctor was indicted under section 58 for inserting an intrauterine device (IUD) into a woman with intent to procure her miscarriage. Wright J ruled that the word "miscarriage" related to "spontaneous expulsion of the products of pregnancy"; that a pregnancy could not commence until the embryo had implanted in the womb; and that the insertion of an IUD "before a pregnancy has become established," and with the intent to prevent implantation, did not amount to an offense under the section.[50] Having heard medical evidence about the stage of the woman's menstrual cycle when the defendant had inserted the IUD, the judge withdrew the case from the jury on the ground that it was highly unlikely that any embryo had begun to implant.[51] As a decision of a High Court judge in a case in which Crown counsel declined to argue the point in question,[52] *Dhingra* is of scant precedential value.

---

[46] Ibid para 195. And by Professor Drife: see text at n 25.
[47] *Smeaton* para 241 (emphasis added).
[48] Ibid para 242.
[49] Keown (n 8) 611, nn 42–3.
[50] Quoted by Munby J in *Smeaton* para 249.
[51] Ibid para 248.
[52] Ibid para 249, although Wright J did base his judgment on research by counsel and himself: ibid.

Wright J relied largely on evidently limited evidence by two doctors that in modern medical usage "miscarriage" related "to the spontaneous loss of an established pregnancy" and not to the prevention of implantation.[53] Moreover, if the propositions on which Wright J relied in his judgment had been challenged, few could have survived unscathed. For example, he said that his tentative support for the restricted interpretation was "greatly reinforced" by the fact that the discussion in the case of *Royal College of Nursing v DHSS*[54] was "entirely in terms of pregnancy and the effect upon the foetus."[55] This is hardly surprising: that case concerned the lawfulness of a method of abortion in advanced pregnancy. Again, Wright J cited the Attorney-General's statement in 1983 but, as we have seen, that statement was the merest assertion.[56] And Wright J seemed unaware of the apparently tautologous expression of his own ruling: "that the insertion of an intrauterine contraceptive device before a pregnancy has become established" did not breach section 58. This phraseology echoes the tautology in the medical evidence before him that "miscarriage" related to the loss of an "established pregnancy."[57] The unrestricted interpretation was implicit in the very testimony seeking to supplant it. Munby J stated that the fact that Crown counsel did not seek to argue for the unrestricted construction "in no sense diminishes the authority of the court's ruling, which was reached after full consideration of the competing arguments of construction...."[58] Full consideration of the competing arguments? Judging from Munby J's own account of the case, it appears that Wright J considered neither of the two articles on the very question which had appeared not very long before in the country's leading journal of criminal law.[59] Further, the fact that Crown counsel did not wish to argue for the unrestricted construction surely enervates what limited precedential value *Dhingra* might otherwise have had. Munby J did fully consider the arguments, but his observation that Wright J had done so appears to have been largely judicial comity.

---

[53] Quoted by Munby J in *Smeaton* para 245.

[54] [1981] AC 800.

[55] Quoted by Munby J in *Smeaton* para 249.

[56] See text at nn 7–8. Moreover, the Attorney said that "miscarriage" should be interpreted as it was understood in 1861.

[57] Quoted by Munby J in *Smeaton* para 245.

[58] *Smeaton* para 254.

[59] V Tunkel, "Modern Anti-Pregnancy Techniques and the Criminal Law" [1974] Crim LR 461; Keown (n 8).

D Commentators

Munby J considered the views of several academic commentators, a majority of whom supported the restricted interpretation. The reasons of the majority were, however, far from cogent. It will suffice to examine the reasons given by two leading authorities on medical law: Professor Glanville Williams and Professor Ian Kennedy.

1 *Williams*

We will recall from Chapter 2 that in his book *The Sanctity of Life and the Criminal Law* Williams captured the scope and purpose of section 58 when he wrote that in Anglo-American criminal law: "The foetus is a human life to be protected by the criminal law from the moment when the ovum is fertilized."[60] There can be little doubt that this would have been regarded at the time as an accurate statement of the law. A quarter of a century later, however, Williams wrote:

Formerly it was thought that the vital point of time was fertilization, the fusion of spermatozoon and ovum, but it is now realised (though the point has not come before the courts) that this position is not maintainable, and that conception for legal purposes must be dated at earliest from implantation.[61]

At no point did Williams advert to his earlier support for the unrestricted interpretation or give any legally relevant reason for his change of opinion. Shortly before the Attorney-General's statement in 1983, a correspondent to *The Times* drew attention to Williams' previous statement of the law.[62] Williams replied that in *The Sanctity of Life*: "I was stating the general opinion as to the law; but my concern was to criticise it."[63] As an outspoken activist for legalized abortion, Williams did indeed criticize the law because he thought it too restrictive. But his statement of what the general opinion as to the law *was* could hardly have been clearer. Readers of *The Times* might well have been misled by Williams into thinking that he had questioned the accuracy of that general opinion, when the truth of the matter was that he had endorsed it. Williams proceeded to expose himself further to a charge of dissimulation. His letter added that *The Sanctity of Life* had noted the medical classification of pregnancy loss before the sixteenth week as "abortion" and as "miscarriage" thereafter. The letter went on:

[60] GL Williams, *The Sanctity of Life and the Criminal Law* (revised edn, Faber and Faber, 1958) ("SLCL") 141. See Ch 2, n 75.
[61] *Textbook of Criminal Law* (2nd edn, Steven & Sons, 1983) 294.
[62] J Finnis, *The Times*, 5 April 1983, Letters.
[63] G Williams, *The Times*, 13 April 1985, Letters.

It can, therefore, be argued with considerable force that when Parliament abolished the limitation for quickening in 1803 it did not mean to extend the law back to the time of fertilisation.... It may be suggested that all that Parliament meant to do was to dispose with the need for proof of the woman's experience of quickening, while retaining the need to prove that the foetus had reached a fairly advanced stage of development—say, four months.

Readers of *The Times* might yet again have been misled, this time into thinking that this was an argument that Williams had raised in his book. On the contrary, any such argument would have been wildly inconsistent with his book.[64] Perhaps the "considerable force" of the contrary argument, that "miscarriage" was intended by the legislature to allow abortion up to the fourth month, occurred to him only a quarter of a century later. In any event, the argument is specious for several reasons, all of which were (or should have been) familiar to Williams. For example, medical writers used "abortion" and "miscarriage" to refer to different stages of pregnancy when they were discussing *spontaneous* abortion, not procured abortion, in which case they used the words interchangeably.[65] In the very footnote in *The Sanctity of Life* where Williams mentioned the medical usage of "miscarriage" he admitted that it was variable and was used "in a sense different from its legal one, namely, the premature expulsion of the contents of the uterus spontaneously."[66] Again, as Williams recognized without equivocation in *The Sanctity of Life*, the defining purpose of the law of abortion has been the protection of unborn life from its beginning. Why should nineteenth-century legislators have undermined this purpose (and the likely allied purpose of protecting women) by punishing abortion only after some unspecified point of foetal formation ("a fairly advanced stage of development—say, four months"), a point utterly unrelated to the child's vitality (and to the mother's safety)? Why, moreover, would they have done so at a time when medical practitioners were berating the law for the significance it attached to the physiologically irrelevant phenomenon of quickening and were urging legislators to protect the embryo from fertilization? In *Smeaton* it was not disputed that "miscarriage" and "abortion" were used synonymously in the nineteenth-century legislation.[67] It is not difficult to see why. It is hard to resist the conclusion that Williams allowed his fervent personal views in favor of relaxed abortion laws to corrupt his legal analysis.

---

[64] SLCL 139, 141, 153, 206.

[65] See eg TH Tanner, *On the Signs and Diseases of Pregnancy* (Henry Renshaw, 1860) 211.

[66] SLCL 139, n 1.

[67] *Smeaton* para 275. Munby J noted (ibid para 353) that miscarriage and abortion are also synonymous in modern usage.

2 Kennedy

The judge considered the meaning of "miscarriage" in a paper by Professor Kennedy in 1982.[68] Kennedy's central argument, which he claimed was supported by Glanville Williams, is captured in the following passage, which was quoted by Munby J:

In the ordinary use of language, we do not think of a fertilized egg as a "child". Nor would we think of a woman as "pregnant" until implantation has taken place.... [Y]ou cannot procure a miscarriage until you have a carriage, and you would not ordinarily use the notion of "carrying" a child until it was implanted in the womb.[69]

Kennedy seemed simply to assume that "miscarriage" should be given its modern meaning, and that its modern meaning was sufficiently obvious not to require the citation of any dictionaries of either English or medicine. Had he tried to cite them, he would have found scant material to clothe his claims. (And as we shall see presently, sources contradicting those claims are not difficult to find.[70]) Suffice it here to comment on his narrow understanding of "child." First, the standard dictionary definition of "child" includes the unborn child, without any qualification about implantation.[71] Second, the law has long used the words "with child" to mean "pregnant"; those words are used in section 58 of the OAPA 1861, and pregnancy was understood in 1861 to start at fertilization. Third, modern illustrations of the same, broad usage are far from scarce. For example, the headnote to a modern English case concerning a father's attempt to prevent the abortion of his unborn child begins: "A wife, who had conceived a child by her husband...."[72] Turning from English usage to English law, Kennedy omitted to mention Williams' statement of the law in *The Sanctity of Life*[73] and the paper by Victor Tunkel, on the very issue in question, which had appeared in the Criminal Law Review only eight years before Kennedy's paper.[74] Kennedy did mention the dissenting

---

[68] I Kennedy, "The Legal and Ethical Implications of Postcoital Birth Control" in *Postcoital Contraception* (1982); reprinted in I Kennedy, *Treat Me Right: Essays in Medical Law and Ethics* (Clarendon Press, 1988) ("TMR") as Ch 3.

[69] TMR 35; quoted in *Smeaton* para 260.

[70] See text at nn 88–96.

[71] The first definition given in the *Oxford English Dictionary* is: "The unborn or newly born human being; foetus, infant. App originally always used in relation to the mother as the 'fruit of the womb'." It continues: "When the application was subsequently extended, the primitive sense was often expressed by *babe, baby, infant*, but 'child' is still the proper term, and retained in phrases such as 'with child'...." (2nd edn, 1989) vol III 113 (emphases in original). It goes on to define "with child" as "pregnant": ibid 114.

[72] *Paton v Trustees of BPAS* [1979] QB 276.

[73] See text at n 60.

[74] V Tunkel, "Modern Anti-Pregnancy Techniques and the Criminal Law" [1974] Crim LR 461.

speech of Lord Wilberforce in *Royal College of Nursing v DHSS*.[75] But this was a case on the interpretation of the Abortion Act 1967, not the OAPA 1861. In any event, the case refuted the proposition for which Kennedy cited it. Kennedy claimed that Lord Wilberforce expressed the opinion that the Abortion Act 1967 should be not given a purposeful construction. So he did. However, the majority held that the Abortion Act 1967 should be given a purposeful construction.

Munby J considered two academic papers favoring the unrestricted construction. The first was by Tunkel in 1974, the second by myself a decade later.

3 Tunkel

Tunkel advanced, *inter alia*, the telling argument that to hold that section 58 did not bite until implantation "would, in effect, give a sort of free-for-all moratorium of a week or more after intercourse during which every sort of abortionist could ply his craft with impunity."[76] Munby J commented that counsel for the Secretary of State had replied that this argument "might be thought" to overlook sections 23 and 24 of the OAPA 1861.[77] These sections prohibit the administration of "any poison or other destructive or noxious thing" so as thereby to endanger life or to inflict grievous bodily harm (section 23), or with intent to injure, aggrieve, or annoy (section 24). If the judge was endorsing counsel's argument, as he appeared to be, his endorsement seems misplaced. If counsel's argument was that in 1861 the legislature did not intend section 58 to protect embryonic life and women until implantation, but that the legislature did intend to protect women, by way of sections 23 and 24, from abortionists[78] plying their trade between fertilization and implantation, it encounters two difficulties. First, why would the legislature, when doctors had known for decades that life began at fertilization and had pressed for its criminalization from that point, have sought to protect it only from implantation? Second, sections 23 and 24 concern the administration of substances. Why would the legislature have intended to protect women from the administration of substances with intent to procure miscarriage, but not the use of instruments with the same intent?

---

[75] [1981] AC 800.

[76] Tunkel (n 74) 465.

[77] *Smeaton* para 271.

[78] Presumably counsel would not have described those destroying the embryo between fertilization and implantation as "abortionists."

4 Keown

Munby J then considered my 1984 paper. As his criticism of my analysis of the nineteenth-century medical and medico-legal sources was considered earlier,[79] it remains only to note his claim that "significant portions" of my paper appeared to be principally directed towards establishing that by 1861 it was recognized that miscarriage could occur before as well as after quickening. He agreed with the claim of Professors Kennedy and Grubb that the arguments in my paper:

> do not appear to be relevant to the discussion concerning the difference between pre-implantation and implantation. They appear to be more concerned with the difference between 'conception' and 'quickening', particularly in the light of the fact that the nineteenth century authorities were unaware of the detail of the physiological processes between conception and birth, save in the most general terms.[80]

First, it is mysterious how Kennedy and Grubb could question the relevance of nineteenth-century sources on the very point in question, sources which consistently supported an unrestricted definition of miscarriage. Some of these sources explicitly described the loss of the embryo before implantation (not simply before quickening) as "miscarriage," others did so implicitly through definitions which dated the beginning of life and gestation from fertilization. Second, Kennedy and Grubb's failure to engage with these sources, and to produce a single source the other way, is compounded by their enigmatic comment about the state of nineteenth-century medicine. Precisely what lack of knowledge about which physiological process are they alleging hampered medical understanding concerning early pregnancy in 1861?

5 Brazier

The judge claimed that other commentators "albeit with differing degrees of confidence" took essentially the same position as Kennedy and Grubb.[81] Among these he included another eminent authority on medical law, Professor Margaret Brazier. However, in the source cited by the judge,[82] she did not take the same position as Kennedy and Grubb. She carefully outlined the arguments about the meaning of "miscarriage," noted the decision in *Dhingra*, and, putting that weak authority in its

---

[79] See text at nn 11–22.
[80] I Kennedy and A Grubb (eds), *Medical Law: Text with Materials* (2nd edn, Lexis Law Publishing, 1994) ("KGII") 1412; quoted in *Smeaton* para 271.
[81] *Smeaton* para 266.
[82] M Brazier, *Medicine, Patients and the Law* (Penguin, 1992) 293–5; cited in *Smeaton* para 266.

proper place, concluded that the question had yet to be resolved by higher judicial authority. This is some way from supporting the restricted construction.

In short, the so-called "weight of legal writing" supporting a restricted opinion turns out on closer inspection to be little more than assertion. Far from supporting the restricted interpretation it serves only, through its evasive or contrived reasoning, to expose the inherent artificiality of that interpretation. The "weight of legal writing" either accepts that "miscarriage" should be given the meaning it had in 1861 and fails to engage with the relevant authorities, or assumes that it should be given its modern meaning and fails to engage with the relevant authorities.

E "Updating" construction

Munby J held that the true answer to the problem of statutory interpretation with which he was faced lay in "the principle of updating construction." He illustrated that principle by considering a number of cases. He concluded that, applying that principle, the correct approach to the instant case could be set out in the form of four propositions:

- the 1861 Act is an 'always speaking' Act;
- the word 'miscarriage' is an ordinary English word of flexible meaning which Parliament in 1861 chose to leave undefined;
- it should accordingly be interpreted as it would be *currently* understood;
- it should be interpreted in the light of the best current scientific and medical knowledge that is available to the court.[83]

Even if the "updating" principle is sound,[84] it is doubtful whether this was an appropriate case for its application. Attempting to procure abortion before implantation falls squarely within the mischief that the legislature had it in mind to suppress when enacting the statute. Moreover, the judge's conclusion about the modern usage of "miscarriage" was questionable.

1 The current meaning of "miscarriage"
Munby J stated that there was "in truth no substantial dispute" as to the present meaning of "miscarriage": pregnancy began once the blastocyst had implanted in the lining of the womb, and "miscarriage is the

---

[83] *Smeaton* para 350 (emphasis in original).
[84] For criticism of the principle see R Ekins, "*Yemshaw* and the constitutionality of updating statutes" (unpublished paper delivered at a meeting of the Statute Law Society, London, 9 May 2011). I am grateful to Dr Ekins for sending me a copy of his paper.

termination of such a post-implantation pregnancy."[85] That this was the current medical understanding was clear, he said, from the evidence of Professor Drife and the medical dictionaries to which the judge had referred. It was also, Munby J added, the current lay understanding of the word. He concluded: "At the end of the day—and despite the length of this judgment—the resolution of this case is as short and simple as that."[86] He went on to add that his interpretation of "miscarriage" accorded with the meaning "properly attributed" by "linguistic analysis." The word "miscarriage" presupposed prior "carriage," and by far the more natural meaning of "carriage" involved not merely presence in the woman's body and interaction with it, but "attachment to it in a real sense such as occurs only with implantation."[87] With respect, the matter is neither as short nor as simple as the judge supposed.

First, we may recall that although the judge appeared to base his restricted definition on the evidence of Professor Drife, Drife defined "miscarriage" not as the loss of an implanted embryo but of a "clinically recognised" pregnancy.[88] Second, the current medical dictionaries which Munby J cited not only cast doubt on his claim that there is "no substantial dispute" about the modern medical understanding of "miscarriage" but, by a significant majority, supported an unrestricted construction.[89] Third, to claim that "carriage" requires implantation or "attachment" seems the merest assertion and the judge cited no dictionary to support it. The dictionary meaning of "carry" is simply "To transport..." as in "running water carries bodies floating on it, or suspended in it, wind carries leaves, balloons, slates, etc."[90] There is no requirement here of physical "attachment." Moreover, hypothetical examples illustrate the inappropriateness of any such requirement. Is a drug smuggler who has swallowed a cocaine-filled condom not "carrying" it if it is floating in his or her stomach or being swept through his or her intestines? And if one contracts a particular bacterium which merely circulates through one's bloodstream, is one not "carrying" the bacterium? Again, *The Times* reported in January 2004 that advances in nanotechnology may result

---

[85] *Smeaton* para 351.
[86] Ibid 352.
[87] Ibid 353.
[88] See text at n 28.
[89] See text at n 38.
[90] *OED* (2nd edn, 1989) vol II 919. "Carriage" is defined simply as "The action of carrying": ibid 914. Similarly, a definition of "carry" in another dictionary is: "To serve as a means for the conveyance of; transmit," as in *"pipes that carry waste water...."* <http://dictionary.reference.com/search?q=carry> (emphasis in original).

in micro-submarines being introduced into the human arterial system.[91] Would it not be perfectly natural to describe the micro-submarines as being "carried" by patients? Indeed, it is not easy to think of a synonym which could be used in these three instances, let alone one which could be used as naturally. For good measure, examples of the unrestricted usage of "miscarriage" in ordinary, contemporary English are far from uncommon. Three examples will suffice. First, the very same issue of *The Times* carried a report of a scientific paper which suggested that a mother's lack of a particular protein may be associated with a heightened risk of miscarriage. The report observed:

Many pregnancies end in miscarriage, usually before the woman realizes she is pregnant. As many as half of pregnancies miscarry before the fertilised egg is implanted in the wall of the womb. Others occur after implantation but before the pregnancy is detected.[92]

Second, counsel for the Secretary of State for Health urged the restricted meaning upon the judge. Yet the Department of Health's own website uses the unrestricted definition. The website carries a Department of Health publication, *The Pregnancy Book*,[93] written with the assistance of expert bodies including the Royal College of Obstetricians and Gynaecologists. This lucid publication explaining pregnancy attaches definitional significance not to implantation but to fertilization.[94] Third, the website of *Women's Health UK* states:

When you conceive and a baby is created, it takes half its genes from the sperm and half from the egg that ovulated that month. At the exact time of conception, the cross-over of these genes takes place. Sometimes, for no reason other than bad luck, some information is lost and the pregnancy is destined from that point not to be.

It observes: "The risk of miscarriage decreases as pregnancy progresses. It is possible that as many as 50 per cent of pregnancies miscarry before implantation in the womb occurs."[95] Finally, we may recall that Professor Edwards, the pioneer of in vitro fertilization,[96] and Sir David Steel MP, the architect of the Abortion Act 1967,[97] have both explicitly described the

---

[91] *The Times*, 9 January 2004, 16.
[92] "Protein clue may help to end agony of miscarriage", *The Times*, 9 January 2004, 10.
[93] *The Pregnancy Book* <http://www.doh.govuk/pregnancybook>.
[94] Ibid 92, 23, 28, 104.
[95] <http://www.womens-health.co.uk/miscarr.htm>. The author is Dr DE Tucker, a clinical lecturer in medicine at Oxford University.
[96] See text at n 34.
[97] See text n 1.

MAP as an "abortifacient." Nor were the above examples of unrestricted usage buried in obscure sources. Indeed, all were found in widely available publications and several resulted from a simple internet search.[98]

2 Legislative purpose

The six cases cited by Munby J concerning the updating principle illustrated the importance of ascertaining and promoting (or at the very least not restricting) the relevant legislative purpose. Two of these cases will suffice to illustrate the point. The first is *A-G v The Edison Telephone Co of London Ltd.*[99] The Telegraph Act 1869 gave the Postmaster-General a monopoly on transmitting telegrams, which were defined as messages transmitted by "telegraph," which was in turn defined as any apparatus for transmitting messages by means of electrical signals. When the Act was passed the only such method of transmission was Morse code. When the telephone was subsequently invented, it was argued that the Act did not apply to it. The Exchequer Division rejected this argument. Stephen J, delivering the judgment of the court, said:

> Of course no one supposes that the legislature intended to refer specifically to telephones many years before they were invented, but it is highly probable that they would, and it seems to us clear that they actually did, use language embracing future discoveries as to the use of electricity for the purpose of conveying intelligence. The great object of the Act ... was to give special powers to telegraph companies. ... The Act, in short, was intended to confer powers and to impose duties upon companies established for the purpose of communicating information by the action of electricity upon wires, and absurd consequences would follow if the nature and extent of those powers and duties were made dependent upon the means employed for the purpose of giving the information.[100]

Similarly, the fact that in 1861 the legislature did not have in mind the MAP is surely no more relevant than the fact that in 1869 it did not have in mind the telephone. Just as the telephone was a new means of transmitting messages by means of electrical signals and fell within the "great object" of the Telegraph Act 1869, so the MAP is a new means of procuring miscarriage and falls within the "great object" of the OAPA 1861. Far from supporting Munby J's application of the principle of updating construction, the cases he cited, such as *Edison*, seem to

---

[98] Using *Google*.
[99] (1880–81) LR 6 QBD 244.
[100] Quoted by Munby J in *Smeaton* para 305.

undermine it.[101] A second case is *Fitzpatrick v Sterling Housing Association Ltd.*[102] The question in this case was whether the deceased tenant's homosexual partner was either his "spouse" and/or a member of his "family" within the meaning of the Rent Act 1977, a provision which originated in legislation of 1920. The House of Lords held, by a bare majority, that the partner was a member of the deceased's "family." Lord Slynn said that the correct question was not whether people in 1920 would have regarded the partner as a member of the deceased's "family," but rather what were the characteristics of a family in 1920 and whether two same-sex partners could satisfy those characteristics today.[103] He added that as the authorities showed that "family" did not mean only a legal relationship (of blood, marriage, or adoption), it was necessary to ask what the characteristics of "family" in this legislation were and to answer that question to ask further what was Parliament's purpose.[104] It seemed to his Lordship that the intention in 1920 was to include not only the legal wife but also other members of the tenant's family unit occupying the property. Lord Nicholls said:

In the present case Parliament used an ordinary word of flexible meaning and left it undefined. The underlying legislative purpose was to provide a secure home for those who share their lives together with the original tenant in the manner which characterises a family unit. This purpose would be at risk of being stultified if the courts could not have regard to changes in the way people live together and changes in the perception of relationships.[105]

In *Fitzpatrick*, legislative purpose played an important role in the interpretation of "family," the court considering the characteristics of "family" when the legislation was enacted. A consideration of the characteristics of "miscarriage" in 1861 and the purpose of section 58 lends little support to the restricted construction. Indeed, the medical concept of "miscarriage" in 1861 was readily ascertainable in the medical and medico-legal texts of the period, which testify to a clear, biological meaning, far less "flexible" than the inherently vaguer sociological concept of "family" in 1920. In the light of the string of cases he cited on updating construction, Munby

---

[101] The other cases were: *Royal College of Nursing v DHSS* [1981] AC 800; *R v Ireland* [1998] AC 147; *Fitzpatrick v Sterling Housing Association Ltd* [2001] 1 AC 27; *Birmingham City Council v Oakley* [2001] 1 AC 617; *R (Quintavalle) v Secretary of State for Health* [2002] EWCA Civ 29, [2002] 2 WLR 550.

[102] [2001] 1 AC 27.

[103] Quoted by Munby J in *Smeaton* para 316. Lord Slynn added that an alternative question was whether the word "family" in the 1920 Act had to be updated to include persons who today would be regarded as being of each other's family, whatever might have been said in 1920: ibid para 316.

[104] Quoted by Munby J in *Smeaton* para 317.

[105] Quoted by Munby J, ibid para 318.

J ruled that it would be wrong in law to tie the meaning of the word "miscarriage" to the sense in which it was understood in 1861 (whatever that was) and in the limited effect it allows to the principle of updating construction. He went on:

There is nothing in the 1861 Act to demonstrate a Parliamentary intention to protect 'life' from the point of fertilisation. The construction for which the defendants contend does not involve any alteration in the conceptual reach of the 1861 Act. Parliament's intention in 1861 was to criminalise the procuring of 'miscarriages'. The content of that Parliamentary intention has, as a matter of law, to be assessed by reference to current—not nineteenth century—understanding of what that word means.[106]

He added that the first, and determinative, reason for preferring the restricted construction was that it would be wrong to "freeze the frame" in 1861: "Now quite apart from the artificiality of freezing the frame in 1861, when the word had been consistently used in this context ever since the beginning of the century, and the impossibility in fact of ascertaining 'the' meaning of the word in 1861"[107] such an approach would be inconsistent with the principle of updating construction. The judge then set out the four propositions, reproduced above,[108] which led him to a restricted construction.

Munby J observed that it was undisputed that two of the purposes of the Act were the protection of women and the protection of the unborn. He then added: "But the fact that one of the legislative purposes of the 1861 Act was—is—the protection of unborn human life has no direct bearing on the issue before me: how far back does the protection afforded by the Act extend?"[109] The answer to that question surely lay in determining when in 1861 human life was thought to begin. The evidence bearing on that question is as clear in relation to England as the previous chapter showed it to be in relation to the United States.

By 1861 it had been known by medical science for decades that human life began at conception, not implantation. Moreover, physicians had consistently condemned abortion from that point as a heinous wrong. For example, the year in which the very first statutory restriction of the abortion law was enacted (1803) also witnessed the publication of the first, and famous, text on medical ethics, written by Dr Thomas Percival. Percival rejected the ancient notion that the unborn child was merely part of the mother:

---

[106] *Smeaton* para 342.   [107] Ibid para 349.
[108] See text at n 83.   [109] *Smeaton* para 354.

false it must be deemed, since no female can be privileged to injure her own bowels, much less the foetus, which is now well known to constitute no part of them. To extinguish the first spark of life is a crime of the same nature, both against our Maker and society, as to destroy an infant, a child, or a man ...[110]

Texts on forensic medicine were equally forthright. In 1815, OW Bartley, having noted that life began at the "moment of impregnation," commented: "There are in the catalogue of human vices, few more heinous ... so heinous that the utmost power of exaggeration cannot add to its deformity. It is murder...."[111] Medical and medico-legal texts consistently berated the legislature for the lighter punishment it provided for abortion before than after quickening, a distinction which did not disappear from the law until 1837. In 1825 Dr Theodric Beck's leading text on forensic medicine stated that reason and physiology showed that the unborn child was alive from the moment of conception and that laws which punished early abortion less severely were immoral and unjust.[112] In 1836 Dr Michael Ryan's text on medical jurisprudence observed: "Abortion is justly considered a heinous crime—as it is the murder of the foetus in the womb, or in other words, of a human being."[113] He added: "I therefore completely agree with Percival, Beck, and almost the whole profession, that embryocide and foeticide ought to be equally punished with death."[114] In 1861 the *Lancet* described abortion as "one of the most despicable, loathsome, and enormous of human crimes...."[115] It railed that abortion was "getting to infect this land in so virulent a manner as must soon call for some direct interference of the Legislature for the purpose of arresting the crying shame."[116] Munby J asked how far back the protection of section 58 extended. As all the evidence confirms, the answer is fertilization, not implantation. Perhaps he thought that the legislature was unaware of the contemporary medical consensus that life began at fertilization and of the profession's uncompromising condemnation of abortion from that point? Or perhaps that the legislature chose, for some unexplained reason, to disagree with that knowledge and condemnation? His judgment does not say. Whatever the explanation, there can surely be little doubt that, to borrow from Stephen J in the *Edison* case, the

---

[110]   *Medical Ethics* (1803) 79.

[111]   OW Bartley, *A Treatise on Forensic Medicine* (Barry and Son, 1815) 2.

[112]   TR Beck, *Elements of Medical Jurisprudence* (2nd edn, John Anderson, 1825) 140. The text was published in the US but was known in England.

[113]   M Ryan, *A Manual of Medical Jurisprudence, And State Medicine* (2nd edn, Sherwood, Gilbert, and Piper, 1836) 265.

[114]   Ibid 283.

[115]   "More abortionists" [1861] 1 Lancet 295.

[116]   Ibid 121.

"great object" of section 58 was the protection of the unborn child from fertilization[117] (though a secondary purpose may well have been the protection of women[118]). Any suggestion that the legislature which enacted section 58 intended its prohibition on attempted abortion to apply only after implantation is, with respect, unsustainable.

As for the judge's two reasons for concluding that it would be artificial to "freeze the frame" in 1861, neither is convincing. The first, that the word "miscarriage" had been used in previous legislation dating from 1803, seems beside the point: there is nothing to suggest (apart perhaps from the judge's strained reading of sources like Dr John Burns) that the word bore anything other than the unrestricted meaning from 1803 to 1861. The second, the alleged "impossibility" of ascertaining the meaning of the word in 1861, is no stronger. Why was it impossible? The judge's consideration of the historical evidence provided little support for this assertion. Moreover, his denial of the possibility of ascertaining "the" meaning of the word in 1861 contrasts markedly with the ease with which he found "the" meaning of the word today, and on the basis of evidence much more conflicting than even he suggested existed in relation to the nineteenth-century sources.

Just as the core purpose of section 58—to protect unborn life from fertilization—undermines any argument that it bore a restricted meaning in 1861, it also blocks any attempt to arrive at a restricted meaning by way of an "updating" construction. As the cases cited by the judge show, an updating construction would require a consideration of the original "characteristics" of "miscarriage" and the underlying purpose or purposes of the legislation. These authorities confirm that it may be permissible to update the original meaning of a word in line with its underlying "characteristics" and thereby to promote the underlying intention of the legislature. They give no warrant for narrowing the meaning of a word so as to frustrate the intention of Parliament.[119]

---

[117] See generally J Keown, *Abortion, Doctors and the Law* (Cambridge University Press, 1988) Chs 1–2.

[118] As Professor Williams pointed out (n 60) 140, the protection of women was not the law's primary purpose, as the equally severe punishments meted out to qualified and unqualified abortionists illustrated. The fact that the woman who procured her own abortion was liable both at common law and under the anti-abortion legislation of the nineteenth century confirms that law regarded the protection of the unborn child as its chief, if not sole, purpose.

[119] The judge went on to discern further support for the restricted construction by reading it in the context of the Abortion Act 1967, as amended by the Human Fertilisation and Embryology Act 1990. This support was much less significant than the judge thought. For example, he thought that the unrestricted construction was inconsistent with the 1990 Act's authorization of the removal of pre-implantation embryos in vivo by lavage, whether for treatment services or research (*Smeaton* paras 367–75). Counsel for the Secretary of State argued that it was "inconceivable" that Parliament would have considered the removal of the pre-implantation embryo permissible while regarding as

III CONCLUSION

Mr Justice Munby's judgment skillfully summarized many complex, interwoven skeins of interdisciplinary and sometimes conflicting expert evidence bearing on the vital question before him. Moreover, it appreciated that the case advanced by the claimant deserved a detailed rebuttal and it resisted the temptation to take the easy way out by invoking the presumption against doubtful criminalization. It also gave short shrift to several of the more spurious arguments adduced by counsel for the respondents. The judgment also properly observed that the issue was whether the use of the MAP may constitute an offense under the OAPA 1861, not whether the MAP was either morally right or socially desirable, which were questions raising issues of principle which ought properly to be decided by Parliament.[120] And on the importance of the separation of powers he rightly recalled the observations of Lord Diplock in *Duport Steels Ltd v Sirs*:

It endangers continued public confidence in the political impartiality of the judiciary, which is essential to the continuance of the rule of law, if judges, under the guise of interpretation, provide their own preferred amendments to statutes which experience of their operation has shown to have had consequences that members of the court before whom the matter comes consider to be injurious to the public interest.[121]

---

criminal the destruction of a pre-implantation embryo by a woman taking the MAP (*Smeaton* para 376). Munby J found this argument "compelling" (*Smeaton* para 367). He could not believe that the legislature in 1990 created an anomaly as great as that criticized by Dr Tyler Smith in 1849, who praised the law for protecting life from fertilization but berated it for allowing the execution of women before quickening (*Smeaton* para 377).The argument is, however, no more compelling than the argument that "miscarriage" in the 1861 Act does not protect implanted embryos because the Abortion Act 1967 allows implanted embryos to be destroyed. The fact that Parliament in 1990 legislated to allow a doctor to remove and destroy a pre-implantation embryo does not mean that the legislature understood the OAPA 1861 as endorsing the destruction of pre-implantation embryos, whether by doctors or lay people. The only "anomaly" is that the legislature in 1990 allowed one doctor to remove and destroy a pre-implantation in vitro, whereas in 1967 it required two doctors to agree on the destruction of an embryo in vivo. To the extent that this could be described as an "anomaly" at all, to describe it as "every bit as great" as that criticized by Dr Tyler Smith, is wide of the mark. It is sometimes argued that a restricted construction of "miscarriage" is supported by s 2(3) of the 1990 Act, which provides that "For the purposes of this Act, a woman is not to be treated as carrying a child until the embryo has implanted." On the contrary, that definition is limited to the 1990 Act, and the fact that it was thought necessary or desirable could equally be used to support an unrestricted construction of "miscarriage" in the 1861 Act.

[120] *Smeaton* para 51.

[121] *Smeaton* para 52 (*Duport Steels v Sirs* [1980] 1 WLR 142). It is, therefore, surprising that significant portions of Munby J's judgment were devoted to the social implications of the case and disclosed the judge's opinion that the social consequences of finding for the claimant would have been highly undesirable: Smeaton paras 71–6, 209–25, 393–8. He thought that such a finding would implicate the contraceptive pill, which may also operate by preventing implantation (ibid paras 71–3), and would "inevitably" result in more post-implantation abortions (ibid para 74). However, s 58 prohibits procuring miscarriage with intent (not merely foresight), and not even the Family Planning

Nevertheless, it is respectfully submitted that the judgment in *Smeaton* is unconvincing. First, the nineteenth-century medical and medico-legal texts make it clear that "miscarriage" was understood in 1861 to include the prevention of implantation. Second, even if an "updating" construction of section 58 were appropriate (which is highly questionable), it is far from clear that "miscarriage" is now generally understood to exclude the prevention of implantation. Third, an updating construction to the contrary frustrates the core purpose of the legislation: the protection of human life from fertilization.[122]

Association went so far as to claim that an increase in post-implantation abortion would be inevitable (ibid para 217). Interestingly, a survey published after the case concluded: "Women did not report more use of the method once it was made available over the counter: they seem simply to have changed where they obtained it. . . . Over the counter availability is therefore unlikely to have affected unwanted pregnancies.": C Marston et al., "Impact on contraceptive practice of making emergency hormonal contraception available over the counter in Great Britain: repeated cross sectional surveys" (2005) 331 BMJ 271. See also E Raymond et al., "Population Effect of Increased Access to Emergency Contraceptive Pills" (2007) 109 Obstetrics & Gynecology 181.

[122] At the start of this chapter we noted that *Smeaton* has attracted scarcely any academic analysis. For an example of how the judgment has been uncritically accepted, see E Jackson, *Medical Law: Text, Cases and Materials* (Oxford University Press, 2006) 624–7.

CHAPTER 7

THE SCOPE OF THE OFFENSE OF CHILD DESTRUCTION

I INTRODUCTION

The case of *C v S*,[1] in which a man unsuccessfully sought an injunction to prevent his former girlfriend from aborting their child, raised the important question of the extent to which the unborn child is protected by the criminal law. As we saw in Chapter 6, section 58 of the Offences against the Person Act 1861 (OAPA 1861) was intended to protect the unborn child from fertilization (or, in the view Munby J in *Smeaton*,[2] from implantation). This protection is neutralized, however, when an abortion is performed in compliance with the conditions set out in the Abortion Act 1967. Moreover, section 58 does not protect the child once delivery has begun.[3] Nor is a child during delivery safeguarded by the law of homicide for, in the quaint terminology of the common law, it is not yet considered a creature in *rerum natura*. In the words of Park J in 1834: "A child must be actually wholly in the world in a living state to be the subject of a charge of murder....."[4] Protection is, however, afforded by section 1(1) of the Infant Life (Preservation) Act 1929 (ILPA 1929), which provides:

Any person who, with intent to destroy the life of a child capable of being born alive, by any wilful act causes a child to die before it has an existence independent of its mother, shall be guilty of felony, to wit, of child destruction.

---

[1] [1988] QB 135, CA.

[2] *R (Smeaton) v Secretary of State for Health* [2002] EWHC 610 (Admin), [2002] 2 FLR 146.

[3] As Willes J testified to the Capital Punishment Commission: "I do not think that the acts against procuring miscarriage meet the point; it is not a case of abortion, it is the case of a full-grown child; it is not to produce a birth before the natural time.": Report of the Capital Punishment Commission, Parl Pap [1866] XXI 327. Cf ibid 326; ibid 75, per Bramwell B.

[4] *R v Brain* (1834) 6 C & P 349, 349–50. See generally DS Davies, "Child-Killing in English Law" (1937) 1 MLR 203 and SB Atkinson, "Life, Birth and Live-Birth" (1904) 20 LQR 134.

A proviso to the sub-section reads:

Provided that no person shall be found guilty of an offence under this section unless it is proved that the act which caused the death of the child was not done in good faith for the purpose only of preserving the life of the mother.[5]

The maximum punishment for the crime of child destruction is life imprisonment. Section 1(2) adds:

For the purposes of this Act, evidence that a woman had at any material time been pregnant for a period of twenty-eight weeks or more shall be prima facie proof that she was at that time pregnant of a child capable of being born alive.

Clearly, section 1(1) prohibits the destruction of the child during birth. Moreover, the wording of section 1(2) and of the Act's long title, which reads "An act to amend the law with regard to the destruction of children at or before birth," indicates that the Act was also intended to protect the child before the process of delivery has begun. What remains controversial, however, is the precise degree to which the Act, by its use of the words "a child capable of being born alive," confers protection on antenatal life.

In *C v S* the Court of Appeal, dismissing an appeal against the judgment of Heilbron J, held that a child was not "capable of being born alive" unless it was capable of breathing. The Appeal Committee of the House of Lords refused leave to appeal. It is respectfully submitted that the Court of Appeal (which, unfortunately, decided upon the unusual course of not giving a fully reasoned judgment) opted for one of the least persuasive of the competing interpretations. This will become apparent during the following examination of the background to the Act, and of three alternative interpretations of "capable of being born alive."

II THE BACKGROUND TO THE ACT

The ILPA 1929 was introduced by Lord Darling. He, however, was by no means the first to propose legal protection for the child during birth. Concern over its vulnerability had been voiced on several occasions before 1929 by both legal and medical authorities. As early as 1844, for example, Alfred Swaine Taylor, a leading authority on medical jurisprudence, pointed out that the hiatus in the law not only deprived children of protection during birth but also exposed those completely born to the danger of homicidal violence, since it was open to defendants to argue that the child had been killed during delivery.[6] In the latter half of the century,

[5] The Abortion Act 1967 provided by s 5(1) that it did not affect the ILPA 1929.
[6] AS Taylor, *A Manual of Medical Jurisprudence* (J & A Churchill, 1844) 471–2.

a number of unsuccessful bills contained provisions designed to remedy the defect in the law.[7] In 1908 a Bill was introduced into the House of Commons by Lord Robert Cecil with the sole aim of protecting the child during birth. As amended in Standing Committee, clause 1 read:

Any person who shall destroy the life of a child during the birth thereof, and before the same shall have been fully born, in such a manner that he would have been guilty of murder if the child had been fully born, shall be guilty of felony, and being convicted thereof shall be liable to penal servitude for life.[8]

In December 1908, Cecil asked the government to give serious consideration to his measure, but without success.[9] He introduced a virtually identical Bill the following year.[10] Again he expressed the hope that the government would take up his proposal, but he was again rebuffed.[11]

Failure also awaited Lord Darling's first attempt to amend the law almost 20 years later. In June 1928 he introduced an Infanticide Bill designed simply, according to its long title, "to amend the law with regard to the crime of infanticide."[12] Its first section proposed, *inter alia*, to make it an offense to destroy a child "in the course of the delivery of a woman." During the second reading debate, Lord Darling explained that his measure sought to remedy a defect in the law which had been a target of judicial criticism only a few days before.[13] He was referring to a charge delivered by Talbot J to a grand jury at Liverpool Assizes. Criticizing the gap in the law, Talbot J had declared: "The result of the law is that a fully born child in many cases can be destroyed with impunity, and I do not think it is very creditable to our Legislature that the defect in the law should have been left unremedied."[14] The Infanticide Bill was welcomed by both the Lord Chancellor, Lord Hailsham, and Lord Phillimore.[15] It was then referred to a Select Committee consisting of Lords Darling, Phillimore, Desart, Hewart, Merrivale, Hanworth, and Dawson.[16] The Committee convened on 5 July 1928, but consisted only of Lord

---

[7] Eg the Criminal Code (Indictable Offences) Bill (1878) cl 168(a)(iii), Parl Pap [1878] II 5, 88 [Bill 178]; the Criminal Code (Indictable Offences) Bill (1879) cl 212, Parl Pap [1878–79] II 175, 267 [Bill 117]; the Criminal Code Bill (1880) cl 205, Parl Pap [1880] II 1, 82 [Bill 2].

[8] Parl Pap [1908] II 1011 [Bill 327]. The proceedings of the Standing Committee are reported in vol IX 271.

[9] *Hansard*, HC vol 198, cols 499, 500 (1908).

[10] Parl Pap [1909] III 243 [Bill 142].

[11] *Hansard*, HC vol 9, cols 1683, 1684 (1909).

[12] *Sessional papers of the House of Lords*, Lords Sessional Bills [1928] II [Bill 81].

[13] *Hansard*, HL vol 71, cols 616–18 (1928). See also ibid vol 72, cols 436–7 (1928–9).

[14] Quoted by Lord Darling in *Hansard*, HL vol 71, col 618 (1928).

[15] Ibid cols 619–21.

[16] Proceedings of the Select Committee on the Infanticide now Child Destruction Bill: *Sessional papers of the House of Lords*, Lords Sessional Papers [1928] IV, ii.

Merrivale, who took the chair, and Lords Darling and Hanworth.[17] The Bill suffered such radical amendment that it was, in effect, rewritten. The short title was altered to the Child Destruction Bill and the long title, proclaiming the revised Bill's broader scope, now read: "An Act to amend the law with regard to the destruction of children at or before birth."[18] A new first clause was passed which consisted of two sub-clauses. The first, which would be enacted unamended, prohibited the destruction of a child capable of being born alive before it had an existence independent of its mother.[19] The second provided that proof of pregnancy for a period of 28 weeks or more would be prima facie evidence that the child was capable of being born alive.[20] At the report stage on 12 July, Lord Darling secured the amendment of this sub-clause to its present form.[21] His object was to alleviate the burden of proof on the prosecution.[22] The Bill was read for a third time on 16 July and passed to the House of Commons.[23] There, it fell. As Lord Darling subsequently explained, he had been told by the member in charge of the Bill in the Commons that the reference in the title to "Child Destruction" had given rise to the impression that "it had something to do with a method for getting rid of the redundant population ...."[24] When he reintroduced the Bill in November, it was more felicitously entitled the Preservation of Infant Life Bill.[25] It received its second reading on 22 November[26] and on 6 December the House resolved itself into a Committee to consider the Bill, which it passed unamended.[27] After its third reading on 18 December[28] it was passed to the Commons, where the only notable amendment was the alternation of its title to its present form.[29]

---

[17] Ibid iii.

[18] Ibid iv.

[19] Ibid iii.

[20] Ibid iv.

[21] *Hansard*, HL vol 71, col 998 (1928).

[22] Ibid.

[23] Ibid col 1057.

[24] *Hansard*, HL vol 72, col 269 (1928–9).

[25] *Sessional Papers of the House of Lords*, Lords Sessional Bills [1928–29] IV [Bill 4].

[26] *Hansard*, HL vol 72, col 269 (1928–9).

[27] Ibid cols 425, 450.

[28] Ibid col 668.

[29] Parl Pap [1928–29] III 365 [Bill 38]. The apparently cursory treatment of the Bill in the House of Commons is confirmed by the fact that it passed through the Standing Committee, together with two other Bills, in under 15 minutes: *The Times*, 26 April 1929.

III THE SCOPE OF SECTION 1(1): THREE COMPETING INTERPRETATIONS

Does the passage of the Bill through the legislative process cast any light on the intended ambit of section 1(1)? The answer must be that the available evidence is inconclusive: passages can be found to support both narrow and broad interpretations of "a child capable of being born alive." To facilitate the interpretation of the phrase, it is proposed to supplement the available parliamentary evidence with that relating to its pre-1929 usage by both medical and medico-legal authorities. In the light of this combined evidence three possible and competing constructions of the words will be considered. They will be considered in order of increasing breadth, from that limited to the child in the process of birth, to that importing the concept of viability and, finally, to that applying to any foetus capable of birth in a living state.

A The child during birth

The narrowest construction of section 1(1) is that which confines its protection to the child in the process of birth. In support of this interpretation may be cited the modest scope of the Infant Life (Preservation) Bill's less successful predecessors, the incident precipitating the Bill's introduction, and several contributions to the debates surrounding its passage. It will be recalled that in 1908 and 1909 Lord Robert Cecil had attempted in vain to secure the enactment of his proposal to protect the child during delivery.[30] That this was also Lord Darling's original intention is apparent both from the wording of his Infanticide Bill of June 1928[31] and from the reason for its introduction, namely Talbot J's criticism of the gap in the law.[32] It should be stressed that the reform urged by the latter was confined to the correction of this defect. He urged: "What is undoubtedly wanted is a short Act of Parliament to make it an offence to destroy the life of a child when it is being delivered. That would remedy the defect and abolish the anomaly."[33] Moreover, there is further evidence

---

[30] See text at nn 8–11.

[31] See text at nn 12–13. In debate, Lord Darling stated that Cecil's Bill of 1908, as amended by the Standing Committee, was a "vast improvement" on his own, and he declared that had he been aware of the Bill beforehand, his own would have been drafted differently: *Hansard*, HL vol 71, col 619 (1928).

[32] See text at n 14.

[33] *The Times*, 13 June 1928. Interestingly, only two years earlier a medico-legal authority, Dr Godfrey Carter, addressed the Public Health Section of the British Medical Association on the subject of the gap at the Association's Annual Meeting: "The Legal Definition of Live Birth" [1926] 2 BMJ 385. The Section passed a unanimous resolution calling on the Association's Council to approach the government with a view to legislation to protect the child during delivery: ibid 387. However, the Council reported that as the Births and Deaths Registration Act 1926 perpetuated the

that the Bills of Cecil and Darling, as originally introduced, were motivated solely by a common concern to safeguard the child during delivery. The evidence is contained in contemporary Home Office papers and reveals that their concern was inspired by one and the same man—Sir George Talbot.

In 1916 George Talbot KC (as he then was) wrote to the Home Office urging legislation to fill the lacuna in the law and enclosing a copy of Cecil's Bill.[34] He explained that the Bill was designed "to stop a scandalous hole in the law" and that he had been responsible for urging Cecil to take an interest in the matter.[35] However, Talbot's petition failed to persuade the Home Office, which felt that the defect to which he had drawn attention was not of sufficient importance, in the context of wartime conditions, to merit the amendment of the Criminal Justice Bill of that year.[36] Talbot repeated his call for legislation in 1923, but again without success.[37] Only in June 1928, when his opinion was invested with judicial authority, was his suggestion acted upon.[38]

The narrow focus of Lord Darling's Bill is also confirmed by contributions to the second reading debate by both its sponsor[39] and others. Lord Phillimore agreed that it was "desirable to cover the gap between the offence of procuring abortion and the offence of killing a fully-born child with separate existence."[40] Similarly, Lord Hailsham remarked: "obviously it is a gap which ought to be closed."[41]Although the Bill was redrafted by the Select Committee to protect the child "capable of being born alive" rather than merely "in the course of delivery," the latter continued to be the focus of debate when the Bill was reintroduced in November. In the words of its sponsor: "It really is a bill designed to prevent children being destroyed at birth."[42] Lord Hailsham repeated his support for the protection of the child during birth and entered the stern caveat that the Bill should be carefully drafted "to make sure that it does

rule that a child was not born until totally delivered, no useful purpose would be served by taking action at that time, which would require fresh legislation: "Annual Report of Council: Protection of Unborn Children" [1928] 1 BMJ Supp 137.

[34] Public Record Office (PRO), HO 45 13291 165 493/6.
[35] Ibid.
[36] Ibid.
[37] Ibid 493/11.
[38] The reaction of the Home Office to his charge to the grand jury appears unenthusiastic. A minute in the records commenting on the charge as reported in *The Times* reads: "It is always a pity to expose this gap—and difficult to fill it.": ibid 493/14A.
[39] See text at n 13.
[40] *Hansard*, HL vol 71, col 619 (1928).
[41] Ibid col 620.
[42] *Hansard*, HL vol 72, col 269 (1928–9).

not go further than is necessary to close the gap . . . ."[43] Lord Atkin agreed that the gap ought to be closed[44] but he challenged Lord Darling's proposed remedy. A cardinal criticism was that the Bill protected the child not only during but also before delivery and thereby overlapped the law against abortion. Referring to clause 1(2) he remarked: "The provision as to twenty-eight weeks after conception seems to be quite unnecessary, because such an act as that would . . . always be covered by the law as to procuring abortion."[45] He elaborated: "It is impossible in practice to kill the unborn child while still in the body of a mother without in fact procuring, and intending to procure, a miscarriage."[46] Consequently, he proposed an entirely new first clause which extended the offense of infanticide to cover the case where the mother killed her child in the course of delivery.[47] In so doing, he reiterated his objection that the Bill as it stood weakened the law of abortion by requiring, in relation to the child capable of being born alive, an intention to destroy.[48] Clearly, then, Lord Atkin was of the opinion that "capable of being born alive" could apply to the child before delivery. The reactions to his criticism of the Bill, however, suggest that his opinion was not universally shared. Lord Darling, for one, retorted that the offense he proposed to create was "one for which, unfortunately, the law at present provides no punishment."[49] He added:

My noble and learned friend opposite said that this Bill overlaps the existing law about abortion. If it does that, then Mr Justice Talbot was absolutely wrong in what he said to a Grand Jury. Abortion is a punishable offence already, punishable with penal servitude for life under the Offences against the Person Act. If this does overlap, then it is no new offence at all but an old offence that is punishable very severely.[50]

Similarly, a note in the Home Office records, criticizing Lord Atkin's amendment, remarks that he seemed to think that the destruction of a child during delivery was already prohibited by the law of abortion and cites the passage, quoted above,[51] in which Lord Atkin criticized clause 1(2)

[43] Ibid col 278.
[44] Ibid cols 425–6.
[45] Ibid cols 270–72.
[46] Ibid.
[47] Ibid col 425.
[48] Ibid col 428. See also ibid cols 446–7.
[49] Ibid col 437.
[50] Ibid cols 437–8. See also Lord Merrivale's criticism of Lord Atkins' proposed amendment to reduce the crime "which is abortion at present according to his view" to a misdemeanor: ibid col 430.
[51] See text at nn 45–6.

as otiose.[52] Although Lord Atkin was referring to the destruction of the child before delivery, his critics evidently understood him to be referring also to the child during delivery. His foremost objection to the Bill appears to have fallen victim to the ambiguity of its own expression and to have frustrated any serious consideration of the crucial issue it raised, namely the degree to which, if any, clause 1(1) protected the child before delivery. With the dismissal of Lord Atkin's objection, the focus of debate continued to be the protection of the child during rather than before delivery. Lord Merrivale stressed that the goal of the Bill was to plug "a loophole in the law of abortion."[53] Again, Lord Hailsham, having described the lacuna in the law as that "very appreciable interval of time after the commencement of labour before it can be said that the child has become a separate person...,"[54] read clause 1 of the Bill as making it a felony "for any person to take the life of a child in the course of its being born...."[55] He added: "What we are hitting at is something which, at the moment, is not punishable by law...."[56]

A final consideration which may be invoked in favor of the limitation of section 1(1) to the child during delivery is the presence in the subsection of the words "before it has an existence independent of its mother." Unless these words focus attention on the child at birth, it could be argued, they are mere surplusage, for it is difficult to imagine how a child "capable of being born alive" could be destroyed otherwise than before it enjoyed such an existence.

The evidence clearly indicates that Lord Darling's original intention in introducing his Infanticide Bill in June 1928 was to remedy the defect in the law which had been consistently exposed by Sir George Talbot and to extend the protection of the law to the child during delivery. The evidence also suggests that although this intention probably persisted,

[52]   PRO, HO 45 13291 165 493/18B.
[53]   *Hansard*, HL vol 72, cols 429–1 (1928–9).
[54]   Ibid cols 438–9.
[55]   Ibid col 440.
[56]   Ibid col 442. Moreover, the exception of therapeutic foeticide from the scope of the Bill was not discussed outside the context of killings during delivery. See *Hansard*, HL vol 71, col 620 (1928) (Lord Hailsham); ibid col 621 (Lord Darling); ibid vol 72, col 271 (1928–9) (Lord Atkin); ibid col 669 (Lord Darling). These discussions of the desirability of a therapeutic proviso also reflect a profound and persistent concern over the need to safeguard the position of doctors and midwives. In its report for 1928–9, the BMA Council welcomed the Bill's aim of protecting the child at birth ("a position which the Association has always considered should be remedied") and its amendment by Lord Darling to ensure that the burden of proving that a given case fell outside the therapeutic proviso rested on the Crown: "Annual Report of Council: Preservation of Infant Life Bill" [1929] 1 BMJ Supp 97, 106. A therapeutic proviso was also inserted into Cecil's Bill of 1908 in Standing Committee, in the wake of objections from the BMA: "Report of Medico-Political Committee: Infant Life Protection" [1908] 1 BMJ Supp 421, 423; "Annual Representative Meeting" [1908] 2 BMJ Supp 89, 132.

he surrendered control of the wording of the Bill in committee, possibly to the draftsman. In fact, speaking of the proceedings of the Select Committee he said that it had given very careful consideration to the Bill and that as it stood the wording was not his but the Committee's, and he revealed that the change of title to the Child Destruction Bill had been due to the parliamentary draftsman.[57] Unfortunately, the report of the Committee's proceedings is perfunctory and fails to illuminate either the reasons for the redrafting of the Bill or the intended scope of the revised first clause.[58] According to its chairman, Lord Merrivale, the Committee resolved upon the wording of the Bill after hearing from both a government draftsman and a representative of the Home Office.[59] This fact can only serve to heighten the interpretative significance of the Home Office papers relating to the Bill.

It is from these papers that persuasive evidence emerges that the Bill, as amended by the Committee, was undoubtedly intended to exceed Darling's limited aim of protecting the child during delivery. A comment on the Bill, dated 5 December 1928, not only recognizes this fact but explains it. It reads: "... Lord Darling's Bill intentionally abstains from limiting the punishable acts to acts done 'in the course of delivery' so as to avoid putting upon the prosecution the onus of proving when 'delivery' in fact began—an almost impossible task . . . ."[60] Recognizing in addition that the proposed offense overlapped the law on abortion it continued:

There is no need for such a limit as there can be no harm in overlapping between the Bill and section 58 of the Offences against the Person Act, 1861; for the maximum punishment for abortion is the same as that proposed for "child destruction" and a person may be convicted for either upon an indictment for the other.[61]

The applicability of the Bill to children before delivery is fortified by its long title, which referred to children "at or before birth." Further, certain judicial members of the Upper House also interpreted the amended Bill as protecting the child even before delivery had begun. It will be recalled that this formed the basis of one of Lord Atkin's central objections to the Bill.[62] Again, at one point Lord Merrivale observed: "I was a little

---

[57] *Hansard*, HL vol 72, cols 269–70 (1928–9).

[58] A search in the library of the House of Lords and of the Public Records Office revealed no further evidence bearing on these questions.

[59] *Hansard*, HL vol 72, col 429 (1928–9). See also Lord Darling's intriguing reference, when moving further amendments to the Child Destruction Bill on report, to "Those who have considered very carefully" the words which he proposed to insert: ibid vol 71, col 998 (1928).

[60] PRO, HO 45 13291 165 493/18B.

[61] Ibid.

[62] See text at nn 45–8.

surprised to see in one part of the clause that the offence aimed at by the bill could be an act of abortion."[63]

In sum, it would appear that although the original intention of the Bill's sponsor persisted throughout its passage, the form in which his intention was expressed was amended in order to facilitate the task of prosecution. The price paid for this alleviation of the evidentiary burden was, however, the broadening of the scope of the Bill to protect children even before the onset of labor, provided they were "capable of being born alive." The question which remains to be considered concerns the scope of this phrase. Does it include any child who might be alive after birth or only one who might survive?

B The "viable" child

The second construction of "a child capable of being born alive" limits the protection of section 1(1) to the child capable of survival after birth. Support for this interpretation can be drawn from several sources.

First, section 5(1) of the Abortion Act 1967 provided: "Nothing in this Act shall affect the provisions of the Infant Life (Preservation) Act 1929 (protecting the life of the viable foetus)." Second, this interpretation has been favored by leading authorities on criminal law. Smith and Hogan, having remarked that the offenses of abortion and child destruction overlap, stated: "Procuring a miscarriage so as to kill a viable child may amount to both offences."[64] Third, this interpretation has been advanced by a Law Officer. In December 1979, in the course of discussing the phrases "capable of being born alive," "viable child," and "viable foetus" for the benefit of the Standing Committee considering Mr John Corrie's Abortion (Amendment) Bill, the Solicitor-General, Sir Ian Percival QC, stated: "My advice is that all those who have considered these phrases have regarded 'capable of being born alive' as being cotermin[o]us with 'viable foetus.'"[65] Addressing himself to section 5(1) of the Abortion Act he opined:

As a matter of law it would be held that "capable of being born alive" means more than simply being born alive in the sense that the body may draw one breath or

---

[63] *Hansard*, HL vol 72, cols 429–30 (1928–9).

[64] J Smith and B Hogan, *Criminal Law* (5th edn, Oxford University Press, 1983) 340. See also G Williams, *Textbook of Criminal Law* (2nd edn, Steven & Sons, 1983) 291; BM Dickens, *Abortion and the Law* (MacGibbon & Kee, 1966) 30; PDG Skegg, *Law, Ethics and Medicine: Studies in Medical Law* (revised edn, Clarendon Press, 1988) 7–12.

[65] *Hansard*, HC Standing Committee C 369 (1979).

make one sound. In law it would be held to mean more than that and something very akin to the concept of "viable foetus"...[66]

He added, somewhat optimistically, that the words would not present a court with any difficulty.[67] Finally, and perhaps most significantly, there is the presumption contained in section 1(2) of the Act that the child of a woman who has been pregnant for 28 weeks or more is "capable of being born alive." When read together, subsections 1 and 2 tend to narrow the focus of the Act to the more advanced stages of pregnancy, when the child is capable not only of living at birth, but of maintaining an existence independent of its mother. As it is of crucial importance to determine the exact interpretative value of the presumption contained in section 1(2), the significance which was attached by medical and medico-legal authorities before 1929 to the twenty-eighth week of pregnancy and, more precisely, whether it was equated with the onset of viability, will be examined by surveying the leading works on both obstetrics and medical jurisprudence before the passage of the Act.

An essential preliminary question, and one too often overlooked, concerns the meaning of "viability." According to the medical consensus before 1929, the word connoted the capacity of a child to survive after birth. Quain's medical dictionary, for example, published in 1882, described the term as: "An epithet applied to a newly-born child, to indicate its capacity for maintaining an independent existence."[68] Medico-legal authorities concurred that viability implied a capacity for survival. In 1893 J Dixon Mann wrote that a viable child was one "endowed with the capacity of continuing to live."[69]

In short, the bulk of medical and medico-legal opinion defined viability in terms of a capacity for survival. Even those authorities who, when discussing viability, spoke simply of a capacity to live, appear to have meant a capacity for sustained life. Although, for example, Hooper's early nineteenth-century medical dictionary at one point defines a viable foetus as one "properly organised and sufficiently developed to live,"[70] it also refers to its "capacity of sustaining extra[-]uterine and independent

---

[66] Ibid.

[67] Ibid. See also *McKay v Essex Area Health Authority and another* [1982] QB 1166, 1180, per Stephenson LJ. Further, Dr Carter's proposals for reform in 1926 concerned the viable child: "The Legal Definition of Live Birth" [1926] 2 BMJ 385, 386.

[68] "Viable" in *A Dictionary of Medicine* (R Quain ed, Longman Green, 1882) vol II, 1748. Quain was representative of other authorities in omitting to lay down a minimum period of survival after which a child could be considered viable.

[69] JD Mann, *Forensic Medicine and Toxicology* (P Blackinston's Sons & Co., 1893) 171.

[70] "Viable" in R Hooper, *Lexicon Medicum: or Medical Dictionary* (7th edn, K Grant, Longman, Hurst, Rees, Orme, and Co, 1839) 1354.

life."[71] There existed, then, a general consensus that viability connoted a capacity to survive. Did this agreement extend to the age at which a foetus qualified as viable? Significantly, the evidence suggests that the bulk of medical and medico-legal authorities dated viability from the period specified in section 1(2), namely 28 weeks. As early as 1822 Good wrote: "At seven months the foetus will often live."[72] Similarly, Severn declared that a seven-month-old child was "capable of being reared."[73] In 1864 Philp's medical dictionary stated: "The earliest age at which a child is likely to live is at seven months; an infant born before the completion of the seventh month is said to be *non-viable*."[74] Several medico-legal authorities subscribed to the same opinion. Writing one year before Good, John Gordon Smith remarked: "Abortion may occur at any period of pregnancy, previous to the evolution of the foetus to that degree which enables it to support existence separate from the mother—in other words, during the first seven months."[75] The medical and medico-legal usage of the nineteenth and early twentieth century, together with the other evidence besides, lends strong support to a construction of section 1 restricting its protection to the viable child.

C The child capable of being born alive

A third possible construction of section 1 is less restricted than the preceding two and involves a literal interpretation of the phrase "a child capable of being born alive." According to this construction section 1(1) prohibits the destruction of any child, whether before or during delivery, who has the capacity to live—however fleetingly—after his or her extrusion from the mother. Central to this approach is the canon of statutory interpretation which requires the words of an enactment to be given their ordinary and natural meaning. Invoking this canon, Gerard Wright QC has argued:

The only way in which the words "a child capable of being born alive" can be construed as meaning "a viable foetus" is by adding to these words other words which are not in the section. Thus if the statute were to read "a child capable of being born alive *and surviving thereafter*," this would indeed mean "a viable foetus,"

---

[71] Ibid.

[72] JM Good, *The Study of Medicine* (Baldwin, Cradock, and Joy, 1822) vol IV, 177.

[73] C Severn, *First Lines of the Practice of Midwifery* (S Highley, 1831) 34.

[74] "Viable" in *The Dictionary of Medical and Surgical Knowledge* (ed RK Philp, Houlston, and Wright, 1864) 712 (emphasis in original).

[75] JG Smith, *The Principles of Forensic Medicine* (T & G Underwood, 1821) 293.

but the italic words are not in the statute and there is no accepted canon of statutory interpretation which permits them to be added.[76]

Bowles and Bell have arrived at the same conclusion.[77] Similarly, the Committee on the Working of the Abortion Act, chaired by Mrs Justice Lane, concluded:

Although the Infant Life (Preservation) Act 1929 was originally intended to deal with child murder and not with late abortion, as a result of the language used it became and still is unlawful for termination of pregnancy to be carried out by a method which destroys a foetus capable of being born alive, *even if its chances of eventual survival are slight or non-existent* . . . [78]

Was this literal usage of "capable of being born alive" recognized before 1929, or did the phrase invariably connote viability?

1 Live-birth in medicine

The available evidence indicates that the phrase in question was used to refer both to the viable child and to the child who was merely capable of being born living. Which definition was intended in a given instance depended upon the context in which the words were used. Undoubtedly, however, the phrase was normally used to refer to an ability to be born living, as opposed to a capacity to survive thereafter. In 1905, for example, Wright's text on obstetrics, in its discussion of a case of premature birth, stated: "While the child was born alive, we doubted whether it could be considered viable . . . ."[79] The distinction was also familiar to medico-legal experts. In 1893 J Dixon Mann remarked: "An infant may have arrived at a sufficiently advanced period of development as to be born alive, but not to be viable—that is, not to be endowed with the capacity of continuing to live."[80] Granted that the distinction between viability and the capacity for live birth was well estab-lished before 1929, the question arises whether a foetus was regarded as capable of being born alive before the twenty-eighth week. If so, then on the literal interpretation of section 1(1), the scope of the Act is correspondingly extended. Arguing along these lines, the Association of Lawyers for the Defence of the Unborn (ALDU) claimed that the Act protects foetuses from as early as the tenth week of pregnancy. The Association declared:

[76] G Wright, "Capable of Being Born Alive?" (1981) 131 NLJ 188 (emphasis in original). See also G Wright, "The Legality of Abortion by Prostaglandin" [1984] Crim LR 347, 349; "Late Abortions and the Crime of Child Destruction: (2) A Rejoinder" [1985] Crim LR 140.
[77] TGA Bowles and MNM Bell, "Abortion—A Clarification" (1979) 129 NLJ 944.
[78] *Report of the Committee on the Working of the Abortion Act* (Cmnd 5579, 1974) vol 1, 88, para 278 (emphasis added). See also P Asterley Jones and RIE Card (eds), *Cross and Jones' Introduction to Criminal Law* (10th edn, 1984) 193, where identical language is used.
[79] AH Wright, *A Text-Book of Obstetrics* (D Appleton & Co, 1905) 167.
[80] JD Mann, *Forensic Medicine and Toxicology* (P Blackinston's Sons & Co, 1893) 171.

ALDU has obtained the opinion of a leading Gynaecologist on this point. He advises that with, e.g., a prostaglandin-induced labour, he would expect the baby to be alive when born, provided that the baby was aged 10 weeks or more. It would seem, therefore, that all abortions of babies aged 10 weeks or more are completely illegal.[81]

This opinion is not as fanciful as it might at first appear, for as early as 1836 Dr Michael Ryan remarked that the French obstetrician Mauriceau had, among others, claimed to have seen 10-week-old foetuses alive, moving their arms and legs and opening their mouths, and added that this was a claim no physiologist could doubt.[82] In 1841, Edward Rigby wrote: "A foetus may be expelled, at a very early stage of pregnancy, not only alive, but capable of moving its limbs briskly for a short time afterwards, but it is unable to prolong its existence separate from the mother beyond a few hours."[83] In 1920 one medical author remarked: "At four and a half months, a living child may be born and even heard to utter a cry, but such a child is not viable...."[84] Among medico-legal authorities, too, there was a consensus that a child might be born living and yet be insufficiently developed to qualify as viable. After a comprehensive review of data on prematurity, Tidy concluded in 1882: "living children have been born between the fourth and fifth month of uterine life."[85] He stressed that the minimum age for live birth was the fourth month:

Allowing that from the first moment of impregnation the ovum is truly alive and, further, that mere motion of the limbs, or evidence of circulation, without active respiration, are sufficient to constitute live birth, nevertheless there is no evidence to show that a foetus, born at an earlier period than between the fourth or fifth month of uterine existence, can in any sense be said to be born alive, much less lead an independent life, i.e. a life apart from its mother.[86]

2 Live-birth in law
Just as medical and medico-legal opinion pre-1929 drew a distinction between viability and live birth, so too did the law, both criminal and civil. It will be recalled that the criminal law does not punish as homicide

---

[81] ALDU Newsletter (1979) no 1, 3. There is an even more extensive interpretation than that advanced by ALDU, namely that "capable" refers to a future as well as an actual capacity, and that therefore the ILPA 1929 protects a child from conception. Not the least difficulty with this interpretation is that it would render that Act and the Abortion Act 1967 inconsistent.

[82] M Ryan, *A Manual of Medical Jurisprudence and State Medicine* (2nd edn, Sherwood, Gilbert and Piper, 1836) 277–82.

[83] E Rigby, *A System of Midwifery* (Lea & Blanchard, 1841) 87.

[84] O St J Moses, *Manual of Obstetrics* (J & A Churchill, 1920) 131.

[85] CM Tidy, *Legal Medicine* (Smith, Elder, and Co, 1882) vol 2, 50.

[86] Ibid.

the destruction of a child either before or during birth: only when completely born alive is the child reckoned a creature in *rerum natura*.[87] Significantly, however, once the child has been born alive, it is protected from destruction by the law, irrespective of viability. This is illustrated by a case tried at York Assizes in 1812 before Bayley J.[88] The defendants, Elizabeth Woodger and Susannah Lyall, were indicted for the murder of a newly-born male infant. The evidence showed that the child suffered from a cranial abnormality which left part of its brain protected only by a covering of membrane. Concluding that the child was not likely to live, the defendants drowned it in an earthen vessel. A surgeon testified that the child could only have survived for a few hours. It appeared that the defendants, in ignorance of the law, had believed their action justifiable. However, in his direction to the jury, the judge made no allowance for the fact that the child was not viable. On the contrary, he declared:

I think this prosecution may be of great use to the public, in removing an erroneous opinion, that the law allows the right of deliberately taking away the life of a human being under any circumstances whatsoever. It is therefore highly necessary that the contrary should be known.[89]

The legal irrelevance of viability was familiar to medico-legal authorities. Taylor declared: "Infanticide requires only that the child should be living. The crime implies the destruction of a new-born child, 'born living,' whatever may be its age, state of development, strength, or capacity to live."[90] Again, after a thorough analysis of both criminal and civil branches of the law, Atkinson concluded in 1904: "A child is live-born in the legal sense, when, after entire birth, it exhibits a clear sign of independent vitality; in practice, at least the evanescently persistent activity of the heart. *Vitae habilitas (viabilité)* need not be proved in English law."[91] Granted, then, that the idea of "live birth" was well established in both medicine and law before 1929, the question arises whether there is any evidence in the legislative history of the ILPA 1929 to suggest that Parliament intended to incorporate this familiar concept into the proposed offense of child destruction.

---

[87] See text at n 4.

[88] *The Annual Register...for the Year 1812* (1813) Chronicle, 96.

[89] Ibid. The defendants were convicted but the jury recommended clemency.

[90] AS Taylor, *The Principles and Practice of Medical Jurisprudence* (2nd edn, J & A Churchill, 1873) vol 2, 318.

[91] SB Atkinson, "Life, Birth and Live-Birth" (1904) 20 LQR 134, 135. Glanville Williams would later write: "If an aborted fetus is alive it is a person, no matter how short the period of gestation, and using it for an experiment would in law be at least as assault upon it. If doctors wish to perform these experiments legally they must seek statutory authority.": *Textbook of Criminal Law* (1st edn, Steven & Sons, 1978) 263, n 8.

The history of the Act does in fact yield some evidence which may be used to support a literal construction of section 1(1). First, at one point in debate, Lord Darling referred to a child "born alive and continuing to exist."[92] If, it might be argued, he was sufficiently particular to describe the viable child in debate, then, on the assumption that he was indeed legislating to protect such a child, it would be reasonable to expect an equal degree of precision in the wording of his Bill. The fact that the Bill used the more general words "capable of being born alive" might be taken to imply that his proposal was designed to embrace both the viable and the pre-viable child. (On the other hand, it could of course be argued that Lord Darling's language in debate provides the more accurate representation of his intention, which the wording of section 1 faithfully encapsulates.) Second, the long title of the Act refers to children "at or before birth." Clearly, this is sufficiently general to apply even to pre-viable children. A third line of argument favoring a literal interpretation originates in a contribution to the debate by Lord Hailsham. Referring to clause 1 of the Preservation of Infant Life Bill, he remarked: "The offence which we are asked to create is an offence which was made penal in the Indian [Penal] Code a great many years ago."[93] He explained:

In that Code, Section 312 has an offence of causing a miscarriage, and Section 315 has an offence which is described as acts done with the intent to prevent a child being born alive or to cause it to die after birth which, when one comes to read the section, is the sort of offence we are dealing with here.[94]

As the Lord Chancellor considered section 315 to be analogous to clause 1, a closer examination of the former ought to illuminate the intended scope of the latter. Significantly, section 315 was broadly drafted. It provided:

Whoever before the birth of any child does any act with the intention of thereby preventing that child from being born alive, or causing it to die after its birth, and does by such act prevent that child from being born alive, or causes it to die after its birth shall, if such act be not caused in good faith for the purpose of saving the life of the mother, be punished with imprisonment ... which may extend to ten years, or with fine, or with both.

Clearly, this provision differs from section 1 in several important respects. Not only is the punishment more lenient, but the offense itself is both broader and narrower. It is not limited to the destruction of the child

---

[92] *Hansard*, HL vol 72, cols 435–6 (1928–9).
[93] Ibid cols 438, 443.
[94] Ibid.

before it enjoys a separate existence, and yet does not obviously extend to the protection of the child during delivery.[95] Finally, the Indian provision lacks an equivalent to section 1(2). Without such a presumption of capacity for live birth, the words "before the birth of any child" would seem to have protected both the viable and the pre-viable child. This impression is fortified by one commentary on the Code, which states: "The offence is one which will ordinarily be committed where the woman is in an advanced state of pregnancy. But the section is not expressly confined to causing the death of quick unborn children."[96] In spite of these differences between the two sections, their underlying similarity, namely the prohibition of acts which prevent children from being born alive, permits instructive comparison. Both sections are sufficiently broad to overlap the offense of abortion, contained respectively in section 312 of the Indian Penal Code 1860 and section 58 of the Offences Against the Person Act 1861 (OAPA 1861) and, as the concept of viability is absent from section 315, this might be used to support the literal construction of "capable of being born alive." This line of interpretation is reinforced by a comment on Lord Darling's Bill in the records of the Home Office. The comment, dated 5 December 1928, criticizes the view, which it attributes to Lord Atkin, that the destruction of the child during delivery was already prohibited by the law of abortion. The comment states that delivery might take place spontaneously and not necessarily as a result of interference.[97] In recognition of this fact, the comment continues, the Indian Penal Code contained not only section 312 to prohibit abortion but also section 315 to prohibit the destruction of children during birth. The note then explains: "It is because acts done in the circumstances mentioned in the second of the above quoted Articles [section 315] do not constitute any crime under English Law unless the child has had a separate existence that Lord Darling's Bill has been introduced."[98] If this note accurately represents the aim of the Bill as it emerged from the Select Committee—which, it will be recalled, heard from a representative of the Home Office[99]—then it tends to support a literal construction of section 1.

---

[95] On emergence, the child was protected by the law of homicide: the third explanatory clause to s 299, which created the offence of "culpable homicide," stated that the offence could be committed by killing a child if any part of the child had been brought forth.

[96] W Morgan and AG Macpherson, *The Indian Penal Code* (GC Hay & Co, 1861) 281.

[97] PRO, HO 45 13291 165 493/18B.

[98] Ibid.

[99] See text at n 59.

3 The significance of section 1(2)

From the evidence hitherto considered, it is clear that respectable legal arguments can be deployed in support of both the second ("viable") and third ("born living") interpretations of "capable of being born alive" in section 1(1). In order to attempt a resolution of the dilemma, it is now proposed to focus more closely on the main obstacle to the "born living" interpretation, namely the 28-week presumption embodied in section 1(2). If the legislature intended section 1(1) to be literally construed, why was section 1(2) enacted at all? This is a question the literal interpretation needs to answer.

One response might be that the subsection relates merely to evidentiary considerations and has no real interpretative bearing on the preceding and substantive subsection. In other words, the 28-week presumption is by no means inconsistent with a recognition that a child was capable of being born alive before that time and was merely an attempt to alleviate the burden on the prosecution in cases where the child had reached the stage at which doctors universally agreed that it was capable of live birth. Why, then, was the twenty-eighth week chosen as opposed to an earlier time at which, according to the same medical opinion, a child could be born living? Perhaps the answer lies in a statute enacted three years before the ILPA 1929, namely the Births and Deaths Registration Act 1926.[100] Section 7 of this Act required the compulsory registration of still-births. "Still-birth" was defined in section 12 as follows: "'Still-born' and 'still-birth' shall apply to any child which has issued forth from its mother after the twenty-eighth week of pregnancy and which did not at any time after being completely expelled from its mother, breathe or show any other signs of life."[101] The possibility that this section provided a model for the presumption contained in section 1(2) of the ILPA 1929 is reinforced by a note in the Home Office records which reads: "For a statutory precedent for choosing that point, cf. last item in section 12 of the Births and Deaths Registration Act 1926."[102] May it not reasonably be argued that, just as the figure of 28 weeks in section 1(2) was borrowed from section 12, so too was the latter's concept of live birth, which was sufficiently extensive to embrace even the pre-viable foetus? Against this contention, however, must be set further evidence relating to the background to the 1926 Act which suggests that the figure of 28 weeks contained in section 12 was intended to import the concept of viability.

---

[100] 16 & 17 Geo V c 48.
[101] See also the Births and Deaths Registration Act 1953, s 41.
[102] PRO, HO 45 13291 165 493/18A.

During the second reading of the Births and Deaths Registration Bill in February 1926, its sponsor remarked that it embodied the recommendations of a Select Committee which had reported in 1893.[103] He was referring to the Select Committee on Death Certification, which had been appointed "to inquire into the sufficiency of the existing law as to the disposal of the dead, for securing an accurate record of the causes of death in all cases, and especially for detecting them where death may have been due to poison, violence, or criminal neglect . . . ."[104] In its second report, the Committee voiced its concern over the number of allegedly still-born children who were buried without any reliable certification of still-birth, and observed that the facility of disposal afforded an opportunity to conceal foul play.[105] Consequently, it recommended the compulsory registration of still-births. In the absence of any internationally accepted definition of still-birth, the Committee concluded that the period of seven months—as accepted in Denmark and Germany—provided "a convenient starting-point" for registration.[106] The Danish definition ran: "By a still-born child is understood a child which has issued forth from its mother's womb after the expiration of the 28th week of gestation as dead, or as apparently dead, and is not called back to life."[107] That the concept of viability dictated the figure of 28 weeks is more apparent from the German approach, which was explained as follows:

A legal definition of a stillborn child is nowhere given; the legislator has expressly abstained from elucidating this point. In science, only a viable foetus is recognised as a "child," and in practice only a foetus of seven months is considered to be capable of living. Before attaining that age they are regarded as immature: the separation of such a foetus (birth) need not be brought to the knowledge of the competent authorities, who would, moreover, reject an announcement of that kind.[108]

That the Committee framed its definition of still-birth in the light of the contemporary notion of viability is confirmed by the Committee's minutes of evidence. In his testimony to the Committee, Dr Robert Rentoul urged that registration should be required from the end of the fourth month.[109] He was then asked whether he considered a child of that age viable, to

[103] *Hansard*, HC vol 192, col 977 (1926).
[104] First and second reports from the select committee on death certification, Parl Pap [1893–94] XI 195, 197.
[105] Ibid 217.
[106] Ibid 218.
[107] Still-Births in England and Other Countries, Parl Pap [1893–94] LXVIII 355, 393.
[108] Ibid 363.
[109] First and second reports from the select committee on death certification, Parl Pap (1893–94) XI 409.

which he replied: "The law does not ask that. A child may have property left to it or inherit a legacy provided it is born alive, it is not a question of living, it is simply the fact of its being born alive."[110] The Committee's preoccupation with viability as opposed to mere live birth is again evidence in an exchange with another medical witness, Dr Tatham, who, like Rentoul, recommended registration from the fourth month. Unlike Rentoul, however, his recommendation was tailored to protect the viable rather than the pre-viable child. He testified: "I would have the death of what medical men call a viable foetus certified, or made a subject of the medical certifier's inquiry."[111] Asked why he advocated registration from the fourth month, when the child was not viable, he replied: "I know a child is not viable at four months, but I should like to have a good safe margin."[112] These exchanges tend to confirm the suggestion that the Committee was concerned to establish the age at which a foetus might not only be born living, but might also survive. This, coupled with the fact that their figure of 28 weeks was embodied in the Act of 1926 and thence evidently transplanted into section 1(2) of the ILPA 1929, can only support the narrower construction of section 1 which limits its protection to the viable child. Moreover, this construction might also claim support from a further fragment of evidence in the Home Office records. A note in the records, commenting upon the presumption contained in section 1(2), reads: "This draws the line between a mere foetus and a child capable of being born alive at the end of the 28th week of pregnancy."[113] The distinction between such a child and a "mere foetus" was not, unfortunately, elucidated.[114]

IV CONCLUSION

Three plausible interpretations of section 1 of the ILPA 1929 have been analysed. The first, limiting the Act's protection to the child during birth, can be rejected with some degree of confidence on the grounds of its inconsistency with the intention of the legislature as gathered from the wording of the Act as a whole and the records of the Home Office. Neither

---

[110] Ibid.

[111] Ibid 368.

[112] Ibid.

[113] PRO HO 45 13291 165 493/18A. An as yet unanswered question is whether the twenty-eighth week of pregnancy is to be calculated from the woman's last menstrual period, or from conception. For one view see G Williams, *Textbook of Criminal Law* (2nd edn, Steven & Sons, 1983) 291, n 1.

[114] The authorities on the meaning of "child" in relation to the offence of concealment of birth fail to clarify the matter: *Berriman* (1854) 6 Cox CC 388, 390; *Colmer* (1864) 9 Cox CC 506, 507; *Hewitt and Smith* (1866) 4 F & F 1011.

of the remaining interpretations can be rejected with the same degree of confidence. The wording of section 1 and, in particular, its use of the phrase "a child capable of being born alive" is sufficiently ambiguous to accommodate either the construction focusing protection exclusively on the viable child, or that extending protection to any child capable of being born living. It is, however, suggested that this very ambiguity tells against the latter interpretation, which purports to give the words in question a plain meaning they do not possess. To resolve the ambiguity it is necessary to examine the words in the context of the Act as a whole, and the Act itself against the backcloth of its parliamentary history. This examination reveals not only that the figure of 28 weeks which appears in the presumption contained in section 1(2) related to the contemporary conception of viability, but that the presumption as originally drafted would have required the prosecution to prove that even a 28-week foetus was "capable of being born alive." Both these considerations tend to militate in favor of confining the protection of section 1 to the viable child. This interpretation can only be strengthened by the parliamentary history of the Act itself, which reveals that both the introduction of the measure and its eventual passage were inspired by a concern for the safety of the child at and around the time of birth. It is submitted, therefore, that the protection afforded by section 1 of the ILPA 1929 is confined to the viable foetus.

This interpretation was almost, but not quite, adopted by the Court of Appeal in *C v S*. The court, it will be recalled, interpreted "a child capable of being born alive" to mean a child capable of breathing, and capacity to breathe is a necessary but not a sufficient condition of viability. The upshot of the ruling would appear to be that the protection of the ILPA 1929 applies, at the earliest, from the twenty-fourth week (which is evidently the stage at which an unborn child develops the capacity to breathe). Why the court preferred this interpretation is not apparent from its brief judgment, and its subsequent decision not to deliver its reasons[115] is, therefore, all the more regrettable. A clue to the court's reasoning may, however, be found in the judgment of Heilbron J, which it affirmed. Heilbron J referred to several of the nineteenth-century cases on homicide which established that, to bring home a charge of child murder the prosecution had to prove that the child had been completely born alive

---

[115] The court stated that its expanded reasons would have been concerned with "technical arguments on the construction and interrelation of the Births and Deaths Registration Acts 1836–1926, the Births and Deaths Registration Act 1953 and the Infant Life (Preservation) Act 1929.": [1988] QB 135, 153.

before it had been killed.[116] She observed that in *Handley*, Brett J directed the jury that a child was born alive "when it existed as a live child, that is to say, breathing and living by reason of breathing through its own lungs alone, without deriving any of its living or power of living by or through any connection with its mother."[117] The courts in *C v S* appear to have imported this criterion of capacity to breathe from the offense of murder into that of child destruction, a course favored by Victor Tunkel in 1985.[118] If this is a basis of the courts' decision, then it would appear to encounter two objections. First, the remaining cases on child murder (including those referred to by Heilbron J) are at most authority for the proposition that breathing was merely one proof of live birth.[119] Indeed, in *Brain*, Park J directed the jury: "A child must be wholly in the world in a living state to be the subject of a charge of murder; but if it has been wholly born, and is alive, it is not essential that it should have breathed at the time it was killed; as many children are born alive, and yet do not breathe for some time after their birth."[120] Nor did he direct that the prosecution had to prove that the child had the capacity to breathe. Park J's direction is, moreover, in line with another rule of law relating to child murder. Having, in his third *Institute*, given the classic definition of murder, Sir Edward Coke proceeded to lay down that if a man beat a woman who was "quick with child" so that the child died after live birth from the wounds received while in the womb, the man was guilty of murder.[121] As quickening takes place well before the child is capable of breathing, this rule of law (which was followed by later commentators[122]) is difficult to square with the ruling that it is necessary to prove a capacity to breathe to bring home a charge of child murder.[123] A second objection to the reasoning in *C v S* is that even if the courts were correct in their apparent belief that proof of a capacity to breathe is required on a charge of child murder, it would still be necessary to justify the importation of this requirement into the offense of child destruction and show why the competing interpretations of "capable of being born alive" examined in this chapter are less persuasive.

---

[116] [1988] QB 135, 146.
[117] (1879) 13 Cox CC 79, 81.
[118] V Tunkel, "Late Abortions and the Crime of Child Destruction: (1) A Reply" [1985] Crim LR 133, 135.
[119] See generally DS Davies, "Child-Killing in English Law" (1937) 1 MLR 203; and SB Atkinson, "Life, Birth and Live-Birth" (1904) 20 LQR 134.
[120] (1834) 6 C & P 349, 350.
[121] 3 Co Inst 50 (1641). See *Sim's Case* (1603) Gouldsborough 176.
[122] Eg W Hawkins, *A Treatise of the Pleas of the Crown* [1716] Book 1 c 31 s 16.
[123] See also *West* (1848) 2 Cox CC 500.

As the Abortion Act 1967 did not affect the ILPA 1929, the abortion of a viable foetus or, after *C v S*, one capable of breathing, remained unlawful unless it came within the proviso to section 1(1) of the 1929 Act, that is, unless it was performed for the purpose only of preserving the life of the mother. The protection afforded to the child capable of breathing was, however, significantly weakened by the Human Fertilisation and Embryology Act 1990. Section 37 of that Act amended the Abortion Act to allow abortion after the twenty-fourth week in a wider range of circumstances, including where there is a "substantial risk" that the child, if born, would be "seriously handicapped."[124] (Indeed, the law has been interpreted by some doctors—as was predicted during the passage of what became the 1990 Act[125]—to allow the destruction of a viable child merely because the child has a cleft palate.) Although the focus of this chapter has been the legal interpretation of the ILPA, it is difficult to conclude without noting the strikingly misshapen ethical state in which the law now stands. A doctor who intentionally kills a child who has been completely born alive commits homicide and is liable to mandatory life imprisonment. But a doctor who intentionally kills a child during birth commits no offence whatever provided the doctor complies with the Abortion Act as amended by section 37 of the Human Fertilisation and Embryology Act. This is so even if the delivery of the child alive, rather than dead, would involve no risk to the life or health of the mother and the child is destroyed simply because he or she is unwanted by the mother. It is not easy to see how the criteria of viability and birth, to which the current law attaches so much moral weight, can bear it. Indeed, the moral irrelevance of viability and birth to the ethics of killing is accepted by many philosophers, whether "pro-life"[126] or "pro-choice."[127]

---

[124] Abortion Act 1967, s 1(1)(d).

[125] J Finnis, "We warned them, they mocked us, now we've been proved right", *Sunday Telegraph*, 7 December 2003.

[126] See eg C Kaczor, *The Ethics of Abortion* (Routledge, 2010) chs 3, 4.

[127] Professor John Harris, questioning whether there is a moral difference between abortion and infanticide, has rightly observed: "The geographical location of the developing human, whether it is inside the womb or not, is not the sort of thing that can make a moral difference.": "Adviser sparks infanticide debate", BBC News Channel, 26 January 2004 <http://news.bbc.co.uk/1/hi/health/3429269.stm>.

CHAPTER 8

THE HUMAN EMBRYO IN VITRO: PERSON, CHATTEL, OR DOLPHIN?

I INTRODUCTION

The three previous chapters have considered the legal status of the unborn child in utero (in vivo). This chapter considers the status, in Anglo-American law, of the human embryo in vitro. The literature on the question is not voluminous. The predominant opinion among the few academic lawyers who have considered it is that the in vitro embryo is not a "person" but is either a form of property or falls into some third category, such as that occupied by wild creatures like dolphins. The few courts which have addressed the question have also tended to categorize the embryo as property, or at least to have invested the gamete contributors with rights over the embryo akin to property rights. Further, the Human Fertilisation and Embryology Act 1990 (HFEA 1990), the first statute comprehensively to regulate in vitro fertilization, implicitly treats the embryo as or like property. This chapter suggests that jurists, courts, and legislatures have, with very few exceptions, failed to do justice to the case for categorizing the in vitro embryo as a person.

A Legal categories

Before considering whether the human in vitro embryo is a "person" or a "chattel," it may be helpful to define these terms. *Salmond on Jurisprudence* states that in law a "person" is any being the law regards as capable of rights or duties and that it does not mean simply a human being, for there are persons, such as companies, which are not human beings and human beings, such as slaves, who have been denied legal personality.[1] *Salmond* continues that there are two types of person, namely a "natural person," that is, "a human being," and "legal persons," that is, "beings, real or

---

[1] G Williams (ed), *Salmond on Jurisprudence* (11th edn, Sweet & Maxwell, 1957) 350.

imaginary, who for the purpose of legal reasoning are treated in greater or lesser degree in the same way as human beings."[2] The relevant definition of "chattel" given by *Salmond* is "A movable physical object...."[3] Professors Kennedy and Grubb write that "The law seems to permit two models of analysis: that the [human embryo in vitro] is either *a chattel* or *a person*."[4] Similarly, Mason and McCall Smith describe the alternatives as "full human being" or "laboratory artefact."[5] However, some lawyers, like George Annas, have questioned the dichotomy between person and property. He has written:

embryos could just as easily be considered neither products nor people, but in some other category altogether. There are many things, such as dogs, dolphins, and redwoods that are neither products nor people. We nonetheless legally protect these entities by limiting what their owners or custodians can do with them.[6]

This is unconvincing. First, the legal categories are not "products" and "people" but "property" and "persons": not all "property" is a "product." Second, entities like "dogs, dolphins and redwoods" may or may not be owned by anyone but they are all capable of being owned. They do not form a third legal category. Indeed, Annas acknowledges as much when he refers to them as "things" which may have "owners." Is then his supposed third category characterized by the fact that the owner's rights may be circumscribed in order to protect the property (or for other reasons)? If so, the fact that the dog owner's rights over the dog may be circumscribed to protect it (from, say, unnecessary suffering) no more takes the dog into a third legal category than listing a building to protect it from demolition by its owner takes it into a third legal category. Could it not be argued that the unborn child in vivo demonstrates the existence of a third (and highly relevant) legal category? Surprisingly overlooked by Annas in favor of dolphins, the foetus is neither property nor, it seems, at least until live birth, a legal person, and it is arguable that the embryo in vitro should be classified like the embryo in vivo. However, as our discussion of the unborn child in English criminal law will indicate, the under-determinate, inchoate, legal status of the unborn child in vivo is attributable to the fact that it is in the uterus rather than the fact that it is

[2] Ibid 350–1.
[3] Ibid 460.
[4] I Kennedy and A Grubb (eds), *Medical Law: Text and Materials* (Lexis Law Publishing, 1989) ("KGI") 682 (emphasis in original).
[5] JK Mason and RA McCall Smith, *Law and Medical Ethics* (2nd edn, Oxford University Press, 1987) 49. What they mean by "full" is unclear.
[6] GJ Annas, "A French Homunculus in a Tennessee Court" (1989) 19 Hastings Center Report 20.

unborn, and there is a powerful case, given the law's historic purpose of protecting human life from its beginning (demonstrated in the previous three chapters), for the law to recognize the legal personality of the human embryo in vitro. (There is also a powerful case for regarding the embryo in vivo as a person.[7]) If two children were conceived, one in vivo and the other in vitro, and both grew to 40 weeks, could the law sensibly recognize the former as a person, because he or she had been born alive, but not the latter?

Let us begin by considering the analysis of the legal status of the unborn child, both in vivo and in vitro, in the pioneering but flawed report in 1984 of the Committee of Inquiry into Human Fertilisation and Embryology, chaired by Dame (now Baroness) Warnock.[8]

B The Warnock Report

The Warnock report's analysis of the ethical status of the human embryo in vitro was brief. Its analysis of its legal status was briefer still. The report began by considering the legal status of the unborn child in vivo. It asserted (inaccurately) that it has "no legal status," before proceeding (accurately) to note that it is protected by legislation by sections 58 and 59 of the Offences Against the Person Act 1861 (OAPA 1861) and by the Infant Life (Preservation) Act 1929 (ILPA 1929).[9] The report's consideration of the legal status of the human embryo in vitro consisted of the bare assertion that it is not "under the present law in the United Kingdom accorded the same status as a living child or an adult. . . ."[10] Although the report did not explicitly conclude that the anti-abortion legislation did not protect the embryo in vitro, its implicit conclusion to this effect seems correct. If a scientist in a laboratory flattens an embryo it is difficult to maintain that this is procuring a "miscarriage" contrary to section 58 of the OAPA 1861[11] let alone destroying a child "capable of being born alive" contrary to section 1 of the ILPA 1929.[12] Is, then, the human embryo in vitro bereft of protection by the criminal law? Let us consider an analysis which would recognize the personhood of the embryo in vitro from conception.

---

[7]   See eg EW Keyserlingk, *The Unborn Child's Right to Prenatal Care* (Quebec Research Centre of Private and Comparative Law, 1984).
[8]   *Report of the Committee of Inquiry into Human Fertilisation and Embryology* (Cmnd 9314, 1984) ("Warnock").
[9]   Warnock para 11.16.
[10]   Ibid para 11.17.
[11]   BM Dickens, *Medico-Legal Aspects of Family Law* (Butterworths, 1979) 78–9.
[12]   For the reach of these provisions see Chs 6 and 7 respectively.

II A PROTECTIVE ANALYSIS: PROFESSOR FINNIS

In an illuminating but unpublished memorandum predating the HFEA 1990, Professor John Finnis considered possible criminal liability for not transferring a human in vitro embryo to the womb.[13] He observed that such conduct might offend section 27 of the OAPA 1861, under which it is an offense to "unlawfully abandon or expose any child, being under the age of two years" whereby its life shall be endangered or its health shall be likely to be permanently injured. In arguing that the word "child" is capable of covering an in vitro embryo, Finnis pointed out that the first meaning of "child" in the *Oxford English Dictionary* is "The unborn or newly born human being; foetus, infant . . . ,"[14] that the words "with child" in section 58 of the same Act refer to a woman at any stage of pregnancy, and that "a child en ventre sa mere" was a well-known expression when the Act was passed. In addition to liability under section 27, Professor Finnis considered liability for manslaughter. He cited *Archbold*:

If a grown-up person chooses to undertake the charge of a human creature helpless . . . from infancy . . . he is bound to execute that charge without gross neglect; and if he lets the person whose charge he has undertaken die by gross neglect, he is guilty of manslaughter.[15]

Finnis pointed out that the applicability of the crime of assault (and therefore presumably of homicide) to even the child outside the womb who is not yet viable was clearly affirmed in 1978 by Glanville Williams when he wrote:

If an aborted fetus is alive it is a person, no matter how short the period of gestation, and using it for an experiment would in law be at least as assault upon it. If doctors wish to perform these experiments legally they must seek statutory authority.[16]

As Finnis observed, Williams was treating the criterion of legal protection not as age, viability, or appearance, but as extra-uterine live

---

[13] JM Finnis, "The Possibility of Criminal Proceedings in respect of Human Embryos Conceived In Vitro and Deliberately not Transferred to the Womb" (unpublished memorandum, 1984). I am grateful to Professor Finnis for a copy of the memorandum.

[14] It continues: "When the application was subsequently extended, the primitive sense was often expressed by *babe, baby, infant*; but 'child' is still the proper term, and retained in phrases such as 'with child'...." (2nd edn, Oxford University Press, 1989) vol III 113 (italics in original). It goes on to define "with child" as "pregnant": ibid 114. See Ch 6, n 71.

[15] *Archbold* (43rd edn, Sweet & Maxwell, 1988) vol 2, §20–59.

[16] G Williams, *Textbook of Criminal Law* (1st edn, Steven & Sons, 1978) 263, n 8. This passage does not appear in the second edition but the proposition it contains is neither withdrawn nor controverted.

existence. Finnis added that this criterion is consistent with the whole course of the common law, as revealed by the offenses of homicide and abortion.

A Homicide

The classic definition of murder was laid down in the seventeenth century by Sir Edward Coke as the unlawful killing with "malice aforethought" of "any reasonable creature *in rerum natura*."[17] *Smith and Hogan* state that "reasonable creature" includes "any human being."[18] The phrase *"in rerum natura"* means (in this context) "in being"—"out in the world", so to speak. The child in the womb has historically not been regarded as "in being" for the purposes of the crime of homicide. Coke added, however, that if an attempt were made to kill the child before birth and it were born alive and died as a result of the injuries received in the womb, this was murder, for when it died it was "in being."[19] The reason for the distinction was the greater difficulty of proving causation when the child died before birth. As the Court of Queen's Bench explained (contemporaneously with Coke), whereas in the case of a stillborn child it could not be known whether it had been alive at the time of its attempted destruction, this problem of proof did not arise when the child died after live birth.[20] Finnis concluded that the law of homicide has always been concerned to protect any living human "in being."

B Abortion

Finnis also considered the common law crime of abortion, which has never been abrogated. Coke wrote that it was an offense to kill an unborn child, at least if the woman was "quick with childe."[21] The rationale of the offense was the protection of unborn human life from the time it was believed to have begun.[22] This rationale of the law, Finnis argued, justified the extension of the offense to protect the human embryo in vitro. An obvious objection is that the protection of the common law applied to

---

[17] 3 Co Inst 47 (1641).

[18] JC Smith and B Hogan, *Criminal Law* (6th edn, Oxford University Press, 1988) 310. *Archbold* states that "reasonable" relates to appearance rather than the mental capacity of the victim and is apt to exclude monstrous births (n 15) §20–10. See Ch 2, text at nn 114–21.

[19] 3 Co Inst 50.

[20] *Sims's Case* (1601) Gould 176; Eng Rep 1075.

[21] 3 Co Inst 50.

[22] Coke observed that the crime was based on the law of God, and in a side-note cited Genesis 9,6: "Whoever sheds the blood of man, by man shall his blood be shed; for God made man in his own image.": ibid 50–1. Similarly, Blackstone wrote that life was a gift from God, "a right inherent by nature in every individual," which began in law as soon as an infant was able to stir in the mother's womb: *Commentaries* (1765) vol 1, 125.

children who were in the womb and after "quickening." However, Finnis pointed out that in the light of recently discovered indictments for the offense at common law[23] it was now doubtful whether the offense was ever confined to post-quickening destruction, and he added that, even if it were, it was only to facilitate proof that the unborn child had been alive at the time of the abortifacient act and had been killed by it. In other words, the law of abortion may have been no less sensitive to the need to prove that a live human being had been killed than the law of homicide: just as the latter required proof of death after live birth, so the former may have required proof of quickening. Finnis concluded that where, as with an in vitro embryo, there is no comparable problem of proving the existence of a live human being, there is no reason why the protection afforded by the common law should not be extended to it.

Such an extension could prove difficult if the common law crime of abortion is obsolete. In *R v Tait* Mustill LJ (as he then was), delivering the judgment of the Court of Appeal, remarked, citing *Smith and Hogan*, that it may have been obsolete by 1861 and that "In the light of all that has happened in the way of legislation, prosecution and debate in the past 100 years, it seems scarcely possible that any court would hold that the common law offense is still in existence."[24] However, his Lordship's remark was obiter and preceded by only a cursory examination of the history of the offense of abortion. Moreover, *Smith and Hogan* did not deal at any length with the question of obsolescence and merely observed by way of introduction to their discussion of the current law: "Though the killing of the child in the womb after quickening was a misdemeanour at common law, the present law on the subject is statutory."[25] Further, the wording of the Abortion Act 1967 appears to recognize the continued existence of the common law crime: section 1(1) provides that a person who complies with the Act shall not be guilty of an offense under "the law relating to abortion," which is defined by section 6 and sections 58 and 59 of the OAPA 1861 as "any rule of law relating to the procurement of abortion." Professor Skegg has observed that this phrase was probably included to preclude any liability at common law.[26] And as late as 1961 the House of Lords held in *Sykes v DPP* that misprision of felony, an offense at least as ancient as abortion, was not obsolete.[27] In reply to the

---

[23] In particular *R v Webb* (1601) and *R v Beare* (1732), discussed in J Keown, *Abortion, Doctors and the Law* (Cambridge University Press, 1988) 7–10. See Ch 5, text at nn 44–5.
[24] [1989] 3 WLR 891, 898.
[25] *Smith and Hogan* (n 18) 363–4.
[26] PDG Skegg, *Law, Ethics and Medicine* (revised edn, Clarendon Press, 1988) 24–5.
[27] [1962] AC 528.

argument that misprision had fallen into obsolescence, Lord Goddard stated:[28] "If [a] maxim expresses a positive rule of law, once established, though long ago, time cannot abolish it nor disfavour make it obsolete." Lord Denning also cited several modern authorities for its existence.[29] Although there would appear to have been no prosecutions for abortion at common law since 1803, when the first statutory prohibition of abortion was enacted, this is explicable by the fact that it has since then been much easier to prosecute for the statutory rather than the common law offense. Rather than impliedly abrogating the common law crime, the intervention of statute, as Professor Winfield observed, merely "made it needless to rely on the common law."[30] And Mustill LJ's comment was made in the context of protecting the child in vivo, not in vitro. Even if the function of the law in protecting unborn life from abortion has been superseded by statute in relation to the child in vivo this is clearly not so in relation to the child in vitro. Finally, even if the common law offense of abortion is obsolete, the common law crime of homicide is not and Professor Finnis' argument that to cause the death of an in vitro embryo may be homicide still stands.

III SOME CONTRARY ANALYSES

Against the view that it may be homicide to destroy an in vitro embryo stand the opinions of several authorities on criminal and medical law, not least Professor Glanville Williams.

A Glanville Williams

Williams considered whether the scientist who discards an in vitro embryo is guilty of murder and concluded: "The sensible solution is to say that the embryo has not reached a sufficient stage of development to be a 'reasonable creature' within the law of homicide."[31] However, this "sensible" approach appears vulnerable to the objection that it is inconsistent with Williams' own observation, noted above, that an aborted foetus is a person "no matter how short the period of gestation."[32] Moreover, Williams failed to offer any reason why the embryo is not a "reasonable

---

[28] Ibid 568, quoting Lord Sumner in *Bowman v Secular Society Ltd* [1917] AC 406.
[29] Ibid 560.
[30] PH Winfield, "The Unborn Child" (1942) 8 CLJ 76, 79.
[31] Williams, *Textbook of Criminal Law* (2nd edn, Steven & Sons, 1983) 290, n 6.
[32] See text at n 16.

creature" which, as we also noted above, *Smith and Hogan* define as including "any human being."[33]

B Mason and McCall Smith

The view that it is not homicide to destroy an in vitro embryo also enjoys the support of Professors Mason and McCall Smith. They have concluded that it is not murder to dispose of an in vitro embryo because it can "in no way be considered to have achieved a separate existence in a legal sense" and that even if it became possible for the embryo to grow to maturity it is difficult to see that any offense would be committed by disposing of it.[34] They contend that the question of the embryo's status is therefore "purely ethical" and turns on the nature of the embryo, and that it seems "scarcely tenable" to regard it as a human being. Their reasoning is that ensoulment and humanity are inseparable, that humanity depends upon a natural human environment, and that the embryo only derives its humanity after establishing normal unity with its mother. Prior to such an "infusion of humanity" it appears both "kinder" and more practical to look upon the embryo, which cannot (they hold) possess a soul, as a laboratory artifact.[35]

Their argument is unpersuasive. To begin with, the relevance to the modern criminal law of theological questions about the timing of ensoulment is not obvious. And, in law, the correct test for personhood is not whether the embryo has achieved a separate existence but whether it is "in being." Although it may be appropriate when referring to the birth of a child to describe the requirement in terms of achieving a separate existence, it is clearly inappropriate in the ectogenetic context. A child who has been completely born alive has achieved a separate existence. But a child conceived in vitro also enjoys a separate existence. If birth were a requirement of legal protection, then a child born alive after 40 weeks would be protected by the law of homicide but not a child of the identical age which had been conceived in vitro and which had grown ectogenetically (as may one day be possible). The implication of their position, that a mature ectogenetic child would not be protected by the law and could, for example, be subjected to lethal experiments, is surely untenable. Moreover, their assertion that humanity depends on a "natural human environment" is neither explained nor defended. Would a baby, infant, or adult who had been conceived and who had developed ectogenetically thereby

---

[33] See text at n 18.
[34] Mason and McCall Smith (n 5) 48.
[35] Ibid 48–9.

forfeit his or her humanity? Is a human child brought up in the wild not a human being? May he or she be hunted, caged, or eaten?

C Kennedy and Grubb

Professors Kennedy and Grubb, having referred to Williams' view that the embryo is not a "reasonable creature," conclude that the in vitro embryo is not a person for the purposes of the law of homicide.[36] They do not, however, address any of the objections to Williams' "sensible solution" and base their conclusion on a questionable extrapolation from the *ratio* in *Tait*. In that case the defendant threatened a woman who was five months pregnant that he would kill her baby. He was convicted under section 16 of the OAPA 1861 of making a threat to another, intending that that other would fear that it would be carried out, to kill that other "or a third person." The Court of Appeal allowed his appeal, holding that although the section seemed to prohibit a threat to kill an unborn child when it was born, it was not an offense to threaten to cause a mother to miscarry because the unborn child "was not, in the ordinary sense, 'another person', distinct from its mother...."[37] As the trial judge had left it to the jury to decide whether the unborn child was a "third person," the conviction was quashed. The reasoning of the Court of the Appeal is questionable. It is not difficult to find references, in both ordinary and legal discourse, to the unborn child as a "person." Crown counsel pointed out[38] that people in common speech talk of the unborn child as one who can die or be killed and pertinently asked why the interpretation of "person" should be strained in some different sense. The dictionary definition of "person" is certainly wide enough to include an unborn child: "a human being regarded as an individual..."[39] or "a man, woman or child"[40] or "a human being, whether man, woman, or child...."[41] The United Kingdom Department of Health's guide to pregnancy is replete with references to the foetus as a "baby."[42] Turning to legal usage, we will recall that section 58 of the OAPA 1861 refers to the pregnant woman as being "with child" and punishes its destruction with life imprisonment. Why should it be protected by section 58 but not section 16? We will recall that *Salmond*

---

[36] Kennedy and Grubb (n 4) 656.
[37] [1989] 3 WLR 891.
[38] Ibid 897.
[39] "Person" in Oxford Dictionaries <http://oxforddictionaries.com/definition/person>.
[40] "Person" in Cambridge Dictionaries Online <http://dictionary.cambridge.org/dictionary/british/person_1?q = person>.
[41] <http://dictionary.reference.com/browse/person>.
[42] UK Department of Health, *The Pregnancy Book* (2009) <http://www.dh.gov.uk/en/Publicationsandstatistics/Publications/PublicationsPolicyAndGuidance/DH_107302>.

defines a "natural person" as "a human being."[43] It also discusses the "Legal Status of Unborn Persons" and observes that although the dead possess no legal personality "it is otherwise with the unborn" who enjoy "legal personality attributed . . . by way of anticipation" of live birth.[44] Further, no fewer than 38 United States states have enacted foetal homicide laws. The Alabama statute, for example, contains the following definition: "PERSON. The term, when referring to the victim of a criminal homicide or assault, means a human being, including an unborn child in utero at any stage of development, regardless of viability."[45]

Even if *Tait* were rightly decided, it is not an authority for the proposition that a human embryo in vitro is not protected by the law of homicide. It is one thing to conclude that an unborn child is not a "person" within section 16, quite another to claim, like Kennedy and Grubb, that a human embryo in vitro is not a "reasonable creature" for the purposes of the law of homicide (and another still to claim, as they do, that this is so *a fortiori*). If a "reasonable creature" means a human being, and the law of homicide protects human beings who are "in being," enjoying a separate physical existence, why are human embryos in vitro not protected by the law of homicide?

Professor Grubb has argued that such law as there is relating to the status of the in vitro embryo supports its categorization as a chattel and that "the pragmatism of the common law would see that to treat an extra-corporeal embryo as a chattel is more consistent with common-sense than for it to be given the rights of a person."[46] The common law is pragmatic, but it is also principled. Despite the enormous pragmatic difficulties of punishing abortion, the common law nevertheless consistently did so. Similarly, in the eighteenth century there were pragmatic arguments, not least economic, for treating black people as chattels. Nevertheless, in *Somersett*'s case, Lord Mansfield famously rejected slavery as "odious" to the common law.[47] Given that the common law has historically sought to safeguard human life from its beginning, is it not treating in vitro embryos as property, rather than persons, that offends "common sense"? Grubb mentions the argument that personhood begins at conception but he nowhere explains why the argument should not prevail. He writes:

---

[43] See text at n 2.

[44] *Salmond* (n 1) 354–5.

[45] Ala. Code 13-A-6-1 (a) 3 (2006): National Conference of State Legislatures, "Fetal Homicide Laws" (updated March 2010) <http://www.ncsl.org/default.aspx?tabid = 14386>.

[46] A Grubb, "The legal status of the frozen human embryo" in A Grubb (ed), *Challenges in Medical Care* (John Wiley & Sons, 1992) 69, 72.

[47] *R v Knowles, ex p Somersett* (1772) 20 State Tr 1.

"Whatever the merits of the medical/philosophical proposition that life/ personhood begins at conception . . . the common law does not adopt it."[48] To illustrate this proposition he cites English cases such as *Paton*, in which Sir George Baker P concluded: "A foetus cannot, in English law, in my view, have any rights of its own at least until it is born and has a separate existence from the mother. That permeates the whole of the civil law of this country. . . ."[49] But such authorities (to which we shall return) relate to the unborn child in vivo. Grubb argues that although these cases arguably involved a conflict between the mother and her unborn child, it would be wrong to see this as the only reason the courts did not recognize the personhood of the unborn.[50] He concludes that "If an unborn child is not a legal person, it cannot seriously be argued that a frozen two-, four- or eight-cell embryo is a legal person. . . ."[51] However, the child's location inside the mother, the potential conflict of interest between the two, and the difficulty of controlling the mother in the interests of the child, featured prominently in the courts' reasoning in these cases. The cases are, therefore, distinguishable from the case of the in vitro embryo. Moreover, these were civil, not criminal, cases. The ellipsis at the end of Grubb's quotation from Sir George Baker P excludes the following significant words: "(I except the criminal law, which is now irrelevant)."[52] The criminal law is far from irrelevant to a proper determination of the legal status of the unborn child, whether in vivo or in vitro. Grubb observes that abortion is an offense absent compliance with the Abortion Act 1967, but that "little, if anything," can be gained from an analysis of the law of abortion.[53] This is to overlook the driving purpose of the law against abortion, both common and statute, across seven centuries: the protection of human life from its beginning. The Abortion Act is a recent exception (albeit a very broad one) to the rule, and only in the circumstances it specifies. The fact that the Abortion Act allows the destruction of human life in vivo tells us "little, if anything" about the status of human life in vitro or, indeed, in vivo. The fact that the law allows killing in certain circumstances does not establish that the being killed is not a legal person. The law allows killing in self-defense without denying personhood to the assailant. Nor does it follow that because the Abortion Act permits the destruction of the unborn child in vivo, the law does or should

[48] Grubb (n 46) 74.
[49] Ibid 75. *Paton v British Pregnancy Advisory Service Trustees* [1979] QB 276.
[50] Grubb (n 46) 75.
[51] Ibid.
[52] *Paton v British Pregnancy Advisory Service Trustees* [1979] QB 276, 279.
[53] Grubb (n 46) 76.

give even less protection to the unborn child in vitro. Somersett was a chattel inside the colonies; it did not follow that he was a chattel outside the colonies. The Abortion Act must be read against the historical prohibition of abortion by the common law and section 58 of the OAPA 1861, which remains in force. Moreover, whereas the Abortion Act clearly has no application to the embryo in vitro, the same cannot be said of the common law. In short, like the previous commentators we have mentioned, Grubb fails to engage with the argument that the embryo in vitro is a human being and that a core purpose of the law has long been, and remains, the protection of human beings. It is no answer to cite *Paton* or the Abortion Act. Whatever inroads may have been made by statute into the protection of children in vivo, they do not apply to the child in vitro. Supporting the property classification of the embryo in vitro, Grubb argues that human gametes are property and asks: "Surely the genetic unification of the gametes to produce a unique human structure should not change our analysis completely?"[54] But to equate gametes and embryos is to overlook a key biological fact: that after unification of the gametes there is a "unique human structure" which has, then and there, the active, radical capacity, not shared by either sperm or egg, to develop as a member of the human species. This is the difference between an egg, which by itself has no capacity to develop as a human being, and an embryo, which does. It is the difference between potential for a new living being and a new living being with potential. This is precisely why a woman commits no offense if she destroys a sperm or an egg in her body but why, if she destroys an embryo in her body, she commits an offense punishable with life imprisonment.

D *Robertson*

Another legal commentator who rejects the argument that the in vitro embryo is a person is Professor John Robertson.[55] He claims: "The central problem in determining the legal status of early embryos is reconciling respect for human life and personhood with competing concerns of bodily integrity and procreative choice."[56] He adds: "To answer the questions that define the early embryo's legal status, the competing interests at stake in any particular definition of legal status must be carefully analyzed."[57] These interests, he continues, fall into two main groups. One

---

[54] Ibid 77.
[55] JA Robertson, "In the Beginning: the Legal Status of Early Embryos" (1990) 76 Virginia Law Review 437.
[56] Ibid.
[57] Ibid 453.

group concerns the embryo, viewing it either as an entity with interests and perhaps rights in itself or as a symbol of human rights; the other group concerns "the array of reproductive and family interests that early embryos may serve."[58] Robertson concludes:

The legal status of the fertilized egg and early embryo will thus be determined by the balance struck among the competing interests of gamete providers, embryo protection, and others as they arise in many different situations. In many cases the embryo's resulting legal status will be as genetic material to be used or not as the gamete providers choose in pursuing their own reproductive goals. In other instances, the state will give the embryo a protected status, by limiting the dispositions available to gamete providers and others.[59]

This approach is highly questionable. If an embryo has "rights in itself," is it not a person? If so, why will its status be determined by a balance struck with the competing interests of others? Would we adopt the same reasoning if we were considering the status not of an "embryo" but of a "newborn baby," or "woman," or "African-American"? Robertson appears to conflate two questions which should be kept distinct. One is the question what legal status an entity has. If that entity is a person, then certain consequences surely follow from that categorization. Should it not be the categorization which determines the balance of interests rather than the balance of interests which determines the categorization? It may well serve the interests of some human beings, such as slave-owners in pre-Civil War America, for other human beings, such as African-Americans, to be categorized as chattels. Lest the example be thought fanciful, this is of course precisely how they were categorized by the United States Supreme Court in *Dred Scott v Sandford*.[60] It is precisely what Lord Mansfield, in *Somersett*'s case, had refused to do, cognizant though he was that his decision liberating Somersett would undermine the vast economic institution of slavery on which the financial interests of many depended. It may be that Robertson would only propose a balancing test in relation to human embryos and not older humans, on the ground that older humans are persons. But, if so, this would beg the question.

To assess the claims of the embryo to legal personhood, Professor Robertson rightly turns for guidance to the Anglo-American legal tradition relating to the unborn. His interpretation of that tradition is (as will be apparent in the light of our discussion of that tradition in Chapter 5) inaccurate. He writes: "Until very recently, positive law had very few

---

[58] Ibid.
[59] Ibid (footnote omitted).
[60] *Dred Scott v Sandford* 60 US 393 (1857).

things to say" about early embryos[61] and that "The law of prenatal and preconception torts, estate law's concept of being 'en ventre sa mere,' and criminal prohibitions on abortion did define in important ways some aspects of the legal status of fetuses, though not necessarily the status of preimplantation embryos."[62] Robertson fails to show that the civil law relating to the embryo in vivo drew any distinction at implantation, and the criminal law certainly did not. The statutory prohibition of abortion in nineteenth-century England and the United States, a cardinal indicator of the legal status of the embryo, protected the embryo from fertilization (as we saw in Chapter 5). Robertson continues that because Anglo-American law developed before in vitro fertilization (IVF) "it has limited relevance" to answering the questions arising from the technological developments that make the early embryo a subject of such intense interest.[63] Why does this follow? If it became technologically possible to grow an embryo to term in the laboratory, would the law of homicide have "limited relevance" to the question whether it was murder to kill the infant? The law has long sought to protect embryonic life, even though hidden from view in the womb. Why would it not protect it when *in rerum natura*? Robertson continues:

In the Anglo-American legal tradition, fertilized eggs and embryos have never had an independent legal status. Only at quickening were they invested with rights (perhaps because there was no way to know that they existed before then) against abortion, although abortion was not the equivalent of homicide. A live-born infant, separate from the mother, was necessary for homicide liability.[64]

While the common law may have prohibited abortion only after quickening (a limitation which, as we noted earlier, is now doubtful given the absence of any mentioning of quickening in a number of common law indictments for the crime[65]), anti-abortion legislation in England and the United State in the nineteenth century abolished the quickening distinction and prohibited abortion from conception. To borrow Robertson's words, the Anglo-American legal tradition, therefore, "invested" unborn embryos with "rights" against abortion. Moreover, if the common law, through its prohibition of abortion, gave a child in the womb a right against being destroyed as soon as the law knew of its existence, why

---

[61] Robertson (n 55) 450. Similarly, he writes: "Since technological change has only recently made early embryos independent objects of interest, there is no well-established tradition defining special respect for the embryo.": ibid 449.
[62] Ibid 450.
[63] Ibid 451.
[64] Ibid 451, n 39.
[65] See text at n 23; and see Ch 5, n 45.

should the common law not protect a child outside the womb of whose existence it knows? And if the law against homicide protects a child born alive who is separate from its mother, why should it not equally protect a child who is alive and separate from its mother even though it has not gone through the process of birth? Robertson writes that early embryos are a long way from the quickening stage.[66] But this answers neither question. In short, Robertson acknowledges that the law's protection of the unborn child has historically tracked its awareness of the child's existence but fails to attend to the implication of this key insight for protection of the existing child in vitro.

Further, he notes that various states have through judicial decision or legislation extended homicide protection to the foetus. He adds that although a majority require the foetus to have reached viability or at least quickening, some define the unborn child whose death in non-abortion situations may be punished as homicide as existing from conception, and appear to apply to the embryo in vitro.[67] Do not these statutes follow the historical trend of the Anglo-American legal tradition in extending protection to the unborn from conception, at least outside the context of abortion? And is not the in vitro embryo outside the context of abortion? Robertson has surprisingly little to say about these relevant and significant developments in United States law.

Robertson concludes that the relationship between the gamete providers and the embryo is not one of parenthood but one of ownership:

Although the bundle of property rights attached to one's ownership of an embryo may be more circumscribed than for other things, it is an ownership or property interest nonetheless.[68]

Of the gamete contributors' ownership he writes:

Their decisional authority (or ownership) gives them discretion to create, store, discard, transfer, donate, screen, use in research, and make other decisions affecting early embryos. Their authority includes the right to give advance instructions for disposition of embryos and to transfer their ownership interest to others, or to prevent or terminate implantation in the uterus.[69]

He writes that such ownership is strongly supported by traditions concerning property in body parts and products, particularly those with reproductive significance. If individuals own their gametes "it follows that

---

[66] Robertson (n 55) 451, n 39.
[67] Ibid 452.
[68] Ibid 455 (footnote omitted).
[69] Ibid 516.

they would have joint authority over the intended product that results...."[70]
The gamete providers are "the rightful owners of the resulting embryo, just
as *the owners of chemical X and chemical Y* are the owners of the new compound
XY that results when the expert chemist they have hired for the purpose
combines X and Y to form XY."[71] Robertson, like Grubb, seems to assume
that there is no substantial difference between a gamete and an embryo. But
this is to beg the question. A gamete has no capacity to develop as a human
being; an embryo does. This is precisely why the Anglo-American legal
tradition has long drawn a clear distinction between the two. There is,
moreover, little support in Anglo-American legal jurisprudence for the
categorization of living human subjects as property, apart of course from
slavery, affirmed by the infamous decision in *Dred Scott*.

Finally, Professor Robertson writes that answers to questions about
the locus and scope of decisional authority over embryos "will depend
very little on one's particular view of the moral status of early embryos."[72]
He explains:

The assignment of property or decisional authority in external embryos is
independent of any particular view as to whether the fertilized egg and early
embryo are themselves right-bearing entities or persons. Whether viewed as an
actual or potential person, the answer to the ownership question is the same.[73]

But whether gamete providers should be allowed to dispose of an embryo
surely depends in no small degree on whether that embryo is a person or
merely a chattel. Does Professor Robertson think that some human
persons can and should be owned, frozen, and flattened ? He writes that
a "useful parallel" between the dispositional authority that gamete providers have over their embryo is parental authority over children. But, as he
rightly notes,[74] parents do not "own" their children and have much more
limited authority over their children than gamete providers do over their
embryos. This is because parents are bound to use their authority to serve
the interests of their children and, unlike gamete providers, have no
authority to have their children put into cold storage, experimented
upon, or disposed of. It is not, therefore, easy to see a parallel. Let us
now turn to consider two leading cases on the legal status of the in vitro
embryo, in the first of which Professor Robertson was an expert witness.

---

[70] Ibid 457.
[71] Ibid 458 (emphasis added).
[72] Ibid 452.
[73] Ibid 456.
[74] Ibid 455, n 48.

IV TWO LEADING CASES: *DAVIS* AND *EVANS*

Judicial decisions on the status of the in vitro embryo are sparse. As our two leading cases will illustrate, most have classified the rights of gamete providers as proprietary rather than parental.[75] The reasoning offered in support of that classification by the courts is no stronger than that which has been offered by legal academics.

A Davis v Davis

Davis v Davis[76] was a family law case before a circuit court in Tennessee. The defendant, Mary Sue Davis, was infertile and she and her husband, Junior Lewis Davis, the plaintiff, had resorted to IVF. In December 1988 nine ova were removed from Mrs Davis and fertilized with her husband's sperm. Two of the resulting embryos were inserted into Mrs Davis but neither resulted in a successful pregnancy; the remaining seven were frozen for the purpose of future implantation.[77] Proceedings for divorce were initiated and the parties disagreed on the disposition of the frozen embryos. The defendant viewed them as her children and asked the court to award her custody so that they could be implanted in her womb.[78] The plaintiff opposed the transfer of the embryos on the ground that it would impose unwanted parenthood on him and condemn the children to being raised by a single parent.[79] The judge ruled in favor of the defendant and awarded her temporary custody of the seven embryos for the purpose of implantation. In arriving at this decision he considered the central issue to be when life begins and, in resolving this issue, he addressed three questions: "Are the embryos human?"; "Does a difference exist between a preembryo and an embryo?"; and "Are the embryos beings... [or] property that may become human beings?"

The court answered the first question by concluding that the embryos were human. It noted that all four expert witnesses who ventured an opinion as to when life begins—Dr King (a specialist in infertility/reproductive endocrinology), Dr Shivers (an embryologist), Professor Lejeune (a geneticist), and Professor Robertson—agreed with this conclusion.[80] As for the second question, the court found that there is no such term as

---

[75] Ibid 72–8; BM Dickens and RJ Cook, "The legal status of in vitro embryos" (2010) 111 International Journal of Gynaecology and Obstetrics 91.

[76] (1989) 15 Family Law Reporter 2097.

[77] Ibid 2098.

[78] Ibid 2110.

[79] Ibid 2108.

[80] Ibid 2099.

"preembryo." Having made a thorough search of encyclopedias and dictionaries of which it could take judicial notice, the court could find no reference to the term. To use it was to create a distinction which did not exist.[81] To the third question the court gave the answer, despite the conflicting testimony of the expert witnesses, that the embryos were human beings.

Professor Lejeune's evidence was that each human has a unique beginning which occurs at the moment of conception; and that when the ovum is fertilized by the sperm the result is "the most specialized cell under the sun" in that no other cell will ever have the same instructions in the life of the individual being created. By contrast, Professor Robertson's evidence was that a human "preembryo" was an entity composed of a group of undifferentiated cells and that it was "not clear" that it was a unique individual.[82] The court observed that the area of most acute disagreement between the witnesses related to cell differentiation: Dr Shivers and Professor Robertson testified that the "preembryo" is not a being because he or she has no (observable) organs, nervous system, and body parts, but Professor Lejeune testified that upon fertilization the entire constitution of a human being is clearly and unequivocally laid out, including arms, legs, and nervous system, and that upon inspection by DNA manipulation the life codes for each of these otherwise unobservable elements of the unique individual are visible. The court preferred his testimony:

The testimony of Dr. Lejeune stands unrebutted in the record; the Court accepts his testimony founded on the fact that DNA manipulation of the molecules of human chromosomes reliably detect[s] these features of man; that the life codes for each special, unique individual are resident at conception and animate the new person very soon after fertilisation occurs.[83]

The court rejected the argument that the embryo is not a human being because it might not realize its potential: the same could be said of a newborn baby. It also dismissed the plaintiff's argument that the frozen embryos were property jointly owned by the parties, an argument supported by Professor Robertson, who said that they might properly be designated fungible property.[84] The court concluded that the embryos were not property but human beings and, returning to the issue identified by the court as central, that their life began at conception.[85]

---

[81] Ibid 2101.
[82] Ibid 2100.
[83] Ibid 2102.
[84] Ibid.
[85] Ibid 2103.

The court proceeded to consider the legal status to be accorded to a human being existing as an embryo in vitro in a divorce case in Tennessee. The court noted the Supreme Court abortion cases of *Roe v Wade*[86] and *Webster and Reproductive Health Services*[87] and observed that they related to abortion, not the status of the embryo in vitro. The court held that there was no public policy reason to prevent the continuing development of the common law to protect the seven embryonic human beings in vitro.[88] Consequently, just as the doctrine of parens patriae ("that power of the sovereign to watch over the interests of those who are incapable of protecting themselves"[89]) applied to protect live-born children in domestic relations cases in that state, it applied equally to protect children in vitro.[90] The thrust of the doctrine was to focus fully on the best interests of the child rather than on those who sought custody and its sole objective was to achieve justice for the child. As it served the best interests of the children in vitro for the defendant to be permitted the opportunity to bring them to term through implantation, the court awarded her temporary custody for that purpose.[91]

The judge's decision was reversed by the Tennessee Court of Appeal, whose decision was affirmed by the Tennessee Supreme Court.[92] By the time the case had reached the Supreme Court, both parties had remarried. The appellant, Mary Sue, no longer wanted to use the embryos herself but wanted to donate them to a childless couple; Junior Davis opposed such donation and wanted the embryos discarded.[93] Appellate courts are of course normally reluctant to interfere with the findings of fact by a trial judge, who has seen and heard the witnesses. Why did the Supreme Court overturn the trial judge's finding of fact that the embryos were human beings? The court's reasons were far from compelling. The court criticized the testimony of Professor Lejeune. Although recognizing that he was "an internationally recognized geneticist" (he discovered the genetic cause of Down's syndrome) the court stated that his background failed to reflect "any degree of expertise in obstetrics and gynaecology (specifically in the field of infertility) or in medical ethics."[94] It added that his testimony revealed "a profound confusion between science and religion,"

---

[86] 410 US 113 (1973).
[87] 492 US 490 (1989).
[88] (1989) 15 Family Law Reporter 2097, 2103.
[89] Ibid 2104.
[90] Ibid 2103.
[91] Ibid 2104.
[92] *Davis v Davis* 842 SW 2d 588 (1992).
[93] Ibid para 19.
[94] Ibid para 34.

quoting his testimony that he was deeply moved that Mary Sue Davis wanted "to rescue babies from this concentration can" and that Junior Davis had a moral duty to bring these "tiny human beings" to term.[95] The court failed to explain why Lejeune's international distinction in human genetics did not eminently qualify him as an expert witness on the nature and development of the early embryo, or why it thought that his lack of expertise in obstetrics and gynecology (specifically infertility) or in medical ethics in any way detracted from the authority of his scientific testimony. The central question identified and decided by the trial judge concerned the nature of the early embryo, not the treatment of infertility or the divergent moral evaluations which ethicists give to the early human embryo. Moreover, the Supreme Court's accusation that Lejeune confused "science and religion" is not borne out by its quotations from his testimony. Those quotations reflect moral (not religious) judgments based on his scientific conclusion that the embryos were human beings. If he was right that the embryos were human beings then his moral judgment that their mother ought to be allowed to implant them was entirely consistent with the respect historically accorded to human beings by professional medical ethics and the law.

The court preferred the testimony of Dr King, the gynecologist who had created the embryos. It noted his testimony that "the currently accepted term" for the zygote immediately from cell division until the fourteenth day was "preembryo," that this was "the accepted period for preembryo research," and that at "about 14 days...the group of cells begins to differentiate in a process that permits the eventual development of the different body parts which will become an individual."[96] This evidence was misleading. "Preembryo" was not the "currently accepted term" for the embryo until the fourteenth day; the ethics of embryo research 20 years ago was then, as now, hotly contested; and the process of cell differentiation which permits the eventual development of the different body parts which will become an individual begins well before the fourteenth day. The court stated that Dr King's testimony was supported by the other expert witnesses and by the American Fertility Society, an organization of 10,000 physicians and scientists who specialize in problems of infertility. The court quoted the Society's report, *Ethical Considerations of the New Reproductive Technologies*, published in 1990. The report, observed the court, stated that at the eight-cell stage each blastomere, if separated, has the potential to develop into a complete adult and

---

[95] Ibid.
[96] Ibid para 34.

that at that stage "the developmental singleness of one person has not been established."[97] But this is a non sequitur. The fact that a worm may be divided to produce two worms does not mean that beforehand there was not a single worm. The fact that a cell may be taken from one animal and cloned to produce another does not mean that beforehand there was not a single animal. The court went on to quote the report's statement that by the thirty-two cell stage it is more like a multi-cellular entity "than a loose packet of identical cells."[98] But even at the eight-cell stage the embryonic human is a dynamic, self-organizing, and self-directed entity oriented toward further development, hardly a "loose packet of identical cells." The report continued that at the blastocyst stage cells form into inner and outer layers which will respectively form the placenta and the embryo and concluded: "Thus, the first cellular differentiation of the new generation relates to physiologic interaction with the mother, rather than to the establishment of the embryo itself. It is for this reason that it is appropriate to refer to the developing entity up to this point as a preembryo, rather than an embryo."[99] However, on the report's own description of this cell differentiation, it is concerned as much with the establishment of the body of the embryo as with the formation of the placenta, and the generation of the placenta by the embryo is an event concerned with the establishment and continuing development of the embryo in utero. Further, given that the formation of the placenta, like other stages of development, is programmed from conception, why should the appearance of that stage warrant a difference in classification based on when that stage is reached?[100] A few years after *Davis v Davis*, Professor Lee Silver, of the Department of Molecular Biology at Princeton and a prominent supporter of embryo research, wrote:

I'll let you in on a secret. The term pre-embryo has been embraced wholeheartedly by IVF practitioners for reasons that are political, not scientific. The new term is used to provide the illusion that there is something profoundly different between what we nonmedical biologists still call a six-day-old embryo and what we and everyone else call a sixteen-day-old embryo.

He added:

The term pre-embryo is useful in the political arena—where decisions are made about whether to allow early embryo (now called pre-embryo) experimentation—as well as in the confines of a doctor's office, where it can be used to allay moral

---

[97] Ibid para 37.
[98] Ibid para 38.
[99] Ibid para 40.
[100] Ibid.

concerns that might be expressed by IVF patients. "Don't worry," a doctor might say, "it's only pre-embryos we're manipulating or freezing. They won't turn into real human embryos until after we've put them back into your body".[101]

Notably, the Warnock Report, which recommended that research on embryos be permitted, used the standard term "embryo" throughout. So too does the HFEA 1990, which implemented the report's main recommendations. The Tennessee Supreme Court referred to neither.

In any event, as the court admitted, the distinction between "embryo" and "preembryo" was "not dispositive" of the case.[102] It deserved emphasis, it said, only because inaccuracy could lead to misanalysis. The court claimed that the trial judge had reasoned that if there was no distinction between embryos and pre-embryos, as Professor Lejeune testified, then Lejeune must also have been correct when he asserted that "human life begins at the moment of conception."[103] But why was the judge not correct? What relevant evidence had he failed to take into account, or what irrelevant evidence had he taken into account? Why was his finding of fact that the lives of the embryos began at conception and that they were human beings, mistaken? Instead of offering anything like a sufficient answer to that key question, the Supreme Court turned to the question of the legal status of the embryos. One of the fundamental questions posed by the case was, said the court, whether the "preembryos" were, in law "persons" or "property." It affirmed the Court of Appeal's ruling that they were not "persons" because the foetus in the womb was not so regarded either by state law or by federal law. The state's wrongful death statute did not allow recovery unless a viable foetus was first born alive. Its abortion law adopted the trimester framework laid down by the United States Supreme Court in *Roe*, a framework which indicated that "as embryos develop, they are accorded more respect than mere human cells because of their burgeoning potential for life."[104] Though the state's murder and assault statutes did protect the viable foetus, even a viable foetus could be aborted.[105] Nor were "preembryos" regarded as "persons" under federal law. In *Roe* the United States Supreme Court, after consideration of the United States Constitution, "relevant common law principles, and the lack of scientific consensus as to when life begins," concluded that the unborn have never been

---

[101] L Silver, *Remaking Eden: Cloning and Beyond in a Brave New World* (William Morrow, 1997) 39. See also R O'Rahilly and F Muller, *Human Embryology and Teratology* (3rd edn, Wiley-Liss, 2001) 88. See also n 133.
[102] *Davis v Davis* 842 SW 2d 588 (1992) para 42.
[103] Ibid.
[104] Ibid para 46.
[105] Ibid.

recognized "as persons in the whole sense." And although the United States Supreme Court recognized a compelling state interest in "potential life" after viability, that stage was far removed from that of the four-to-eight-cell "preembryos" in this case.[106] To classify "preembryos" as "persons" would, moreover, doubtless have the effect of outlawing IVF.[107]

The Tennessee Supreme Court's reasoning is problematic. To assume that the status of the embryo in vitro should be determined by precedents concerning its status in vivo, whether in relation to abortion or wrongful death, is, as we suggested earlier, to beg the question. The trial judge aptly observed that *Roe* related to the question of abortion, not the status of embryos in vitro, and held, rightly, that there was no public policy reason to prevent the continuing development of the common law to protect human embryos in vitro.[108] As Professor Robertson repeatedly observes in his paper, it does not follow that *Roe* should govern in the case of an embryo outside the woman's body. *Roe* establishes, he observes, a right of privacy to be free from unwanted physical intrusions or burdens, a right that trumps the state's compelling interest in the life of the foetus, at least until viability.[109] It does not establish a right to destroy the embryo if the woman's bodily integrity may otherwise be protected, or a right to destroy embryos in vitro if she refuses to have them implanted in her body.[110] He writes that the constitutionality of state laws preventing the destruction of in vitro embryos does not depend on the reversal of *Roe*: "*Roe* would not directly apply to state restrictions on external embryos that do not interfere with a woman's interest in bodily integrity. Under *Roe*, the state would be free to treat external embryos as persons or give as much protection to their potential life as it chooses...."[111] He also points out that in the later abortion case of *Webster v Reproductive Health Services*, five justices of the United States Supreme Court opined that the state has a compelling interest in protecting pre-natal life throughout pregnancy, not just from viability.[112]

The Tennessee Supreme Court was also mistaken in assuming that there were no statutory or common law precedents to guide it.[113] It therefore showed little understanding of the historical sweep of Anglo-American law toward increasing protection of the unborn child, not least

---

[106] Ibid para 48.
[107] Ibid para 49.
[108] (1989) 15 Family Law Reporter 2097, 2103.
[109] Robertson (n 55) 484–5, n 118.
[110] Ibid 487. See also ibid 456, n 50; 467.
[111] Ibid 499. See also ibid 499, n 162; 500.
[112] Ibid 485.
[113] *Davis v Davis* 842 SW 2d 588 (1992) para 22.

as a result of growing scientific understanding in the nineteenth century that human life began at conception, an understanding vastly enriched by twentieth-century discoveries about the intricate genetic code which controls the organization of the constitution and life of each human being from that point. And, despite the frustration of that trend in the context of abortion, where *Roe* and the Abortion Act have effectively elevated the woman's wish to divest herself of an unwanted pregnancy above the interest of the unborn child in continued survival, it does not follow that the trend should be frustrated in the context of IVF, where no pregnancy is involved. The embryo in vivo is growing inside a woman's body; the embryo in vitro is not. Nor does it follow that recognizing the personhood of the embryo in vitro would outlaw IVF, but it would require embryos so conceived to be treated as persons, not property. They would at least enjoy the most fundamental right enjoyed by persons: the right not to be intentionally destroyed.

The Tennessee Supreme Court noted that the Court of Appeal had, without explicitly holding that the embryos were "property," nevertheless awarded "joint custody" to Mary Sue and Junior Davis, citing *York v Jones* for the proposition that they shared "an interest" in the embryos.[114] The Supreme Court observed that that case involved a dispute between a married couple and a clinic in Virginia, which refused to send their frozen embryo to a clinic in California for implantation there. The federal district court assumed without deciding that the subject matter of the dispute was "property" and that the cryopreservation agreement between the Yorks and the clinic created a bailment relationship which obligated the clinic to return the subject matter of the bailment to the Yorks once the purpose of the bailment had come to an end.[115] The Supreme Court decided that the Court of Appeal had, by citing this case, but by failing precisely to define the "interest" that Mary Sue and Junior Davis had in the "preembryos," implied that it was a property interest.[116]

The Supreme Court observed that the "most helpful" discussion of the status of in vitro embryos was to be found in the ethical standards laid down by the American Fertility Society. The Society had canvassed three ethical positions. The first was that the embryo was a person. The second was that the embryo was like any other human tissue. The third and "most widely held" view was that the embryo merited "greater respect than other human tissue because of its potential to become a person and

---

[114] Ibid para 50. *York v Jones* 717 F Supp 421 (E D Va 1989).
[115] *Davis v Davis* 842 SW 2d 588 (1992) para 52.
[116] Ibid para 53.

because of its symbolic meaning for many people." It should not, however, be treated as a person "because it has not yet developed the features of personhood, is not yet established as developmentally individual, and may never realize its biologic potential."[117] The Society concluded that "pre-embryos" were entitled to "special respect"[118] and that "decision-making authority regarding preembryos should reside with the persons who have provided the gametes.... A person's liberty to procreate or to avoid procreation is directly involved in most decisions involving embryos."[119] Accordingly, the Supreme Court concluded that the "preembyos" were not "strictly speaking, either 'persons' or 'property,' but occupy an interim category that entitles them to special respect because of their potential for human life." Mary Sue and Junior David did, however, "have an interest in the nature of ownership, to the extent that they have decision-making authority concerning Disposition of the preembryos, within the scope of policy set by law."[120] What of situations where, as here, there was no agreement between the parties? The "essential dispute" was not where or how long to store the embryos "but whether the parties will become parents."[121] In resolving this dispute, the court invoked the "right of procreational autonomy" which was inherent in the "right to privacy" in both state and federal law.[122] The right was enjoyed by the gamete providers and the state's interest in "potential human life" was insufficient to justify an infringement on their procreational autonomy: state statutes revealed a policy decision to recognize that "persons born alive or capable of sustaining life ex utero have a higher status" than do foetuses in utero.[123] The state's abortion statute, adopting *Roe*'s trimester frame-work, which reflected a growing state interest as pregnancy developed, supported the conclusion that the state's interest in the four-to-eight-cell "preembryos" was "at best slight."[124] It added:

When weighed against the interests of the individuals and the burdens inherent in parenthood, the state's interest in the potential life of these preembryos is not sufficient to justify any infringement upon the freedom of these individuals to make their own decisions as to whether to allow a process to continue that may result in such a dramatic change to their lives as becoming parents.[125]

[117] Ibid para 57.
[118] Ibid para 60.
[119] Ibid para 61.
[120] Ibid para 63.
[121] Ibid para 73.
[122] Ibid para 90.
[123] Ibid para 100.
[124] Ibid para 101.
[125] Ibid.

Balancing the parties' interests, the Supreme Court held that the interest of Junior Davis in "avoiding parenthood" was greater than that of Mary Ann Davis in donating the embryos for implantation: "he would face a lifetime of wondering about his parental status or knowing about his parental status but having no control over it."[126]

The Supreme Court's analysis of the law was scarcely more convincing than its analysis of the scientific evidence. The court criticized the Court of Appeal for ruling that the couple had a property interest in the embryos, and for invoking *York v Jones*, but itself proceeded to rule that they had "an interest in the nature of ownership" in deciding the disposition of the embryos. What is a right to freeze, flatten, or alienate if not a property right? Moreover, the court again assumed that the legal status of the unborn child in the laboratory should be no greater than that of the unborn child in the womb, which does not follow. As the court itself stated: "None of the concerns about a woman's bodily integrity that have previously precluded men from controlling abortion decisions is applicable here."[127] Further, the ethical reasoning of the American Fertility Society quoted by the court and which it thought "most helpful" was flawed. First, why is the fact that an embryo may "never realize its biologic potential" morally (and legally) relevant? A newborn baby may never do so, but the law acknowledges that the baby is a person. Could it be argued that whereas an embryo in vivo has the ability to develop, the embryo in vitro does not, unless implanted? This argument, which confuses the ability to develop with the opportunity to develop, was answered in a report of the President's Council on Bioethics. In that report, members of the Council opposed to human cloning pointed out:

The fact that embryos have been created outside their natural environment—which is to say, outside the woman's body—and are therefore limited in their ability to realize their natural capacities, does not affect either the potential or the moral status of the beings themselves. A bird forced to live in a cage its entire life may never learn to fly. But this does not mean it is less of a bird, or that it lacks the immanent potentiality to fly on feathered wings. It means only that a caged bird—like an in vitro human embryo—has been deprived of its proper environment. There may, of course, be good human reasons to create embryos outside their natural environments—most obviously, to aid infertile couples. But doing so does not obliterate the moral status of the embryos themselves.[128]

---

[126] Ibid para 108.
[127] Ibid para 98 (footnote omitted).
[128] President's Council on Bioethics, *Human Cloning and Human Dignity* (2002) Ch 6.IV.A.

Second, if the Fertility Society's reference to "established as developmentally individual" refers to the possibility that early embryos may twin, why is this morally (and legally) relevant? As the same members of the President's Council observed:

There is the obvious rejoinder that if one locus of moral status can become two, its moral standing does not thereby diminish but rather increases. More specifically, the possibility of twinning does not rebut the individuality of the early embryo from its beginning. The fact that where "John" alone once was there are now both "John" and "Jim" does not call into question the presence of "John" at the outset. Hence, we need not doubt that even the earliest cloned embryo is an individual human organism in its germinal stage. Its capacity for twinning may simply be one of the characteristic capacities of an individual human organism at that particular stage of development, just as the capacity for crawling, walking, and running, or cooing, babbling, and speaking are capacities that are also unique to particular stages of human development. Alternatively, from a developmental science perspective, twinning may not turn out to be an intrinsic process within embryogenesis. Rather, it may be a response to a disruption of normal development from which the embryo recovers and then forms two. Twinning would thus be a testament to the resilience of self-regulation and compensatory repair within early life, not the lack of individuation in the early embryo. From this perspective, twinning is further testimony to the potency of the individual (in this case two) to fullness of form.[129]

Third, what are the "features of personhood" that the Fertility Society thought to be morally key, and why? Why is the *decisive* criterion of personhood not the one which accounts for the exhibition of *all* the features of personhood, namely the embryo's human nature? To quote the members of the President's Council again, the human embryo, whether resulting from natural conception or cloning:

is not just a 'clump of cells' but an integrated, self-developing whole, capable (if all goes well) of the continued organic development characteristic of human beings. To be sure, the embryo does not yet have, except in potential, the full range of characteristics that distinguish the human species from others, but one need not have those characteristics in evidence in order to belong to the species. And of course human beings at some other stages of development—early in life, late in life, at any stage of life if severely disabled—do not forfeit their humanity simply for want of these distinguishing characteristics. We may observe different points in the life story of any human being—a beginning filled mostly with potential, a zenith at which the organism is in full flower, a decline in which only a residue remains of what is most distinctively human. But none of these points is itself the

---

[129] Ibid.

human being. That being is, rather, an organism with a continuous history. From zygote to irreversible coma, each human life is a single personal history.[130]

They added:

attempts to ground the special respect owed to a maturing embryo in certain of its developmental features do not succeed. And the invoking of a "special respect" owed to nascent human life seems to have little or no operative meaning once one sees what those who take this position are willing to countenance.[131]

Furthermore:

Because the embryo's human and individual genetic identity is present from the start, nothing that happens later during the continuous development that follows—at fourteen days or any other time—is responsible for suddenly conferring a novel human individuality or identity. The scientific evidence suggests that the fourteen-day marker does not represent a biological event of moral significance; rather, changes that occur at fourteen days are merely the visibly evident culmination of more subtle changes that have taken place earlier and that are driving the organism toward maturity. Indeed, many advocates of cloning-for-biomedical-research implicitly recognize the arbitrariness of the fourteen-day line.[132]

In short, the trial judge's finding that the embryos were human beings was soundly based on scientific evidence adduced by one of the world's foremost experts on human genetics. His evidence confirmed and, with the benefit of modern genetic knowledge, elaborated upon what was known to nineteenth-century doctors when, not least in the United States, they successfully campaigned for the law to protect unborn human beings from conception. The Tennessee Supreme Court failed to give any cogent reason for rejecting what has been known to medical science for generations: that human life begins not at 14 days, or implantation, but at conception. It also overlooked the relevant legal precedents offered by both common and statute law from which it could have discerned the law's core historical purpose of protecting human life from that point, and could have seen *Roe* as an obvious aberration. Instead, the court was distracted by the politically motivated neologism "preembryo", by a questionable analogy with the status of the embryo in vivo post *Roe*, and by the flawed ethical reasoning of the American Fertility Society.[133] If

---

[130] Ibid.

[131] Ibid.

[132] Ibid.

[133] That Society is now called the American Society of Reproductive Medicine. Its website refers to the human "embryo" not "preembryo." See eg <https://www.asrm.org/topics/detail.aspx?id = 1278>. It is also noteworthy that the title and text of Professor Robertson's paper use "embryo." See Robertson (n 55) n 2.

the Supreme Court had affirmed the trial judge's finding of fact that the embryos were human beings, it is difficult to see how it could have failed to affirm his ruling that they were, in law, persons, instead of finding that they were in effect mere chattels. The Supreme Court therefore mischaracterized the "essential dispute" being "whether the parties will become parents."[134] On the facts as rightly found by trial judge in the light of the scientific evidence, they already were. At least the court recognized that the key question is whether the embryo in vitro is a human being. A future court may demonstrate a better grasp of the scientific evidence (and legal tradition).

B Evans v Amicus Healthcare Ltd

This English case was factually similar to *Davis v Davis*, involving a dispute between a couple, who had undergone IVF and who later separated, over their frozen embryos.[135] The applicant, Ms Evans, sought an order from the High Court authorizing the implantation of the embryos. Her former partner objected. The court looked to the statute governing the use of in vitro embryos for infertility treatment or for scientific research, the HFEA 1990. This Act broadly implemented the recommendations of the Warnock Report, not least by providing a comprehensive regulatory framework for IVF and the use of in vitro embryos. An important principle underlying the Act is the continuing consent of the gamete providers to the use of their embryo. By section 3(1), no person shall bring about the creation of an embryo, or keep or use an embryo, except in pursuance of a license, and section 12(c) makes compliance with Schedule 3 to the Act, which deals with consent, a condition of every license. An embryo may be implanted, stored, discarded, or used for research only with the consent of the gamete contributors. Paragraph 6(3) of Schedule 3 provides that an embryo created in vitro must not be used for any purpose unless there is an effective consent by each gamete provider to the use of the embryo for that purpose. Paragraph 1(1) provides that an "effective consent" is a consent under the Schedule which has not been withdrawn. Paragraph 8(2) provides that an embryo must not be kept in storage unless there is an effective consent by the gamete contributors. As Ms Evans' former partner did not consent to the continued storage of the embryos, or to their implantation, the judge

---

[134] See text at n 121.
[135] *Evans v Amicus Healthcare Ltd and others (Secretary of State for Health and another Intervening)* [2003] EWHC 2161 (Fam), [2005] Fam 1.

(Wall J, as he then was) held that the embryos could no longer be stored nor be implanted in Ms Evans.

What of the argument that the embryos were persons, and that they therefore enjoyed a right to life under Article 2 of the European Convention on Human Rights? Astonishingly, counsel for the applicant elected not to advance it. Instead, he conceded that "an embryo is not a human life,"[136] a concession which was described by the judge as "proper."[137] Counsel submitted instead that the embryo had a sufficiently "special status" to attract a "qualified" right to life, "a right consistent with his mother's wishes."[138] Wall J held, however, that counsel's concession was "fatal" to the engagement of Article 2.[139] The judge cited two authorities for the conclusion that the embryo in vitro was not protected by Article 2. The first was *Re F* in which the Court of Appeal held that there was no jurisdiction to make an unborn child a ward of court.[140] Wall J quoted from the judgment of Balcombe LJ in that case, who noted that in *Paton* the European Court of Human Rights had ruled that Article 2 applied to those already born and not to a foetus. The European Court had stated:

The "life" of the foetus is intimately connected with, and cannot be regarded in isolation from, the life of the pregnant woman. If article 2 were held to cover the foetus and its protection under this article were, in the absence of any express limitation, seen as absolute, an abortion would have to be considered as prohibited even where the continuance of the pregnancy would involve a serious risk to the life of the pregnant woman. This would mean that the "unborn life" of the foetus would be regarded as being of a higher value than the life of the pregnant woman. The "right to life" of a person already born would thus be considered as subject not only to the express limitations mentioned [in Article 2] but also to a further, implied limitation.[141]

Wall J also cited the judgment of Butler-Sloss LJ in *Re MB*, where the Court of Appeal upheld a pregnant woman's absolute right to refuse a Caesarean section.[142] Butler-Sloss LJ said: "The foetus up to the moment of birth does not have any separate interests capable of being taken into account when a court has to consider an application for a declaration in

---

[136] Ibid para 174.
[137] Ibid para 175.
[138] [2004] EWCA Civ 727, [2005] Fam 72, para 106 per Arden LJ in the Court of Appeal.
[139] [2003] EWHC 2161 (Fam), [2005] Fam 1, para 175.
[140] Ibid para 176. *Re F* [1988] Fam 122.
[141] [2003] EWHC 2161 (Fam), [2005] Fam 1, para 176. *Paton v United Kingdom* (1980) 3 EHRR 408.
[142] [2003] EWHC 2161 (Fam), [2005] Fam 1, para 177. *In re MB (Medical Treatment)* [1997] 2 FLR 426.

respect of a caesarean section operation."[143] Wall J stated that, unlike the foetus, the in vitro embryo exists outside the womb, where it is governed by the HFEA 1990. He observed:

There is no property in an embryo, but in contrast to a foetus, both gamete donors have an interest in, and rights over, the embryos they have created. Those rights are governed by the Act. The embryo, however, cannot be considered a person, or to have a "qualified" right to life.[144]

The introduction of Article 2 into the argument was, he thought, "an unhelpful diversion."[145]

The Court of Appeal gave the claimant leave to appeal on a number of grounds, but not on the ground that the embryos enjoyed even a "qualified" right to life under Article 2.[146] Thorpe and Sedley LJJ explained that this ground of appeal held no realistic prospect of success because *Re F* and *Re MB* established that a foetus prior to the moment of birth has no independent rights or interests.[147] They went on: "Thus even more clearly can there be no independent rights or interests in stored embryos."[148] They added that counsel was prepared to accept that a stored embryo would not be protected by Article 2 if both gamete providers wanted it destroyed, but the right to life could not be waived by its possessor, let alone by others. This, they said, illustrated the fallacy of invoking Article 2.[149] Arden LJ concurred that the embryo did not have a qualified right under Article 2. She observed: "We do not have any scientific detail and so I proceed on the basis that while an embryo has the potential to become a person it is not itself that person: further changes must take place."[150] *Re F* showed that a foetus did not have a right to life, so the claim of an embryo "must be weaker."[151] Moreover, the HFEA 1990 recognized no such right, whether absolute or qualified, because it provided that the embryo must be destroyed if either party withdrew consent to storage.[152] The court dismissed the appeal.

Ms Evans appealed to the European Court of Human Rights.[153] One of her grounds of appeal was that in requiring the embryos to be destroyed

---

[143] *In re MB (Medical Treatment)* [1997] 2 FLR 426, 444.
[144] *Evans v Amicus Healthcare and others (Secretary of State for Health and another Intervening)* [2003] EWHC 2161 (Fam), [2005] Fam 1, para 178.
[145] Ibid.
[146] [2004] EWCA Civ 727, [2005] Fam 72, 73 (CA).
[147] Ibid para 19.
[148] Ibid.
[149] Ibid.
[150] Ibid para 106.
[151] Ibid para 107.
[152] Ibid.
[153] *Evans v United Kingdom* (2006) 43 EHRR 21.

once her former partner withdrew his consent to their continued storage, English law violated their right to life under Article 2. Her argument failed. The Court noted that in *Vo v France*[154] it had held that in the absence of any European consensus on the scientific and legal definition of the beginning of life, the issue of when the right to life begins comes within the margin of appreciation which states should enjoy in this sphere and, as the English courts had made clear in the case before it, an embryo did not have independent rights or interests and could not claim, or have claimed on its behalf, a right to life under Article 2.[155] A further appeal to the Grand Chamber also failed.[156] The applicant did not pursue her complaint under Article 2 but the Grand Chamber affirmed the Court's rejection of that complaint for the reasons it had given.[157]

Evans is hardly a sound authority against the legal personhood of the in vitro embryo. First, unlike in *Davis v Davis*, the courts did not consider the scientific evidence bearing on the nature of the human embryo. As we have noted above (especially in Chapter 6), medical science has known since the early nineteenth century that human life begins at conception, which is why anti-abortion legislation from that era, in both England and the United States, punished the destruction of the embryonic human being from that point. More recently, the IVF pioneers Edwards and Steptoe have aptly described the early in vitro embryo as a "microscopic human being."[158] Yet we will recall that in the Court of Appeal in *Evans*, Arden LJ noted the absence of "any scientific detail" available to the court. She proceeded on the basis that while an embryo "has the potential to become a person it is not itself that person: further changes must take place."[159] But on what evidence did she base this key finding? And are they *qualitative* changes which are thought to convert the embryo from a non-personal being into a personal being (and, if so, what are they?) or rather only *quantitative* changes which reflect the different developmental stages through which a personal being grows? Her Ladyship seems to have confused *what kind* of a being the human embryo is with *what stage* of development it is at. As Professors George and Gómez-Lobo have explained:

The proximate, or immediately exercisable, capacity for mental functions is only the development of an underlying potentiality that the human being possesses

---

[154] (2005) 40 EHRR 12 at [82].

[155] (2006) 43 EHRR 21 para 46.

[156] *Evans v United Kingdom* (2008) 46 EHRR 34 para 56.

[157] Ibid para 355–6.

[158] R Edwards and P Steptoe, *A Matter of Life* (Sphere Books, 1981) 83.

[159] See text at n 150.

simply by virtue of the kind of entity it is. The capacities for reasoning, deliberating, and making choices are gradually developed, or brought toward maturation, through gestation, childhood, adolescence, and so on. But the difference between a being that deserves full moral respect and a being that does not (and can therefore legitimately be dismembered as a means of benefiting others) cannot consist only in the fact that, while both have some feature, one has more of it than the other. A mere quantitative difference (having more or less of the same feature, such as the development of a basic natural capacity) cannot by itself be a justificatory basis for treating different entities in radically different ways. Between the ovum and the approaching thousands of sperm, on the one hand, and the embryonic human being, on the other hand, there is a clear difference in kind. But between the embryonic human being and that same human being at any later stage of its maturation, there is only a difference in degree.[160]

Lord Denning, the former Master of the Rolls, demonstrated a grasp of this crucial point when he said in the House of Lords debate on the Warnock Report:

I would suggest that the only logical point at which the law could start is that the child, the human being, starts at the moment of conception and fertilisation. From that point onwards there is a gradual development in its environment. So I would hold—and I hope the judges would hold—that from that moment there is a living, human being which is entitled to protection just as much as the law protects a child.[161]

Second, not only did the courts in *Evans* lack scientific evidence, they lacked legal argument. Counsel for *Evans* conceded at first instance that the embryo did not enjoy a right to life under Article 2, a concession which Wall J rightly observed was "fatal." The Court of Appeal refused leave to appeal on this ground, noting that counsel's argument for a "qualified" right was fallacious.

Third, consideration of the rights of the in vitro embryo comprised only a fraction of the judgments at each level. In the judgment of the Chamber of the European Court, it occupied only one short paragraph in a judgment running to 77.[162] The judgments were concerned mainly with the compatibility of the 1990 Act with Article 8 and, to a lesser extent, Article 14.

---

[160] President's Council on Bioethics, *Human Cloning and Human Dignity: An Ethical Inquiry* (2002) Appendix, statement of Professor George (joined by Dr Gómez-Lobo) (emphasis in original). See generally R George and C Tollefsen, *Embryo: A Defense of Human Life* (2nd edn, The Witherspoon Institute, 2011); C Kaczor, *The Ethics of Abortion* (Routledge, 2011) Ch 6.

[161] *Hansard*, HL vol 456, cols 541, 542 (1983–4).

[162] (2006) 43 EHRR 21 para 46.

Fourth, none of the judgments showed any awareness of the historical purpose of English law of protecting human life from its beginning. No judge mentioned that for a woman to procure the abortion of her embryo from conception (or at least, according to the unreliable ruling in *Smeaton*, from implantation[163]) renders her liable to life imprisonment under section 58 of the OAPA 1861.

Fifth, the judgments all seemed to assume, perhaps aided by that lack of awareness, that the legal status of the embryo in vitro could simply be read off from the legal status of the embryo in vivo, as decided in cases concerning conflict or potential conflict with the mother. *Re F*, *Re MB*, *Paton*, and *Vo* were all decided in that context. To assume that if the embryo in vivo in such a context has no right to life then neither has the embryo in vitro in an entirely different context, is simply to beg the question. In any event, the reasons given by the European Court in *Paton* for denying a right to life to the embryo in vivo were unsound. We will recall that the Court reasoned that if Article 2 protected the foetus, abortion would have to be considered as prohibited even where the continuance of the pregnancy would involve a serious risk to the life of the pregnant woman, and that this would accord the foetus a higher value than the mother.[164] Neither conclusion follows. First, to prohibit the intentional killing of A to save B, on the ground that both have a right to life, does not accord A a higher value than B. Second, Article 2 prohibits the intentional deprivation of life. An intention to remove an unborn child where the continuation of the pregnancy would involve a serious risk to the mother's life need involve no intention to deprive the unborn child of life. Such cases could be justified by the principle of double effect. Even if the risk of death of the unborn child were foreseen, exposing the child to that risk in order to save the life of its mother could be justified (especially if both would otherwise die), at least if there is no reasonable alternative. And, to repeat, the Court was concerned with a scenario where the life of the foetus was "intimately connected with, and cannot be regarded in isolation from, the life of the pregnant woman."[165] This is not so with the embryo in vitro. The embryo in vivo is located inside its mother; its interests may conflict with those of the mother; and a resolution of such a conflict may raise the problem of controlling the mother. None of these factors, which have been key to the cases denying the in vivo embryo legal

[163] See Ch 6.
[164] See text at n 141.
[165] Ibid.

personality, applies to the embryo in vitro. The cases are clearly distinguishable.

V CONCLUSION

As Kennedy and Grubb rightly recognized, the human embryo in vitro must be categorized in law as either a person or as a chattel. The arguments in favor of some third category, such as wild animals, are unconvincing. The fact that a rat in the wild is not yet property does not alter the fact that that property is the appropriate category once it is reduced into possession. Nor does the fact that the criminal law may prohibit a rat owner from mistreating the creature convert it from chattel to person. Nor does the fact that a scientist wishing to research on a rat may need a license to do so, and that the license may stipulate that certain conditions be observed, alter the rat's status as property. If the law allows the human in vitro embryo to be subjected to destructive experimentation then the law is clearly treating the in vitro embryo like a lab rat. No amount of talk of "special respect" can disguise this fact. How is a being accorded "respect," let alone "special" respect, by being flattened for research, frozen for later research, or by being discarded as "surplus to requirements"?[166] As Kennedy and Grubb pertinently enquire:

What special status does an embryo have if it may be the subject of research during the first fourteen days ... and thereafter destroyed? What is ownership if it is not the right to control, including to dispose of by sale, or otherwise? ... Why require the "informed consent" of the donors unless to do otherwise would be to infringe some property right of theirs?[167]

The question of the in vitro embryo's legal status has too often been evaded. Just as the Warnock Report fudged the question of the embryonic human's moral status by going "straight to the question of *how it is right to treat the embryo*,"[168] so too the House of Lords evaded the question of its legal status by defeating an amendment to the HFEA 1990 which would have classified it as either a person or as a chattel.[169] This chapter has argued that, even when the question has been addressed, most

---

[166] Since the HFEA 1990 came into force, over three million human embryos have been produced in vitro in the UK, of whom almost half have been discarded. See <http://services.parliament.uk/hansard/Lords/bydate/20110720/writtenanswers/part025.html>.

[167] KGI 682–3.

[168] *Report of the Committee of Inquiry into Human Fertilisation and Embryology* (Cmnd 9314, 1984) para 11.9 (emphasis in original).

[169] *Hansard*, HL vol 515, col 748 (1989–90).

commentators,[170] courts, and legislators have failed to appreciate the strength of the case for recognizing the personhood of the human embryo in vitro. Even in the earliest stages we are, as Edwards and Steptoe put it, "microscopic human beings," requiring nothing to develop ourselves through the various stages of our lives—embryonic, foetal, infant, child, adolescent, and adult—except a hospitable environment. By categorizing the in vitro embryo as a person, the law would be promoting the same protective purpose which has historically informed the Anglo-American legal tradition. By failing to do so, and by treating the embryo as property which may be destroyed or discarded, it frustrates that purpose.

Largely because they have overlooked the key significance of the historical protection of the unborn child in Anglo-American criminal law, most commentators and courts have tended to make two questionable assumptions. The first is that the relevant law is civil, not criminal. However, it does not follow that because the civil law denies recovery to a child who is not born alive, an unborn child in vitro is not a legal person. There may be many reasons, such as the desirability of certainty in relation to the disposition of property, for the civil law to require proof of live birth before recognizing a cause of action and granting a remedy. It does not follow that having a right of action in the civil law is a prerequisite to having a right to protection by the criminal law.

The second questionable assumption is that because it is now no longer a crime to procure abortion in many cases, as a result of the Abortion Act 1967 in England and *Roe* in the United States, it cannot be a crime to destroy the embryo in vitro. But it does not follow that because the law allows a woman (in certain circumstances) to terminate the embryo inside her body, it allows her to terminate the embryo outside her body. Whatever arguments may be used to justify abortion, whether the argument that the presence of the embryo threatens her life (an argument long accepted by the common law) or, more radically, that a woman has "a right to control her own body" (which of course means a right to control the embryo's body), neither applies to the embryo outside her body. We will recall from Professor Finnis' memorandum that whatever pragmatic reasons the criminal law may historically have had for not punishing the destruction of the embryo in vivo as homicide, those reasons have no application to the embryo in vitro. And, as Professor Robertson agrees,[171]

---

[170] Cf EW Keyserlingk, *The Unborn Child's Right to Prenatal Care* (Quebec Research Centre for Private and Comparative Law, 1984) for an argument in favor of legal personhood for the unborn child.

[171] See text at nn 109–12.

Roe does not prevent a state from legislating to protect the embryo in vitro as a person, as indeed the state of Louisiana has done.[172]

Misled by these two questionable assumptions, commentators, courts, and legislators have too often failed to appreciate the strength of the case for the personhood of the in vitro embryo and have tended to categorize the embryo as (or as akin to) a chattel. As we noted above,[173] there is a legal precedent for treating human beings like chattels. It is not one which any civilized society should wish to follow.

---

[172] LA-RS 9 §121–133 (1986). See <http://biotech.law.lsu.edu/cases/la/health/embryo_rs. htm>. LA-RS 9 §123 provides: "An in vitro fertilized human ovum exists as a juridical person until such time as the in vitro fertilized ovum is implanted in the womb; or at any other time when rights attach to an unborn child in accordance with law."

[173] See text at n 60.

Part Three
The End(ing) of Life

CHAPTER 9

THE EUTHANASIA DEBATE IN THE
HOUSE OF LORDS

I INTRODUCTION

Few, if any, legislative bodies can claim to have debated voluntary, active euthanasia and/or physician-assisted suicide (VAE/PAS) over so many years, and in such depth, and drawing on such a wide range of expertise, as the House of Lords. The House first considered the issue three quarters of a century ago when a "Voluntary Euthanasia (Legalisation) Bill" was introduced by Lord Ponsonby.[1] In 1969 another Bill was introduced by Lord Raglan.[2] In 1993 the House established a Select Committee, chaired by Lord Walton, which considered, in depth, the case for decriminalizing VAE/PAS. In its valuable report, published in 1994, the Walton Committee unanimously rejected that case. The Committee grounded its rejection in both principle and prudence. It concluded that the prohibition of intentional killing was the "cornerstone of law and of social relationships" which "protects each one of us impartially, embodying the belief that all are equal."[3] It also concluded that it would be "next to impossible to ensure that all acts of euthanasia were truly voluntary, and that any liberalization of the law was not abused."[4] The Committee was "also concerned that vulnerable people—the elderly, lonely, sick, or distressed—would feel pressure, whether real or imagined, to request early death."[5] In arriving at its conclusions, the Committee took full account of the experience of the Netherlands, where VAE and PAS have been legally permitted and widely practiced since 1984. To assist its deliberations, the Committee sent a delegation there. In the debate on the report in the

---

[1] *Hansard*, HL vol 103, cols 465–506 (1 December 1936).
[2] *Hansard*, HL vol 300, cols 1143–254 (25 March 1969).
[3] *Report of the Select Committee on Medical Ethics* (HL Paper 21-I of 1993–4) para 237.
[4] Ibid para 238.
[5] Ibid para 239.

House of Lords, Lord Walton commented that the delegation had returned "feeling uncomfortable, especially in the light of evidence indicating that non-voluntary euthanasia... was commonly performed."[6] He added that it was "particularly uncomfortable"[7] about a case which involved the prosecution of a doctor for assisting a woman, who was grieving at the loss of her sons, to commit suicide. The Dutch Supreme Court had held that such suffering, albeit purely mental, could justify VAE/PAS. Another member of the Select Committee, Lord Meston, also commented unfavorably on the Dutch experience. He said that the evidence was "not encouraging" and that there appeared to be a gap between theory and practice. He said: "it did not seem possible to find any other place beyond the existing law for a firm foothold on an otherwise slippery slope."[8]

In 2004 Lord Joffe introduced his Bill on Assisted Dying for the Terminally Ill, which sought to permit PAS for the terminally ill. The Bill was given a second reading and referred to a Select Committee, chaired by Lord Mackay, a former Lord Chancellor. The Committee produced its report ("the Mackay Report") in April 2005. The following November Lord Joffe introduced a revised Bill.[9] The report was accompanied by two volumes of evidence, much of which concerned the experience of VAE/PAS in the Netherlands and of PAS in the US state of Oregon. This chapter assesses the Mackay Report's contribution to the VAE/PAS debate, not least in relation to the useful evidence it gleaned from the Netherlands and Oregon.

II THE MACKAY REPORT

The Report stated that it aimed to summarize, in as balanced a manner as possible, the evidence the Committee received on both the principles underlying the Joffe Bill and on the practical implications such legislation

---

[6] *Hansard*, HL vol 554, col 1346 (1993–4).

[7] Ibid.

[8] Ibid col 1398.

[9] The revised Bill is available at <http://www.publications.parliament.uk/pa/ld200506/ldbills/036/06036.i.html>. The Mackay Report (HL Paper 86 I), together with its substantial volume of oral and written evidence (Paper 86 II) and with its slighter volume of selected individual submissions (Paper 86 III), is available at <http://www.publications.parliament.uk/pa/ld/ldasdy.htm>. References to the report's "volume of evidence" will relate to Paper 86 II. References to volume I ("the Report") will take the form "MI paragraph number." References to volume II (the evidence) will take the form "MII page number" when the citation refers to written evidence submitted by witnesses who testified, and "MII page number question number (Q)" when the citation refers to an oral question or answer to a question.

would have, and to draw the attention of the House to a number of key issues arising from this which seemed to be pertinent to the consideration of any future Bill.[10] Producing a report on such a complex issue is an unenviable task involving as it typically does the sifting of a mountain of often conflicting written and oral evidence. Moreover, in addition to conflicts in the evidence submitted, there may also be conflicts among Committee members about the proper interpretation and weight to be placed on that evidence. It is no secret that the final report may be influenced by political compromise. It is therefore important to read not only volume I, the relatively brief Report, but also volume II, the much more substantial volume of oral and written evidence tendered to the Committee, as well as other evidence.

In the debate on the Report in the House of Lords in October 2005, both the Report and its chairman attracted general praise.[11] The Report can certainly boast a number of strengths, such as its analysis of two of the major arguments for relaxation of the law: the allegedly common practice of VAE/PAS and the allegedly popular support for relaxation of the law. The Committee usefully commissioned a review of opinion surveys over the preceding 10 to 20 years. It also solicited views from anyone who wished to write in and by the end of September 2004 it had received over 14,000 letters and emails and some 83,000 cards or emails which formed part of organized petitions.[12] Interestingly, the expressions of opinion it received were fairly evenly divided. Of those who sent individual letters or emails, 50.6 per cent supported the Bill, with the remainder opposed. The balance of opinion was broadly the same if the other communications were included.[13] As for the commissioned review of opinion surveys, the Report concluded that the research carried out hitherto into public and public health sector attitudes to the legalization of euthanasia was limited in value and could not be accepted at face value as an authentic account of opinion in the United Kingdom.[14] The Report continued that this was particularly the case with regard to the attitudes of the general public, whose views on euthanasia were obscured by a lack of information and by the lack of opportunity to reflect in an informed way upon the implications of any change in the law for themselves and for society. Polls reflected a "knee-jerk" reaction to the simple options they

---

[10] MI para 268.
[11] *Hansard*, HL vol 674, col 12 (2005).
[12] MI para 216.
[13] Ibid para 231.
[14] Ibid para 232.

offered and did not form a very useful guide to public opinion as support for legislative change.[15]

The Report's examination of the current incidence of illegal life-shortening by doctors was also illuminating. Referring to studies allegedly showing a significant incidence, the Report concluded that "it would be unsafe for us to assume that there has been no exaggeration or misunderstanding in any of these surveys," such as a confusion between intentional and merely foreseen life-shortening.[16] The Committee concluded that, bearing in mind a number of such factors, "we would be surprised if covert euthanasia were being practised on anything like the scale which some of these surveys suggest."[17] The Committee's skepticism has been borne out by two subsequent surveys of end-of-life decision-making, carried out by Professor Clive Seale. In 2006 Seale reported that the proportion of deaths in the United Kingdom from VAE, PAS, and NVAE (non-voluntary active euthanasia—the euthanasia of incompetent patients) was "extremely low" and that this finding suggested a culture of decision-making informed by a philosophy of palliative care. He also found that only 4.6 per cent of doctors thought that the existing law had inhibited or interfered with their preferred management of patients, and that only 2.6 per cent thought that relaxing the law would have facilitated management.[18] In 2009 a second survey by Seale concluded that "Euthanasia, physician-assisted suicide and the ending of life without an explicit patient request . . . are rare or non-existent at both time points . . . ."[19] He also found "non-treatment decisions . . . and double effect measures . . . to be much less common than suggested in earlier estimates, rarely involving intent to end life or being judged to have shortened life by more than a day."[20]

There were, then, informed insights in the Mackay Report. Whether the Report succeeded in its aim of providing a balanced summary of all the relevant evidence is, however, less clear. This is essentially because, in gathering evidence about the experience of laws permitting VAE and PAS in the Netherlands and PAS in Oregon—a centerpiece of the Report—the Committee relied very largely on the testimony of those who defend those laws. The Report's account of the law and practice in those jurisdictions

---

[15] Ibid.

[16] Ibid para 238.

[17] Ibid para 239.

[18] C Seale, "National survey of end-of-life decisions made by UK medical practitioners" (2006) 20 Palliative Medicine 3, 6–8.

[19] C Seale, "End-of-life decisions in the UK involving medical practitioners" (2009) 23 Palliative Medicine 198, 201.

[20] Ibid 198.

tended, therefore, to lack balance. As an analysis of volume II of the Report (the volume of oral and written evidence) indicates, critics of the laws were outnumbered more than four to one.[21] The Report suffers from a corresponding imbalance. This source of imbalance is, moreover, compounded by another. Some disturbing evidence which was brought to the Committee's attention about the Netherlands and Oregon, often but not always by critics, was omitted from the Report.[22] Even so, as we shall now see, the evidence helpfully elicited by the Committee indicated that in neither the Netherlands nor in Oregon has the law succeeded in ensuring effective control. By "effective" is meant sufficient to achieve the degree of control and protection that is warranted by the importance of the rights and interests to be protected, and that has been regularly accepted by proponents of these laws (and of proposed measures like them) to be desirable and asserted by them to be attainable by virtue of the safeguards stipulated in the laws themselves.

III THE NETHERLANDS

The long experience of the Netherlands is central to the ongoing debate about whether VAE/PAS in the sort of "hard cases" typically portrayed by campaigners could (even if those cases were morally unproblematic) be subjected to effective control. To emphasize, "effective" means evening the degree of control and protection that is warranted by the importance of the rights and interests to be protected and that has been regularly accepted by proponents of VAE/PAS to be desirable and asserted by them to be attainable in virtue of the legal safeguards they propose. Whereas the law allowing PAS in Oregon has been in operation since only 1997, Dutch law has permitted VAE/PAS since 1984. Again, the Dutch experience has generated much more literature and data. The Dutch have long claimed that their regulatory regime has effectively controlled the

---

[21] 23 to 4 in the Netherlands (MII 390–439; 451–87; 440–50) and 24 to 5 in Oregon (MII 255–328; 344–61; 329–43; 593–602).

[22] Although the Report's imbalance in its representation of practice abroad is a focus of this chapter, apparent lack of balance in at least one other respect should not be overlooked: the Report's identification of "key" issues. All of the issues identified as "key" by the Report (MI paras 268–9) concerned the scope of possible legislation permitting VAE/PAS. The Report did not appear to consider as a key issue the question whether such legislation would be, irrespective of its scope, defensible in principle, even though this might well be thought key and was an issue on which the Committee properly solicited much evidence. It is also worth mentioning that the first chapter of the Report claimed that the Report avoided euphemistic terminology such as "assisted dying": ibid para 18. That phrase was, however, used five times in that chapter: ibid paras 1, 5, 7, 9, 10. Ms Vicky Robinson, a nurse consultant in palliative care, testified that "assisting dying" was a misnomer and offensive to those who provided care to the dying: MII 151 Q354.

practice of VAE/PAS and has forestalled any slide down the "slippery slope." Their claim is, however, not easy to square with the evidence, not least the data generated by their four valuable national surveys of medical practice at the end of life, published in 1991, 1996, 2003, and 2007.[23]

A Legalization in 1984

It merits mention, as a preliminary matter, that the Mackay Report described the Dutch Termination of Life on Request and Assisted Suicide (Review Procedures) Act, which came into force in 2002, as "legalizing" VAE/PAS, and quotes a witness (from the Dutch Voluntary Euthanasia Society) that under the previous law it was "a criminal act".[24] This is misleading. In 1984 the Dutch Supreme Court held that VAE/PAS were in certain circumstances justified by the defense of necessity. In other words, in those circumstances VAE/PAS were lawful: it was not that the doctor was merely excused punishment for what remained a criminal act. Consequently, the Dutch legislation was essentially a change of form rather than substance. As the Royal Dutch Medical Association (KNMG) told the Committee, the change effected by the statute was "symbolic."[25]

B A voluntary and carefully considered request?

The Dutch law requires a "voluntary and carefully considered" request (often called an "explicit request") from the patient. How voluntary and carefully considered are requests in reality?

In a key statement against the Joffe Bill, the Royal College of Psychiatrists observed in an important statement in 2006 that studies of the terminally ill had clearly shown that depression is strongly associated with the desire for a hastened death, including VAE/PAS, and that once a patients' depression is effectively treated, 98–99 per cent change their mind about wanting to die. It also cautioned:

---

[23] PJ van der Maas et al., *Medische beslissingen rond het levenseinde. Het onderzoek voor de Commissie onderzoek medische praktijk inzake euthanasia* (SDU Uitgeverij Plantijnstraat, 1991); G van der Wal et al., *Euthanasie en andere medische beslissingen rond het levenseinde. De praktijk en de meldingsprocedure* (SDU Uitgevers, 1996); G van der Wal et al., *Medische besluitvorming aan het einde van het leven* (De Tijdstroom, 2003); B Onwuteaka-Philipsen et al., *Evaluatie Wet toetsing levensbeeindiging op verzoek en hulp bij zelfdoding* (ZonMW, 2007) ("First," "second," "third," and "fourth" surveys respectively.) For an analysis of the first two surveys see J Keown, *Euthanasia, Ethics and Public Policy* (2002) ("Keown") Chs 9–12. For an analysis of the third see R Fenigsen, "Dutch Euthanasia: the new government ordered survey" (2004) 20 Issues in Law and Medicine 73.

[24] MI para 166.

[25] MII 392.

Many doctors do not recognise depression or know how to assess for its presence in terminally ill patients ... Even when recognized, doctors often take the view that "understandable depression" cannot be treated, does not count or is in some way not real depression.[26]

Only three per cent of patients accessing VAE/PAS are referred for psychiatric evaluation in the Netherlands.[27] This clearly raises questions about the extent to which the requests made by the remaining 97 per cent are voluntary and carefully considered.

C The logical slide from VAE to NVAE

As we shall see, the Dutch experience confirms not only the *practical* difficulty of ensuring compliance with guidelines—the confidential nature of the doctor–patient relationship resists independent supervision and control—but also the *logical* slippery slope from VAE to NVAE. The fact that many requests for VAE/PAS are refused in the Netherlands confirms that it is the doctor who decides whether requests are granted. As a Dutch witness explained to the Select Committee: "It is ... the exclusive competence of the doctor, and the doctor only, to decide whether or not he will terminate a patient's life on request."[28] And the doctor surely grants requests in the light of whether, in his or her judgment, death would benefit the patient. But, if the doctor can make this judgment in relation to a patient who can ask for euthanasia, why cannot the doctor make the same judgment in relation to a patient who is incompetent? Why should incompetent patients be denied the "benefit" of death merely because they cannot request it? Is it not the duty of doctors to act in the best interests of all their patients, competent and incompetent? There is, then, a logical slippery slope from VAE to NVAE. This is illustrated by the fact that prominent philosophers who support VAE, such as Professors John Harris and Jonathan Glover (both of whom appeared before the Select Committee[29]), generally also support NVAE.[30]

---

[26] Statement from the Royal College of Psychiatrists on Physician-Assisted Suicide (2006) para 2.4. The guidance is under review.

[27] J Griffiths et al., *Euthanasia and Law in Europe* (Hart Publishing, 2008) 174 ("Griffiths II").

[28] MII 433 Q1439.

[29] MII 12; 32.

[30] J Harris, *The Value of Life* (Routledge & Kegan Paul, 1985); J Glover, *Causing Death and Saving Lives* (Penguin, 1990). For an attempted refutation of the argument see H Lillehammer, "Voluntary Euthanasia and the Logical Slippery Slope Argument" (2002) 61(3) CLJ 545. He argues that the defender of VAE can claim that a request by and benefit to the patient are individually necessary and jointly sufficient conditions for VAE: ibid 548. He does not explain why benefit to an incompetent patient would not by itself be sufficient. Even if the presence of a request were a justification for VAE, its absence would not be a reason against NVAE. See DA Jones, "Is there a Logical Slippery

The Chief Executive of the Dutch Voluntary Euthanasia Society assured the Committee that: "No doctor in The Netherlands—even if the whole family asks for it and everyone sees that there is hopeless and unbearable suffering—will ever terminate a life, because there is no request."[31] The reality is, however, that doctors have ended the lives of thousands of patients without request. The Mackay Report noted[32] the stark statistic, contained in the first three surveys which had by then been published, that every year in the Netherlands lethal injections were administered to around 1000 patients without an explicit request. The Report quoted a witness from the Dutch Ministry of Health who testified that about half of these patients were incompetent, "25 per cent are people who could have made a request but did not (so we are wondering about those), 15 per cent are newborn babies, and 10 per cent are other categories."[33] The legal requirement of an explicit request was, then, ignored in around 1000 cases per year, in 250 of which (those about whom, some 15 years after they were first uncovered, the Dutch were still "wondering") the patient was either wholly or partly competent. The fourth survey, published in 2007, indicated that the number of cases had fallen to around 550, but each case remains a violation of the requirement of a voluntary request and, in Dutch law, murder.[34] Moreover, Dutch law has changed to permit NVAE in certain circumstances. The Mackay Report omitted to mention[35] that in 1996 two courts of appeal in the Netherlands held it lawful to administer lethal injections to disabled babies in certain circumstances.[36] This aspect of Dutch euthanasia, among others, drew criticism from the United Nations Human Rights Committee in 2001.[37] Notwithstanding this criticism, in 2005 the NVAE of newborn babies was approved by the Dutch Paediatric Society and a protocol (referred to as the "Groningen protocol" after the hospital where it was formulated) was approved by the Dutch prosecution service to allow doctors to report

Slope from Voluntary to Nonvoluntary Euthanasia?' (2011) 21(4) Journal of the Kennedy Institute of Ethics 379 .

[31] MII 459 Q1566.
[32] MI para 178.
[33] Ibid.
[34] Griffiths II 154, Table 5.1; 180.
[35] Even though it was drawn to the Committee's attention: MII 411 Q1287.
[36] H Jochemsen, "Dutch Court Decisions on Nonvoluntary Euthanasia Critically Reviewed" (1998) 13(4) Issues in Law & Medicine 447; Keown 119–20.
[37] See <http://www.unhchr.ch/tbs/doc.nsf/(Symbol)/CCPR.CO.72.NET.En?Opendocument> paras 5–6. This criticism was drawn to the Mackay Committee's attention (MII 393) but is not mentioned in its Report.

such cases of NVAE without being prosecuted.[38] The slide from VAE to NVAE is hardly surprising. This is not only because of the logical link between VAE and NVAE but also because, since VAE became lawful in 1984, important figures in the Dutch establishment have openly expressed approval of NVAE. For example, the first survey to disclose the 1000 cases (published in 1991) was commissioned by a government committee of inquiry (known as the Remmelink committee, after its chairman). This committee, far from condemning the cases of NVAE, condoned them. Describing them as "care for the dying," it concluded that ending life in these cases was justified because of the patient's "unbearable suffering."[39] Also endorsing NVAE, the lead authors of the survey, Professor van der Maas et al., have candidly written:

[Is] it not true that once one accepts [voluntary] euthanasia and assisted suicide, the principle of universalizability forces one to accept termination of life without explicit request, at least in some circumstances, as well? In our view the answer to this question must be affirmative.[40]

Mackay omits a further disturbing piece of evidence relating to the 1000 cases. The evidence was drawn to the Select Committee's attention in oral testimony by Professor Finnis. Drawing on a paper by Dutch doctor Richard Fenigsen, which critically analyzes the third Dutch survey, published in 2003, Professor Finnis testified that page 201 of this survey repeated the "eye-opening assertion" made in the second survey, published in 1996, that:

it is the patient who is now responsible in the Netherlands for avoiding termination of his life; if he does not wish to be killed by his doctor then he must state it clearly orally and in writing, well in advance.[41]

Challenging this evidence, Lord Joffe replied: "We took this back and referred it back to the people who prepared the report and they said they had never stated this and on page 201 I cannot find anything like this. So perhaps you could explore that . . . ."[42] Professor Finnis duly supplied the

    [38] E Verhagen and P Sauer, "The Groningen Protocol—Euthanasia in Severely Ill Newborns" (2005) 352 New England Journal of Medicine 959. A Select Committee member's observation that there had been talk about a protocol for neonatal euthanasia was met with a misleading response from a Dutch witness that the protocol concerned palliative care and the withdrawal of futile treatment: MII 484–5 Q1737–41.
    [39] Griffiths II 180, n 101; *Medische beslissingen rond het levenseinde. Rapport van de Commissie onderzoek medische praktijk inzake euthanasie* (1991).
    [40] JJM van Delden et al., "The Remmelink Study: Two Years Later" (1993) 23(6) Hastings Center Report 24, 25.
    [41] MII 554 Q1973. R Fenigsen, "Dutch Enthanasia: The New Government Ordered Study" (2004) 20 (1) Issues in Law and Medicine 73, 75.
    [42] MII 563 Q2009.

Committee with a copy of the relevant passages in the second and third surveys, together with a translation of those passages. The passage referred to on page 201 of the third survey reads:

Due consideration should be give to the question how termination of life without explicit request can be prevented. It should be the responsibility of the patients, (their) next of kin, the doctors, the nurses, and the management, to clarify, well in advance, orally and in writing what are the wishes of the patient concerning the end of his life; for example, as a statement of will or as advance care planning.[43]

Finnis' revelation was indeed "eye-opening" and clearly raises serious questions, yet it was omitted from the Mackay Report.[44] Finally, the Report also omitted to note, first, the rarity of prosecutions of doctors for performing NVAE and, second, the striking leniency of punishments imposed when doctors have, even more rarely, been convicted of murder or assisted suicide. As Professor John Griffiths, a law professor in the Netherlands (and defender of the Dutch experience) noted in 1998, the Dutch regulatory system seemed to be "all bark and no bite."[45] A graphic illustration of the leniency of the system was provided by the conviction of Dr Wilfred van Oijen for the murder of one of his patients, a comatose, dying, 84-year-old woman. Both her daughters had urged the doctor to end her life but the patient had said she did not want to die. Nevertheless, van Oijen administered a lethal injection. He did not seek a second opinion and he reported the cause of death as natural. He was convicted of murder but his conviction attracted no punishment. The court stated that he had made an "error of judgment" and had acted "honourably and according to his conscience" in what he considered the interests of his patient. The KNMG defended his actions as exhibiting "complete integrity." Van Oijen was also convicted of having reported the case as death by natural causes, for which he received a suspended fine.[46] On appeal the court affirmed the convictions and for both offenses imposed a sentence of one week's imprisonment, suspended for two years. The KNMG called for doctors

---

[43] G van der Wal et al., *Medische besluitvorming aan het einde van het leven* (De Tijdstroom, 2003) 201 (lines 22–27) translated by Dr Richard Fenigsen. The Dutch reads: "Het verdient overweging om na te gaan op welke wijze levensbeeindigend handelen zonder uitdrukkelijk verzoek kan worden voorkomen. Hier ligt een veraantwoordelijkheid voor patienten, naasten, artsen, verpleging en management, om vroegtijdig, mondeling en schriftelijk, duidelijkheid te creeren over de wensen van de patient met betrekking tot diens levenseinde, bijvoorbeeld door middel van wilsverklaringen en advance care planning."

[44] Perhaps the Report's failure to explore the Dutch slide from VAE to NVAE is not accidental. One Dutch witness, when asked about NVAE, replied: "We should leave this out, because you explicitly said that we would be talking about competent people.": MII 416 Q1311.

[45] J Griffiths et al., *Euthanasia and Law in the Netherlands* (Amsterdam University Press, 1998) 268. ("Griffiths I").

[46] T Sheldon, "Dutch GP found guilty of murder faces no penalty" (2001) BMJ 509.

who ended patients' lives without request to be allowed to report their actions and have them judged outside courts of law.[47] On further appeal, the Supreme Court affirmed van Oijen's convictions, noting that his patient was in a coma and was not suffering unbearably.[48] He continued to practice and his appearance before a medical disciplinary board resulted in only a warning.[49]

In 2008 Griffiths et al. discussed the continuing trend in Dutch law toward endorsement of NVAE. Commenting on the courts' approval of infanticide, they wrote:

The applicable norms in the Netherlands have assuredly changed in the direction of open acceptance of the legitimacy of termination of life of severely defective newborn babies.... [T]he influence on these changes of the way euthanasia had earlier been legalised and regulated is obvious. In this sense, one might speak of a normative slippery slope.[50]

Of the van Oijen case they observed: "the Supreme Court ruled that the justification of necessity in principle can be available in a case of ending the life of a dying patient without the patient's request...."[51] The courts are, then, indicating that the same defense, necessity, which they invoked to justify VAE, can also justify NVAE in the case of disabled babies and comatose adults. This is the logical slippery slope argument in action. Griffiths et al. forecast:

If one may venture a prediction, it would be this: the idea of an "inhumane death" will, in one form or another, come increasingly to be accepted not only as a legitimate (prospective) reason for requesting euthanasia but as a justification for "help in dying" [NVAE]...[52]

They reasonably suggested, in the light of these developments, that Dutch law is slowly but steadily moving in the direction of explicit recognition of a doctor's duty to ensure that his or her patient dies a "humane" or "dignified" death.[53] The ease with which such an arbitrary notion could be extended to vulnerable groups, including the elderly, the demented, and the disabled, scarcely needs emphasis.

---

[47] T Sheldon, "Court upholds murder verdict on doctor who ended woman's life" (2003) BMJ 1351.

[48] T Sheldon, "Two test cases in Holland clarify law on murder and palliative care" (2004) BMJ 1206.

[49] Ibid.

[50] Griffiths II 252.

[51] Ibid 41.

[52] Ibid 73. See also ibid 142.

[53] Ibid 143.

D The extension of "unbearable suffering"

The Mackay Report also omitted to note another way in which the Dutch criteria have been loosened. The guidelines have long required that in addition to making a request the patient be "suffering unbearably" and that VAE/PAS be a "last resort." Evidence of how widely these criteria have been interpreted in the Netherlands was provided in 1989 by a leading and widely respected Dutch practitioner of VAE. Asked whether he would rule out VAE for an old man who requested it because he felt a nuisance to his relatives who wanted him dead so they could enjoy his estate, the doctor replied: "I ... think in the end I wouldn't, because that kind of influence—these children wanting the money now—is the same kind of power from the past that ... shaped us all."[54] Again, "unbearable suffering" has been held by the Dutch Supreme Court in the *Chabot* case (the case which so troubled the Walton Committee[55]) to justify PAS for a mother who was not terminally ill, or even physically ill, but who wanted PAS to put an end to her grief over the death of her two sons.[56] Fear of the effects of dementia may also qualify as "unbearable suffering."[57] Moreover, "last resort" includes cases where palliative care could have alleviated the patient's suffering but the patient declined it.[58] Further, doubts have been expressed about the availability of adequate palliative care in the Netherlands. In its evidence to the Select Committee the Dutch Voluntary Euthanasia Society stated: "The practice of euthanasia developed in the Netherlands in the early 1970s. Palliative care as such did not really exist at this time...."[59] The Report observed[60] that palliative care is not recognized as a clinical specialty there. One Dutch doctor (who is involved in the practice of VAE/PAS) was quoted in the Report[61] as accepting that such care had been "at a low level" but as claiming that it had improved over the previous five years to a standard at least as high as in England.[62] Whether palliative care in the Netherlands has improved as substantially as this witness claimed is open to question. Another witness, the medical director of a hospice, testified[63] that hospitals in general were "totally devoid of input from palliative care specialists." He added that the fact that

---

[54] Dr H Cohen, quoted in Keown 87.
[55] See text at n 7.
[56] Nederlandse Jurisprudentie 1995 no 656.
[57] Griffiths II 45–6.
[58] First survey 45, Table 5.7.
[59] MII 454.
[60] MI para 183.
[61] MI para 184.
[62] MII 415 Q1305.
[63] MI para 183.

palliative care is not regarded as a medical specialty explained why he had lost his job and was moving to the United Kingdom.[64] He noted that increased funding had come to an end, that hospices were under-resourced, and that many people were losing their jobs.[65] Illustrating the use of VAE in place of palliative care, he referred to a case in which he had been consulted by a GP. The GP said that the problem was that the patient was refusing euthanasia:

I said, "What happened?". He said, "In the past, all these kinds of situations, when people were intractably vomiting, I solved by offering euthanasia. Now this patient does not want it, and I do not know what to do". That was really striking.... This GP was not even aware of all the possibilities we have to control this kind of suffering.[66]

Another witness commented that although the number of palliative care units had risen in the light of increased funding, the increased quantity did not mean improved quality:

many institutions which were providing nursing care in general were opening palliative care units, because they got more money for the patients.... but these people are mostly just continuing what they were doing—in the sense that there is no real specialist understanding, knowledge and practice of palliative care.[67]

Further, the Report's presentation of the reasons why patients request VAE/PAS calls for qualification. It quotes one witness who testified that 84 per cent of such patients have pain (which raises questions about what palliative care they were receiving, if any); 70 per cent extreme fatigue; 50 per cent gastrointestinal complaints and loss of weight; 70 per cent coughing, dyspnoea, or suffocation; and almost 70 per cent feeling extremely weak. The witness said that each of these symptoms or combination of symptoms may lead to unbearable suffering.[68] However, the Dutch surveys have included vaguer reasons. Doctors surveyed replied that for 57 per cent of patients it was "loss of dignity"; for 46 per cent "not dying in a dignified way"; for 33 per cent "dependence"; and for 23 per cent "tiredness of life." For only 46 per cent was "pain" a reason[69] (and this again raises questions about the quality of any palliative care they were receiving).

[64] MII 446 Q1515.
[65] MII 442 Q1491.
[66] MII 449 Q1535.
[67] MI para 185.
[68] MI para 185.
[69] First survey 45, Table 5.8.

The Report also omits to convey the substantial support in the Netherlands for VAE/PAS for those with "existential" suffering, ie those who are "tired of life." As early as 1991 a former Vice-President of the Dutch Supreme Court argued that doctors should be able to provide elderly people over 75 who were living alone with the means to commit suicide.[70] In 2001 Dr Els Borst, the former Minister of Health who steered the euthanasia legislation through the Dutch Parliament, stated that very old people who were "tired of life" should be allowed to obtain a suicide pill.[71] In 2004 an advisory committee of the KNMG agreed that existential suffering should qualify.[72] And the Chair of the Medical Committee of the Dutch Society for Voluntary Euthanasia told the Select Committee that an "end-of-life pill" for healthy old people, which could be obtained without consulting a doctor, was "the ultimate goal" and "one of the ideals of Dutch society in general at the moment."[73] The third national survey disclosed that 45 per cent of the Dutch population and 29 per cent of Dutch physicians thought that older people who wanted to end their lives should have access to the means to do so.[74] The KNMG informed the Mackay Committee: "It is likely that, under the influence of 'tired of life' cases, the emphasis of the debate will shift from physician-assisted death . . . to possibilities and options which limit or even rule out the role and influence of physicians."[75] One of the few critics of Dutch euthanasia who testified commented generally on the Dutch slippery slope:

Just look at what has been debated in the Netherlands from the summer until the present time [16 December 2004]. First of all, it was again about life-terminating actions in newborn babies . . . . Second, euthanasia or assisted suicide for those who have the beginnings of dementia has been accepted by the authorities. A debate is starting whether this should not be done more generally. Just today, a KNMG committee has published its report on an investigation into the possibility of accepting "tired of life" as an indication for euthanasia . . . . [T]his committee is now saying that . . . "tired of life" could, in certain circumstances, be

[70] "Obituary: Huibert Drion" (2004) 328 BMJ 1204.

[71] "Dutch minister favours suicide pill" CNN, 14 April 2001 <http://archives.cnn.com/2001/WORLD/europe/04/14/netherlands.suicide/>.

[72] KNMG, *Op zoek naar normen voor het handelen van artsen bij vragen om hulp bij levensbeëindiging in geval van lijden aan het leven: verslag van de werkzaamheden van een commissie onder voorzitterschap van prof. J Dijkhaus* (2004).

[73] MII 418 Q1323. Though the Voluntary Euthanasia Society was "not actively campaigning for it at the moment," he said that its membership would very much support this goal: MII 424 Q1355.

[74] R Fenigsen, "Dutch Euthanasia: the new government ordered survey" (2004) 20 Issues in Law and Medicine 73, 76.

[75] MII 393.

an indication for performing euthanasia. We therefore see that...the groups which are open to the possibility of getting euthanasia are definitely extending.[76]

He also stated: "social pressure is leading people to ask for euthanasia. Not asking for euthanasia has become an option...which you have to defend."[77] About these significant developments and concerns the Mackay Report had surprisingly little to say.

Developments since the publication of the Report have done little to assuage concerns about the looseness of the criteria and their gradual extension. In 2009 Dr Borst, interviewed by euthanasia researcher Dr Anne-Marie The, reportedly admitted that the legalization of euthanasia had been followed by a decline in the quality of care for the terminally ill, and Dr The commented that palliative care was so poor that patients "often ask for euthanasia out of fear" of dying in agony.[78] "Tiredness of life" was rejected as justification for VAE/PAS by the Supreme Court in 2003[79] and in 2011 a KNMG report stated that requests must be "motivated in part by a medical ground."[80] However, the report agreed that "it is wholly justifiable that vulnerability—extending to such dimensions as loss of function, loneliness, and loss of autonomy—should be part of the equation" physicians use to assess requests.[81] And what, in practice, is to prevent a patient (with or without the doctor's collusion) misrepresenting existential suffering as "in part" medical? Many people with existential suffering will be able to point to some medical condition. The KNMG report continued that even if a physician concluded that the patient's suffering was not "unbearable," the patient had the option of ending life by refusing food and drink, and that there were some 2500 such cases per year (approximately as many as there are cases of VAE/PAS). The report stated that "the conscious denial of food and drink, when combined with effective palliative care, can offer a dignified death."[82] It added that physicians were under a "duty to supervise their patient and offer support in steps to deny food and drink" and that if a patient decided to hasten death in this way, "the physician must arrange for effective palliative care, such as in the form of an anti-decubitus mattress, oral care and control

---

[76] MII 445 Q1510. Another witness, a Dutch nursing home doctor with no evident objection to VAE, also pointed to a widening of the criteria: MII 481 Q1712.

[77] MII 441–2 Q1488.

[78] S Caldwell, "Now the Dutch turn against legalised mercy killing", *Daily Mail*, 9 December 2009.

[79] In the *Brongersma* case, Nederlandse Jurisprudentie 2003 no 167; Griffiths II 35–9.

[80] KNMG, *The role of the physician in the voluntary termination of life* (2011) 25.

[81] Ibid 22.

[82] Ibid 34.

measures against pain, confusion and other complaints."[83] A physician could, moreover, raise the possibility of stopping eating and drinking.[84] The report also advised that physicians may provide information to patients about suicide, by referring them to information available on the Internet, by lending materials to patients, and by discussing the stopping of life-prolonging drugs.[85] The KNMG took the view that deaths resulting from self-starvation were "natural,"[86] and that doctors incurred no liability for providing information about suicide.[87] The report appears, then, to endorse a right to assisted suicide, by self-starvation, which bypasses the conditions for PAS stipulated by the Dutch legislation. The report also appears to invite yet further relaxation of those conditions. If physicians are under a duty to "offer support," "supervise," and "alleviate suffering"[88] when patients end their lives by self-starvation, why may physicians not assist patients to end their lives by providing a lethal prescription or a lethal injection? Why are physicians *duty-bound* to help patients end their lives slowly and uncomfortably but *may not* help them end their lives swiftly and comfortably? If the answer is that the patients are not thought to be experiencing "unbearable suffering," what if the patients say that they are experiencing "unbearable suffering" while thirsting to death, or through fear of thirsting to death? If fear of future dementia qualifies as "unbearable suffering," why not fear of dying of thirst?

E Under-reporting

The KNMG told the Mackay Committee that "now and again" doctors ignored the guidelines but that "evidence for abuse on a larger scale is lacking." It added: "it is not easy to neglect the core requirements and get away with it."[89] However, the undisputed evidence from the Netherlands is that in thousands of cases doctors have, with virtual impunity, violated the requirement of an explicit request and the requirement to report VAE/PAS to the proper authority, the local medical examiner. Before 1998 the local medical examiner would send a report to the local prosecutor. Since 1998 the report is sent to one of five regional review committees, comprising a lawyer, doctor, and ethicist, who do their

[83] Ibid 35–6.
[84] Ibid 35.
[85] Ibid 36–7.
[86] Ibid 36.
[87] Ibid 36–7.
[88] Ibid 36.
[89] MII 393–6.

committee work "on the side."[90] The first three surveys disclosed non-reporting rates of 82 per cent (in 1990), 59 per cent (in 1995), and 46 per cent (in 2001).[91] The fourth survey (into practice in 2005) showed an improvement to 20 per cent, but this means that one in five cases was still illegally covered up by doctors as death by "natural causes."[92] Prosecutions for murder or for non-reporting are, moreover, rare. Griffiths et al. pointed out that of the 1800 cases reported each year to the regional review committees, the committees found "in only a tiny handful" that the doctor has not met the legal requirements, and no such case had resulted in prosecution.[93] The "handful" of prosecutions in recent years had been of non-reported cases which "happen accidentally" to come to prosecutorial attention.[94] And there were many unreported cases. For example, Griffiths et al. observed that although there were known to be "a considerable number" of cases of NVAE, "hardly any" had been reported.[95] In relation to the NVAE of infants they wrote that "control over termination of life of severely defective newborn babies cannot yet be regarded as legally adequate" and "because of an apparently low reporting rate, it is certainly not effective."[96] In 1998 Griffiths et al., having aptly noted the "intrinsic ineffectiveness of control based on self-reporting,"[97] observed that the control regime did not provide "effective control," that the results of the first two national surveys which had by then been published had been "pretty devastating," and that the regulatory regime was "as leaky as a sieve"[98] and seemed "all bark and no bite."[99] The enforcement mechanism was "essentially an exercise in self-deception" because of the absence of any real prospect of detecting offending doctors.[100] "Such an enforcement system is by its very nature ineffective; one could as well enforce speed limits by asking drivers to report whether they have obeyed the law or not."[101] And as for the proposal that doctors should report to regional

[90] Griffiths II 138.

[91] Ibid 199. The Mackay Report ventilated the suggestion that the number of cases of euthanasia may have been exaggerated because cases defined as "euthanasia" by the surveys may not have been regarded as "euthanasia" by the doctors: MI para 181. But it is the definition used by the surveys which is key. The evidence tendered to the Committee by the lead researcher of the second and third surveys, Professor van der Wal, repeated without qualification the low reporting rates as found by the first three surveys: MII 469.

[92] Griffiths II 199.

[93] Ibid 128.

[94] Ibid.

[95] Ibid 127.

[96] Ibid. 252.

[97] Griffiths I 257.

[98] Ibid 289.

[99] Ibid 268.

[100] Ibid 274.

[101] Ibid.

review committees instead of to prosecutors, Griffiths et al. opined that "any additional reporting will be limited to non-problematic cases in which the doctor is satisfied that he runs no risk of prosecution"[102] and that the added value of such committees therefore seemed doubtful.

In 2008, by contrast, they claimed that there is now a "well-developed system of control, consisting of expert consultation before euthanasia is carried out and assessment afterwards by the regional review committees, which have been designed to be acceptable to doctors."[103] The system of consultation has indeed improved: most doctors now consult with another doctor who has undergone a training course in euthanasia consultation.[104] But a requirement of independent consultation is not new, and there is still no requirement to consult a specialist in psychiatry, palliative care, or the patient's condition. And as for the replacement of prosecutors by regional review committees, how can a system of review by part-timers who rely on what they are told by those who report, and who are not told anything by those who do not, sensibly be described as a "well-developed system of control"? How does reporting to a committee instead of a prosecutor cure the "intrinsic ineffectiveness of control based on self-reporting"? As Judge Gorsuch has asked of the Dutch regime in his impressive treatise on euthanasia published in 2006:

Does a regime dependent on self-reporting by physicians who have no interest in recording any case falling outside the guidelines adequately protect against lives taken erroneously, mistakenly, or as a result of abuse or coercion? How would we ever know?[105]

Griffiths et al. have even suggested that to encourage doctors to report NVAE it should be classified as "normal medical practice." Gorsuch notes that, curiously, Griffiths does not give any significant consideration to the question whether allowing doctors to kill patients without consent might also lead to additional cases of abusive, coercive, and mistaken killings, and that Griffiths' proposal would appear to rule out prosecution whether the doctor's motives were compassionate or cruel. Gorsuch adds:

In Griffiths' preferred regime, only professional and civil sanctions would be available as remedies when doctors kill without consent—and even these reme-dies would be available only if and when doctors kill in the absence of what he

---

[102] Ibid 280.
[103] Griffiths II 49.
[104] Ibid 139–40; 195.
[105] NM Gorsuch, *The Future of Assisted Suicide and Euthanasia* (Princeton University Press, 2006) 114.

calls "normal medical practice"—although Griffiths fails to specify when he thinks killing a patient without consent should be considered "normal".[106]

In short, nothing Griffiths et al. wrote in 2008 detracts from their telling observation in 1998 that a regime which relies on self-reporting by doctors "is by its very nature ineffective . . . ."[107]

The Select Committee heard from a member of one of the regional review committees. He testified: "we must be sure there has been no manipulation, no pressure or undue influence, and that the request is well-considered."[108] But how can the review committee be sure when it relies to such an extent on information provided by the very doctor who ended the patient's life? As the same witness testified: "[I]it is a paperwork exercise. On the basis of what is in the paper, we need to assess whether the requirements have been fulfilled."[109] And how extensive is the information supplied? The same witness stated: "if you are ever going to develop a form, you should certainly not follow our form. The typography of it is limiting in the amount of information that you can provide." He added that the form "certainly does not invite you to be extensive."[110]

Underlining the ineffectiveness of the Dutch law, Griffiths et al. have also pointed to a sizeable incidence of illicit assistance in suicide by doctors and laypeople. They cite research suggesting that some 1600 people per year commit assisted suicide outwith the legislation, by taking sleeping pills which were supplied by a doctor or prepared for ingestion by a layperson, or both. They observe that "a considerable number of serious crimes" are committed over which "control seems to be essentially non-existent."[111]

In conclusion, the Mackay Report's portrayal of the Dutch experience was insufficiently critical. In view of the Report's heavy reliance on evidence tendered largely by leading defenders of Dutch euthanasia, this is perhaps not surprising. The Committee would have done better to have balanced the evidence from these witnesses against the several book-length critiques of the Dutch experience, based on empirical research by their authors. For example, the year the Committee was established witnessed the publication of Professor Raphael Cohen-

[106] Ibid 115.
[107] See text at n 97. See also J Keown, 'Five Flawed Arguments for Decriminalising Euthanasia' in A Alghrani et al. (eds), *The Criminal Law and Bioethical Conflict: Walking the Tightrope* (Cambridge University Press, forthcoming).
[108] MI para 175.
[109] MII 435 Q1441.
[110] MII 437 Q1454.
[111] Griffiths II 184.

Almagor's *Euthanasia in the Netherlands.* Though a supporter of VAE/PAS, Cohen-Almagor concluded that the Dutch regime suffered from serious flaws, that all of the guidelines were regularly broken, and that the Dutch tended to condone NVAE. The high number of unreported cases, and the fact that many physicians did not wish to be bothered with the procedures, was, he found, "alarming."[112] It is also surprising that the Mackay Report did not refer to the criticisms leveled at the Netherlands by the United Nations Human Rights Committee in 2001. That Committee expressed concern that the Dutch system might not detect "undue pressure"; that the review process operated after the fact; that minors as young as twelve could access VAE/PAS with (and from sixteen without) parental approval; and that infanticide was practiced.[113] (In 2009 the Committee again expressed concerns, not only "at the extent of euthanasia and assisted suicides" but also that a physician can terminate a patient's life "without any independent review by a judge or magistrate to guarantee that this decision was not the subject of undue influence or misapprehension."[114])

The Select Committee may not have been aware that the Dutch portrayal of euthanasia in the Netherlands has not been free from "spin."[115] Dr Borst's frank statement about the decline in care for the terminally ill since the passage of the euthanasia legislation[116] is, therefore, all the more significant. She also acknowledged that more should have been done legally to protect those who want to die naturally, adding: "In the Netherlands, we first listened to the political and social demand in favour of euthanasia" adding, "Obviously, this was not in the proper order."[117]

IV OREGON

Like its treatment of the Netherlands, the Mackay Report's treatment of the law and practice of PAS in Oregon, though useful, needs to be read alongside the oral and written evidence the Committee canvassed, and other evidence besides.

---

[112] R Cohen-Almagor, *Euthanasia in the Netherlands* (Springer, 2004) 175–9. See also C Gomez, *Regulating Death: Euthanasia and the Case of the Netherlands* (The Free Press, 1991); H Hendin, *Seduced by Death: Doctors: Patients and Assisted Suicide: Patients and Assisted Suicide* (WW Norton, 1998); Keown.

[113] Human Rights Committee, "Concluding Observations of the Human Rights Committee: Netherlands" (2001) CCPR/CO/72/NET <http://www.unhchr.ch/tbs/doc.nsf/0/dbab71-d01e02db11c1256a950041d732?Opendocument>.

[114] UN Human Rights Committee, "Consideration of Reports Submitted by States Parties Under Article 40 of the Covenant" CCPR/C/NLD/CO/4 (25 August 2009) para 7 <http://www.unhcr.org/refworld/publisher,HRC,,,4aa7aa642,0.html>.

[115] Keown 99–101, 139–41.

[116] See text at n 78.

[117] Ibid.

A The Death with Dignity Act (DWDA)

The Death with Dignity Act (DWDA), which was passed by a voter referendum in 1994 and which came into force in 1997, provides:

An adult who is capable, is a resident of Oregon, and has been determined by the attending physician and consulting physician to be suffering from a terminal disease, and who has voluntarily expressed his or her wish to die, may make a written request for medication for the purpose of ending his or her life in a humane and dignified manner.[118]

The patient must make two oral requests to a physician separated by at least 15 days, and sign a written request witnessed by two people. The prescribing physician and a second physician must confirm the patient's diagnosis and prognosis and confirm that the patient is competent. If either physician thinks a patient "may be suffering from a psychiatric or psychological disorder or depression causing impaired judgment"[119] the patient must be referred for counseling. The prescribing physician must inform the patient of certain matters, including feasible alternatives such as hospice care; request the patient to inform next-of-kin; and file a report with the Public Health Division of the Oregon Health Authority (OHA). The OHA must annually "review a sample" of reports and publish a statistical report.[120] Finally, "No person shall be subject to civil or criminal liability or professional disciplinary action for participating in good faith compliance" with the DWDA.[121]

B Strict safeguards?

The Mackay Report's summary of the DWDA[122] does not convey the laxity of the legislation. Although the Act is narrower than Dutch law in requiring that the patient have a "terminal illness" and in permitting only PAS, not VAE, it is wider in not requiring that the patient be suffering, unbearably or otherwise.[123] Its regulatory regime is, moreover, even weaker than that in the Netherlands. Professor Alexander Capron has

---

[118] DWDA 127.805 s.2.01(1) <http://public.health.oregon.gov/ProviderPartnerResources/EvaluationResearch/DeathwithDignityAct/Pages/ors.aspx>. See Keown Ch 15; Gorsuch (n 105) Ch 7.

[119] DWDA 127.825 s.3.03.

[120] 127.865 s.3.11.

[121] 127.885 s.4.01(1).

[122] MI para 144.

[123] "Terminal illness" is defined as an incurable and irreversible disease that will, in reasonable medical judgment, produce death within six months. Whether this means with or without treatment is unclear.

observed that the safeguards in Oregon are "largely illusory."[124] Daniel Callahan has described them as "a Potemkin-village form of regulatory obfuscation. They look good, sound good, feel good, but have nothing behind them."[125] Their assessments are sound. The Act is so loosely drafted that it would allow a "terminally ill" patient who is depressed (though not so as to cause "impaired judgment") to obtain a prescription for lethal drugs, having "shopped around" for any two doctors, even though neither doctor has seen the patient before or has any expertise in palliative care or psychiatry or the patient's condition, and even though the doctors' diagnosis, prognosis and evaluation of competence are grossly negligent. The written request could be witnessed by the patient's heir and the heir's best friend.[126] And, even if the patient is not suffering from depression causing impaired judgment when he or she obtains the prescription, there is nothing in the Act to ensure that when the lethal drugs are taken, which may be months later, the patient is not then so suffering. Echoing the concerns of the Royal College of Psychiatrists,[127] palliative care expert Professor Kathleen Foley and psychiatrist Professor Herbert Hendin have noted that, despite the fact that two-thirds of all suicides and two-thirds of those requesting physician-assisted suicide are suffering from depression,[128] the DWDA does not require consultation with a psychiatrist to see whether relievable depression or anxiety is at the source of the patient's request to die. They add that physicians are not reliably able to diagnose depression, let alone whether depression is causing "impaired judgment," and that in one study only six per cent of Oregon psychiatrists were very confident that in the absence of a long-term relationship with a patient they could satisfactorily determine in a single visit whether that patient was competent to commit suicide.[129] Judge Gorsuch has noted that when the state of Oregon wishes to confine for a maximum of five days a patient with suicidal impulses, the patient is entitled to an examination by a mental health expert. "How," he asks, "can one coherently explain and defend a regulatory regime that affords terminally ill patients less protection against the possibility of a mistaken death due to a psychiatric ailment than it affords all patients against the

---

[124] AM Capron, "Legalizing Physician-Aided Death" (1996) 5(1) Cambridge Quarterly of Healthcare Ethics 10.
[125] D Callahan, "Organized Obfuscation: Advocacy for Physician-Assisted Suicide" (2008) 38(5) Hastings Center Report 30, 32.
[126] DWDA 127.810 s.2.02.
[127] See text at n 26.
[128] K Foley and H Hendin, "The Oregon Report: Don't Ask, Don't Tell" (1999) 29(3) Hastings Center Report 37, 39.
[129] Ibid 39–40.

possibility of a mistaken five-day confinement from the same cause?"[130]
When Lord Mackay put it to a witness from the OHA that the Act
prescribes "minimal conditions," and that a good doctor might, but need
not, do more than the law requires, the witness replied "Very well said."[131]
As with the Netherlands, the Report's account of the evidence from
Oregon reflects the fact that the evidence was tendered largely by those
who either campaigned for the law or who are involved in its implementation. Critics were, as in the Netherlands, outnumbered more than four
to one.

C Effective control?

The incidence of PAS since the DWDA came into operation in 1997 is
significantly lower than the incidence of VAE and PAS in the Netherlands. The latest report, for 2010, indicates that from 1998 to 2010 only
525 patients have used the law to commit suicide.[132] The trend of
reported cases has, however, been upward, from sixteen in 1998 to
sixty-five in 2010. How effective is Oregon's control over PAS? First,
there is no guarantee that all cases have been reported. One critic of the
Act testified: "It is much easier to simply give a couple of prescriptions
that are supposedly for sleep and say 'Just keep these for a couple of
months and then you will have enough to do yourself in', why would a
doctor bother to report it?"[133] Asked whether the number of reported
cases could be relied upon as accurate, a witness from the OHA replied
that it received "pretty good data" because physicians had a vested
interest in complying with the law: if they reported they were protected.[134] However, Dutch doctors could be said to have the same "vested
interest" in reporting, yet many have not. The same witness testified
that"there have not been any really egregious events."[135] It is difficult
to see how she could claim to know. The role of the OHA is one of
passive recording rather than active investigation. As the Mackay
Report recognizes, its role "is simply to record what is happening,
which includes compiling an annual report giving the number of
lethal prescriptions issued and the number actually ingested."[136] Even

---

[130] Gorsuch (n 105) 179.
[131] MII 264 Q606.
[132] Oregon Public Health Division, "Characteristics and end-of-life care of 525 DWDA patients
who died after ingesting a lethal dose of medication as of 7 January 2011, by year, Oregon, 1998–
2010" Table 1 <http://public.health.oregon.gov/ProviderPartnerResources/EvaluationResearch/
DeathwithDignityAct/Documents/yr13-tbl-1.pdf> ("Table 1").
[133] MII 341 Q1007.
[134] MI para 152.
[135] MI para 148.
[136] Ibid.

more accurately, the authority's role is to record what doctors who report say is happening. If the doctors involved in issuing lethal prescriptions report that the legal criteria have been fulfilled (and the doctor's involvement may well end with the writing of the prescription) there is simply no reason for the authority to refer the case for possible investigation to the Oregon Board of Medical Examiners (OBME), the doctors' regulatory body. As a witness from the OHA testified:

[W]e are not a regulatory agency ... so if we see that there are any problems ... our role is to report that to the Board of Medical Examiners .... We do not call the police or take away their licence, we are not regulatory in that regard.[137]

The OBME has no more of a proactive investigatory role than the OHA. As a representative of the OBME told the Committee: "There may be instances in which there are problems, but if they are not brought to our attention there is no way for us to investigate them. In any area of medical practice, we do not go out and affirmatively go looking for trouble, so to speak."[138] Similarly, the representative of the Oregon Medical Association (OMA) testified: "the Board has very little jurisdiction over this Act because in essence, assuming the physician is following the law, they cannot take action against the physician based on his or her participation under this law."[139] He added:

I am not aware of any evidence that things have either gone extraordinarily smoothly or extremely badly in any of the cases. As you are aware, the way the law is set up there is really no way to determine that unless there is some kind of disaster.[140]

Judge Gorsuch writes:

even if a doctor were actually to take the extraordinary step of reporting himself or herself as having violated the law, Oregon's statute imposes no duty on the health division to investigate or pursue such cases, let alone root them out in the absence of any such self-reports.[141]

The OHA has, then, an administrative rather than an investigatory role. Further, one of its staff told the Committee that it operated "on a shoestring."[142] She added that it had neither the legal authority nor the resources to investigate cases.[143]

---

[137] MII 257 Q555.
[138] MII 323 Q897.
[139] MII 346 Q1029.
[140] MII 347 Q1035.
[141] Gorsuch (n 105) 118–19.
[142] MII 258 Q557.
[143] MII 266 Q615.

The Report quotes testimony by Ann Jackson from the Oregon Hospice Association (who is an advocate of PAS) that if there were any abuses they would come to light because there were hospices all over Oregon "and they have big mouths!"[144] She added: "We know that no-one has awakened, there have been no problems, and every outcome has been as it was supposed to have been...."[145] These were bold assertions. She omitted to provide evidence of complaints by staff about non-compliance with this (or any other) legislation, or to explain the incentive for any member of staff to blow the whistle on a failure by a superior or a colleague to comply with the law. And, as she noted, only two per cent of United States hospice patients die in an inpatient facility (where there might be some opportunity for oversight) rather than at home.[146] There is, moreover, no legal requirement on anyone, whether doctor or nurse, to be present when the patient takes the lethal substance. Indeed, the prescribing doctor has been present in only around a quarter of cases.[147] When anyone is present, it is often a member of the pressure group, Compassion in Dying, which agitated for the DWDA and which is unlikely to be eager to report problems with its implementation. The president of this group testified that it has "participated in a consultative way with about three-quarters of the patients who have made a request" under the Act.[148] Further, the doctors' notifications about the prescriptions they have written are confidential. In light of the above, how Jackson could claim to know that there have been "no problems," not least patients availing themselves of the DWDA even though they were suffering from impaired judgment at the time of obtaining the prescription, or at the time of taking it, is unclear. Ninety-two per cent of patients who have used the Act have not been referred for psychiatric or psychological evaluation. Moreover, the representative of the Oregon Nurses Association revealed that some of its members had admitted actually assisting patients to take the lethal substance,[149] which appears, not surprisingly, to have gone undetected by the authorities. Another witness testified: "It took six years before the Oregon Health Division's flawed tracking system even reported one case of vomiting."[150] Lord McColl, an eminent surgeon on the Mackay Committee's delegation to Oregon, commented: "If any surgeon or physician

[144] MI para 152.
[145] MII 309 Q834.
[146] MII 302 Q797.
[147] Table 1.
[148] MII 310 Q837. See also MII 338 Q982.
[149] MII 353 Q1058.
[150] MII 334 Q954.

told me that he did 200 procedures without any complications I knew that he possibly needed counselling and had no insight. We come here and I am told there are no complications. There is something strange going on."[151] In the Netherlands, a complication rate of almost one in five cases of PAS has been reported.[152] How tenable, then, is the claim that there have been "no problems" in Oregon? Another witness, a psychiatrist from the Oregon Health and Science University who is studying the working of the DWDA (and who expressed no opposition to the Act) was asked by Lord Joffe whether after seven years of operation the safeguards appeared to be working adequately and the legislation was generally accepted. She replied: "I think it needs more study...."[153]

Evidence of non-compliance with the Act is unlikely to come to light because the Act is not designed to detect non-compliance. And absence of evidence of abuse is not, of course, evidence of absence of abuse. It was only some seven years after the courts in the Netherlands permitted VAE/PAS, and after a comprehensive government-sponsored survey, that the reality of widespread abuse in the Netherlands came to light. Such comprehensive research, involving in-depth interviews with doctors granted immunity from prosecution, has yet to be carried out in Oregon. Callahan has noted that the assurances from Oregon that there is no abuse are, in their confidence and firmness, "the equal of those expressed in the Netherlands prior to its confidential surveys."[154] The OHA has admitted the limitations of the regulatory framework. For example, its first report admitted that the department's duty to report any evidence of non-compliance to the OBME "makes it difficult, if not impossible, to detect accurately and comment on underreporting," and acknowledged: "We cannot determine whether physician-assisted suicide is being practiced outside the framework of the Death with Dignity Act."[155]

D Concerns about practice

The few critics of the DWDA who were interviewed by the Select Committee expressed grave concerns about its operation. Dr Gregory Hamilton, a psychiatrist, related the case of one patient, Michael Freeland.

---

[151] MII 334 Q956.

[152] See text at n 183.

[153] MII 289 Q756.

[154] D Callahan, "Organized Obfuscation: Advocacy for Physician-Assisted Suicide" (2008) 38(5) Hastings Center Report 30, 32.

[155] AE Chin et al., "Legalized Physician-Assisted Suicide in Oregon—the First Year's Experience" (1999) 340 New England Journal of Medicine 577, 583.

Freeland was depressed, had a lifelong history of depression and previous suicide attempts, had been found incompetent by a judge, and was left by his assisted suicide doctor with 90 barbiturate tablets with which to commit suicide. Freeland told Hamilton that when he rang the doctor to complain of pain, the doctor replied "I will come and sit with you while you take your overdose." Hamilton added that volunteers went to his house where Freeland "was found alone in a deplorable condition in uncontrolled pain, delirious, and afraid to take his pain medicine. We had to physically give him his pain medicine. We did. The hospice did not do it. The assisted suicide doctors did not do it, volunteers did it." Dr Hamilton went on: "This man was not in pain because his pain was not treatable, he was in pain because nobody bothered." He added that the patient's palliative care doctor wondered whether he should be offered palliative care because he had drugs for assisted suicide at hand. "This is," Hamilton commented, "just one case among many."[156]

Two other cases which have managed to pierce the DWDA's veil of confidentiality also raise serious questions. The first was presented by Compassion in Dying as a model of how well the law supposedly works. It concerned "Helen," a woman in her mid-80s with metastatic breast cancer. Her own doctor had refused to assist her in suicide and a second doctor had also refused on the ground that Helen was depressed. Helen's husband phoned Compassion in Dying and was referred to a doctor willing to assist. In their critical analysis of this case Professors Foley and Hendin comment that even the limited details supplied by Compassion in Dying and by the prescribing physician give cause for concern. The physicians who evaluated Helen offered two contradictory sets of opinions about the appropriateness of her decision. As the decision-making process progressed, it provided no mechanism for resolving the disagreement and the views of the two doctors who did not support the patient's decision— one who had known her for some time and another who considered that she was depressed—were essentially ignored. The prescribing doctor admitted that he did not discuss Helen's case with her regular doctor, and had only very cursory contact with the second doctor who thought that Helen was depressed. The prescribing doctor also revealed that although he liked Helen and found the thought of her dying so soon "almost too much to bear," he found even worse "the thought of disappointing this family. If I backed out, they'd feel about me the way they felt about her previous doctor, that I had strung them along...."[157]

---

[156] MII 331–2 Q949.
[157] K Foley and H Hendin, "The Oregon Experiment" in K Foley and H Hendin (eds), *The Case Against Assisted Suicide: For the Right to End-of-Life Care* (The Johns Hopkins University Press, 2002) 144, 146–50.

A second case analyzed by Foley and Hendin concerned Kate Cheney, an 85-year-old widow terminally ill with stomach cancer. Kate, accompanied by her daughter Erika, who had moved from Arizona to care for her, requested assisted suicide from her physician at her health maintenance organization (HMO), Kaiser Permanente. Erika described this doctor as "dismissive" and obtained a referral to another doctor with Kaiser. This doctor arranged for Kate to be psychiatrically examined. The psychiatrist concluded that Kate did not seem to be explicitly pushing for assisted suicide, that she lacked the high level of capacity to weigh options about it, and that although Kate seemed to accept this assessment, her daughter became very angry. Kaiser then suggested a further assessment from an outside consultant. This consultant concluded that Kate was able to decide, although her choices might have been influenced by her family and that Erika might have been "somewhat coercive." Kate received the lethal drugs and later took them. Foley and Hendin observe:

Caregiver burden leading to depression in the caregiver has now been identified as a serious issue, particularly for women like Erika who are asked to shoulder the work and responsibility of providing twenty-four hour care to a parent. This particular case raises the question of what real meaning or value is Oregon's prohibition of coercion if it can be circumvented so easily.[158]

Judge Gorsuch comments that these two cases:

encapsulate and illustrate some of the difficult questions about Oregon's assisted suicide regime alluded to by the [Oregon] data...: what role is depression, as opposed to terminal illness, actually playing in patient decisions to die in Oregon? Are alternative options, including treatment for depression, being fully presented (or presented at all)? Are the doctors that prescribe death even knowledgeable about the alternatives that exist? To what extent are family members unduly influencing patient choices and physician evaluations? What would have happened if family members in each case had argued *against* the request to die and offered care? Should patients be allowed to 'shop' around for physicians and psychologists who will find them competent? Do psychologists and physicians have an obligation to do more than a cursory examination? Should they consult the patient's primary care providers and other doctors and psychologists who may have refused prior requests for lethal medication by the patient? Would Cheney's HMO have offered to pay for a second opinion if the first opinion had found Cheney competent? Do HMOs have a conflict of interest—given that assisted suicide is unquestionably cheaper than continuing care—that may provide an incentive for them to encourage patients to seek death?[159]

---

[158] Ibid 156–7.
[159] Gorsuch (n 105) 125 (emphasis in original).

Foley and Hendin have concluded that the monitoring process is essentially a case of "don't ask, don't tell," yielding limited data which does not reveal what happened in any particular case.[160] Critics' concerns have not been assuaged by that data, published in the form of annual statistical reports.[161] One in five patients has expressed concern about inadequate pain control and one in three about being a burden on others. The three most common reasons for seeking a lethal prescription have been "losing autonomy" (91 per cent), a decreasing ability "to engage in activities making life enjoyable" (88 per cent), and "loss of dignity" (84 per cent). These reasons seem some way from the sort of "hard cases" of "unbearable suffering" typically used to illustrate the alleged need for VAE/PAS.

A paper by Professor Margaret Battin et al. in 2007 claimed that, statistically, there is no evidence from Oregon or the Netherlands that decriminalization has had a disproportionate impact on vulnerable groups.[162] However, to show that the proportion from these groups who accessed VAE/PAS is statistically similar to the proportion who died naturally is not to show that their vulnerability was not exploited, or that their deaths were not the result of malice or mistake. Moreover, Baroness Ilora Finlay and Dr Rob George have responded that the notion of "vulnerability" used by Battin et al. is problematic; that subsequent Oregon data show that PAS is in fact more common among the elderly (the median age being over 70); and that research by Ganzini[163] has shown that some patients approved for PAS in Oregon were suffering from undiagnosed depression.[164]

In an overview of the DWDA published in 2008, Hendin and Foley concluded that Oregon physicians appear to have been given great power without being in a position to exercise it responsibly:

They are expected to inform patients that alternatives are possible without being required to be knowledgeable about such alternatives or to consult someone who is. They are expected to evaluate patient decision-making capacity and judgment

---

[160] K Foley and H Hendin, "The Oregon Report: Don't Ask, Don't Tell" (1999) 29(3) Hastings Center Report 37. They also claim that, as in the Netherlands, those administering the law have become its advocates: ibid 42.

[161] Oregon Health Authority, "Death with Dignity Act, Current Annual Reports" <http://public.health.oregon.gov/ProviderPartnerResources/Evaluationresearch/deathwithdignityact/Pages/index.aspx>.

[162] MP Battin et al., "Legal Physician-assisted dying in Oregon and the Netherlands: evidence concerning the impact on patients in 'vulnerable' groups'" (2007) 33 Journal of Medical Ethics 591.

[163] L Ganzini et al., "Prevalence of Depression and Anxiety in Patients Requesting Physicians' Aid in Dying: Cross-Sectional Survey" (2008) 337 BMJ 1682.

[164] IG Finlay and R George, "Legal physician-assisted suicide in Oregon and The Netherlands: evidence concerning the impact on patients in vulnerable groups—another perspective on Oregon's data" (2011) 37 Journal of Medical Ethics 171.

without a requirement for psychiatric expertise or consultation. They are expected to make decisions about voluntariness without having to see those close to the patient who may exert a variety of pressures, from subtle to coercive.

They add:

They are expected to do all of this without necessarily knowing the patient for more than fifteen days. Since physicians cannot be held responsible for wrongful deaths if they have acted in good faith, substandard medical practice is permitted, physicians are protected from the consequences, and patients are left unprotected while believing they have acquired a new right.[165]

Finally, even if the DWDA were effectively controlling PAS in Oregon, a sparsely populated and affluent state, it does not follow that PAS could be effectively controlled in other, more densely populated and less-affluent United States states, or in the United Kingdom. While neighboring Washington state has, as a result of a voter referendum, decided to follow Oregon, many others have voted not to do so.[166]

V THE COMMITTEE'S RECOMMENDATIONS

The members of the Select Committee differed on the importance of the issues it considered and on the interpretation of the evidence it had received. The Committee therefore confined itself to summarizing the evidence it had received on the principles underlying Lord Joffe's Bill and on its practical implications and, given that that version of the Bill could not proceed due to lack of parliamentary time, to drawing the attention of the House to certain key issues relevant to the consideration of any future Bill.[167] It recommended that any Bill should take account of several considerations. It should:

- clearly distinguish between VAE and PAS to give the House the opportunity to support one or the other, or both;
- set out clearly the actions which a doctor may and may not take in providing VAE or PAS;
- define "terminal illness" (if a Bill contained such a qualifying condition) in such a way as to reflect the realities of clinical practice as regards accurate prognosis;

---

[165] H Hendin and K Foley, "Physician-Assisted Suicide in Oregon: A Medical Perspective" (2008) 106 Michigan Law Review 1613, 1639. Also in 2008, the state-run Oregon Health Plan wrote to a cancer patient informing her that it would not fund her therapy, but it would fund PAS: S Donaldson James, "Death Drugs Cause Uproar in Oregon", abcnews, 6 August 2008.

[166] RL Marker, "Assisted Suicide: The Continuing Debate" <http://www.patientsrightscouncil.org/site/assisted-suicide-the-continuing-debate/>.

[167] MI para 268.

- define "mental competence" so as to take into account the need to identify applicants suffering from psychological or psychiatric disorder as well as a need for mental capacity;
- consider requiring every applicant for PAS (or VAE) to be given a psychiatric assessment "in order both to confirm that the request is based on a reasoned decision and is free from external pressure and that the applicant is not suffering from a psychiatric or psychological disorder causing impaired judgment";[168]
- consider including "unrelievable" or "intractable" rather than "unbearable" suffering or distress;
- consider how patients seeking to end their lives might experience palliative care before taking a final decision;
- seek, in setting a waiting period between an application for VAE or PAS and their implementation, to balance the need to avoid increased suffering for determined applicants against the desirability of providing time for reflection for the less resolute;
- not place on a physician with a conscientious objection the duty to refer an applicant for assisted suicide or voluntary euthanasia to another physician without such objection;
- provide adequate protection for all health care professionals who may be involved in any way in such an application, and ensure that the position of persons working in multi-disciplinary teams is adequately protected;
- not include provisions governing the administration of pain relief by doctors.

VI PAS OR VAE?

Given that recent attempts to relax the law in the United Kingdom and the United States, such as Lord Joffe's Bill, have sought to decriminalize PAS rather than VAE, the Committee's first recommendation merits some discussion. It reflects the view that permitting only PAS would be a way of limiting accelerated death to those most determined to obtain it, be less objectionable to the medical profession, and involve less risk of slippage to NVAE.[169] However, the case for permitting only PAS raises several questions.

First, the line between PAS and VAE is blurred. Writing a prescription for a lethal substance is an instance of the former, but what of placing the lethal substance on the patient's tongue or helping the patient to keep the substance down once taken? The Director of the Oregon State Board of Nursing told the Committee that the Board was fielding very detailed

---

[168] MI para 254.
[169] MI paras 244–5.

questions about the extent to which a nurse could assist the patient in taking the lethal substance and that it was a "very grey area."[170]

Second, it does not follow from the fact that the patient took a lethal substance that he or she did so volitionally. One Oregon doctor who has assisted suicide testified that the fact of self-administration "provides a final piece of clear evidence that this is completely volitional...."[171] This does not follow. It is just as possible to pressure a patient into swallowing a lethal substance as it is to pressure them into accepting its injection, and patients swallowing a drug may be just as depressed as patients who request an injection.

Third, a law permitting only PAS may be held unlawfully to discriminate against those physically incapable of self-administering lethal drugs. Indeed, the deputy Attorney-General in Oregon has evidently issued an opinion that the law may violate the Americans with Disabilities Act and may therefore need to be extended to allow for lethal injections.[172]

Fourth, it does not follow (as the Mackay Report seems to imply) that the take-up rate for PAS in the United Kingdom would be as low as it appears to have been in Oregon. One Oregon witness testified: "I do not want to say that because it has played a certain way here in Oregon ... it would play out the same way in the United Kingdom, because it might not."[173] If the law were relaxed in the United Kingdom the experience might well be much closer to that of another densely populated Western European country—the Netherlands—than to a sparsely populated west coast state of three-and-a-half million people. As Professor Finnis testified, Oregon is "a very intermediate stage and a very curious, isolated bubble." He added:

It is a state which exists in a rather special set of circumstances, very advantageous, well-off, isolated in many respects from the rest of the country. I have no doubt whatsoever that if the Oregon ... regime were to be adopted in the wider United States it would soon prove impracticable to hold the line in the way that it has been held in the few years since Oregon's law has been in force, and we would have a movement towards the Dutch experience, extensively.[174]

Why, then, was a line drawn between PAS and VAE in Oregon? The answer would appear to lie in political expediency. Campaigners for relaxation of the law realized (correctly) that PAS stood a greater chance

---

[170] MII 354 Q1068–9.

[171] MII 315 Q849.

[172] NG Hamilton, "Oregon's culture of silence" in K Foley and H Hendin (eds), *The Case against Assisted Suicide: For the Right to End-of-Life Care* (The Johns Hopkins University Press, 2002) 175, 179.

[173] MII 284 Q724.

[174] MII 559 Q1981.

of winning public acceptance than VAE. As Finnis informed the Committee, the campaign which narrowly succeeded in Oregon was one of several run "by people who make no secret in their own publications, although it is not generally publicised, that they regard assisted suicide as simply one stage in a progressive liberation of society from its present taboo."[175] Against this, the Report quotes a witness who said: "in the US we are quite a way in our community dialogue from discussing active euthanasia or injected medication to end life. We are decades away from that."[176]

This witness was, however, mistaken. Proposals for euthanasia have been discussed in the United States since the early twentieth century.[177] The campaign for the legalization of VAE/PAS intensified with the founding in 1980 of the Hemlock Society, a leading pro-euthanasia pressure group, by Derek Humphry. Hemlock provided substantial financial backing to the campaign for the relaxation of the law in Oregon.[178] Humphry and Hemlock have long advocated the legalization not only of PAS but also of VAE. Indeed, in a letter to the *New York Times* in 1994, Humphry commented that the Oregon law "could be disastrous" because it did not permit lethal injections. Referring to research in the Netherlands showing that self-administered drugs often failed, he wrote:

[A]bout 25 percent of assisted suicides fail, which casts doubts on the effectiveness of the new Oregon law . . . . The new Oregon way to die will only work if in every instance a doctor is standing by to administer the coup de grâce if necessary.

He observed: "The only two 100 percent ways of accelerated dying are the lethal injection of barbiturates and curare or donning a plastic bag."[179] He has also commented: "This law doesn't help the people who need it most—the people who cannot keep drugs down, because of their terrible diseases, or cannot put hand to mouth" and added: "In a few years the law is going to have to be adapted to allow for lethal injection."[180] The current limitation of the Oregon law to PAS appears to lie not, therefore, in moral principle but in political tactics. The same applies to the narrowing of Hemlock's proposals to accommodate only the "terminally ill." As Humphry's own website explains:

---

[175] MII 559 Q1981. See also MI para 144.

[176] MI para 145.

[177] EK Emanuel, "The History of Euthanasia Debates in the United States and Britain" (1994) 121 (10) Annals of Internal Medicine 793.

[178] "About Derek Humphry" <http://www.finalexit.org/dhumphry>.

[179] D Humphry, "Oregon's Assisted Suicide Law Gives No Sure Comfort in Dying", *New York Times*, 3 December 1994, Letters.

[180] T Appleby, "Suicide law falls short, activist says", *Globe & Mail*, 7 December 1994, A10.

When Humphry started Hemlock, and for its first ten years of existence, the Society's credo embraced assisted dying (preferably medical) for the terminally ill and the hopelessly ill, such as patients with advanced ALS or MS, or extreme old age with severe health problems. But as Hemlock became more involved in state politics in its drive to change the law to secure physician-assisted suicide, it dropped the other illnesses and spoke only for "the advanced terminally ill." While recognizing this as necessary political expediency, Humphry stays firm in his belief that many more persons also deserve assisted dying.[181]

Only "necessary political expediency" is, then, holding back "assisted dying" for a wider range of patients (and, perhaps, by a wider range of providers).

Fourth, like Humphry, the Dutch have long recognized that permitting PAS but not VAE has little to recommend it either in principle or in practice. In principle, if PAS is to be allowed out of respect for patient autonomy, or to relieve suffering, why not VAE? Dr Gerrit Kimsma, a member of a Dutch regional review committee who gave evidence to the Select Committee, has written:

Thinking that physician-assisted suicide is the entire answer to the question of ending of life of a suffering patient . . . is a fantasy. There will always be patients who cannot drink, or are semiconscious, or prefer that a physician perform this act. Experience has taught us that there are many cases of assisted suicide in which the suicide fails. Physicians need to be aware of the necessity to intervene before patients awaken.[182]

A Dutch study revealed that in 18 per cent of cases in which the doctor intended to assist in suicide the doctor ended up administering a lethal injection because of complications. The study commented:

In most of these cases, the patient did not die as soon as expected or awoke from coma, and the physician felt compelled to administer a lethal injection because of the anticipated failure of the assisted suicide. In some cases, the physician administered a lethal injection because the patient had difficulty swallowing the oral medication, vomited after swallowing it, or became unconscious before swallowing all of it.[183]

Dr Gideonse, an Oregon doctor who has assisted suicide, told the Committee of several cases where the limitation to PAS had proved "extremely frustrating for the patient and family" and that the provision in Lord

---

[181] "About Derek Humphry" <http://www.finalexit.org/dhumphry>.
[182] GK Kimsma, "Euthanasia Drugs in the Netherlands" in David C Thomasma et al. (eds), *Asking to Die: Inside the Dutch Debate about Euthanasia* (Springer, 1998) 135, 142–3.
[183] JH Groenewoud et al., "Clinical Problems with the Performance of Euthanasia and Physician-Assisted Suicide in the Netherlands" (2000) 342 New England Journal of Medicine 551, 554–5.

Joffe's Bill (as it then stood) allowing for VAE made "a lot of sense" and was an option which should be made available.[184] If it is right that the patient's life should be brought to an end, why require an uncomfortable exit? Finally, in 2000 the British Medical Association held a conference to develop a consensus on PAS. A discussion paper written by its Medical Ethics Department considered the argument for distinguishing PAS from VAE and concluded that in many cases there was little practical difference between the two and that similar arguments against abuse applied to both.[185]

The above arguments questioning the defensibility of drawing a line between PAS and VAE, arguments accessible in the academic literature,[186] are surprisingly absent from the Mackay Report.

VII LORD JOFFE'S BILL

Lord Joffe's revised Bill,[187] modeled on the DWDA with the addition of a Dutch-style review system, failed to incorporate several of the key recommendations made by Mackay. For example, it did not require applicants for PAS to be referred for psychiatric assessment, even if the patient was thought to be suffering from a psychiatric disorder impairing judgment. Lord Joffe claimed that his Bill contained more safeguards than the laws in the Netherlands and Oregon.[188] In some respects, the Bill was more restrictive: unlike Oregon it required "unbearable suffering" and unlike the Netherlands it did not permit VAE. But in other respects the Bill was less restrictive. The Oregon law does not allow PAS for those suffering "a psychiatric or psychological disorder or depression causing impaired judgment."[189] The Dutch law requires doctors who have performed VAE/PAS to be interviewed by the local medical examiner. Further, the Dutch guidelines require VAE/PAS to be a "last resort." Even though this guideline has been loosely interpreted in practice to include cases where palliative care could have alleviated pain but was refused by the patient, it nevertheless reflects some attempt to rule out

---

[184] MII 315 Q849. The president of Compassion in Dying defended the limitation to PAS "in this society, in this state, at this time.": MII 316 Q849. See also MII 333 Q954.

[185] British Medical Association, "Euthanasia and Physician-Assisted Suicide: Do the Moral Arguments Differ?" in Physician-Assisted Suicide Debating Pack PAS4 (2000) 1, 4.

[186] eg Y Kamisar, "Physician-assisted suicide: the last bridge to active voluntary euthanasia" in J Keown (ed), *Euthanasia Examined: Ethical, Clinical and Legal Perspectives* (Cambridge University Press, 1995) Ch 15.

[187] The revised Bill is available at <http://www.publications.parliament.uk/pa/ld200506/ldbills/036/06036.i.html>.

[188] MII 48 Q70, referring to the previous version of his Bill.

[189] DWDA 127.825 s.3.03.

premature VAE/PAS. Lord Joffe's Bill did not require PAS to be a last resort or the patient to have tried palliative care. And, although the Bill required the patient to be "suffering unbearably," this seemed to remain an essentially subjective criterion.

Moreover, the Bill carried the seeds of its own extension from assisted suicide for the terminally ill suffering unbearably to active euthanasia on request and, in due course, without request. Lord Joffe told the Select Committee (referring to the Bill as it then stood): "The Bill is based on the principle of personal autonomy and patient choice, the right of each individual to decide for themselves how best he or she should lead their lives."[190] But if personal autonomy was the key principle, why should patients have to be "terminally ill" to qualify for PAS? Indeed, Lord Joffe, noting that the Bill had been criticized by some for not being more permissive, told the Select Committee:

[W]e are starting off; this is a first stage; it is new territory.... [N]ormally with new legislation one should go forward in incremental stages. I believe that this Bill should initially be limited, although I would prefer it to be of much wider application.[191]

He admitted that the limitation of the Bill to the terminally ill was due simply to the strength of opposition encountered by the previous Bill which was not so limited, and he added: "I can assure you that I would prefer that the law did apply to patients who were younger and who were not terminally ill but who were suffering unbearably, and if there is a move to insert that into the Bill I would certainly support it."[192] Terminal illness would not be the only limit to fall victim to the principle of autonomy. If individual autonomy were key, why permit PAS but not VAE? And why deny PAS or VAE to those who were not suffering unbearably or even at all? Further, the Bill limited PAS to those who had attained the age of majority. Why did it not respect the autonomous requests of legally competent patients under eighteen, as do the Dutch?

Another reason the Bill carried the seeds of its own extension is that a second principle underlay the Bill. Although Lord Joffe placed autonomy centre stage, the principle of beneficence was waiting in the wings. Indeed, he testified that the Bill was a "deeply humane piece of legislation...."[193] Lord Mackay pointed out: "Your Bill is also based on the principle of

---

[190] MII 47 Q70. See also MII 50 Q70; MII 52 Q73; MII 56 Q104.
[191] MII 53 Q89. Later, during the second reading debate on the Bill, he said that he no longer wished to widen the criteria: *Hansard*, HL vol 681, col 1188 (2006).
[192] MII 58 Q124.
[193] MI 51 Q70.

humanity, you have explained to us, and that would apply to the incompetent as well as the competent."[194] If "beneficence" was thought to justify ending suffering on request, why was it not thought to justify ending suffering without request? Further, "beneficence" (like autonomy) undermines the limitation of PAS to those suffering unbearably with six months or less to live. If it is humane to assist such patients, why is it not even more humane to assist those who face longer periods of unbearable suffering? Moreover, "beneficence" (like autonomy) undermines the requirement that the patient be suffering "unbearably." If it justifies ending suffering which the patient finds unbearable, why does it not justify ending suffering which the patient could bear but would much rather not? Again, "beneficence" (like autonomy) sees little justification for limiting accelerated death to those whose suffering arises from an illness, terminal or otherwise. Illness is one, but by no means the only, source of human suffering. Finally, why would "beneficence" not permit PAS or VAE for those who are suffering but are under eighteen?

Third, it seems that Lord Joffe, like many advocates of VAE/PAS, sees little, if any, moral difference between PAS and other end-of-life decisions which shorten life, such as withholding and withdrawing treatment.[195] But if what matters morally to Lord Joffe is the shortening of life rather than the doctor's intention, and if he accepts the shortening of the lives of patients, competent and incompetent, by the withholding/withdrawal of treatment, must he not logically accept the shortening of the lives of patients, competent and incompetent, by lethal injection? In his testimony, he certainly voiced no objection to NVAE in principle. He stated: "For people who are mentally incompetent there needs to be, perhaps, a different system, but it cannot be based ... on personal autonomy."[196]

In short, the Bill's "safeguards," being an amalgam of the ineffectual provisions in the Dutch and Oregon laws, were no more capable than they of providing effective control of PAS. Moreover, the Bill's limitations, like those in the DWDA, appeared little more than political expediency, temporary concessions designed to coax the legislature to take the first step onto the slippery slope. If that step were taken, the limitations would surely sooner or later have buckled under the pressure of the very same principles, "autonomy" and "beneficence," which were invoked to justify that first step.

[194] MI 56 Q109.
[195] MI 54 Q98; MI 316 Q854.
[196] MII 56 Q108.

The second reading debate took place on 12 May 2006.[197] The Bill was rejected by 148 votes to 100. Pertinently, several of their Lordships in the majority commented on the implicit judgment about the worthwhileness of life linking both the voluntary and the non-voluntary ending of life. Lord Williams, echoing the concerns of the Disability Rights Commission, said:

[T]o specify, even in the fairly broad terms of the Bill, conditions under which it would be reasonable and legal to end your life, is to say that certain kinds of human life are not worth living. As soon as this is publicly granted, we put at risk the security of all who experience such conditions.[198]

Also speaking against the Bill, Lord Mackay recalled the anxieties that had been expressed by witnesses with serious disabilities. He told of a meeting with a woman who said that if doctors could help to end a "heavily burdened life" in the circumstances set out in the Bill, then that involved a judgment on such a life, and that her life fell into that category. Lord Mackay said that there are many more disabled people than there are likely to be beneficiaries from the Bill, if the evidence from Oregon was to be relied on, and that he felt strongly that he did not wish to add to their burden.[199] The evidence to which he was referring was the general agreement of witnesses to his Committee that the number of people who were serious about wanting to end their lives, who were not psychiatrically ill, and who were unlikely to be deflected from their purpose was "very small indeed" and largely comprised terminally ill people with strong personalities who were used to being in control of their lives and whose suffering derived more from loss of control than from the symptoms of their illness.[200] Baroness O'Neill, the eminent philosopher, opposed the Bill on the ground that changing the law to accommodate this minority would expose others to pressure:

Legalising "assisted dying" amounts to adopting a principle of indifference towards a special and acute form of vulnerability: in order to get a few independent folk to get others to kill them on demand, we are to be indifferent to the fact that many less independent people would come under pressure to request the same.[201]

---

[197] *Hansard*, HL vol 681, col 1184 (2006) <http://www.publications.parliament.uk/pa/ld200506/ldhansrd/vo060512/text/60512-01.htm>. For the debate on the Report of the Mackay Committee see *Hansard*, HL vol 674, col 12 (2005).
[198] *Hansard*, HL vol 681, col 1197.
[199] Ibid col 1277 (2006).
[200] MI para 244.
[201] *Hansard*, HL vol 681, col 1266 (2006).

Baroness Campbell, a disabled peer, has commented that a law allowing PAS would undoubtedly place people with disabilities under pressure to end their lives early to relieve the burden on relatives, carers, or the state. She wrote:

The concerns are not side issues that only affect disabled people. We are like society's "canaries in the coalmine" who can often see the dangers of potentially discriminatory legislation before others, as it impacts on us even before the deed is done. We are scared now; we will be terrified if assisted suicide becomes state-sanctioned.[202]

Baroness Campbell will not have been reassured by comments made in 2008 by another member of the House, which outraged disability rights groups. Baroness Warnock, perhaps the most influential ethicist in government circles, said: "If you're demented, you're wasting people's lives—your family's lives—and you're wasting the resources of the National Health Service."[203] Nor by the entirely reasonable prediction made (in a book edited by Professor Battin, a leading advocate of VAE/PAS) by Professor Patricia Mann. Professor Mann predicted that decriminalizing PAS would have profound social and cultural consequences and that strong social expectations are likely to develop for individuals to choose assisted suicide as soon as their physical capacities decline to a point where they become extremely dependent on others in an expensive, inconvenient way.[204]

VIII CONCLUSION

The House of Lords has, particularly through the Select Committees chaired by Lord Walton and by Lord Mackay, and the wealth of evidence they garnered, made a valuable contribution to the continuing euthanasia debate. The repeated rejection of the case for VAE/PAS by the House, after exhaustive and informed debate, is indicative of the fact that the case for relaxation of the law is much less cogent than it may superficially appear to be.

This chapter has focused on the Mackay Report, with particular reference to its analysis of the experience of the Netherlands and Oregon. There is much that repays study in the Report, such as the research it

---

[202] Baroness Campbell et al., "Open Letter from Leaders of Disabled People's Movement in UK and USA" <http://www.carenotkilling.org.uk/?show = 775.>

[203] J Macadam, "A Duty to Die?", *Life and Work*, October 2008, 23, 24.

[204] PS Mann, "Meanings of Death" in M Battin et al (eds), *Physician-Assisted Suicide: Expanding the Debate* (Routledge, 1998) 11, 25.

commissioned into opinion polls. Whether the Report's account of the experience of the Netherlands and Oregon meets the Committee's aim of providing a balanced account is, however, open to question, not least because the Committee heard from relatively few critics. This source of imbalance is compounded by the fact that some critical evidence which was brought to the Committee's attention is omitted. A more rounded understanding requires familiarity not only with the Mackay Report but also with its accompanying volumes of evidence, and with other evidence besides. Taken together, that evidence indicates that the law in both jurisdictions has fallen well short of ensuring effective control. Despite the clear association, pointed out by the Royal College of Psychiatrists, between a desire for a hastened death and depression, neither jurisdiction requires patients to undergo psychiatric evaluation. Nor does either jurisdiction require patients to consult a specialist in palliative care or a specialist in the patient's condition. Crucially, both legal regimes rely on self-reporting which is, to recall Professor Griffiths' analogy, like enforcing the speed limit by asking people to report if they have exceeded it. Not surprisingly, the Dutch surveys have disclosed widespread breach of the guidelines, with virtual impunity. NVAE has not only been widely practised but is now officially condoned, at least in the case of disabled babies. It is not surprising that the Dutch regime has now been twice criticized by the United Nations Human Rights Committee. The regime in Oregon is even more lax.

Lord Joffe's Bill, being an amalgam of the two regimes, offered no greater assurance of effective control. Its failure to adopt key recommendations of the Mackay Report exposed it to even greater criticism. Moreover, as used by Lord Joffe to justify PAS for the terminally ill, the principles of autonomy and beneficence which underlay the Bill would equally justify VAE and NVAE, and in a wide range of cases. The Bill would have been but a first step. Its underlying acceptance of the notion that certain lives are no longer worth living, and the dangers of that notion to the vulnerable, not least those with disabilities, played no small part in its deserved demise.

CHAPTER 10

TOWARDS EUTHANASIA IN EUROPE?: MARTY, *PRETTY*, AND *PURDY*

I INTRODUCTION

As we saw in Chapter 9, the modern euthanasia debate in England has generated two House of Lords Select Committees. The debate in continental Europe has been scarcely less lively. The Netherlands has now been followed, in permitting voluntary euthanasia, by Belgium and Luxembourg.[1] Whether this presages a more widespread trend may well depend in no small measure on the positions of two key bodies: the Council of Europe[2] and the European Court of Human Rights. This chapter analyzes, first, an attempt by one of its committees to persuade the Council of Europe to endorse euthanasia; second, an attempt to persuade the European Court of Human Rights that the European Convention on Human Rights contains a right to be assisted in suicide; and, third, an attempt (invoking the decision of the European Court in that case) to persuade the Law Lords to order the Director of Public Prosecutions to issue guidelines setting out the factors he takes into account in deciding whether to prosecute the crime of assisting suicide.

II THE COUNCIL OF EUROPE: THE MARTY REPORT

In the European debate, a significant starting-point is the recommendation against legalizing euthanasia passed in 1999 by the Parliamentary Assembly of the Council of Europe. Recommendation 1418 urged member

---

[1] See J Griffiths et al., *Euthanasia and Law in Europe* (Hart Publishing, 2008) 174 ("Griffiths II") Chs 7–10; <http://www.legilux.public.lu/leg/a/archives/2009/0046/a046.pdf#page=7>.

[2] The Council of Europe was established in 1949 and currently comprises 47 countries. It "seeks to develop throughout Europe common and democratic principles based on the European Convention on Human Rights and other reference texts on the protection of individuals" <http://www.coe.int/lportal/web/coe-portal>. It should not be confused with the European Union.

states "to respect and protect the dignity of terminally ill or dying persons in all respects."[3] To this end it recommended a trio of means:

- recognizing and protecting a terminally ill or dying person's right to comprehensive palliative care;
- protecting the terminally ill or dying person's right to self-determination;
- upholding the prohibition against intentionally taking the life of terminally ill or dying persons.[4]

In relation to this third means it added:

- recognizing that the right to life, especially with regard to a terminally ill or dying person, is guaranteed by the member states, in accordance with Article 2 of the European Convention on Human Rights which states that "no one shall be deprived of his life intentionally."[5]

More recently, moves have been made to revise the Council's position. In September 2003 a report on euthanasia was passed by a narrow majority of the Council's Social, Health and Family Affairs Committee.[6] The report comprised a Draft Resolution (of nine paragraphs) and an Explanatory Memorandum (of sixty-three paragraphs). The Memorandum was written by Mr Dick Marty, a "radical-liberal" member of the Parliamentary Assembly and the Committee's Rapporteur. In April 2004 the Parliamentary Assembly of the Council of Europe voted to send the report back to the Social, Health and Family Affairs Committee, which produced a revised report in February 2005.[7] We shall analyze these reports in turn.

A Marty I

1 The report's reasoning and recommendations

The report stated that some doctors practiced active, voluntary euthanasia on, or assisted in suicide, terminally ill patients who experienced "constant, unbearable pain and suffering without hope of any improvement."[8] It added that this practice was usually "confined to the shadows of

---

[3] Council of Europe, "Protection of the human rights and dignity of the terminally ill and the dying", Recommendation 1418 (1999) para 9 <http://assembly.coe.int/Documents/AdoptedText/ta99/erec1418.htm1>.

[4] Ibid.

[5] Ibid.

[6] Report of the Social, Health and Family Affairs Committee of the Council of Europe, *Euthanasia* Doc 9898, 10 September 2003 ("Marty I") <http://assembly.coe.int/Documents/WorkingDocs/Doc03/EDOC9898.htm>.

[7] Report of the Social, Health and Family Affairs Committee, *Assistance to patients at end of life* Doc 10455, 9 February 2005 ("Marty II") <http://assembly.coe.int/Documents/WorkingDocs/Doc05/EDOC10455.htm>.

[8] Marty I (Draft Resolution) para 1.

discretion or secrecy," that decisions could be taken in an arbitrary manner, that pressures from the family could be more pernicious "if exercised in the dark and beyond any procedures or control," and that it was "this reality" that carried "the greatest risk of abuse."[9] Further, penal and professional sanctions were very rare. Hence, there was a "striking divergence" between law and practice and this gap had to be reconciled if respect for the rule of law was to be maintained.[10] The closure of this gap was one reason, it claimed, why legislation had been passed in the Netherlands and in Belgium to permit voluntary euthanasia subject to "rigorously regulated and controlled conditions." Such legislation was designed:

to bring such practices out of the grey area of uncertainty and potential abuse by establishing strict and transparent procedures, mechanisms and criteria which doctors and nursing staff have to observe in their decision-making.[11]

Further, it was difficult to distinguish ethically between active voluntary euthanasia and the withholding or withdrawal of life-sustaining treatment when it was known that as a result the patient would die sooner, which the report described as "passive euthanasia."[12] The report continued:

Nobody has the right to impose on the terminally-ill and the dying the obligation to live out their life in unbearable suffering and anguish where they themselves have persistently expressed the wish to end it.[13]

Its argument continued that we now respected "a person's choice to take their own life" and avoided making value judgments about it, a development which could in no way be interpreted as a devaluation of human life. Moreover, palliative care could not take away unbearable pain and suffering in all cases and, in any event, the issues went beyond the alleviation of pain:

the degree of patients' own suffering, including mental anguish and loss of dignity that they feel, is something that only they can assess. Individuals suffering in the same situation may take different end-of-life decisions, but each human being's choice is deserving of respect.[14]

In light of the above considerations the Draft Resolution recommended that member states:

[9] Ibid para 2.
[10] Ibid para 3.
[11] Ibid para 4.
[12] Ibid para 5.
[13] Ibid para 7.
[14] Ibid para 8.

- collect and analyze empirical evidence about end-of-life decisions;
- promote public discussion of such evidence;
- promote comparative analysis taking into account in particular the results of the legislation in the Netherlands and Belgium, "notably their effects on practice in the matter of euthanasia"; and
- in the light of the evidence and public discussion, consider whether legislation should be envisaged, where it has not already been introduced, to exempt from prosecution doctors who agree to help terminally ill patients undergoing constant, unbearable pain and suffering without hope of any improvement in their condition, to end their lives at their persistent, voluntary, and well-considered request, subject to prescribed rigorous and transparent conditions and procedures.[15]

2 Some criticisms

The report was flawed, not least because it overstated the arguments for legalization and downplayed or even ignored the arguments against it.

a Arguments advanced by the report

I THE RULE OF LAW   The report claimed that the rule of law supported legalization. However, just as the opening paragraph of Recommendation 1418 noted that it is the vocation of the Council of Europe "to protect the dignity of all human beings and the rights which stem therefrom," so too the rule of law affords protection to all citizens, recognizing their fundamental equality-in-dignity. Just as no one is above the law, so no one is outwith the law. A law permitting voluntary, active euthanasia (VAE) allows certain private citizens to kill other private citizens on the basis of the arbitrary judgment, historically denied in Western law and medical ethics, that they would be "better off dead." In short, the rule of law, to which the arbitrary exercise of power is repugnant, not least the power of life and death, tells not for but against legalization.

II "CLOSING THE GAP"   The argument that there is a "striking divergence" between the law and medical practice and that the gap must be closed if respect for the rule of law is to be maintained is unconvincing. First, the assertion that there is a "striking" discrepancy between law and practice is controversial. Obtaining reliable data on the incidence of the offenses of murder and assisted suicide by medical practitioners is, not surprisingly, difficult. The surveys cited by the report allegedly demonstrating a "striking" discrepancy in countries where euthanasia and assisted suicide are illegal must be read with caution. For example, the

---

[15] Ibid para 9.

report pointed out that according to a survey of United Kingdom doctors[16] almost 60 per cent replied that they had been asked to hasten death and 32 per cent had complied. However, the 60 per cent includes 14 per cent who were asked to let the patient die "through deliberate inaction" which the survey defined as "passive euthanasia." And the 32 per cent who said they had taken active steps to end a patient's life represented only nine per cent of all of the doctors who had been sent a questionnaire. Moreover, unlike the comprehensive surveys into end-of-life decision-making in the Netherlands, which have been carried out since 1990, the United Kingdom survey, as its definition of "passive euthanasia" indicates, did not consistently define "euthanasia" in terms of the *intentional* hastening of death, which may have led to some confusion.[17] As we saw in Chapter 9, more recent and reliable United Kingdom surveys by Professor Clive Seale in 2006 and 2009 have concluded: "Euthanasia, physician-assisted suicide and the ending of life without an explicit patient request...are rare or non-existent at both time points...."[18] Similarly, a United States survey found that only six per cent of physicians had performed euthanasia or assisted suicide, the author of the survey concluding that it was a "rare" event.[19] And Professor van der Maas has written that the proportion of deaths in the United States from euthanasia and physician-assisted suicide (PAS) is likely to be "small."[20]

Second, even if there were a serious discrepancy between the law and practice of voluntary euthanasia it would not follow that the gap should be narrowed by relaxing the law. Many criminal laws, such as those against perjury and possessing illicit drugs, are doubtless frequently broken without detection, but it does not follow that those laws should therefore be relaxed. The report seemed simply to assume that if VAE is practiced it should therefore be condoned.[21] But what if whatever VAE is practiced is performed on patients whose autonomy is compromised by

[16] BJ Ward and PA Tate, "Attitudes among NHS doctors to requests for euthanasia" (1994) 308 BMJ 1332.

[17] J Keown, *Euthanasia, Ethics and Public Policy* (2002) ("Keown") 94, n 22.

[18] C Seale, "End-of-life decisions in the UK involving medical practitioners" (2009) 23 Palliative Medicine 198, 201.

[19] DE Meier et al., "A National Survey of Physician-Assisted Suicide and Euthanasia in the United States" (1998) 338 New England Journal of Medicine 1193.

[20] PJ van der Maas and LL Emanuel, "Factual Findings" in LL Emanuel (ed), *Regulating How We Die* (Harvard University Press, 1998) 151.

[21] Revealingly, the Draft Resolution did not propose that in the light of whatever evidence might emerge from studies into the incidence of euthanasia there should be a review of various options, including improving the provision of quality palliative care and/or tighter enforcement of the criminal law. It proposed solely that member states consider legalizing euthanasia. That this appeared to be the report's not too skillfully hidden agenda was also suggested by its underlying argument in principle for reform. For: if there is a right to VAE, why should it not be recognized by law whatever the evidence about the current illegal incidence of VAE?

clinical depression or whose suffering could have been alleviated by palliative care? As we saw in Chapter 9, the Royal College of Psychiatrists has pointed out that there is a clear association between depression and a desire for a hastened death, and that when the depression is treated, almost all patients change their mind about wanting to die.[22] Why did the report seem to assume that the problem with the alleged gap between the criminal law and medical practice lay with the former rather than the latter, that the law was bad and the practice good? Was Dr Kevorkian a model of good medical practice? Of the 69 people he assisted in suicide, only a quarter were in fact terminally ill.[23] Why assume that the law's response to Kevorkians should be accommodation rather than incarceration?

Third, if the law against VAE is broken, so too is the law against NVAE (non-voluntary euthanasia—the killing of incompetent patients), both in jurisdictions where, like the United Kingdom and the United States, VAE is illegal and in jurisdictions, most notably the Netherlands, where it is legally permitted. If the report believed that the gap between the law and practice of VAE militated in favor of legalization, then would not the gap between the law and practice of NVAE militate in favor of legalizing NVAE?

Fourth, relaxing the law to allow euthanasia to be performed in certain circumstances would not mean that euthanasia would be performed only in those circumstances. Legislative proposals for regulating euthanasia typically set out procedural requirements aimed at *monitoring* the practice of euthanasia; they do not seek to *prohibit* the practice of euthanasia which fails to satisfy those requirements. In other words the potential for abuse, for breaking the law against murder and assisted suicide, remains. Indeed, it may well be that legalizing euthanasia in certain circumstances would result in euthanasia in other circumstances being regarded by the criminal justice system as less, not more, serious; a lower, not a higher priority. It is noteworthy that in the Netherlands very few doctors have been prosecuted for breaching the requirements for lawful euthanasia and that doctors who have been convicted of murder have typically received very lenient sentences.

Finally, advocates of legalization often allege that in countries where VAE is illegal there is a higher incidence of NVAE than in countries where VAE is lawful, and that legalizing VAE would reduce the incidence

---

[22] See text at Ch 9, 91–2.
[23] L Roscoe et al., "Dr. Jack Kevorkian and Cases of Euthanasia in Oakland County, Michigan, 1990–1998" (2000) 343 New England Journal of Medicine 1735–6, Correspondence.

of NVAE. Euthanasia advocates argue that doctors are currently "forced" to practice NVAE precisely because VAE is unlawful. This is unpersuasive. If VAE is unlawful then so too is NVAE. How can the same prohibition which deters doctors from performing the former encourage them to perform the latter? Legalizing VAE, far from discouraging NVAE, would surely do the opposite. For it would send out a signal that killing patients, at their request, can benefit them. Many doctors would then reasonably ask why patients should be denied this benefit merely because they are unable to request it.

III THE DUTCH EXPERIENCE   The report implicitly endorsed the Dutch (and Belgian) legislation permitting VAE. It described the procedures prescribed by the legislation as "strict and transparent" and claimed that the Dutch surveys have shown that "close monitoring" is possible. On the contrary, as we noted in Chapter 9, Dutch doctors have covered up thousands of cases by illegally certifying them as deaths by "natural causes."[24] In other words, in the bulk of cases there has not even been an opportunity for control. Even in relation to those cases which are reported, the report is filed by the doctors, who are hardly likely to disclose that they have breached the guidelines. We will also recall that Dutch doctors, in violation of the cardinal guideline requiring a free and informed request from the patient, have euthanized thousands of patients without request, so much so that patients are now advised that it is their responsibility to make it clear while competent if they do *not* want a lethal injection when incompetent.[25] Marty cited the first two Dutch surveys[26] but, remarkably, made no mention of these disturbing revelations and developments. In addition, the report made no mention of the serious concerns which had been expressed about the Netherlands by the United Nations Human Rights Committee in 2001. Given that a key role of the Council of Europe is to promote human rights, this omission is striking.[27] Nor did the report mention academic research critical of the Dutch experience.[28]

In short, there does indeed appear to be a "striking divergence." The empirical sources invoked by Marty do not, however, establish that this divergence is between the law and practice in the United Kingdom, where

[24] See Ch 9, text at nn 32–4.
[25] See Ch 9, text at nn 41–43.
[26] Marty I (Explanatory Memorandum) paras 20–4.
[27] <http://www.unhchr.ch/tbs/doc.nsf/(Symbol)/CCPR.CO.72.NET.En?Opendocument> paras 5–6; Ch 9, text at n 37.
[28] Eg H Hendin, *Seduced by Death: Doctors, Patients and Assisted Suicide* (WW Norton, 1998); Keown.

VAE is illegal. Those sources indicate, on the contrary, that it is between the law and practice in the Netherlands, where it is legal.

IV CHANGING ATTITUDES TOWARD SUICIDE   In claiming that "we" now "respected a person's choice to take their own life" and avoided making value judgments about it, the report advanced a contentious interpretation of changing attitudes to suicide. As we noted in Chapter 1, the decriminalization of suicide in England by the Suicide Act 1961 reflected not a condonation of suicide but a realization that criminal punishment was not the best way of dealing with the suicidal,[29] and as Lord Bingham confirmed in *R (Pretty) v Director of Public Prosecutions*, the Act conferred no right on anyone to commit suicide.[30]

V PUBLIC OPINION   The report claimed that public opinion polls showed a majority in favor of legalization. Such polls must, however, be read with no little reserve. As we saw in Chapter 9, the research into opinion polls commissioned by the Mackay Committee found that they were "limited in value"[31] and that this was particularly the case with regard to the attitudes of the general public, whose real views on euthanasia were obscured by a lack of information on the subject and by the lack of opportunity to reflect in an informed way upon the implications of any change in the law for themselves and for society.[32] In any event, even if it were the case that a majority of the public favored the decriminalization of VAE/PAS, it could hardly be allowed to dictate law and public policy any more than a finding that a majority of people favored capital or corporal punishment.

VI CONFLATING EUTHANASIA WITH NON-TREATMENT   The report's equation of "euthanasia" with the withdrawal of life-sustaining treatment when the shortening of life is foreseen, which it described as "passive euthanasia," was misleading. The report defined "euthanasia" as: "any medical act intended to end a patient's life at his or her persistent, carefully considered and voluntary request in order to relieve unbearable suffering."[33] How, then, could the withdrawal of treatment when the doctor merely *foresees* that it will shorten life count, on the report's own definition, as "euthanasia"? For one thing, it is not obvious that withdrawal, and particularly withholding, can properly be characterized as an

---

[29] See Ch 1, text at n 46.
[30] [2002] UKHL 61, para [35]. See ch 1, text at n 47.
[31] See Ch 9, text at n 14.
[32] See Ch 9, text at n 15.
[33] Marty I (Explanatory Memorandum) para 8.

"act."[34] For another, even if there were foresight of death it would not follow that there was also an intention (purpose) to end life. For the report to conflate these two forms of conduct, which there are cogent ethical reasons to regard as distinct, invites confusion. Moreover, by defining "euthanasia" as "active, voluntary euthanasia" the report adopted the controversially narrow Dutch definition. One danger of this definition is that it can be used (as has been in the Netherlands) to deflect concerns about a slippery slope from VAE to NVAE on the ground that NVAE, because it does not involve a request, is not "euthanasia" and therefore lies outside the boundaries of the euthanasia debate.

VII MISREPRESENTING THE CASE AGAINST EUTHANASIA   The report stated that opponents of legalization reject the claim that:

each individual, out of respect for his or her dignity and value, has a right to take decisions concerning his or her own life and death in accordance with his or her own values and beliefs, as long as no harm is done to others, and not to have these imposed.[35]

It would have been less misleading to have stated that opponents of euthanasia, while supporting the right of patients to make a wide range of decisions concerning their medical treatment, reject *one* decision as being incompatible with the patient's dignity and value: the decision to be intentionally killed, or to be helped to kill oneself. Moreover, to prohibit that choice does not deny the patient's dignity but affirms it, just as disallowing other choices which a person may want to make, such as to be executed rather than imprisoned or enslaved rather than free, equally respects his or her dignity. The fact that, through depression, pain, or loneliness, some patients may lose sight of their worth, is no argument for endorsing their misguided judgment that their life is no longer worth living. Were the law to allow patients to be intentionally killed by their doctors the law would be accepting that there are two categories of patients: those whose lives are "worth living" and those who would be "better off dead." Once society accepts that judgment, the implications for vulnerable groups, including the dying, the demented, and the disabled, are stark.

The report went on to imply that opponents of euthanasia are imposing on the terminally ill "the obligation to live out their life in unbearable suffering and anguish...."[36] On the contrary, many of the leading

---

[34] Marty boldly asserted that withdrawal is "an act of commission, if ever there was one.": ibid para 59.
[35] Ibid para 55.
[36] Ibid para 56.

opponents of euthanasia, such as the late Dame Cicely Saunders, founder of the United Kingdom hospice movement, have devoted their lives to the alleviation of suffering and anguish. The standard case against euthanasia recognizes the right of patients to refuse treatments because they are futile or too burdensome, and to be treated with palliative drugs, even if it is foreseen that death will come sooner. It does not hold that life should be preserved at all costs. That is (as we saw in Chapter 4) a caricature.

b Counter-arguments not met

In addition to advancing strained arguments in favor of VAE, the report glossed over important counter-arguments. For example, it mentioned but nowhere rebutted the counter-argument that legalizing VAE leads as a matter of practice and of logic to NVAE. This counter-argument runs that the slide will occur as a matter of practice because "safeguards" to prevent it cannot be made effective, and as a matter of logic because the case for VAE for the terminally ill contains the seeds of its own extension to those who are not terminally ill or to those who cannot request it. The failure of "safeguards" as a matter of *practice* is amply demonstrated by the Dutch guidelines. The Dutch experience also illustrates the force of the *logical* "slippery slope," which is a product of the unresolved tension in the argument for VAE between patient autonomy and patient welfare.

I RESPECT FOR PATIENT AUTONOMY   The report stated that opponents of euthanasia denied "the individual's right to take decisions concerning his or her own life and death in accordance with his or her own beliefs and values, as long as no harm is done to others...."[37] It concluded that consideration should be given to exempt from prosecution doctors who agree to help "terminally-ill patients undergoing constant, unbearable pain and suffering without hope of any improvement in their condition, to end their lives at their persistent, voluntary and well-considered request...."[38]

If, however, there is a right to make decisions concerning life and death in accordance with one's own values and beliefs, why should euthanasia not be available to any autonomous person who believes for whatever reason (terminal illness, chronic physical or mental illness, "tiredness of life") that his or her life is no longer "worth living"? By requiring candidates for VAE to satisfy conditions such as "terminal illness," why was the report not denying each individual's "right to take decisions concerning his or her own life and death in accordance with his or her

---

[37] Ibid para 62. See text at n 35.
[38] Ibid (Draft Resolution) para 9(iv).

own values and beliefs"? We will recall from Chapter 9 the influential voices in the Netherlands calling for VAE/PAS to be made available to those who are simply "tired of life," including that of Mrs Borst, the former Minister of Health.[39] Mr Marty could not claim to be unaware of her viewpoint: it was pointed out by the author in my response to Mrs Borst's speech at a hearing on euthanasia held by his Committee in Paris in 2002.[40]

II RESPECT FOR PATIENT WELFARE: THE LIFE "NOT WORTH LIVING"   If the doctor thinks that he or she can make the judgment (that the patient would be better off dead) in relation to a patient who asks for euthanasia, why cannot the doctor make that decision in relation to a patient in the same situation who is unable to request it? In the 1980s, leading Dutch advocates of VAE/PAS sought to assuage concerns about the slippery slope to NVAE. For example, the Dutch Voluntary Euthanasia Society claimed that NVAE was "murder, and will be prosecuted and sentenced as such."[41] However, as we saw in Chapter 9, Dutch doctors have performed NVAE in thousands of cases without prosecution; Dutch law has moved from endorsing VAE to endorsing NVAE, at least in the case of disabled newborns; and there is widespread condonation of NVAE in the case of incompetent adults.[42] In short, the Dutch experience nicely illustrates the logical slippery slope argument.

III EXPERT COMMITTEES   Marty's Explanatory Memorandum concluded:

As a lawyer and a legislator, I note that all over the world, doctors are ending the lives of patients, often in secrecy and with a sense of guilt. The law seems to want to ignore this fact of life, whereas it ought to have the courage to address it. Decriminalising euthanasia, rather than keeping the ban, might enable us to better supervise it and also prevent it.[43]

Marty seemed unaware that around the world the case for legalizing voluntary euthanasia has been considered by "lawyers and legislators" time and again and that they have, with few exceptions, rejected that case. He omitted to mention the Report of the Select Committee on Medical Ethics (HL Paper 21-I of 1993–4). He also omitted to mention the report of the New York State Task Force, whose members,

---

[39] See Ch 9, text at nn 71–2.
[40] A hearing which, like the report, was unbalanced: invited speakers in favor of legalization markedly outnumbered those against.
[41] Keown 122.
[42] Ch 9.III.C.
[43] Marty I (Explanatory Memorandum) para 62

both pro- and anti-euthanasia in principle, unanimously rejected legalization on the ground that it would be socially disastrous.[44]

The Marty Report appeared in September 2003. It was criticized by the Council's Committee on Legal Affairs and Human Rights later that month.[45] The Committee's Rapporteur[46] called in his Explanatory Memorandum for the Parliamentary Assembly to reaffirm Recommendation 1418 rather than to adopt the Marty Report.[47] The Marty Report was debated in April 2004 by the Parliamentary Assembly, which decided not to vote on the text and charged the Social, Health and Family Affairs Committee to prepare a new text bringing together the widely diverging viewpoints expressed in the debate. In February 2005, the Committee produced a revised report.

B Marty II

The revised report comprised a Draft Resolution of six paragraphs and an Explanatory Memorandum by Mr Marty running to fifty-one paragraphs and four Appendices (which outlined respectively the law in the Netherlands, Belgium, Switzerland, and proposed legislation in France).[48] The revised Draft Resolution was noticeably more conservative than the original. The original's focus on euthanasia, including its explicit recommendation that member states consider the legalization of euthanasia, was replaced by an emphasis on the promotion of palliative care and on the prevention of euthanasia in secret. However, not least when read in the light of the accompanying revised Explanatory Memorandum (which was, by contrast, barely amended), the revised Draft Resolution remained open to serious objection.

1 The revised Draft Resolution

The more conservative tone of the report was reflected in its change of title, from "Euthanasia" to "Assistance to patients at end of life." Moreover, its opening paragraph affirmed that it was "important and necessary" to reaffirm the "fundamental principle" in Recommendation 1418 of

---

[44] New York State Task Force on Life and the Law, *When Death is Sought: Assisted Suicide and Euthanasia in the Medical Context* (New York State Task Force on Life and the Law, 1994).

[45] Euthanasia: *An opinion by the committee on legal affairs and human rights* Doc 9923, 23 September 2003; Rapporteur, Kevin McNamara, United Kingdom, Socialist Group ("Legal Opinion") <http://assembly.coe.int/Documents/WorkingDocs/Doc03/EDOC9923.htm>.

[46] K McNamara, United Kingdom, Socialist Group: Legal Opinion (Explanatory Memorandum) para 4.

[47] Legal Opinion (Explanatory Memorandum) para 4.

[48] Report of the Social, Health and Family Affairs Committee, *Assistance to patients at end of life* Doc 10455, 9 February 2005 ("Marty II") <http://assembly.coe.int/Documents/WorkingDocs/Doc05/EDOC10455.htm>.

protecting the dignity and rights of all human beings. The paragraph continued: "The Assembly takes this opportunity to reiterate its unwavering belief that this principle means, *inter alia*, that it is forbidden to cause someone's death deliberately."[49] However, the remainder of the Draft Resolution proceeded, by leaving open the option of legalizing VAE, to saw off the branch on which this reaffirmation sat. No sooner had the first paragraph of the Draft Resolution reaffirmed Recommendation 1418's opposition to intentional killing than paragraph two stated that the Assembly could not ignore certain facts, such as that the Netherlands and Belgium had enacted laws which permitted euthanasia; that Bills to legalize it had been introduced in "numerous" other countries; that in several countries opinion polls suggested that a majority favored legalization; and that euthanasia was practiced in countries where it was illegal "in proportions well in excess of what was previously believed." Further undermining the Draft Resolution's stated opposition to intentional killing, paragraph three stated that euthanasia was a "very delicate" issue which touched on the "moral, religious and cultural values of our societies" and that it therefore followed that the solution to the problem "cannot be the same for all countries." It was "essential" that these "different sensitivities" be respected "while reiterating the inviolable principle that human rights and dignity must be respected."

Paragraph four recommended that member states should implement a genuine policy of assistance to patients at the end of life which did not cause them to want to die, as by promoting palliative care (including care in their own homes) and the avoidance of superfluous treatment. However, paragraph five proposed that "greater transparency" be achieved so as to reduce as far as possible the practice of euthanasia "in secret or in a legal vacuum" and that procedures be introduced, where they did not already exist, clearly defining the responsibilities of medical and nursing staff and ensuring the traceability of all decisions, thus facilitating effective monitoring. That the Draft Resolution was open to the legalization of euthanasia became even clearer in paragraph six, which reiterated that in view of the "diversity of cultural and religious sensitivities" among member states it was "hardly possible to recommend a universal model for all to follow" and that member states should analyze the Dutch and Belgian experience and relevant Bills currently being discussed in other countries, and "prevent euthanasia from developing in a shroud of secrecy because of legal uncertainties or outdated norms."[50]

---

[49] Marty II (Draft Resolution) para 1.
[50] Ibid para 6(v).

In short, the Draft Resolution's first paragraph was progressively undermined by its subsequent paragraphs. Moreover, neither the report nor the accompanying Draft Explanatory Memorandum pointed out why, if euthanasia was a "very delicate" issue which touched on the "moral, religious and cultural values of our societies," it therefore followed that the solution to the problem could not be the same for all countries. Until very recently, it *has* been the same and, with few exceptions, still is. Capital punishment is an issue which touches on moral and cultural values and yet it is totally prohibited by the Council of Europe.

The Draft Resolution's suggestion that euthanasia is practised in secret because of "legal uncertainties and outdated norms" was unsubstantiated. Leaving aside that it did not explain what these "uncertainties" were, why they were "outdated," or how they promoted secret euthanasia, the reality is that the legal norms in the Netherlands, which are of relatively recent vintage, have conspicuously failed to prevent the practice of euthanasia in secret.

That the revised report remained sympathetic to the legalization of euthanasia, despite its opening paragraph, becomes even clearer when the revised Draft Resolution is read in the light of the revised Explanatory Memorandum.

2 Revised Explanatory Memorandum

As has been noted, the revised Draft Resolution was more conservative in tone than its original version. Not so the revised Explanatory Memorandum (again drafted by Marty) which remained a polemic for legalization.[51] Given that the revised version is vulnerable to the same objections leveled above at the original, only three additional points need to be made.

First, the revised Memorandum criticized "the silence in which this issue is more often than not enshrouded"[52] and announced that a "long-repressed debate" had now been launched in several countries.[53] The reality is that the legalization of euthanasia has been debated for decades. Bills were introduced in the United States from the early twentieth century and in the United Kingdom from the 1930s.[54] The debate has

---

[51] Marty concluded that the answer to the questions he raised about patient autonomy, dignity, and the practice of secret euthanasia should "not necessarily" be the legalization of euthanasia, at least as a solution applicable to all member states (revised Explanatory Memorandum para 49). It seems clear, however, that "not necessarily" for "everyone" did not mean "not" for "anyone."

[52] Ibid para 12.

[53] Ibid para 49.

[54] EK Emanuel, "The History of Euthanasia Debates in the United States and Britain" (1994) 121 (10) Annals of Internal Medicine 793. See also I Dowbiggin, *A Merciful End: the Euthanasia Movement in Modern America* (Oxford University Press, 2003); I Dowbiggin, *A Concise History of Euthanasia: Life, Death, God and Medicine* (Rowman & Littlefield Publishers, 2007).

intensified over the last 20 years, not least as a result of the legalization of euthanasia by the Dutch Supreme Court in 1984 and of the euthanasia legislation enacted in the Netherlands in 2001 and in Belgium in 2002. The intensification has been reflected by the publication of reports of expert bodies such as the New York State Task Force in 1994[55]and the House of Lords Select Committees in 1994 and 2005;[56] by widespread and high-profile media coverage of cases like that of Dianne Pretty in 2002;[57] and by the voluminous and growing academic literature on the subject. The debate has been anything but "long-repressed."

A second point concerns the revised Memorandum's claim, in relation to the Netherlands and Belgium, that "[t]he initial indications would not seem to point to any increase in the number of cases of euthanasia or any other types of abuse."[58] The first two Dutch surveys cited by Marty did, in fact, show an increase in VAE/PAS from 2700 cases in 1990 to 3800 in 2001 (and only a slight decrease in NVAE from a little over 1000 cases per year to a little under 1000 cases).[59]

A third point concerns the persistence of errors in the revised Memorandum even though they had been exposed by the Legal Affairs and Human Rights Committee. For example, the Committee concluded that the Dutch euthanasia surveys had demonstrated: "a disturbingly high incidence of euthanasia ... without the patient's explicit request and an equally disturbing failure by medical practitioners to report euthanasia cases to the proper regulatory authority."[60] Marty's revised Memorandum did not respond to such objections and persisted in its misrepresentation of the Dutch experience.[61] Similarly, the Legal Affairs Committee urged that the withholding or withdrawal of treatment because its burdens outweighed its benefits "should not be confused with voluntary active euthanasia or physician assisted suicide where the intention is to accelerate or cause death by withholding or withdrawing treatment."[62] The revised Memorandum, however, maintained its controversial definition of withholding or withdrawing life-support as "passive euthanasia." Indeed, it even compounded matters by asserting that "euthanasia" was commonly practiced, and supported this with a comment by the French

---

[55] NYSTF.
[56] *Report of the Select Committee on Medical Ethics* (HL Paper 21-I of 1993–4)and *Report of the Select Committee on the Assisted Dying for the Terminally Ill Bill* (HL Paper 86-I of 2004–5).
[57] *R (Pretty) v Director of Public Prosecutions* [2002] UKHL 61.
[58] Revised Explanatory Memorandum para 51.
[59] Griffiths II 154, Table 5.1.
[60] Legal Opinion (Conclusions of the Committee) Amendment D.
[61] Revised Explanatory Memorandum paras 26–30, 51.
[62] Legal Opinion (Conclusions of the Committee) Amendment E.

Health Minister that many life-support machines were switched off every year. The Minister was further quoted as saying that an end should be brought to this "unacceptable hypocrisy."[63] There is no hypocrisy in prohibiting intentional killing while allowing the withholding or withdrawal of treatment which is futile or too burdensome. It was hardly prudent for a report which affirmed the prohibition on intentional killing, while scarcely concealing its support for VAE, to have accused the present law of hypocrisy. On 27 April 2005 the Parliamentary Assembly of the Council of Europe voted, by 138 votes to twenty-six, to reject the Marty Report.

Dutch philosopher Professor Guy Widdershoven has offered a partial defense of the Marty Report.[64] He addresses only two of the arguments it advanced, namely the "gap" it alleged between law and practice and the need to alleviate unbearable pain and suffering. In an attempt to improve the first argument, he writes that laws against euthanasia are different from other crimes because it is committed by "well-respected" people (doctors) with the support of many, including their patients. But does it follow that a law should be relaxed if it is broken by "well respected" people with the support of many? If doctors in a particular ethnic community practised female genital mutilation at the request of their female patients, and with the support of many in that community, should the law against it be repealed? And there is no evidence that VAE/PAS is commonly practised by doctors in a country like England: on the contrary. Widdershoven continues that the Marty Report was proposing VAE/PAS only in "proper" cases, and he claims that in the Netherlands euthanasia is "excluded in cases where depression influences the patient's ability to make a well considered request" and that palliative options have to be "thoroughly investigated."[65] He omits to explain how this is achieved without a requirement of specialist psychiatric and palliative care consultation. He also omits even to mention the 1000 cases of NVAE. He writes that Dutch law enables a "clear distinction" to be made between VAE and NVAE and that "no definite legal arrangement has been made."[66] However clear the definitional distinction may be, this has not prevented thousands of patients being killed without request. And the endorsement of infanticide by the courts in 1996 indicates not only that a "definite" legal change has indeed been made but also that the distinction is not so clear after all: NVAE has been legalized on the very

    [63] Revised Explanatory Memorandum para 48, n 15.
    [64] G Widdershoven, "Commentary: Euthanasia in Europe: a critique of the Marty report" (2006) 32 Journal of Medical Ethics 34.
    [65] Ibid.
    [66] Ibid 35.

same ground used initially to justify only VAE, namely the doctor's alleged "conflict of duties."[67]

He continues that each case known not to be in accordance with the legal requirements is examined by a prosecutor. But, as he notes, many cases are not in fact reported (only around half at the time he was writing[68]). And even those cases which are reported are reported by the doctor and are hardly likely to disclose breach of the requirements. He states that the doctor is required to consult an independent doctor, but he omits to point out the inadequacy of this requirement to ensure effective control. For example, the second doctor, like the first, need have no expertise whatever in psychiatry, palliative care, or the patient's condition; the first doctor need not accept the opinion of the second; and a failure to consult by no means automatically results in prosecution.[69]

Turning to the second argument in the Marty Report which he seeks to defend, Widdershoven writes that when patients claim that they can no longer bear their situation, this is not to say that their life has no worth: "They may highly value life, but see no way to live it out any more."[70] To suggest that they must suffer from depression, pain, or loneliness[71] does no justice to the fact that many patients who have a realistic view of their situation may still want to have their lives ended because of the suffering they are currently experiencing, and the future they face. He adds that a physician who decides to follow the patient's request does not act on the basis of a judgment about the worth of the patient's life, but on the basis of the judgment that the patient is suffering unbearably and without prospect of any improvement. This judgment is not necessarily arbitrary. It requires medical knowledge about the future course of the disease and understanding of the patient's experiences of the situation as being unbearable. The first criterion refers to medical expertise and scientific evidence. The latter acknowledges that there are differences between

---

[67] He also denies (ibid) that the Dutch try to deflect discussion of NVAE by the definitional device that as it involves no request, it is not, therefore, "euthanasia." See, however, Ch 9, n 44 and Keown 122–4.

[68] Ibid 34. He contrasts my claim that the bulk of cases "are" not reported with the finding of the third survey, published in 2003, that just over half were reported in 2001. But I did not write that the bulk "are" not reported. I wrote that the first three surveys had shown that bulk had not been reported: "...in the bulk of cases there has not even been an opportunity for control.": J Keown, 'Mr Marty's Muddle: A Superficial and Selective Case for Euthanasia in Europe' (2006) 32 Journal of Medical Ethics 29, 31. Widdershoven's change of tense misleads.

[69] Griffiths II 94–9.

[70] Ibid 35.

[71] Ibid. I wrote: "The fact that, through depression or pain or loneliness, some patients may lose sight of their worth is no argument for endorsing their misguided judgement that their life is no longer worth living.": Keown (n 68 above) 31. To say that some may be suffering from depression is not to say that all must be suffering from depression.

patients, but that does not imply that such experiences are arbitrary. The fact that for each patient the limit may be different does not mean that patients have no grounds for saying that they cannot bear the situation any longer, or that physicians have no grounds for accepting this.

Widdershoven's defense of the Marty Report's second argument fares little better than his defense of its first. If patients seeking VAE/PAS "highly value" their lives, why are they seeking to destroy them? Is it not precisely because they think that life now has for them a negative, rather than a positive, net value and that death would be preferable to life? And is this not precisely why the doctor who ends their lives does so, because he or she believes that the patient would indeed be "better off dead"? Second, the notion of "unbearable suffering" is inherently arbitrary, as the Dutch experience has shown. For some patients it may mean pain of a certain type and to a certain degree; for others grief; for others fear of dementia or simply "tiredness of life." And, once one accepts that certain people would indeed be "better off dead," why limit euthanasia to "unbearable suffering"? Why not extend it to suffering which the patient could bear but does not want to? Why require suffering at all? Why not euthanize those in persistent vegetative state (PVS)? As early as 1991 a committee of the KNMG condoned euthanasia for patients in a persistent coma.[72] When asked whether he saw any moral distinction between removing artificial feeding from a comatose patient and actively killing him, Dr Pieter Admiraal, one of the leading Dutch advocates of voluntary euthanasia, replied:

No, I should kill the patient as well.... In a coma there is no...suffering...and there is no consciousness so there is no...reason to stop life immediately but I should do [so] and not wait for the starving of that patient for the next weeks. Oh no, I should say if I made the decision to stop tube-feeding, I should give active euthanasia.[73]

Third, Widdershoven claims that doctors in other countries also make judgments about their patients' suffering in so far as they are allowed to prescribe palliative drugs. But there is a clear difference, recognized by medical professionals and laws around the world, between a clinical decision to eliminate pain and a moral judgment, because of pain (or suffering or whatever), to eliminate the patient. Finally, he adds that so long as there are certain forms of suffering that cannot be alleviated by palliative care, patients will have to endure it unless euthanasia is allowed.

---

[72] J Keown, "The Law and Practice of Euthanasia in the Netherlands" (1992) 108 LQR 51, 75.
[73] Ibid 76.

He does not consider the option of palliative sedation. Moreover, in the Netherlands, the law allows patients to access VAE/PAS even if palliative care options are available.

In short, Professor Widdershoven's attempted defense of the Marty Report serves only to highlight the inadvisability of the report's reliance on the Dutch experience.

III THE EUROPEAN COURT OF HUMAN RIGHTS:
THE *PRETTY* CASE

In 1993, in the *Rodriguez* case, the Supreme Court of Canada considered and rejected (albeit by a narrow majority[74]) the argument that Canada's law against assisted suicide, which contains no exceptions, breached the Canadian Charter of Rights and Fundamental Freedoms.[75] In 1997, in the *Glucksberg* and *Quill* cases, the United States Supreme Court unanimously rejected the argument that blanket bans on assisted suicide breached the United States Constitution.[76] In 2001 the House of Lords rebuffed the argument, advanced by a terminally ill woman, Dianne Pretty, that the English law prohibiting assisted suicide was incompatible with the European Convention on Human Rights.[77] Pretty's appeal to the European Court of Human Rights in Strasbourg was dismissed.[78]

Dianne Pretty was diagnosed with motor neurone disease ("ALS" or "Lou Gehrig's disease" in North America) in November 1999 and her condition deteriorated rapidly. Though her intellect remained unimpaired, she became paralyzed from the neck down. She had only months to live. Frightened at the prospect of a distressing death, she wanted her husband to help her commit suicide at a time of her choosing. Her husband, however, was fearful of prosecution. Although the Suicide Act 1961 decriminalized suicide, section 2(1) preserved the crime of assisting or encouraging suicide. Under section 2(4) prosecutions may be brought only with the consent of the DPP. Dianne Pretty asked the DPP to give an undertaking that he would not prosecute her husband. He declined. She challenged his refusal by way of judicial review, seeking an order quashing his decision and ordering him to give the undertaking or, alternatively, a declaration that the Suicide Act was incompatible with the European

---

[74] 5—4.

[75] *Rodriguez v British Columbia (Attorney-General)* (1994) 107 DLR (4th) 342.

[76] *Washington v Glucksberg* 521 US 702 (1997); *Vacco, Attorney-General of New York v Quill* 521 US 793 (1997).

[77] *R (Pretty) v Director of Public Prosecutions* [2002] UKHL 61.

[78] *Pretty v United Kingdom* (2002) 35 EHRR 1.

Convention on Human Rights. The Divisional Court unanimously dismissed her claim.[79] It held that the DPP had no power to give the undertaking sought. It also rejected her argument that the Suicide Act was incompatible with the Convention. She appealed to the House of Lords. Unanimously, the Law Lords dismissed her appeal.[80] Their Lordships agreed with the Divisional Court that the DPP lacked power to grant such an undertaking. The power to dispense with and suspend laws and the execution of laws without the consent of Parliament was denied to the Crown and its servants by the Bill of Rights of 1689.[81] The Law Lords also rejected Pretty's claim that the Convention contained a right to assisted suicide. Pretty appealed to the European Court of Human Rights. In seeking to persuade the Court of the existence of a right to assisted suicide, counsel for Pretty relied principally on Articles 2 and 3 of the Convention, and on Articles 8, 9, and 14.

A Article 2

Article 2 provides that "[E]veryone's right to life shall be protected by law. No one shall be deprived of his life intentionally" save for certain purposes connected with criminal justice. Pretty argued that the article protected individuals from third parties but not from themselves, and that it contained a right to choose whether or not to go on living. The Court disagreed. Article 2 protected the right to life and could not, without a distortion of language, be interpreted as conferring a diametrically opposite right, namely a right to die or a right to choose death rather than life.[82] The Court was confirmed in its view by Recommendation 1418 (1999) of the Parliamentary Assembly of the Council of Europe.[83]

B Article 3

The applicant also invoked Article 3, which provides that "[N]o one shall be subjected to torture or to inhuman or degrading treatment or punishment." She argued that the state's prohibition on assisting suicide and the DPP's refusal to give an undertaking not to prosecute her husband constituted inhuman and degrading treatment for which the state was responsible because it was failing to protect her from the suffering in the illness's final stages. The Court replied that it was beyond dispute that the

---

[79] [2001] EWHC Admin 788.
[80] [2001] UKHL 61, [2002] 1 AC 800.
[81] [2001] UHKL 61, para 39.
[82] (2002) 35 EHRR 1 para 39.
[83] Ibid para 40. See text at nn 4–5.

United Kingdom had not inflicted ill-treatment on the applicant. Nor did she complain that she was not receiving adequate medical care from the state. Her argument placed a new and extended construction on the concept of "treatment" which, as the House of Lords had held, went beyond the ordinary meaning of the word. While the Court must take a dynamic and flexible approach to the interpretation of the Convention, which is a living instrument, any interpretation has to comport with the fundamental objectives of the Convention and its coherence as a system of human rights protection. Article 3 has to be construed in harmony with Article 2, which contains a prohibition on the intentional deprivation of life and does not confer a right on an individual to require a state to permit or facilitate her death. There had been no violation of Article 3.[84]

C Article 8

Article 8(1) prohibits interference with anyone's "right to respect for his private and family life," although Article 8(2) excepts interference that is in accordance with the law and is necessary in a democratic society in the furtherance of certain specified interests, including the protection of the rights of others. Pretty claimed that Article 8 protected the right to self-determination, and that this right embraced the right to choose when and how to die. The Court held that personal autonomy was indeed an important principle in interpreting the article. The very essence of the Convention was respect for human dignity and freedom.[85] The Court observed that, without wishing to undermine the principle of the sanctity of life, considerations of "quality of life" were relevant under Article 8.[86] As the ban on assisting suicide prevented the applicant from exercising her choice to avoid what she considered would be an undignified and distressing end to her life, the Court was "not prepared to exclude" the possibility that the ban constituted an interference with her right to respect for her private life under Article 8(1).[87]

Was this interference justified under article 8(2)? In its discussion of whether the blanket ban was "necessary in a democratic society" to protect the lives of others, the Court observed that the notion of necessity implied that the interference corresponded to a pressing social need and that it was proportionate to the legitimate aim pursued. In determining the necessity of interference, the Court would take into account the fact

[84] (2002) 35 EHRR 1 paras 53–4.
[85] Ibid para 65.
[86] Ibid.
[87] Ibid para 67.

that national authorities enjoyed a certain margin of appreciation.[88] The applicant argued that the blanket ban was disproportionate as it failed to take into account that she was not vulnerable and in need of protection: she was a mentally competent woman who was free from pressure and who had made an informed and voluntary decision. The Court agreed that the evidence did not establish that she was vulnerable. Nevertheless, it held that the interference with her private life was justified under Article 8(2): states were entitled to use the criminal law to regulate activities that were detrimental to the lives and safety of others. And the more serious the harm involved, the more heavily public health and safety weighed against individual autonomy. The Court observed:

The law in issue in this case, section 2 of the 1961 Act, was designed to safeguard life by protecting the weak and vulnerable and especially those who are not in a condition to take informed decisions against acts intended to end life or to assist in ending life. Doubtless the conditions of terminally ill individuals will vary. But many will be vulnerable and it is the vulnerability of the class which provides the rationale for the law in question. It is primarily for States to assess the risk and the likely incidence of abuse if the general prohibition on assisted suicides were relaxed or if exceptions were to be created. Clear risks of abuse do exist, notwithstanding arguments as to the possibility of safeguards and protective procedures.[89]

The Court also noted that the English law against assisted suicide was flexible in that it required the consent of the DPP for prosecution and allowed courts to impose sentences below the stipulated maximum.[90]

D Article 9

The Court rejected the applicant's argument that the prohibition on assisted suicide violated her right to "freedom of thought, conscience and religion," protected by Article 9. Not all opinions constituted beliefs in the sense protected by this article, and her claim did not involve a manifestation of a belief or religion in "worship, teaching, practice and observance" within Article 9(1). To the extent that her views reflected her commitment to the principle of personal autonomy, this was simply a restatement of her complaint under Article 8.[91]

---

[88] Ibid para 70.
[89] Ibid para 74.
[90] Iibid para 76.
[91] Ibid para 82.

E Article 14

Article 14 provides that the enjoyment of the rights set out in the Convention shall be secured "without discrimination on any ground...." Pretty submitted that the law against assisted suicide discriminated against her because it treated her in the same way as those whose situations were significantly different: she was prevented from exercising a right enjoyed by others who could end their lives without assistance because they were not prevented by any disability from doing so. The Court observed that Article 14 came into play only if a substantive right protected by the Convention were engaged. Because her right to respect for her private life had been engaged, Article 14 was thereby activated.[92] The Court concluded, however, that just as it had found, when considering Article 8, sound reasons for not allowing assisted suicide for the non-vulnerable, similar cogent reasons existed under Article 14 for not distinguishing between those who could, and those who could not, commit suicide unaided. The borderline between those two categories would often be very fine and to try to build it into law would seriously undermine the law's protection of life and would greatly increase the risk of abuse.[93]

F An Evaluation

Pretty was, like *Rodriguez*, *Glucksberg*, and *Quill*, a setback for those seeking to establish a legal right to assisted suicide through the courts. Critics of the Court's reasoning argue that it attached insufficient importance to individual autonomy and to the alleviation of human suffering, and exaggerated the difficulties of framing and enforcing adequate safeguards against abuse.[94] Even critics, however, would surely have to concede that Pretty's case was far from the strongest that could have been brought before the Court. Pretty did not argue that her suffering could not be alleviated by palliative care. Moreover, she was claiming a right to *non* physician-assisted suicide. As the Divisional Court observed, it was not being asked to permit assisted suicide in carefully defined circumstances with carefully defined safeguards.[95]

The rejection of Pretty's appeal by the European Court was defensible in terms of both principle and prudence. It was principled because the

[92] Ibid para 87.
[93] Ibid para 89.
[94] Eg M Freeman, "Denying Death its Dominion: Thoughts on the Dianne Pretty Case" (2002) 10 MLR 245.
[95] [2001] EWHC Admin 788 para 60.

Convention protects the right to life, which is primarily the right not to be intentionally killed. As the European Court recognized, Article 2 could not, without a distortion of language, be interpreted as conferring a right to be helped to kill oneself. Pretty's attempted to stand Article 2 on its head was rightly dismissed. The Court's rejection of her application was prudent because there would be serious risks to the vulnerable were a right to assisted suicide acknowledged. The Court's concern that clear risks of abuse do exist[96] was well-founded. As we saw in Chapter 9, expert committees worldwide, such as the House of Lords Select Committee on Medical Ethics, whose report was noted by the Court,[97] have concluded that it would not be possible to frame adequate safeguards were the law to be relaxed, even if only for physicians. The risks of abuse involved in granting a right to laypeople to assist suicide, the right demanded by Pretty, would be exponentially greater. As Lord Bingham pointed out, even the Dutch do not permit lay assistance in suicide.[98] Another Law Lord, Lord Steyn, remarked on the serious concerns that had been raised about the Dutch experience, not least by the United Nations Human Rights Committee.[99] Lord Bingham observed:

If the criminal law sought to proscribe the conduct of those who assisted the suicide of the vulnerable, but exonerated those who assisted the suicide of the non-vulnerable, it could not be administered fairly and in a way that could command respect.[100]

Indeed, the reality of the "slippery slope" was evident in the very arguments advanced by counsel for Pretty. He submitted that she had a right to assisted suicide, though not to voluntary euthanasia, because she had a right to decide when to die. But, as Lord Bingham responded:

If article 2 does confer a right to self-determination in relation to life and death, and if a person were so gravely disabled as to be unable to perform any act whatever to cause his or her own death, it would necessarily follow in logic that such a person would have a right to be killed at the hands of a third party without giving any help to the third party and the state would be in breach of the convention if it were to interfere with the exercise of that right.[101]

---

[96] (2002) 35 EHRR para 74.
[97] Ibid paras 21–3.
[98] [2001] UKHL 61, [2002] 1 AC 800 para 28.
[99] Ibid para 55.
[100] Ibid para 36.
[101] Ibid para 5.

Indeed, His Lordship could have gone further. If there is a right to decide when to die, why is it not enjoyed by those who are neither dying nor disabled?

The judgment of the European Court does, however, invite at least one criticism: its holding that Article 8(1) was engaged. The Court observed that "[w]ithout in any way negating the principle of [the] sanctity of life," considerations of "quality of life" were relevant under that article, adding that in an era of increasing medical technology, "many people are concerned that they should not be forced to linger on in old age or in states of advanced physical or mental decrepitude which conflict with strongly held ideas of self and personal identity."[102] It also noted that in domestic law a person may exercise a "choice to die" by refusing life-prolonging treatment.[103] The Court failed to make a vital distinction between two ethically different sorts of choice. There is, on the one hand, the ethically uncontroversial choice to refuse life-prolonging treatment that is either futile or too burdensome. On the other, there is the ethically contentious choice to refuse life-prolonging treatment precisely in order to kill oneself because one no longer thinks one's life worth living. To endorse the latter choice, as the Court implicitly appeared to do, is to endorse suicide and, thereby, to undermine the law against assisting suicide. If one has a right to commit suicide (whether by refusing treatment or otherwise), how can the law consistently prohibit someone from assisting one to exercise that right? So, despite the Court's disclaimer that its reasoning was not "negating the principle of the sanctity of life,"[104] its apparent endorsement not only of choices intended to put an end to worthless treatments but also choices intended to put an end to worthless lives, risks doing just that. The Court should have adopted the reasoning of Lord Bingham and of the submission it had received from the Archbishop of Wales.[105] Both had concluded that there is no right to commit suicide and that the law against assisting suicide does not engage Article 8(1). The Archbishop observed: "[t]he ending of a life is *not* a private matter, but is a legitimate concern of public authorities whose duty is to protect the lives of citizens within their jurisdiction."[106] The Court led up to its conclusion that Article 8 was engaged by asserting that individual autonomy is an important principle underlying the article and

---

[102] (2002) 35 EHRR 1 para 65.
[103] Ibid para 63.
[104] Ibid para 65.
[105] Ibid paras 14 and 31 respectively.
[106] "Intervention of the Catholic Bishops' Conference of England and Wales pursuant to Art. 36 § 2 of the Convention" (available online using this search parameter).

by citing the holding of the Canadian Supreme Court in the *Rodriguez* case that, although the Canadian prohibition on assisting suicide did not violate the Canadian Charter of Rights and Freedoms, it did interfere with Rodriguez's right to "life, liberty and security of the person" under section 7 of the Charter. However, these observations by the European Court were incautious, for three reasons. First, importing the principle of autonomy into Article 8 threatens unreasonably to stretch the article's bounds (as happened in *Pretty*): an interference with autonomy may, but need not, involve any interference with privacy. Second, as the brief for the Archbishop noted:

Article 8 does not encompass a right to self-determination *as such*. Rather, Article 8 relates to the right to private and family life in respect of the manner in which a person *conducts* his life. Where rights under Article 8 are engaged, it is to protect the physical, moral and/or psychological integrity of the individual: cf. Appl. 8978/80 *X and Y v. The Netherlands* (Series A, No.91; 26th March 1985; (1985) 7 EHRR 152) at para. 22 of the Court's judgment. Such rights may—indeed, sometimes do—include rights over the individual's own body. However, the alleged right claimed by Mrs. Pretty would ineluctably and necessarily extinguish the very benefit on which it was purportedly based, namely respect for her private *life*.[107]

Third, as Lord Bingham noted, section 7 of the Canadian Charter, which expressly protects personal "liberty," has "no close analogy" with Article 8.[108]

Moreover, one consequence of finding that Article 8(1) was engaged was to bring Article 14 into play. In its reply to the applicant's argument that the prohibition on assisting suicide discriminated against those physically unable to commit suicide, the Court's earlier failure to hold that there is no right to commit suicide deprived it of the riposte, deployed by Lord Bingham, that the blanket prohibition on assisted suicide treats everyone, able-bodied or disabled, equally. The law could not be criticized as discriminatory because it applied to everyone. As he pointed out, the policy of the law remained firmly opposed to suicide, as its continuing prohibition on assisting suicide made clear.[109] His Lordship also observed that English law's prohibition on assisting suicide was consistent with a "very broad international consensus."[110]

---

[107] Ibid (emphases in original).
[108] [2001] UKHL 61, [2002] 1 AC 800 para 23.
[109] Ibid para 35.
[110] Ibid para 28.

IV THE LAW LORDS: THE *PURDY* CASE

On 1 October 2009 the Justices of the United Kingdom's new Supreme Court, which replaced the ancient jurisdiction of the Appellate Committee of the House of Lords, were sworn in. The Law Lords' final ruling, in the *Purdy* case,[111] could scarcely have been more controversial: it undermined the law against assisting suicide.

Although the Suicide Act 1961 maintained the law's prohibition on assisting suicide it provided that no proceedings should be instituted for this crime except by, or with the consent of, the DPP.[112] Debbie Purdy, the claimant in this case, had primary progressive multiple sclerosis. She told the court:

My wish is to be able to ask for and receive assistance to end my life, should living it become unbearable for me. I wish to be able to make the decision to end my life while I am physically able to do so. I consider that this will probably mean either travelling to Zurich, Switzerland, to avail myself of the services of Dignitas ... or to go to Belgium and avail myself of the Belgian Act on Euthanasia ...[113]

She added: "My husband has said he would assist me and if necessary face a prison sentence, but I am not prepared to put him in this position...."[114] Ms Purdy therefore asked the DPP, Keir Starmer QC, to set out the criteria governing the exercise of his discretion under section 2(4), in particular where a relative or friend assists with travel to a country where assisting suicide is not an offense.[115] She said that if the risk of prosecution were sufficiently low, she could wait until the last moment before making the trip with her husband's help, but if the risk were too high she would have to travel without such help and earlier than she would wish.[116] The DPP declined, replying that the policy he applied was that set out in the Code for Crown Prosecutors, which applied to all criminal offenses.[117]

Purdy sought judicial review of the DPP's refusal. She argued that the prohibition on assisting suicide infringed her right to respect for her "private and family life" under Article 8(1) of the European Convention on Human Rights, and that this interference was not, in the absence of an "offence-specific" policy by the DPP concerning the exercise of his discretion, "in accordance with law" as required by Article 8(2).[118] Her

---

[111] *R (Purdy) v Director of Public Prosecutions* [2009] UKHL 45 ("*Purdy* HL").
[112] Section 2(4).
[113] *R (Purdy) v Director of Public Prosecutions* [2009] EWCA Civ 92 ("*Purdy* CA") para 6.
[114] Ibid.
[115] Ibid para 12.
[116] *Purdy* HL para 31.
[117] *Purdy* CA para 12.
[118] Ibid paras 25–6; *Purdy* HL para 28.

application was rejected by the Divisional Court[119] and her appeal to the Court of Appeal was dismissed. Her appeal to the House of Lords was, surprisingly, allowed. Lord Hope stated that the Convention required laws to satisfy the tests of accessibility and foreseeability: individuals were entitled to know which acts and omissions would incur criminal liability and to be able to foresee the consequences a given action may entail. A law conferring a discretion needed to indicate with sufficient clarity the scope of that discretion and the manner of its exercise so as to protect the individual against arbitrary interference.[120] He noted that since the publication of the current version of the Code for Crown Prosecutors in 2004, the DPP had set up a Special Crimes Division staffed by specially trained lawyers to supervise prosecutions of exceptional sensitivity or difficulty, and had published an explanation of his decision not to prosecute in the case of Daniel James, a paralyzed 23-year-old who had been helped by his reluctant parents to travel to Switzerland to commit suicide.[121] Lord Hope concluded, however, that these developments fell short of what was needed to satisfy the Convention tests of accessibility and foreseeability in the case of a person with a severe or incurable disability who was likely to need assistance to travel to a country where assisting suicide is lawful.[122] In a "highly unusual and extremely sensitive case," like Ms Purdy's, the Code offered almost no guidance, and the factors relevant to the Daniel James case might not be relevant to others.[123] Lord Hope held that the Code usually provided sufficient guidance to Crown Prosecutors and the public:

But that cannot be said of cases where the offence in contemplation is aiding or abetting the suicide of a person who is terminally ill or severely and incurably disabled, who wishes to be helped to travel to a country where assisted suicide is lawful and who, having the capacity to take such a decision, does so freely and with a full understanding of the consequences.[124]

The Law Lords ordered the DPP to issue "an offence-specific policy identifying the facts and circumstances which he will take into account in deciding, in a case such as that which Ms Purdy's case exemplifies,

---

[119] [2008] EWHC 2565 (Admin).
[120] *Purdy* HL para 41.
[121] Ibid para 52. Crown Prosecution Service (CPS), "Decision on Prosecution—The Death by Suicide of Daniel James", 9 December 2008.
[122] *Purdy* HL para 53.
[123] Ibid.
[124] Ibid para 54.

whether or not to consent to a prosecution under section 2(1) of the 1961 Act."[125]

A The DPP's policy

The DPP issued his interim policy on 23 September 2009 and launched a public consultation.[126] The response was "overwhelming," resulting in almost 5000 submissions.[127] He published his final policy on 25 February 2010.[128] It applied to all cases of assisting or encouraging suicide, not just the Debbie Purdy scenario. It listed 16 factors indicating when prosecution is in the public interest and six when it is not. These six were:

- that "the victim had reached a voluntary, clear, settled and informed decision to commit suicide"; and that the suspect
- was "wholly motivated by compassion";
- had provided "only minor encouragement or assistance";
- had "sought to dissuade" the victim from suicide;
- had provided "reluctant encouragement or assistance in the face of a determined [suicidal] wish"; and
- had reported the suicide to the police and "fully assisted" them in their enquiries.

The *Purdy* case and the DPP's policy prompt several questions.

B Some concerns

First, did the Law Lords not undermine the Suicide Act's prohibition on assisting suicide by promoting its *de facto* (and ultimately *de jure*) decriminalization? Lord Hope acknowledged that changing the law against assisting suicide was a matter for Parliament, not the courts. However, *Purdy* at least verges on doing just that. As the Lord Chief Justice, Lord Judge, observed, delivering the judgement of the Court of Appeal:

Like this court the DPP cannot dispense with or suspend the operation of s.2(1) of the 1961 Act, and he cannot promulgate a case-specific policy in the kind of

---

[125] Ibid para 56. For a penetrating critique of the decision see J Finnis, "Invoking the Principle of Legality against the Rule of Law" in R Ekins (ed), *Modern Challenges to the Rule of Law* (LexisNexis, 2011) 129.

[126] CPS, "A public consultation on the DPP's interim policy for prosecutors on assisted suicide" <http://www.cps.gov.uk/consultations/as_index.html>.

[127] K Starmer, "'Mercy killing' is not the same as assisted suicide", *The Times*, 25 February 2010.

[128] CPS, "Policy for Prosecutors in Respect of Cases of Encouraging or Assisting Suicide" (2010) <http://www.cps.gov.uk/publications/prosecution/assisted_suicide_policy.html>.

certain terms sought by Ms Purdy which would, in effect, recognise exceptional defences to this offence which Parliament has not chosen to enact.[129]

The Lord Chief Justice could have gone further: Parliament has *chosen not to* enact exceptions, and after repeated and exhaustive consideration of the case *for* making exceptions. Indeed, only weeks before the Law Lords' ruling, the legislative chamber of the House had voted down, by a comfortable majority, an attempt by Lord Falconer to amend the Coroners and Justice Bill so as to decriminalize assisting suicide in circumstances similar to those canvassed in *Purdy.* Moreover, in that very same Bill the government updated the crime of assisting or encouraging suicide.[130] The Law Lords, nevertheless, ordered the DPP to formulate a policy which in effect undermines that prohibition. Lord Falconer recognized this ramification of their ruling:

The DPP will now have to set out in writing what his policy will be in prosecuting cases in enough detail for a person to know whether what he or she does will attract the attention of the law. Requiring that degree of clarity means the DPP will in practice be carving out an exception to the terms of s2(1) of the Suicide Act.[131]

As Professor Conor Gearty has observed: "Throwing everything on to the DPP is not only to ask too much of a single law officer, it is also to impose a legislative duty on him that is beyond his role as director of prosecutions."[132] Further, once assisting suicide is decriminalized *de facto,* the argument for its decriminalization *de jure* becomes all the stronger. This is doubtless the goal motivating Ms Purdy and her fellow campaigners in the pressure-group "Dignity in Dying."

A second question is whether *Purdy* is consistent with the earlier decision of the Law Lords in the not dissimilar case of *Pretty.* True, Ms Purdy was not, like Mrs Pretty, seeking a *guarantee* that the DPP would not prosecute, but she was seeking something close. Is there a substantial difference between demanding *that* the DPP not prosecute and demanding *to know when* he will not prosecute (or even to know all the factors he will take into account in deciding to prosecute)? The Lord Chief Justice said that what Ms Purdy was seeking was "the nearest thing possible to a guarantee" that her husband would not be prosecuted. The judge added that her true objective would not be achieved unless she obtained "what in

---

[129] *Purdy* CA para 79.
[130] Coroners and Justice Act 2009, s 59 and Sch 12.
[131] C Falconer, "A Right to Die—and a right to clarity in the law", *The Times,* 31 July 2009.
[132] C Gearty, "Too much for a single law officer?", *The Tablet,* 8 August 2009.

reality would amount either to immunity from prosecution or the promulgation of a policy which would effectively discount the risk of a prosecution in this particular case...."[133] He went on to observe that the DPP's refusal to issue such a policy was "amply supported" by the House of Lords in *Pretty*, where more than one Law Lord had expressed the view that "whether or not the Director has the power to make such a statement he has no duty to do so...."[134]

Moreover, we will recall that although the European Court of Human Rights held in *Pretty* (unlike the House of Lords in that case) that the Suicide Act's prohibition on assisting suicide engaged Mrs Pretty's right to "private and family life" under Article 8(1), it nevertheless upheld, under Article 8(2), the Act's blanket prohibition, indicating that the existence of prosecutorial discretion was a reason for so doing.[135] It may also be asked whether, even if Ms Purdy had a right to clarity as to the DPP's approach to cases like hers, it had not already been provided (as both the Divisional Court and Court of Appeal indicated) by the Code for Crown Prosecutors and the DPP's detailed explanation of his decision not to prosecute in the comparable case of Daniel James. As one Law Lord, Lord Neuberger, commented: "it can be said with some force that it must be pretty clear"[136] to Ms Purdy and her husband how the DPP exercised his discretion in cases like theirs.

A third question: could the policy the DPP was directed to formulate ever sensibly have been confined to what Lord Hope thought was the "very special and carefully defined class of case"[137] illustrated by Ms Purdy? Why did his Lordship think that travel abroad was special? Providing assistance to travel is, like supplying a plastic bag, simply one of the myriad forms which assistance may take. Again, why did he seem to think that the guidelines should be limited to the "terminally ill or severely and incurably disabled"? And why should they not apply to murder? As Ms Purdy noted in her statement to the court, she might want help to travel not to Switzerland for suicide but to Belgium for euthanasia. The nexus between the two crimes is only reinforced by the opinion of the Senior Law Lord, Lord Phillips,[138] that even helping someone to travel abroad to commit suicide amounts to complicity in the crime of murder.

---

[133] *Purdy* CA para 74.
[134] Ibid para 75.
[135] *Pretty v United Kingdom* (2002) 35 EHRR 1 [76].
[136] *Purdy* HL para 97.
[137] Ibid para 55.
[138] Ibid paras 12, 16.

It is one thing for the courts to protect citizens from the arbitrary use of prosecutorial discretion resulting in abuse of process. It is quite another for courts to order prosecutors to spell out the public interest criteria they will apply in relation to particular crimes, not least hypothetical instances of particular crimes. And even if it could be known for certain that Ms Purdy's husband will assist her in suicide, is it now the law that P1 may make use of the judicial process prospectively to minimize P2's risk of prosecution for the commission of a serious criminal offense? For example, the Female Genital Mutilation Act 2003 makes it an offense to commit or assist female genital mutilation (FGM) on a woman (but it does not make the woman herself liable).[139] If Fatima wants to slice off her own clitoris (surely at least as much an incident of her "right to privacy" as a decision to slit her own throat) and her uncle Faisal wants to fly her to Somalia, or simply to supply her with a razor in Swindon, will the courts at Fatima's behest order the DPP to spell out when he will and will not prosecute Faisal?

Turning to the policy the DPP formulated at the behest of the Law Lords, it too raises important questions. His interim policy had attracted four major criticisms, namely that it failed:

- to state that assisting suicide remained a crime to which only Parliament could make exceptions;
- to recognize that two in particular of the factors it listed against prosecution—that the victim was terminally ill or severely disabled, and was assisted by a spouse, partner, or close relative—discriminated against the disabled and ignored the reality of abuse by relatives;
- to spell out that prosecution would be the rule unless the circumstances were wholly exceptional; and
- to provide that the presence of any one of the major factors in favor of prosecution (such as the victim having no clear, settled, and informed wish to commit suicide) would result in prosecution, irrespective of the number of factors against.

The final policy meets only the first and second criticisms. It fails to meet the third by asking not whether a prosecution is in the public interest but by asking whether it "is required" in the public interest, thereby reversing the normal presumption in favor of prosecution. It fails to meet the fourth by evidently allowing factors against prosecution to outweigh even key factors in favor. Should an assister escape prosecution because of a wholly

---

[139] Female Genital Mutilation Act 2003, ss 1, 2.

compassionate motivation (factor 2 against) even if the victim lacked capacity (factor 2 in favor)?

Launching his final policy the DPP announced: "The policy is now more focused on the motivation of the suspect rather than the characteristics of the victim. The policy does not change the law on assisted suicide. It does not open the door for euthanasia. It does not override the will of Parliament."[140] This has failed to reassure everyone, particularly disability groups,[141] and understandably so. How is the DPP to gainsay the assister who claims that his or her motives were wholly compassionate (especially when the policy allows the assister to gain financially[142])? And if the DPP declines to prosecute Debbie Purdy's husband if he takes her to Switzerland for assisted suicide, will he prosecute if her husband takes her to Belgium for euthanasia, which would clearly involve the crime of complicity in murder? Last but not least, if Parliament has repeatedly refused to make any exceptions for assisting suicide, why should the DPP?

The movement toward the statutory legalization of euthanasia in the Netherlands began with courts, prosecutors, and "guidelines." Have the Law Lords diverted English law onto the same trajectory?

V CONCLUSION

For over three quarters of a century, campaigners for VAE/PAS have, with rare exceptions as in Belgium and Luxembourg, repeatedly failed to persuade legislative and expert bodies of their case.[143] Even in Oregon and Washington State, the law was relaxed as a result of voter referenda. Campaigners have, therefore, increasingly turned their attention to the courts. Even there, however, they have met with little success. Though the Dutch Supreme Court relaxed the law in 1984, the Supreme Courts of Canada, the United States, and the Law Lords have declined to do so.[144]

---

[140] CPS, "Assisted Suicide" (2010) <http://www.cps.gov.uk/publications/prosecution/assisted_suicide.html>.

[141] R Hawkes, *Daily Telegraph*, 26 February 2010, Letters.

[142] "If it is shown that compassion was the only driving force behind his or her actions, the fact that the suspect may have gained some benefit will not usually be treated as a factor tending in favour of prosecution.": CPS, "Policy for Crown Prosecutors in Respect of Cases of Encouraging or Assisting Suicide" (2010) para 44.

[143] For a recent illustration of the arguments in the ongoing debate see E Jackson and J Keown, *Debating Euthanasia* (Hart Publishing, 2012).

[144] In a remarkable decision in 2009 the Supreme Court of Montana held, despite a clear and long-established state criminal prohibition of assisting suicide in the state, that physician-assisted suicide was permissible as not being contrary to public policy: *Baxter v Montana*, 2009 WL 5155363 (Mont. 2009). For telling criticism of the decision see C Kaveny, "Peaceful and Private", Commonweal, 12 March 2010 <http://www.commonwealmagazine.org/%E2%80%98peaceful-private%E2%80%99>.

This is not surprising. To permit VAE/PAS would involve overturning one of the most fundamental and historic prohibitions in the criminal law. Moreover, courts are far less well-equipped than legislatures to resolve an issue that involves contentious moral and complex social policy questions. This is partly why the decision of the Law Lords in *Purdy*, an unsound if not unconstitutional decision, is so surprising. The Canadian case of *Carter v Attorney General of Canada*[145] is but the latest invitation to the judiciary to legalize VAE/PAS. It is unlikely to be the last.

---

[145] *Lee Carter, Hollis Johnson, Dr William Shoichet, the British Columbia Civil Liberties Association and Gloria Taylor v Attorney-General of Canada* No S112688 Vancouver Registry (2011).

CHAPTER 11

PALLIATIVE CARE: AN ETHICAL AND LEGAL DUTY?

I INTRODUCTION

As the two previous chapters have indicated, the question whether the law should permit voluntary, active euthanasia/physician-assisted suicide (VAE/PAS) has been the subject of intense and protracted debate which has taxed legislatures and courts and has spawned a vast and growing literature. Commenting on the debate, Ezekiel Emanuel has observed that if the objective is to improve the quality of care at the end of life then the battle over legalizing euthanasia is "an emotionally charged irrelevance."[1] He adds that legalization might well be counter-productive, diverting attention from reforms needed to help the 90 per cent or more of dying patients who will never even vaguely desire euthanasia, and concludes: "It is time to eschew the spotlight of euthanasia and focus on the unglamorous process of systematic change to help the majority of dying patients."[2] This chapter will address one of many important questions the euthanasia debate has, unfortunately, overshadowed. That question is whether there is an ethical and legal duty to provide palliative care to those who could benefit from it. There is a consensus on both sides of the euthanasia debate that one desirable change would be an improvement in the availability of adequate palliative care, but little consideration has been given to whether the law might not have a valuable role to play in promoting that improvement.

The chapter begins by defining "palliative care." It then notes the inadequate availability of palliative care. It proceeds to argue that there is an ethical duty on doctors and hospitals to remedy that inadequacy. It

---

[1] EJ Emanuel, "Euthanasia: Where the Netherlands Leads Will the World Follow?" (2001) 322 BMJ 1376, 1377.
[2] Ibid.

then considers, in turn, whether the failure to provide palliative care may not constitute a breach of human rights, medical negligence, or a criminal offense. Finally, it considers the desirability of legislation, either by way of a statute focused on palliative care or by extending existing legislation prohibiting wilful neglect, to make it clearly criminal to neglect to provide reasonable palliative care.

II A DEFINITION

The World Health Organization defines "palliative care" as follows:

Palliative care is an approach that improves the quality of life of patients and their families facing the problem associated with life-threatening illness, through the prevention and relief of suffering by means of early identification and impeccable assessment and treatment of pain and other problems, physical, psychosocial and spiritual. Palliative care:

- provides relief from pain and other distressing symptoms;
- affirms life and regards dying as a normal process;
- intends neither to hasten or postpone death;
- integrates the psychological and spiritual aspects of patient care;
- offers a support system to help patients live as actively as possible until death;
- offers a support system to help the family cope during the patient's illness and in their own bereavement;
- uses a team approach to address the needs of patients and their families, including bereavement counselling, if indicated;
- will enhance quality of life, and may also positively influence the course of illness;
- is applicable early in the course of illness, in conjunction with other therapies that are intended to prolong life, such as chemotherapy or radiation therapy, and includes those investigations needed to better understand and manage distressing clinical complications.[3]

This chapter will confine itself to the unreasonable failure to alleviate severe pain in the terminally ill, but its conclusions will have implications for palliative care more broadly understood, to include the alleviation of other symptoms and in patients who are not terminally ill. If there is an ethical and legal duty to alleviate severe pain in the terminally ill, then it is difficult to see why it should not apply to the alleviation of pain in the non-terminally ill, and to the relief of other serious symptoms.

---

[3] "WHO Definition of Palliative Care" <http://www.who.int/cancer/palliative/definition/en/>

III THE INADEQUATE AVAILABILITY OF
PALLIATIVE CARE

The growth of palliative care over the last half century has been one of the most inspirational movements in modern medicine and nursing. The founding in 1967 of St Christopher's Hospice[4] in London by Dr Cicely Saunders was a landmark in the development of the "hospice movement." The Walton Report observed in 1994 that thanks to the increasing dissemination of best practice by means of home-care teams and training for general practitioners, palliative care was becoming more widely available in the hospitals and the community.[5] However, much remained to be done. It concluded: "With the necessary political will such care could be made available to all who could benefit from it. We strongly commend the development and growth of palliative care services."[6]

The same year, the New York State Task Force (NYSTF) observed that many health care professionals lacked the clinical knowledge and experience needed to provide effective palliative care.[7] Educators must convey to nursing and medical students that "pain and symptom management are a basic and essential component of medical care for professionals in all areas of medical practice."[8] Continuing education for health care professionals was also vital.[9] Guidelines for the treatment of pain had been issued by bodies such as the American Pain Society.[10] However, those guidelines would not be effective without institutional commitment to implement them and effective programmes to educate health care professionals.[11] Moreover, hospitals and other health care facilities had "the responsibility to promote high quality medical care" which "should encompass the delivery of adequate pain and symptom management."[12] Doctors and nurses should be trained to ask patients about their pain on a regular basis and hospitals and nursing facilities should address palliative care in their quality-assurance procedures.[13] In 1991 the American Pain Society (APS) proposed "Quality Assurance Standards for Relief of Acute Pain and Cancer Pain." Its recommendations were designed to improve

---

[4] <http://www.stchristophers.org.uk/>.
[5] Report of the Select Committee on Medical Ethics (HL Paper 21-I of 1993–4) para 241.
[6] Ibid.
[7] New York State Task Force on Life and the Law, *When Death is Sought: Assisted Suicide and Euthanasia in the Medical Context* (New York State Task Force, 1994) 165.
[8] Ibid 166.
[9] Ibid.
[10] Ibid.
[11] Ibid 167.
[12] Ibid 168.
[13] Ibid.

treatment of all types of pain. The APS emphasized the need for systems "to assure that the occurrence of pain is recognized and that when pain persists, there is rapid feedback to modify treatment." It recommended: "The education of health care professionals about pain relief and palliative care must be improved. Training in pain relief and palliative care should be included in the curriculum of nursing schools, medical schools, residencies, and continuing education for health care professionals."[14] Good palliative care should be made "standard, not exceptional, treatment for all patients."[15]

We will recall that Walton noted that "much remains to be done." Sadly, it still does. In 2010, in a survey of end-of-life care in forty countries, the United Kingdom was ranked first and the United States third,[16] but there is evidence that, even in the United Kingdom, many people still suffer unnecessarily as a result of the lack of good palliative care. In 2008 the Department of Health launched an End of Life Care Strategy to improve the quality of end-of-life care. It noted:

Some people do indeed die as they would have wished, but many others do not. Some people experience excellent care in hospitals, hospices, care homes and in their own homes. But the reality is that many do not. *Many people experience unnecessary pain and other symptoms.* There are distressing reports of people not being treated with dignity and respect and many people do not die where they would choose to.[17]

In 2011 the Palliative Care Funding Review estimated that "around 92,000 people per year have an unmet palliative care need, or up to 145,500 if using the maximum estimated need."[18] It noted: "Changing demographics, with an ageing population, longer chronic disease trajectories, and greater comorbidity, provide further incentives to improve and expand palliative care provision."[19]

Though the concern of this chapter is the common law, and particularly the law in England and Wales, it merits mention that the lack of palliative care is even graver in poorer nations. A survey by Human Rights Watch published in 2011 concluded: "Every year, tens of millions of people

---

[14] Ibid xvi.
[15] Ibid 121.
[16] "Quality of death", *Economist,* 14 July 2010.
[17] Department of Health, *End of Life Care Strategy* (2008) Executive Summary para 5 (emphasis added). See also *Report of the Select Committee on the Assisted Dying for the Terminally Ill Bill* (HL Paper 86-I) para 35.
[18] T Hughes-Hallett et al., *Palliative Care Funding Review* (www.palliativecarefunding.org, 2011) 64 <http://palliativecarefunding.org.uk/wp-content/uploads/2011/06/PCFRFinal%20Report.pdf>.
[19] Ibid 62. See also *Report of the Select Committee on the Assisted Dying for the Terminally Ill Bill* (HL Paper 86-I) para 35.

around the world with life-threatening illnesses suffer unnecessarily from severe pain and other debilitating symptoms because they lack access to palliative care...."[20] It added: "experts estimate that 60 per cent of those who die each year in the developing world—a staggering 33 million people—need palliative care."[21]

IV PALLIATIVE CARE: AN ETHICAL DUTY?

Betty, 75, lives in London. Six months ago she was diagnosed with terminal cancer of the colon, which has metastasized. As Betty's life reaches its end, she is admitted to the geriatric ward of her local hospital, under the care of Dr Andrews, a consultant geriatrician. The cancer is causing her considerable pain. Dr Andrews fails to bring her pain under control, though he could easily have done so by prescribing an analgesic such as morphine or diamorphine (heroin), or by calling in a palliative specialist to attend her. Betty lingers on in agony. Has Dr Andrews acted ethically?

The following have been traditionally understood as the goals of medicine:

- the maintenance of health;
- cure or healing;
- where cure is not possible, helping patients approximate as far as possible to organic well-functioning; and
- symptom control, so that the symptoms of an organic disorder (such as the pain caused by certain cancers) are kept from unnecessarily obtruding on a person's capacity to enjoy some of the other goods of human life.[22]

Gormally explains that the latter two are justified ends of medicine because health is an instrumental as well as a basic good:

So medicine's dedication to the good of health in patients encompasses a dedication to securing what organic well-functioning is instrumental for, namely, the body's readiness for the pursuit of other human goods—a dedication that reasonably extends to mitigating a damaged or ailing body's unreadiness for the pursuit of other human goods. Hence palliative medicine is a proper part of the practice of medicine though it has no curative *telos*.[23]

---

[20] Human Rights Watch, *Global State of Pain Treatment* (2011) Summary <http://www.hrw. org/node/98902/section/3> ("HRW Report").

[21] Ibid.

[22] See L Gormally, "The Good of Health and the Ends of Medicine" in H Zaborowski (ed), *Natural Moral Law in Contemporary Society* (The Catholic University of America Press, 2010) 264, 281. See also Ch 1, n 31.

[23] Gormally (n 22) 282 (italics in original).

A physician who does not attend to the control of a patient's symptoms ignores the key principle of Hippocratic ethics, to benefit the patient, by ignoring one of the defining goals of medicine. Pain is an all-too-common symptom, which can have serious physical, psychological, and social effects.[24] That physicians are under at least a prima facie ethical duty to palliate pain is a proposition which would surely attract the support of other ethical traditions, including both utilitarianism and "principlism." The utilitarian, whether one who is concerned to maximize pleasure and minimize pain, or to maximize patients' preferences, would surely endorse such a duty. So too would the "principlist," who advocates respect for autonomy, non-maleficence, beneficence, and justice.[25] To fail to provide patients with the pain relief they need and want could be said to offend all four principles. In short, the ethical proposition that hospitals and doctors have a duty to provide adequate pain relief to their patients, at least where hospitals and doctors have the resources to do so, seems to be a proposition which would attract a very wide consensus. There would certainly appear to be such a duty in wealthy developed nations like the United Kingdom and the United States.[26] Dr Andrews has surely acted unethically. Some have argued that relief from pain is not only morally desirable but is a basic human right.

V PALLIATIVE CARE: A HUMAN RIGHT?

Dr Frank Brennan has pioneered the argument that palliative care is a basic human right. He has written that an international consensus is emerging that "the unreasonable failure to treat pain is poor medicine, unethical practice, and is an abrogation of a fundamental human right."[27] Gwyther et al. observe that Article 12.1 of the International Covenant on Economic, Social and Cultural Rights, which came into force in 1976, provides that the states parties recognize "the right of everyone to the

---

[24] HRW Report Part I, text at nn 14–16.
[25] TL Beauchamp and JF Childress, *Principles of Biomedical Ethics* (6th edn, Oxford University Press, 2008).
[26] The duty may of course be qualified in poorer nations where hospitals and doctors may well not have access to the necessary resources. This is not to say that the governments of those poorer countries (and/or of richer countries) may not have an ethical duty to make sufficient resources available. A good case can be made that pain relief is so basic a human need that it should be accorded a high priority, not least given that palliative care need not be costly.
[27] F Brennan et al., "Pain Management: A Fundamental Human Right" (2007) 105 Anaesthesia and Analgesia 205. See also F Brennan et al., "Palliative Care as an International Human Right" (2007) 33(5) Journal of Pain and Symptom Management 494; HRW Report Part VIII; The Declaration of Montreal (International Association for the Study of Pain, 2010) <http://www.iasppain.org/Content/NavigationMenu/Advocacy/DeclarationofMontr233al/default.htm>.

enjoyment of the highest attainable standard of physical and mental health" and that General Comment 14, issued by the committee that oversees the Covenant, has asserted that "in particular, States are under the obligation to respect the right to health by, *inter alia*, refraining from denying or limiting equal access for all persons ... to preventive, curative and palliative health services."[28] Gwyther et al. note a statement made to the United Nations Human Rights Council in 2008 by the Special Rapporteur on the Right to Health that every year millions suffered "horrific, avoidable pain" and that palliative care needed urgent and greater attention,[29] as well as a joint statement by the Special Rapporteur on the Right to Health and the Special Rapporteur on Torture that international human rights law required governments to provide essential medicines, including opioid analgesics, as part of their minimum core obligations under the right to health, and that lack of access to essential medicines, including for pain relief, was a global human rights issue which should be forcefully addressed.[30] In a report the following year to the United Nations Human Rights Council, the Special Rapporteur on Torture wrote that the denial of access to pain relief, if it causes severe pain and suffering, constitutes cruel, inhuman, or degrading treatment or punishment, and that all measures should be taken to overcome current regulatory, educational, and attitudinal obstacles to ensure full access to palliative care.[31] Betty might, therefore, be able to invoke Article 3(1) of the European Convention on Human Rights, which provides, without exception: "No one shall be subjected to torture or to inhuman or degrading treatment or punishment." She might also rely on a number of other relevant European sources. In 2003 the Committee of Ministers adopted a recommendation which stated that palliative care is an "inalienable element of a citizen's right to health care."[32] As we will recall from Chapter 10, Recommendation 1418, passed by the Parliamentary Assembly of the Council of Europe in 1999, urged member states "to respect and protect the dignity of terminally ill or dying persons in all respects" by, *inter alia*, "recognising and protecting a terminally ill or dying person's right to comprehensive palliative care."[33] We will also recall, no less importantly, that in *Pretty* the European Court of Human Rights held that a blanket ban on assisting

---

[28] L Gwyther et al., "Advancing Palliative Care as a Human Right" (2009) 38(5) Journal of Pain and Symptom Management 767, 769.

[29] Ibid 771.

[30] Ibid 772.

[31] HRW Report Part VIII, text at n 140.

[32] Gwyther et al. (n 28) 770. See also F Brennan, "Palliative Care as an International Human Right" (2007) 33(5) Journal of Pain and Symptom Management 494; HRW Report Part VIII.

[33] Chapter 10, n 3.

suicide prevented Dianne Pretty from "exercising her choice to avoid what she considers will be an undignified and distressing end to her life" and was "not prepared to exclude that this constitutes an interference with her right to respect for private life as guaranteed under Article 8(1) of the Convention."[34] The Court went on to uphold the blanket ban under Article 8(2) as it protected the interests of the vulnerable.[35] The Human Rights Act 1998 incorporated the European Convention into English law. The Act provides that it is unlawful for a "public authority" to act in a way which is incompatible with a Convention right.[36] "Public authority" includes "any person certain of whose functions are functions of a public nature,"[37] which would include the government and a National Health Service hospital. An "act" includes a failure to act.[38] If (however erroneously) the denial of assisted suicide was thought by the European Court of Human Rights to engage Dianne Pretty's Article 8(1) right, why could an unreasonable failure to alleviate severe pain not engage Betty's Article 8(1) right? May not Betty equally be said to be suffering "an undignified and distressing end to her life"? And what justification could a public authority (whether the government or a hospital) invoke for failing to provide reasonable palliative care? Could the failure possibly be said to be "in accordance with the law" and "in the interests of national security, public safety or the economic well-being of the country, for the prevention of disorder or crime, for the protection of health or morals, or for the protection of the rights and freedoms of others" under Article 8(2)? Health care resources are not, of course, infinite, but neither is palliative care necessarily costly. It may simply involve the prescription of morphine at the correct dosage. And how many other calls on the health care budget can match the urgent, grave need to keep tens of thousands of patients out of unnecessary pain and distress?[39]

In short, it appears that a right to palliative care may be emerging in international human rights law, if it does not already exist. People in

[34] *Pretty v United Kingdom* (2002) 35 EHRR 1 para 67.
[35] Ibid para 74.
[36] Human Rights Act 1998, s 6(1).
[37] Ibid, s 6(3)(b).
[38] Ibid, s 6(6).
[39] To give some perspective, billions of pounds have been squandered in recent years on a failed National Health Service IT project: A Hough, "'Disastrous' £11.4 bn NHS IT programme to be abandoned", *Daily Telegraph*, 21 September 2011. The Palliative Care Funding Review estimated that improving palliative care could actually save resources. It concluded that "delivering improved recognition of palliative care needs, as well as optimized provision of services outside the hospital setting" could reduce deaths in hospital by up to 60,000 a year by 2021, potentially reducing hospital costs by £180 million per year: T Hughes-Hallett et al., *Palliative Care Funding Review* (http://www.palliativecarefunding.org>, 2011) 9.

Betty's position who obtain no relief from their hospital might, therefore, consider seeking relief from the courts, invoking Articles 3 and 8 of the European Convention. On the other hand, it remains unclear whether, and if so when, a failure to provide palliative care involves a breach of human rights. May a failure to provide reasonable palliative care constitute negligence or even a criminal offense?

VI CIVIL LAW: NEGLIGENCE?

A Vicarious liability

Betty could consider bringing an action in negligence against the hospital on the basis of its vicarious liability for the conduct of its employee, Dr Andrews. To recover, she would have to show, on a balance of probabilities, a breach of the doctor's duty of care which caused her loss. There would be no difficulty showing that Dr Andrews owed her a duty of care: she is his patient. Could she prove breach of duty? The question is whether the doctor satisfied the "*Bolam* test": did Dr Andrews act in accordance with a practice accepted as proper by a responsible body of medical practitioners?[40] This will involve a consideration of the facts of the case in the light of the medical evidence and of professional medical opinion. Depending on those facts and on that opinion, it may well be possible to establish that Dr Andrews fell below the required standard of care. If, for example, he was (or should have been) aware of Betty's serious pain, and if he could easily have taken steps to alleviate it, as by prescribing morphine in appropriate dosages, then it is difficult to see why he would not be in breach of duty. How can it be in accordance with responsible medical practice to allow one's patient to suffer serious pain which could easily be alleviated? If Dr Andrews were to reply that other doctors would also have failed to take steps to alleviate Betty's pain, perhaps because doctors are insufficiently knowledgeable about pain relief, it is doubtful that this would be sufficient to show that he had acted reasonably. First, perhaps he should have had a sufficient knowledge about pain relief, particularly if the knowledge he lacked was basic or if he could easily have accessed the required information. Second, even if he was not unreasonably ignorant of palliative care, and the case called for more expert knowledge, perhaps he should have consulted with or called in an expert in palliative care. Although evidence of medical opinion is important in determining what constitutes medical negligence, the courts

---

[40] *Bolam v Friern HMC* [1957] 1 WLR 582, 587 (McNair J).

may find conduct negligent even if it is endorsed by a body of professional opinion. In *Bolitho v City and Hackney HA* Lord Browne-Wilkinson, delivering the judgment of the House of Lords, said:

[I]n cases of diagnosis and treatment there are cases where, despite a body of professional opinion sanctioning the defendant's conduct, the defendant can properly be held liable for negligence (I am not here considering questions of disclosure of risk). In my judgment that is because, in some cases, it cannot be demonstrated to the judge's satisfaction that the body of opinion relied upon is reasonable or responsible. In the vast majority of cases the fact that distinguished experts in the field are of a particular opinion will demonstrate the reasonableness of that opinion. In particular, where there are questions of assessment of the relative risks and benefits of adopting a particular medical practice, a reasonable view necessarily presupposes that the relative risks and benefits have been weighed by the experts in forming their opinions. But if, in a rare case, it can be demonstrated that the professional opinion is not capable of withstanding logical analysis, the judge is entitled to hold that the body of opinion is not reasonable or responsible.[41]

In a case like Betty's, where the benefits of palliative care are high and the risks, if any, are low, it is not easy to see how Dr Andrews' failure to alleviate her pain could be regarded as having any "logical basis" and as being reasonable or responsible. As for proving causation, if Betty can prove that but for Dr Andrews' failure to treat her pain, or to call in an expert in palliative care who would have done so, she would not have suffered serious pain, she will have satisfied this requirement. Finally, as for Dr Andrews' negligence causing loss, "pain and suffering" is a well-recognized head of damages.

B Direct liability

The hospital may, then, be vicariously liable for any negligence on the part of its employee, Dr Andrews. But it may also be directly liable, which would be a useful avenue for Betty to explore if for any reason, such as acute understaffing, Dr Andrews successfully argues that he was not in breach of duty. Betty could argue that the hospital's failure to ensure that adequate palliative care was provided to her is a breach of the hospital's own duty to ensure that its patients are provided with a reasonable standard of care.[42] Again, liability would turn on the facts, such as

---

[41] [1998] AC 232, 243. See M Brazier and J Miola, "Bye Bye Bolam: a Medical Litigation Revolution?" (2000) 8 Med L Rev 85.

[42] *Wilsher v Essex AHA* [1988] AC 1074. See also M Somerville, *Death Talk* (McGill-Queen's University Press, 2001) 225–6. Professor Somerville was one of the first health lawyers to explore the legal implications of failing to provide reasonable palliative care. See ibid Chs 11–14.

whether it made palliative care expertise readily available, either by ensuring that its staff were sufficiently knowledgeable and/or by employing specialists in palliative care, and whether it complied with any guidance laid down by professional or regulatory bodies or from the Department of Health. It is doubtful that a hospital could simply "toll the bell of tight resources."[43] While courts are understandably reluctant to second-guess resource-allocation decisions, it does not follow that they would uphold a failure to provide reasonable palliative care services, at least where those services are of proven effectiveness in meeting a basic need, the palliation of serious pain, and are not particularly costly. The Human Rights Watch report states that most suffering caused by pain is avoidable as medicines to treat it are "effective, safe, inexpensive, and generally easy to administer"[44] and that, with relatively inexpensive interventions, palliative care can treat other common symptoms of life-threatening illness, including breathlessness, nausea, anxiety, and depression.[45] Moreover, if the United Nations Special Rapporteur on Torture is correct that denial of access to pain relief, if it causes severe pain and suffering, constitutes cruel, inhuman, or degrading treatment or punishment, how could a hospital's failure to ensure at least a basic level of palliative care be other than manifestly unreasonable? In view of the fact that many people experience unnecessary pain and other symptoms,[46] actions in negligence and applications for judicial review for failure to provide reasonable palliative care are surprising by their apparent absence. Dr Andrews, and the hospital, may, then, be liable to Betty in negligence. Is Dr Andrews also guilty of any criminal offense? If not, should he be?

VII CRIMINAL LAW

A Possible criminal liability

1 "Double effect"

It is occasionally suggested that, far from requiring doctors to provide palliative care, the criminal law discourages them from doing so, at least where such care may incidentally shorten life. Lord Joffe, explaining a clause in his Bill on assisted dying for the terminally ill, which would have

---

[43] *R v Cambridge HA, ex p B* [1995] 1 WLR 898, CA. This phrase was used by Laws J at first instance in quashing the health authority's decision to refuse to fund an experimental treatment which had little prospect of success and which would impose significant burdens on the patient. His decision was (with respect, rightly) reversed on appeal.

[44] HRW Report text at n 17.

[45] Ibid text at n 21.

[46] See text at nn 17, 18.

entitled a terminally ill patient to request and receive such medication as
may be necessary to keep him or her as free as possible from pain and
distress, said that it was clear that some doctors were frightened of
prosecution for using "double effect."[47]

First, the evidence from palliative care experts is that, properly administered, analgesics including opioids do not shorten life. One such expert
has described the belief that they do as a "persistent fantasy."[48] Indeed, a
recent survey of patients with lung cancer who received early palliative
care showed that they lived three months longer than those who did not.
The study concluded:

Among patients with metastatic non-small-cell lung cancer, early palliative care
led to significant improvements in both quality of life and mood. As compared
with patients receiving standard care, patients receiving early palliative care had
less aggressive care at the end of life but longer survival.[49]

Second, any fear that some doctors may have of prosecution for the
reasonable use of palliative drugs is entirely misplaced. The courts have
long made it clear that a doctor is entitled to administer palliative
treatment in order to ease the pain and suffering of the dying even if, as
an unintended side-effect, the treatment were to shorten life. The law, in
other words, embraces the principle of "double effect." Lord Goff in *Airedale NHS Trust v Bland* referred to:

the established rule that a doctor may, when caring for a patient who is, for
example, dying of cancer, lawfully administer painkilling drugs despite the fact
that he knows that an incidental effect of that application will be to abbreviate the
patient's life.[50]

In *Cox*—the prosecution of a doctor for the attempted murder of his
patient by injecting her with potassium chloride—Ognall J directed the
jury that if a doctor genuinely believed that a certain course was beneficial
to his patient, either therapeutically or analgesically, then even though he
recognized that that course carried with it a risk to life, he was fully
entitled to pursue it. If in those circumstances the patient died, nobody

---

[47] MI para 35.
[48] R Twycross, "Where there is hope, there is life: a view from the hospice" in J Keown (ed),
Euthanasia Examined: Ethical, Clinical and Legal Perspectives (Cambridge University Press, 1995) 161.
[49] JS Temel et al., "Early Palliative Care for Patients with Metastatic Non-Small-Cell Lung
Cancer" (2010) 363 New England Journal of Medicine 733.
[50] [1993] AC 789, 867. See Ch 1, n 20. See also *R v Adams* [1957] Crim LR 365; P Devlin, *Easing
the Passing: the Trial of Dr John Bodkin Adams* (The Bodley Head, 1985).

could possibly suggest that the doctor was guilty of murder or attempted murder.[51] He continued:

There can be no doubt that the use of drugs to reduce pain and suffering will often be fully justified notwithstanding that it will, in fact, hasten the moment of death. What can never be lawful is the use of drugs with the primary purpose of hastening the moment of death.[52]

In such circumstances, then, a doctor was "entitled" or "justified" in using palliative drugs even if they shortened life as a foreseen side-effect. But Ognall J went further. He said:

It was plainly Dr Cox's *duty* to do all that was medically possible to alleviate her pain and suffering, even if the course adopted carried with it an obvious risk that, as a side effect of that treatment, her death would be rendered likely or even certain.[53]

Therefore, a doctor not only may but *must* try to palliate the patient's pain and suffering. Far from the law inhibiting palliative care, the law requires it.[54] Ognall J's direction serves to reinforce the argument that a doctor who fails to provide reasonable palliative care may incur liability in negligence. Moreover, if the patient is an incompetent adult, the Mental Capacity Act 2005 requires the doctor to act in the patient's "best interests."[55] This must surely require taking reasonable steps to palliate the patient's pain and suffering. Might the doctor who breaches his or her duty to provide reasonable palliative care incur criminal liability? There are a few possibilities.

2 Wilful neglect

The first possibility relates to mentally incapacitated adults. Section 44 of the Mental Capacity Act 2005 provides, *inter alia*, that a person who "has the care of" a person who lacks (or whom he or she reasonably believes to lack) capacity commits an offense if he or she "ill-treats or wilfully

---

[51] *R v Cox* (1992) 12 BMLR 38, 41.

[52] Ibid.

[53] Ibid (emphasis added). See Ch 3, text at n 30.

[54] This is not to say that certain forms of conduct intended to alleviate pain might not incur criminal liability. Just as a doctor, like the defendant in *R v Cox*, will incur liability if there is an intention to alleviate pain by ending the patient's life, "palliative" or "terminal" sedation could equally, if the doctor's intention were to end life, result in liability. However, "palliative sedation" covers many different forms of conduct with different ethical and legal aspects, and is beyond the scope of this chapter. For a useful ethical introduction see L Gormally, "Terminal sedation and the doctrine of the sanctity of life" in Torbjörn Tännsjö (ed), *Terminal Sedation: Euthanasia in Disguise?* (Springer, 2004) 81.

[55] Mental Capacity Act 2005, ss 1, 4.

neglects" that person.[56] The offense is punishable following conviction on indictment by a maximum of five years' imprisonment, or a fine, or both.[57]

The second possibility relates to mentally disordered patients. Section 127(1) of the Mental Health Act 1983 makes it an offense for any person who is an officer on the staff or otherwise employed in, or who is one of the managers of, a hospital or care home, to "ill-treat or wilfully to neglect" a patient receiving treatment for mental disorder as an in-patient or as an out-patient in that hospital or home. Section 127(2) provides that it is an offense for any individual "to ill-treat or wilfully neglect" a mentally disordered patient who is subject to his guardianship or otherwise in his custody or care, whether by virtue of any legal or moral obligation or otherwise. The maximum punishment on indictment is imprisonment for a maximum of five years, or a fine, or both.[58] *Salisu*[59] illustrates the broad reach of section 127. A demented patient in a care home needed constant attention because he lacked spatial awareness. He died of natural causes and no one was with him when he died. The defendant was the staff nurse on duty at the time of death and had failed to ensure that the patient was attended. The defendant was convicted of wilful neglect. He appealed on the ground that the trial judge had failed to distinguish between wilful neglect and mere negligence. The Court of Appeal dismissed the appeal, noting that the judge had properly directed the jury that the Crown had to prove not only an act, or failure to act, which amounted to neglect, but also intention or subjective recklessness. The judge had directed that simple negligence was not enough: the Crown had to prove that the defendant, knowing that the deceased required one-to-one care, ignored that requirement, "knowing or not caring that there might be a risk to his health or welfare...."[60]

A third possibility relates to patients under the age of 16. Section 1(1) of the Children and Young Persons Act 1933 provides that if any person who has attained the age of 16 has responsibility for any child under that age "wilfully assaults, ill-treats, neglects, abandons or exposes him, or causes or procures him to be assaulted, ill-treated, neglected, abandoned, or exposed, in a manner likely to cause him unnecessary suffering or injury to health..." that person shall be guilty of a misdemeanor and

---

[56] Section 44(2).

[57] Section 44(3)(b).

[58] Section 127(3)(b). Section 127(4) states that no proceedings for an offense under the section may be instituted except by or with the consent of the DPP.

[59] *R v Salisu (Musedig)* 2009 WL4666885. I am grateful to Mr Neil Allen for drawing this case to my attention.

[60] Ibid para 19.

shall be liable to imprisonment for a maximum of 10 years, or a fine, or both.[61]

It seems clear that a failure to provide reasonable palliative care may result in liability under these three statutes. If a nurse's failure simply to be with a demented patient can constitute an offense against section 127, as in *Salisu*, then why may not a doctor's failure to palliate serious pain, at least if the doctor is subjectively reckless or indifferent to the risk of the patient suffering unnecessarily? But what of patients outwith these statutes? It is far from clear that an unreasonable failure to palliate their pain will result in criminal liability. It might conceivably involve liability under section 20 of the Offences Against the Person Act 1861, which prohibits the malicious infliction of grievous bodily harm. It is also possible that if a failure is grossly negligent and hastens the patient's death, the doctor may incur liability for manslaughter by gross negligence.[62] But the limitations of these possibilities are plain, and there is much to be said for a clear statutory requirement to alleviate or prevent serious pain or, more generally, to provide reasonable palliative care. It is not easy to see why it should be a crime for a nurse not to be present when a demented patient dies but not for a doctor to knowingly allow a competent patient to suffer agonizing pain when it could easily be prevented, either by the prescription of an opioid or, should the case require specialist intervention, by summoning a specialist in palliative care. It could of course be argued that the three statutory provisions above protect particularly vulnerable groups: the mentally incapacitated, the mentally disordered, and young persons. But many patients are, as a result of their sickness, in a vulnerable position to a greater or a lesser extent. And some groups of patients, such as the frail elderly, are particularly so. Moreover, enacting a clear statutory requirement placing a duty on physicians to palliate pain or provide reasonable palliative care would have an important educative and symbolic effect. It would exorcise any lingering fears that the criminal law in any way prohibits such care; clarify the duty, mentioned by Ognall J, to alleviate pain and suffering; encourage the medical profession, the nursing profession, and hospitals to improve standards; and reaffirm the dignity of all patients. To the objection that the imposition of such a duty would be excessive or difficult to enforce, there is an established precedent. It has

---

[61] Section 1(2) provides that "a parent or other person legally liable to maintain a child" shall be deemed to have neglected him in a manner likely to cause injury to his health "if he has failed to provide adequate food, clothing, medical aid or lodging for him, or if, having been unable otherwise to provide such food, clothing, medical aid or lodging, he has failed to take steps to procure it to be provided...."

[62] *R v Adomako* [1995] 1 AC 171.

long been a crime to allow an animal in one's care to suffer unnecessarily. Why should patients not be afforded at least as much protection as pets?

B Future legislation

There are several possible legislative approaches to improving the provision of reasonable palliative care, only a few of which will be sketched here. One approach would enact a specific duty to provide pain relief. In the Australian Capital Territory the Medical Treatment Act 1994 provides that a patient "has a right to receive relief from pain and suffering to the maximum extent that is reasonable in the circumstances" and that in providing such relief a health professional "shall pay due regard to the patient's account of his or her level of pain and suffering."[63]

Alternatively, legislation could clearly criminalize causing a patient unnecessary suffering, using the existing animal welfare legislation as a template. The Animal Welfare Act 2006 provides that it is an offense for a person, by an act or by a failure to act, to cause a "protected" animal to experience unnecessary suffering, if he knew or ought reasonably to have known that the act or failure to act would have that effect or would be likely to do so.[64] A relevant consideration in deciding whether suffering was "unnecessary" is whether it could reasonably have been avoided or reduced.[65] Accordingly, a palliative care statute could make it an offense for physicians (or perhaps any persons having the care of another) to cause a person in their care to experience unnecessary pain (and perhaps suffering), if they knew or ought to have known that their act or failure to act would have that effect or would be likely to do so. The legislation might expressly provide that physicians would not be liable if they had a "reasonable excuse."

Brennan invokes statutes in Australia and California as models for future legislation. He concludes that the strongest statutory foundation

---

[63] Medical Treatment Act 1994 (ACT), s 23, quoted in F Brennan et al., "Pain Management: A Fundamental Human Right" (2007) 105 Anaesthesia and Analgesia 205, 211.

[64] Section 4. By s 2(a) a "protected animal" includes an animal of a kind which is commonly domesticated in the British Isles. The Department for Environment, Food and Rural Affairs (DEFRA) website points out: "The Act contains a Duty of Care to animals—this means that anyone responsible for an animal must take reasonable steps to make sure the animal's needs are met. This means that a person has to look after an animal's welfare as well as ensure that it does not suffer . . . ." <http://www.defra.gov.uk/food-farm/animals/welfare/on-farm/legislation/>.

[65] Section 4(3)(a). Section 4(4) provides: "Nothing in this section applies to the destruction of an animal in an appropriate and humane manner." Many would defend this provision on the grounds that animals, unlike humans, can make no sense of suffering and do not enjoy a right to life. Whatever the ethical status of animals, a subject not addressed in this book, the question relevant here is: "If it is unethical and a crime to allow an animal in one's care to suffer unnecessarily, should it not be a crime for a doctor to allow his or her patient to so suffer?"

to support best practice in pain relief would involve core aspects of those statutes and would provide that:

- reasonable pain management is a right;
- doctors have a duty to listen to and reasonably respond to a patient's report of pain;
- the provision of necessary pain relief is immune from potential legal liability;
- doctors who are neither able nor willing to ensure adequate analgesia must refer to a colleague with the necessary expertise;
- pain management is a compulsory component of continuing medical education.[66]

There is yet another alternative, however; a still wider approach which would seek to ensure adequate care in general, not just in relation to the prevention and palliation of pain and suffering. This approach would expand the offense of "wilful neglect" to protect all patients, not just those covered by the Mental Health Act 1983 or the Mental Capacity Act 2005. This proposal boasts the attraction of using an existing criminal prohibition which currently protects only some groups of patients, and of prohibiting forms of neglect other than a failure to provide reasonable palliative care. Recent revelations of the appalling neglect of patients in some National Health Service hospitals and in residential "care" homes suggest that there is an urgent need not just for improvements in palliative care, but also in basic care like feeding and bathing. For example, the report into the scandalous neglect of patients by the Mid-Staffordshire NHS Foundation Trust makes grim reading. It disclosed:[67]

The evidence gathered by the Inquiry shows clearly that for many patients the most basic elements of care were neglected. Calls for help to use the bathroom were ignored and patients were left lying in soiled sheeting and sitting on commodes for hours, often feeling ashamed and afraid. Patients were left unwashed, at times for up to a month. Food and drinks were left out of the reach of patients and many were forced to rely on family members for help with feeding. Staff failed to make basic observations and pain relief was provided late or in some cases not at all. Patients were too often discharged before it was appropriate, only to have to be re-admitted shortly afterwards. The standards of hygiene were at times awful, with families forced to remove used bandages and

---

[66] F Brennan et al., "Pain Management: A Fundamental Human Right" (2007) 105 Anaesthesia and Analgesia 205, 218.

[67] See <http://www.midstaffsinquiry.com/pressrelease.html>. For further examples of inadequate care see M Beckford, "Elderly suffer poor care in half of NHS hospitals", *Daily Telegraph*, 13 October 2011; M Evans, "One in seven nursing homes breaking the law on feeding patients", *Daily Telegraph*, 16 October 2011.

dressings from public areas and clean toilets themselves for fear of catching infections.

Amel Alghrani et al. have suggested the extension of the crime of wilful neglect to punish both health care professionals and health care managers for such inattention to patient care. They argue that the crime would not implicate doctors and nurses on a busy, under-staffed ward because it would require proof of indifference to the welfare of the patient.[68] There is much to be said for their suggestion. Many health care managers and professionals can be relied upon to provide a reasonable standard of care to patients, but as the Mid-Staffordshire scandal all too graphically demonstrates, by no means all can. It is difficult to see why their culpable neglect of patients should not attract the attention of the criminal law.

VIII CONCLUSION

Emanuel's point, at the start of this chapter, that the euthanasia debate has served to distract attention from the need to improve end-of-life care for the overwhelming majority of patients, is well made. That so many people in developed societies like the United Kingdom and the United States suffer unnecessary pain at the end of life (and during life) is inexcusable, and if politicians and the media had devoted a fraction of the time to this issue that they have to euthanasia, the problem would be less grave than it is.[69] As the Walton Report pointed out, with the necessary "political will," palliative care could be made available to all who could benefit from it. The answer to the problem is clearly multifaceted: the necessary "political will," backed by the necessary funding; improved education and training for health care professionals and students; and education of the public in what palliative care can achieve. This chapter suggests that the law, both civil and criminal, may have a significant role to play not only in vindicating the rights of those denied reasonable relief from pain and suffering, but also as a fillip to promote reasonable practice. Given that around 100,000 people per year are denied adequate palliative care, it is surprising that there appear to have been no reported cases for the negligent failure to provide reasonable palliative care, or criminal prosecutions for wilful neglect. There is much to be said for legislation to clarify and reinforce the existing common law duty of

---

[68] A Alghrani et al., "Healthcare scandals in the NHS: crime and punishment" (2011) 37 Journal of Medical Ethics 230, 231. I am grateful to Professor Margaret Brazier, one of the co-authors of this paper, for drawing it to my attention.

[69] It is scarcely less inexcusable that developed societies do so little to help those in poorer countries where palliative care is virtually unknown, and where many die in agony.

doctors to palliate pain and to make it an offense to fail to provide adequate pain relief. Whether the better way forward is the enactment of a specific statutory offense of failing to provide reasonable pain relief, or the extension of the existing offense of wilful neglect, is a matter for further consideration. Given the symbolic and educative advantages of the former, and given disclosure(s) of widespread neglect of vulnerable patients in hospitals and nursing homes, there is something to be said for doing both. In any event, the status quo is not an ethical option.[70]

---

[70] Though the focus on this chapter has been on English law, it is noteworthy that in the US, a state's failure to provide palliative care could undermine its prohibition on assisting suicide. In *Washington v Glucksberg* 501 US 702 (1997), the US Supreme Court rejected a facial challenge to a statute prohibiting assisting suicide. It appears that if a state failed to provide palliative care, its prohibition on assisting suicide would be more vulnerable. See eg ibid 792 (Breyer J).

CHAPTER 12

RESTORING MORAL AND INTELLECTUAL SHAPE TO THE LAW AFTER *BLAND*

I INTRODUCTION

In *Airedale NHS Trust v Bland*, the Law Lords held that it was lawful for a doctor to cease tube-feeding his patient who was in a persistent vegetative state (PVS), even though this would inevitably lead to the patient's death and even though, in the opinion of a majority of their Lordships, the doctor's intent was to kill. The implications of the case are profound. A leading utilitarian bioethicist and euthanasia advocate, Professor Peter Singer, claimed that the case marked the collapse of the traditional Western ethic—the inviolability of life (IOL).[1] Although Singer's obituary for the IOL was premature, the case did deal a body blow to the IOL. With few exceptions, notably Professor Finnis' incisive case-note,[2] this cardinal case has inspired strikingly little academic analysis.[3] This chapter argues that *Bland* should be overruled, not least because, as Lord Mustill commented in that case, it left the law in a "morally and intellectually misshapen" state, prohibiting intentional killing of patients by an act, but permitting intentional killing by planned omission.

II THE FACTS

Before his death on 3 March 1993, Tony Bland had lain in Airedale Hospital for over three years in PVS, a state in which, it was believed, he could neither see, hear, nor feel. The medical consensus was that he would never regain consciousness. Neither dead nor dying, his brain stem

---

[1] P Singer, *Rethinking Life and Death: The Collapse of our Traditional Ethics* (St Martin's Griffin, 1995) 1.

[2] JM Finnis, "*Bland*: Crossing the Rubicon?" (1993) 109 LQR 329.

[3] An overview of *Bland* and more recent cases on PVS is provided by JK Mason and GT Laurie, "The Management of the Persistent Vegetative State in the British Isles" (1996) 4 Juridical Review 263.

still functioned and he breathed and digested naturally. He was fed by nasogastric tube, his excretionary functions regulated by catheter and enemas. Infections were treated with antibiotics. His doctor and parents wanted to stop the feeding and antibiotics on the ground that neither served any useful purpose. The hospital trust applied for a declaration that it would be lawful to do so. The application, supported by an amicus curiae instructed by the Attorney-General, was opposed by the Official Solicitor, representing Bland. The declaration was granted by Sir Stephen Brown P, whose decision was unanimously affirmed by the Court of Appeal and by the House of Lords.

III THE LAW

A The ratio

Counsel for the Official Solicitor, James Munby QC (now Munby LJ), argued that stopping treatment and feeding would be murder or at least manslaughter. Three of the members of the House of Lords accepted his submission that the doctor's intention would be to kill Tony Bland, a submission which the remaining two neither rejected nor accepted. As one of the three, Lord Browne-Wilkinson, said:[4]

Murder consists of causing the death of another with intent to do so. What is proposed in the present case is to adopt a course with the intention of bringing about Anthony Bland's death. As to the element of intention . . . in my judgment there can be no real doubt that it is present in this case: the whole purpose of stopping artificial feeding is to bring about the death of Anthony Bland.[5]

Why, then, would it not be murder? Because stopping treatment and feeding was not a positive act but an omission. Lord Goff stated[6] that withdrawing life-support was no different from withholding it in the first place; the doctor was simply allowing the patient to die as a result of his pre-existing condition. Further, tube-feeding was "medical treatment." There was, he said, "overwhelming evidence" that in the medical profession tube-feeding was so regarded and, even if it were not strictly treatment, it formed part of the patient's medical care. The provision of food by tube was, he added, analogous to the provision of air by a ventilator. The House held that the doctor was under no duty to continue tube-feeding.

---

[4] *Airedale NHS Trust v Bland* [1993] AC 789, 881 (*"Bland"*).
[5] Why the majority assumed that it was the doctor's intention to kill is unclear: it did not follow that because Tony Bland's doctor foresaw the patient's death as certain that he therefore intended it.
[6] *Bland* 868.

Re F[7] decided that a doctor could treat an incompetent patient only if it was in the patient's "best interests"; *Bland* held that the same criterion should govern the withdrawal of treatment. As continued feeding was no longer in the patient's interests, the doctor was under no duty to continue it. The tube-feeding was not in Bland's best interests because it was futile and it was futile because, in the words of Lord Goff:[8] "the patient is unconscious and there is no prospect of any improvement in his condition." In deciding whether treatment was futile, the doctor had to act in accordance with a responsible body of medical opinion and thereby satisfy the *"Bolam* test," the test which determines whether, in an action for medical negligence, a doctor has fallen below the standard of care required by the law.[9]

IV A CRITIQUE

Their Lordships' reasoning invites several criticisms.

A Tube-feeding: futile treatment or basic care?

Why was tube-feeding not basic care which the hospital and its medical and nursing staff were under a duty to provide? Their Lordships held that tube-feeding was part of a regime of "medical treatment and care."[10] The insertion of a gastrostomy tube into the stomach requires a minor operation, which is clearly a medical procedure. But it is not at all clear that the insertion of a nasogastric tube is a medical intervention. And, even if it were, the intervention had already been carried out in Tony Bland's case. The question in such a case is why the pouring of food down the tube constitutes "medical treatment." What is it supposed to be treating? Nor does the difficulty evaporate by classifying it, as did the Law Lords, as medical treatment or medical care. As Professor Finnis observes[11]:

The judgments all seem to embrace a fallacious inference, that if tube-feeding is part of medical "treatment or care", tube-feeding is therefore *not* part of the non-medical (home or nursing) care which decent families and communities provide or arrange for their utterly dependent members. The non-sequitur is compounded by failure to note that although naso-gastric tube-feeding will not normally be established without a doctor's decision, no distinctively medical

---

[7] [1990] 2 AC 1.

[8] *Bland* 869.

[9] *Bolam v Friern HMC* [1957] 1 WLR 582. Lord Mustill (see text at n 34) reserved judgment about the appropriateness of this test in this context.

[10] *Bland* 858, per Lord Keith.

[11] JM Finnis, *"Bland*: Crossing the Rubicon?" (1993) 109 LQR 329, 335 (emphasis in original).

skills are needed to insert a naso-gastric tube or to maintain the supply of nutrients through it.

Their Lordships seemed to place great weight on the fact that tube-feeding is regarded by the medical profession as medical treatment.[12] But whether an intervention is "medical" is not a matter to be determined by medical opinion, nor by the mere fact that it is an intervention typically performed by doctors. A doctor may do many things in the course of his or her practice, such as reassuring patients or fitting catheters, which are not distinctively medical in nature. And, if it is opinion which is crucial, the answer one gets may well depend on whom one asks. Tube-feeding may be regarded as medical treatment by many doctors, but many nurses regard it as ordinary care.[13] Further, Lord Goff's analogy between tube-feeding and mechanical ventilation is (although accepted by Mr Munby QC[14]) unpersuasive. Ventilation is standardly part of a therapeutic endeavor to stabilize, treat, and cure: tube-feeding is not. Moreover, ventilation replaces the patient's capacity to breathe but a tube does not replace the capacity to digest and merely delivers food to the stomach. Nor have all patients who are tube-fed (including, it appears, those in PVS) lost the capacity to swallow. Tube-feeding may be instituted solely to minimize the risk of the patient inhaling food and/or because spoon-feeding is thought to be too time consuming. Even if the patient has lost the capacity to swallow, the tube would still not be treating anything. A feeding-tube by which liquid is delivered to the patient's stomach is, at least arguably, no more medical treatment than a catheter by which it is drained from the patient's bladder.

Even if tube-feeding were medical treatment, why was it futile? Was it because it would do nothing to restore Tony Bland to the condition towards which *medical* practice and procedures are directed, namely some level of health, an explanation consistent with the IOL?[15] Or was it rather because Bland's life was thought futile, an explanation inconsistent with it? Dr Keith Andrews, director of medical services at the Royal Hospital for Neurodisability, and a leading authority on PVS, has written:[16]

---

[12] See *Bland* 870 (Lord Goff).

[13] See *Nursing Times*, 10 February 1993, 7.

[14] *Bland* 822.

[15] L Gormally, "Reflections on Horan and Boyle" in L Gormally (ed), *The Dependent Elderly* (1992) 47; L Gormally, "The Good of Health and the Ends of Medicine" in H Zaborowski (ed), *Natural Moral Law in Contemporary Society* (The Catholic University of America Press, 2010) 264; see Ch 11, text at n 22.

[16] (1995) 311 BMJ 1437, Letters.

It is ironic that the only reason that tube-feeding has been identified as "treatment" has been so that it can be withdrawn.... I would argue that tube-feeding is extremely effective since it achieves all the things we intend it to. What is really being argued is whether the patient's life is futile—hence the need to find some way of ending that life.

Are there, then, grounds for concluding that the judges in *Bland* condoned the withdrawal of tube-feeding because they felt the patient's life, rather than his "treatment," was futile?

B *Misunderstanding the IOL*

Lord Mustill, with respect rightly, rejected the notion that the state's interest in preserving life was attenuated "where the 'quality' of the life is diminished by disease or incapacity." If correct, he added, that argument would justify active as well as passive euthanasia and thus require a change in the law of murder.[17] The proposition that because of incapacity or infirmity one life is intrinsically worth less than another was, he said, the first step on a "very dangerous road indeed" and one he was unwilling to take.[18] However, even he held that Tony Bland had no interest in being kept alive[19] and no "best interests" of any kind.[20] How do these propositions differ from a judgment that the patient's life was no longer worthwhile? The notion of a life no longer worth living was even more apparent in passages from other judgments. This was particularly true of passages which adopted what one may call "dualism," the notion that human beings comprise two separate entities: a "body" and a "person," the former being of merely instrumental value as a vehicle for the latter. Sir Stephen Brown P, for example, described Tony Bland thus:[21] "His spirit has left him and all that remains is the shell of his body ... [which is] kept functioning as a biological unit ...." Similarly, Hoffmann LJ said:[22] "His body is alive, but he has no life in the sense that even the most pitifully handicapped but conscious human being has a life." Bland's existence was, he added, a "humiliation"; he was "grotesquely alive."[23] Such judicial endorsement of

---

[17] *Bland* 894.
[18] Ibid.
[19] Ibid 898.
[20] Ibid 897.
[21] Ibid 804.
[22] Ibid 825. He admitted he had been influenced by reading the manuscript of Professor Dworkin's book, *Life's Dominion. An Argument about Abortion and Euthanasia* (Harper Collins Publishers, 1993), which espouses dualism and misrepresents the IOL. See my review in (1994) 110 LQR 671; GV Bradley, *"Life's Dominion*: A Review Essay" (1993) 69(2) Notre Dame L Rev 329; CM Coope, *Worth and Welfare in the Controversy over Abortion* (Palgrave Macmillan, 2006).
[23] See also *Bland* 863 (Lord Goff); ibid 879 (Lord Browne-Wilkinson); ibid 897 (Lord Mustill).

dualism is both novel and surprising, not only because (as Finnis points out[24]) dualism enjoys relatively little support among philosophers but also because the law has hitherto rejected the notion of "biological units" which are "inhabited" by a non-bodily person and has, on the contrary, taken the traditional, common-sense view that human life is personal life, that living human beings are persons, and that persons are, applying standard biological criteria, either alive or dead. As the judges recognized, it would be murder actively to kill Tony Bland, regardless of his permanent unconsciousness. The law does not deny personhood, and the rights it attracts, because the person has lost the ability to think. We are all "biological units" and our mental acts, far from being a separate form of life, something "added to" our body (from where?), intrinsically involve, just like our physical acts, biological processes, and are an expression of our one life as a human being, a human person. For example, the judge who listens to and evaluates an argument from counsel is not a biological machine with a little mental person inside, but an integrated, dynamic unity, a living human body exercising the capacities (intellectual and physical) which are inherent in his or her nature as a human being. It is because we are human beings, human "biological units," that we have the radical capacity for acts both physical and mental. The fact that a human being has lost the ability to think does not mean that he or she has lost his or her life. As Finnis explains:[25]

One's living body is intrinsic, not merely instrumental, to one's personal life. Each of us has a human life (not a vegetable life plus an animal life plus a personal life); when it is flourishing that life includes all one's vital functions including speech, deliberation and choice; when gravely impaired it lacks some of those functions without ceasing to be the life of the person so impaired.

The fact, he adds, that one is in PVS, although a gravely impairing condition which may prevent participation in basic human goods apart from life, such as aesthetic experience, does not mean that one is not participating in the good, the benefit, of life. Was it beneficial to feed and care for Tony Bland even though he could not appreciate it? It is, however, perfectly possible to benefit someone, even if he or she is unaware of it, as where A, unbeknown to B, deposits a large amount in B's bank account, or speaks well of B to C.[26] And to state, as did Lord

---

[24] JM Finnis, "*Bland*: Crossing the Rubicon?" (1993) 109 LQR 329, 334.

[25] Ibid.

[26] J Boyle, "A Case for Sometimes Tube-Feeding Patients in Persistent Vegetative State" in J Keown (ed), *Euthanasia Examined: Ethical, Clinical and Legal Perspectives* (Cambridge University Press, 1995) 189, 193.

Mustill,[27] that Bland had "no best interests of any kind" is, with respect, unconvincing. Would it not have been contrary to his interests to use him as a sideboard? Or to make him a spectacle for the entertainment of ghoulish spectators? Given the dualistic reasoning uncritically engaged in by the judges, their conclusion that Tony's life was of no benefit, indeed may even have been a harm, a humiliation, comes as little surprise. That it was his life, and not his tube-feeding, that was adjudged worthless is clearly illustrated by the following passage from the speech of Lord Keith:

[I]t is, of course, true that in general it would not be lawful for a medical practitioner who assumed responsibility for the care of an unconscious patient simply to give up treatment in circumstances where continuance of it would confer some benefit on the patient. On the other hand a medical practitioner is under no duty to continue to treat such a patient where a large body of informed and responsible medical opinion is to the effect that no benefit at all would be conferred by continuance. *Existence in a vegetative state with no prospect of recovery is by that opinion regarded as not being a benefit*, and that, if not unarguably correct, at least forms a proper basis for the decision to discontinue treatment and care: *Bolam v Friern Hospital Management Committee* [1957] 1 W.L.R. 582.[28]

But why was discontinuance not a breach of the principle of the IOL, a principle which Lord Keith accepted[29] it was the concern of the state, and the judiciary as one of the arms of the state, to uphold? What is remarkable is that, while their Lordships agreed with the fundamental importance of the principle, none of them accurately articulated it. Lord Goff, for example, in setting out the fundamental principles of law relevant to the case, stated[30] that the "fundamental principle is the principle of the sanctity of life." But he then went on to claim[31] that, although it is fundamental, it is "not absolute." In support of this surprising claim, he made a number of observations which suggest that his Lordship conflated the IOL with "vitalism," a common error identified in Chapters 1 to 4 above. He observed, first, that it is lawful to kill in self-defense and, second, that, in the medical context, there is no absolute rule that a patient's life must be prolonged by treatment or care regardless of the circumstances. Both statements are accurate. But they do not show that the IOL is "not absolute" unless one thinks, as his Lordship appears to have, that the principle prohibits all conduct that may hasten death or that requires the preservation of life at all costs. Neither proposition is

---

[27] *Bland* 897.
[28] Ibid 858–9 (emphasis added). See also ibid 878–9, and 884–5 (Lord Browne-Wilkinson).
[29] Ibid 859.
[30] Ibid 863.
[31] Ibid 864.

consistent with the principle as traditionally formulated and understood. His Lordship observed, third, that the fact that a doctor must respect a patient's refusal of life-prolonging treatment showed that the IOL yielded to the right to self-determination. Again, his Lordship seemed to think that the IOL requires the preservation of life even against the competent patient's contemporaneous wishes. Again, this is not so. Fourth, he distinguished between a doctor, on the one hand, omitting to provide life-prolonging treatment or care and, on the other, administering a lethal drug. "So to act," he said,[32] "is to cross the Rubicon which runs between on the one hand the care of the living patient and on the other hand euthanasia—actively causing his death to avoid or to end his suffering." But the intentional killing by one person of another person in his care, even if effected by omission, breaches the IOL.

C *The* Bolam *test*

The Law Lords decided that Tony Bland's doctor was under no duty to continue treatment and tube-feeding if he felt that continuation was no longer in the patient's best interests and if his opinion was supported (as it was) by a responsible body of medical opinion. Indeed, as Lord Browne-Wilkinson pointed out,[33] if the doctor decided that treatment was no longer in the patient's best interests, he was under a *duty* to withdraw it. Since the doctor could lawfully treat the patient only if he believed it was in the patient's best interests, continuing treatment when he did not believe it to be so would constitute the crime and tort of battery.

Why should the judgment about which patients have lives "worth living" be delegated to a "responsible body" of medical opinion? Even assuming this comprehensive judgment can be made about the worth of another (which the IOL denies), what qualifies a doctor to make it? Lord Mustill pertinently observed[34] that the decision could be said to be ethical and that there was no logical reason why the opinions of doctors should be decisive. His was, however, a lone voice. Lord Browne-Wilkinson expressly stated[35] that one doctor could decide, because of his ethical views about the IOL, that his patient was "entitled to stay alive" whereas another doctor who saw "no merit in perpetuating a life of which the patient is unaware" could lawfully stop his patient's treatment. Their Lordships did direct that, for the present, all cases like Tony Bland's

---

[32] Ibid 865.
[33] Ibid 883.
[34] Ibid 898–9.
[35] Ibid 884.

should be brought before the High Court for a declaration. But what is the court's role? Is it, as it appears to be, essentially to confirm that the doctor's opinion is supported by a responsible body of medical opinion? Or is it to lay down judicial criteria for deciding which lives are worth-while? If the latter, what are those criteria?[36]

D A "slippery slope"

Hoffmann LJ said[37] that it was "absurd to conjure up the spectre of eugenics" as a reason against the decision in *Bland*. However, once the "Quality of life" approach (outlined in Chapter 1) supplants the IOL, there is no reason in principle why the Quality threshold should stop at PVS. Finnis has observed that it is one thing to say that one should not treat people in ways which affront their inalienable dignity, but quite another to say that, because of their physical or mental disability, they *have* no dignity or, worse, that they *are* an indignity. How can the latter judgment logically be limited to those in PVS? As he reminds us:[38]

Epithets of indignity and humiliation could easily be applied (as in recent history) to various classes of severely handicapped people, many of whom, moreover, cannot exercise the distinctively human or "personal" forms of understanding and response.

Lord Mustill raised,[39] without resolving, the case of the patient who has "glimmerings of awareness," and Lord Browne-Wilkinson[40] the patient with slight chances of improvement or with "very slight sensate aware-ness." In May 1995, the Irish Supreme Court, following *Bland*, permitted (by a 4–1 majority) the withdrawal of tube-feeding from a patient who was not in PVS and had retained some cognitive function.[41] It affirmed the decision of the first instance judge who stated that if she were aware of her condition "that would be a terrible torment to her and her situation would be *worse* than if she were fully PVS."[42] Leaving aside the reasoning of the judges who favored withdrawal (which is more, rather than less, vulnerable to criticism than the reasoning in *Bland*) the Irish case illus-trates the inherently arbitrary nature of "Quality of life" judgments. The

---

[36] See *Frenchay NHS Healthcare Trust v S* [1994] 1 WLR 601; IJ Keown, "Applying *Bland*" [1994] CLJ 456.

[37] *Bland* 831.

[38] JM Finnis, *"Bland*: Crossing the Rubicon?" (1993) 109 LQR 329, 336.

[39] *Bland* 899.

[40] Ibid 885.

[41] *In the Matter of a Ward of Court* [1995] 2 ILRM 410. See IJ Keown, "Life and Death in Dublin" [1996] CLJ 6.

[42] Cited in [1995] 2 ILRM 401, 432, per O'Flaherty J (emphasis added).

criticism bites even more deeply when the judgment is, via the *Bolam* test, delegated to "responsible" medical opinion. The question then simply becomes whether there is a body of "responsible" medical opinion which supports the doctor's view that the particular patient's life is no longer worthwhile, whether or not a larger body of medical opinion disagrees. The inherent arbitrariness of "Quality of life" judgments, particularly when delegated to doctors, is underlined when it is recalled that medical opinion is often divided and in flux. A patient may be treated by a doctor who thinks his or her life worthwhile, but that doctor's ethical views may change, or the patient may come under the care of a doctor with different ethical views. The upshot would appear to be that if a doctor responsible, say, for a patient with advanced Alzheimer's disease thinks that the patient's life is of no benefit, and the doctor's opinion coincides with that of a "responsible body" of medical opinion, the doctor may, perhaps must, cease treatment (including tube-feeding).

The risk to patients is heightened by the practical difficulties which can be involved in accurately diagnosing the condition which is thought to justify non-treatment. Even PVS is not a clear-cut syndrome and misdiagnoses are not uncommon. A study carried out by Dr Keith Andrews, published in 1996, disclosed that of forty patients referred to the Royal Hospital for Neurodisability as "vegetative" between 1992 and 1995, no fewer than seventeen (43 per cent) had been misdiagnosed. All but one of the 17 had been referred by a hospital consultant, mostly by a neurologist, neurosurgeon, or rehabilitation specialist. The study concluded that accurate diagnosis is possible but requires the skills of a multidisciplinary team experienced in the management of people with complex disabilities.[43] The Practice Note issued to govern applications for declarations in cases of PVS stated that there should be two neurological reports on the patient, one commissioned by the Official Solicitor, but did not require the involvement of such a team.[44] Furthermore, the risks of misdiagnosis must increase if time is short. In one case in which the Court of Appeal declared that it would be lawful not to reinsert a feeding tube which had become disconnected, there had been insufficient time for the Official Solicitor to obtain an independent neurological opinion. It seems doubtful whether the patient in that case was in fact in PVS.[45] More recently, evidence has emerged that some PVS patients have regained

---

[43] K Andrews et al., "Misdiagnosis of the Vegetative State: Retrospective Study in a Rehabilitation Unit" (1996) 313 BMJ 13.

[44] [1996] 2 FLR 375.

[45] IJ Keown, "Applying *Bland*" [1994] CLJ 45.

consciousness after being given a common sleeping pill, zolpidem.[46] Research with brain scanning technology has indicated that some PVS patients are conscious and able to communicate.[47] A recent review of the syndrome confirms that 40 per cent of patients diagnosed as PVS are in fact aware; that standard behavioral assessments cannot distinguish a minimally conscious patient from an unaware patient; and recommends that current diagnostic guidelines should be amended to include functional neuro-imaging.[48]

E A possible explanation

What accounts for the judges' misunderstanding in *Bland* of the IOL, a principle historically foundational to the law? A plausible explanation is that the principle does not appear to have been accurately set out before them by any of the learned counsel who appeared in the case. Even the highly experienced counsel for the Official Solicitor appears to have confused the IOL with vitalism. In the Court of Appeal, for example, he argued that if Tony Bland showed signs of life-threatening failure of, in succession, heart, lungs, liver, kidneys, spleen, bladder, and pancreas, the doctor would be under a duty to perform surgery to rectify the failure. Sir Thomas Bingham MR (as he then was) responded:[49] "Such a suggestion is in my view so repugnant to one's sense of how one individual should behave towards another that I would reject it as possibly representing the law." This response was entirely reasonable, since counsel's argument was vitalistic. *Bland* was not the first time that this distinguished member of the Bar had, as counsel for the Official Solicitor, advanced a vitalistic understanding of the IOL. In *Re J*,[50] an earlier leading case on the withholding or withdrawal of life-prolonging medical treatment, the question was whether a disabled ward should be artificially ventilated. Counsel made two alternative submissions. The first, his "absolute" submission, was:

that a court is never justified in withholding consent to treatment which could enable a child to survive a life-threatening condition, whatever the pain or other side-effects inherent in the treatment, and whatever the quality of life which it would experience thereafter.[51]

---

[46] S Boggan, "Reborn", *Guardian*, 11 September 2006.
[47] R Alleyne and M Beckford, "Patients in 'vegetative' state can think and communicate", *Daily Telegraph*, 3 February 2010.
[48] MM Monti et al, "The Vegetative State" (2010) 341 BMJ c3765.
[49] *Bland* 815. See also ibid 822–3 (Butler-Sloss LJ).
[50] *Re J (A Minor)(Wardship: Medical Treatment)* [1991] 1 FLR 366.
[51] Ibid 370–1.

His alternative, "qualified" submission[52] (based on the reasoning of the Court of Appeal in the earlier case of *Re B*[53]) was that a court could withhold consent to treatment only if it was certain that the "quality" of the child's life would be "intolerable" to the child. In *Re J*, then, the court was presented with only two alternatives: "vitalism" or "Quality of life" (QOL).[54] It preferred the latter, with the rider that QOL was to be judged from the perspective of the child. As Taylor LJ expressed it:[55]

[T]he correct approach is for the court to judge the quality of life the child would have to endure if given the treatment and decide whether in all the circumstances such a life would be so afflicted as to be intolerable to that child.[56]

It appears, then, that in *Bland*, as in *Re J* before it, the IOL was not heard; that the choice as presented and perceived was between vitalism and QOL, and that the judges (unsurprisingly) opted for QOL. Despite the fundamental importance attached to the IOL by the judges who sat in *Bland*, it seems that none had the benefit of an accurate appreciation of it.

V FROM QOL TO IOL

What answer would the traditional ethic, accurately understood and applied, have yielded in the *Bland* case? IOL ethicists are broadly in agreement that since medical treatment, whether antibiotics or ventilation, can do nothing to restore those in PVS to anything approaching a state of health and well-functioning, it is futile and need not be provided. On the question whether tube-feeding is simply medical treatment or also basic care there is not, at least as yet, unanimity. Some classify tube-feeding as medical treatment which may, therefore, be withdrawn; others (probably advancing the more representative viewpoint) that it is basic

---

[52] ibid 373.

[53] [1981] 1 WLR 1421.

[54] In the "Conjoined Twins" case Ward LJ agreed that counsel in *Re J* had confused the IOL with vitalism, and observed that vitalism was "too extreme a position to hold.": *Re A* [2001] Fam 147, 186.

[55] [1991] 1 FLR 366, 383–4. See Ch 1, text at n 25.

[56] Given that the child had never been capable of making any judgment, invoking the child's viewpoint was a fiction. It is perhaps surprising that the courts should have imported "substituted judgment" in the case of a child who had never been competent, but rejected it in the case of an adult like Tony Bland, who had been. Yet even if substituted judgment had been applied in *Bland*, and the court had declared that the feeding should be stopped because he would have preferred to be killed rather than live in PVS, it would still have amounted to the making of a QOL judgment. A QOL judgment remains just that, whether arrived at through "best interests" or "substituted judgment."

care which ought, therefore, to be provided.[57] However, although the traditional ethic does not, as yet, unequivocally rule out the withdrawal of tube-feeding on the ground that it is futile medical treatment, it certainly rules out its withdrawal on the ground that the *patient* is futile. While the ethic may currently allow for a legitimate diversity of answers, it does insist on asking the right question: "Is tube-feeding 'treatment' and, if so, is it worthwhile?" and not "Is the patient's life worthwhile?"

How, then, could their Lordships have developed the law in accordance with the IOL? As Finnis has pointed out, the authorities clearly establish that one who undertakes the care of a dependent person and omits to provide necessary food or clothing with the intention of causing death (or serious harm) commits murder if death results. He adds that the authorities do not confront the argument successfully raised in *Bland*—that one who has undertaken a duty of care may yet have no duty to exercise it so as to sustain life—but that "the proper application or extension of their rule to meet that argument was surely this: those who have a duty to care for someone may never exercise it in a manner intended to bring about that person's death."[58] *Bland* decides the opposite, and does so at the expense of radical inconsistency: prohibiting as murder intentional killing by an act, but permitting intentional killing by omission. Imagine the following scenario. X is a patient in PVS who is free of any suffering and who has made no request to be killed. X's doctor decides that, because X's life is worthless, he would be better off dead, and stops his tube-feeding with intent to kill. In the next bed is Y, a patient dying in agony who, after serious reflection, begs the doctor to kill him by lethal injection. The doctor, fearful of prosecution, refuses. A third patient, Z, moved by Y's predicament, draws a revolver, holds it to the doctor's head and threatens "If you don't give Y a lethal injection, I will shoot you dead." The doctor, to save his own life, administers a lethal drug to Y. The doctor's killing of X is lawful. His killing of Y, to which duress is no defense,[59] is murder. Small wonder that Lord Mustill expressed[60] his "acute unease" about resting his decision on a distinction between acts and omissions given that "however much the terminologies may differ the ethical status of the two courses of action is for all relevant purposes indistinguishable." But it

---

[57] L Gormally, "Definitions of Personhood: Implications for the Care of PVS Patients" (1993) 9.3 Ethics and Medicine 44, 47; J Boyle, "A Case for Sometimes Tube-Feeding Patients in Persistent Vegetative State" in J Keown (ed), *Euthanasia Examined: Ethical, Clinical and Legal Perspectives* (Cambridge University Press, 1995) Ch 13.

[58] JM Finnis, "*Bland*: Crossing the Rubicon?" (1993) 109 LQR 329, 333.

[59] *Howe* [1987] AC 417.

[60] *Bland* 887. See also ibid 865 (Lord Goff); ibid 877 (Lord Lowry); ibid 885 (Lord Browne-Wilkinson).

is, with respect, the judges' reasoning in *Bland* which has distorted the legal structure, not vice versa. *Bland* is the culmination of a series of cases in which the courts have veered away from the traditional ethic, which coherently combines inviolability and quality in a consistent and principled legal opposition to intentional killing or abandonment, toward a new ethic which incoherently combines IOL and QOL and produces a misshapen opposition to intentionally ending life by an act but not by a deliberate omission. One of the few academic articles on *Bland* has, however, sought to defend it. Let us now consider the merits of that defense.

VI A DEFENSE OF *BLAND*

Andrew McGee has ventured a thoughtful response to critics of *Bland*.[61] His defense raises a number of issues, such as the distinction between intention and foresight, and between "quality of life benefits" and "beneficial Quality of life," which have appeared throughout this book, and therefore provides a useful way to end this chapter.

Dr McGee agrees that there is a "cogent and therefore defensible" distinction between intended and merely foreseen consequences.[62] As he points out, both doctor and cancer patient may foresee unpleasant side-effects from chemotherapy but neither therefore intends them.[63] No less sound is his comment that, to the extent that the House of Lords conflated intention and foresight in *Woollin*, their Lordships fell into error.[64] As it develops, however, McGee's defense of the distinction blurs it. He criticizes the "failure test" to distinguish intended from foreseen consequences, that is, the test which asks, if the consequence had not come about, whether the agent would have failed to achieve his or her purpose. His criticism is, however, unpersuasive. Commenting on the hypothetical case of the bomber who blows up a plane solely in order to collect the insurance on the cargo, and who would not on the "failure test" intend to kill the passengers (because the bomber would not regard his enterprise as a failure if the passengers survived), McGee protests that the hypothetical is too divorced from reality.[65] But this is, if anything, a criticism of the hypothetical, not the test, which can be applied to a range of cases

---

[61] A McGee, "Finding a Way through the Ethical and Legal Maze: Withdrawal of Medical Treatment and Euthanasia" (2005) 13 Med L Rev 357.

[62] Ibid 360.

[63] Ibid 365.

[64] Ibid.

[65] Ibid 368.

hypothetical or real. And even factually impossible hypotheticals can play an important role in clarifying concepts. Moreover, fact can be stranger than fiction. A mountaineer, to save himself from being dragged over a precipice by his companion, cut the rope which tied them together. His companion plunged to what both must have thought was certain death, but he miraculously survived. Did the mountaineer intend to kill his companion because his death seemed certain?[66] Further, if McGee rejects the "failure test" what does he propose in its place? Does he think that the bomber intends the passengers' deaths if they are certain to occur? If so, why does the doctor not intend the chemotherapy patient's hair to fall out? And if, as McGee claims, it would be "absurd" to deny that the 9/11 bombers intended to commit suicide, even if they would have been happy to survive to terrorize another day, would it be absurd to deny that the doctor who foresees the certainty that palliative drugs will incidentally hasten death intends to kill the patient? In short, McGee starts by distinguishing intention from foresight but seems to end by conflating them. He then turns to a context in which the law clearly accepts the moral distinction between intending and foreseeing the hastening of death: palliative care. He points out that in this context the criminal law adopts the moral principle of "double effect."[67] He argues that while the distinction between intended and merely foreseen hastening of death is cogent and applicable in the context of palliative care, I and other critics of *Bland* have erred in applying the distinction to all cases of withdrawal of treatment currently permitted by the law. Let us consider the merits of his criticism. McGee charges that attempting to apply the distinction "outside the context of palliative care" is "a species of ethics and law *by categorisation*."[68] His criticism is wide of the mark.

A My argument misunderstood

Dr McGee misstates my argument as to when life-prolonging treatment may ethically be withheld/withdrawn. Nowhere do I state, as he claims,[69] that it is justifiable to withhold/withdraw burdensome treatment only if it is not serving any useful therapeutic purpose. The contrary is clear from a passage he quotes in which I observe: "A treatment may be not worthwhile either because it offers no reasonable hope of benefit or *because, even*

---

[66] The case is discussed in JM Finnis, "Intention and Side-Effects" in RG Frey and CW Morris (eds), *Liability and Responsibility* (Cambridge University Press, 1991) 32.

[67] McGee (n 61) 376. His summary of the principle overlooks its important requirement of proportionality.

[68] Ibid 360 (emphasis in original).

[69] Ibid 360.

though it does, the expected benefit would be outweighed by burdens which the treatment would impose, such as excessive pain."[70] McGee then cites my hypothetical case of a terminally ill infant, Bertha, who is close to death and whose carers decide against ventilation. McGee claims[71] that I do not explain why they do not therefore intend her to die. As I pointed out (in another passage he quotes) their aim is not that she should die but to spare her the futile and burdensome intervention of artificial ventilation: "Given that such efforts could not hope to reverse Bertha's inevitable decline, and might impose significant burdens on her, they decide against ventilation as it would be disproportionate."[72] Deciding to allow Bertha to die in peace is not the same as intending her to die. Her carers would doubtless be delighted if a cure were suddenly discovered for her terminal illness and she survived. Their intention is simply that her dying, which (absent such a discovery) is inevitable, should not be burdened by painful ventilation. Bowing to the inevitability of death, and deciding to make it as comfortable as possible, is not the same as intending that death should occur.

McGee also misrepresents my criticism of *Bland*. He claims, first, that I have argued that the Law Lords were wrong in *Bland* to hold that stopping the patient's tube-feeding was motivated by an intention to kill[73] and, second, that I have argued that: "the way to restore moral and intellectual shape to the law after *Bland* is simply to reject the majority view that, in withdrawing medical treatment from Anthony Bland, the doctors intended to bring about Anthony's death."[74] I have advanced neither argument.[75] My argument has been that, irrespective of whether the majority of their Lordships were right in thinking that Tony Bland's doctor intended to kill him, their reasoning left the law in a morally inconsistent state: doctors may not intentionally end the life of a patient in PVS by an act but they may do so by withholding or withdrawing tube-feeding. The significance of the majority's approval of withdrawal, even on the basis that the doctor's purpose was to kill, lies (even if it does not form part of the *ratio*) in its *blatant* inconsistency with the IOL.[76] As we

---

[70] Ibid 371 (emphasis added).

[71] Ibid 372.

[72] Ibid.

[73] Ibid 369, n 45.

[74] Ibid 363 (footnote omitted).

[75] I wrote that it is unclear why the majority assumed that the doctor's purpose was to kill, not that they were wrong to do so: Keown 218, n 2.

[76] Their reasoning would also have been inconsistent with the IOL, though less blatantly so, had they thought that the doctor's purpose was not to kill Tony, but was to abandon him. The IOL prohibits not only intentionally ending a patient's life, but also recklessly or negligently doing so. See Ch 1.II.C.

saw above, had the House of Lords reasoned, without any reference to the supposed worth of Tony's life, that tube-feeding could lawfully be withdrawn on the ground that it was a futile medical treatment (an approach to which Lord Goff's opinion was closest[77]) the law would arguably have remained consistent with the IOL. It would certainly not have been as "morally and intellectually misshapen" as the House of Lords left it. This is not to suggest that categorizing tube-feeding as a futile treatment, without any reference to the supposed worth of Tony's life, would have been uncontroversial: there is a powerful counter-argument that tube-feeding patients in PVS constitutes basic care, not medical treatment, and ought in general to be provided.[78]

B McGee's four grounds for rejecting my argument

McGee cites four grounds for dismissing my argument that the IOL might allow withdrawal of the tube-feeding as futile medical treatment. The first ground is that the argument is "insufficiently analogous to the case of palliative care" because "no positive benefit can be said to be the purpose of the withdrawal—except perhaps the benefit of not being subjected to any further futile treatment."[79] Even if we leave aside the possibility that being relieved of futile treatment is a benefit, McGee here confuses the principle of double effect with its application in the context of palliative care. The principle applies not only in that context, where there is a benefit to the patient, but also in others, where there is none. For example, a doctor may carry out non-therapeutic research on a consenting patient, research which the doctor foresees will inflict discomfort. The principle may justify such research even though the research confers no benefit whatever on the patient. It is erroneous to conclude (not least for someone concerned about ethics "by categorization") that because benefit to the patient occurs when the principle is applied in one context it is therefore required in others.[80] The presence of benefit in the palliative care context leads McGee to ask the wrong question about withdrawing

---

[77] As his Lordship stated: "[T]he question is not whether it is in the best interests of the patient that he should die. The question is whether it is in the best interests of the patient that his life should be prolonged by the continuance of this form of medical treatment or care.": *Bland* 868. He continued (ibid 869): "As Sir Thomas Bingham MR pointed out ... in the present case, medical treatment or care may be provided for a number of different purposes.... But for my part I cannot see that medical treatment is appropriate or requisite simply to prolong a patient's life, when such treatment has no therapeutic purpose of any kind, as where it is futile because the patient is unconscious and there is no prospect of any improvement in his condition."

[78] See text at n 57.

[79] McGee (n 61) 374.

[80] See text at Ch 1, nn 22–3.

tube-feeding. The question should not be "What benefit is conferred on the patient by withdrawal?" but rather "Does this treatment (if treatment it be) offer any reasonable hope of therapeutic benefit so as to justify any burdens?"

McGee's second ground for doubting the applicability of the intention/ foresight distinction to justify withdrawal of tube-feeding is that the distinction would clash with the law allowing competent refusals of life-prolonging treatment. Citing *Re B*[81] he comments that the patient in that case refused further ventilation not because she thought the treatment too burdensome but because she judged her life too burdensome, and yet the court did not regard her as committing suicide nor her doctors as assisting her in suicide. He states that the law upholds refusals of treatment whether patients merely foresee or even intend death and thinks this "a formidable obstacle to the kind of account proposed by Keown." He adds:

He cannot defend his account by claiming that judges have merely misexplained the lawfulness of competent refusal, and that, in reality, the distinction between intention and foresight is the better rationale. *For the law itself would have to change*—doctors would have to be allowed to perform a medical operation on a person without their consent if they discovered that such a patient intended their own death.[82]

First, it is hardly a strong argument against the validity of the intention/ foresight distinction in one context (withholding/withdrawing treatment from incompetent patients) that it has been overlooked by the courts in another (competent refusals of treatment). The counter-argument would be that the law should no more endorse suicidal refusal of treatment than it should endorse homicidal withdrawal of treatment. Second, it is in any event doubtful that the courts have extended the right to refuse treatment to include suicidal refusals. The courts may well have used incautiously sweeping language to describe the right to refuse treatment but this is not the same as holding that the right extends to committing suicide. Moreover, McGee overlooks authority the other way.[83] Third, McGee's analysis of suicidal refusals, assistance in such refusals, and what a law denying such refusals force would entail, is shaky. He seems to think that a suicidal intention exists when the patient knows that refusal will

---

[81] [2002] 1 FLR 1090.

[82] McGee (n 61) 378 (emphasis in original; footnote omitted).

[83] *R v Collins and Ashworth Hospital Authority, ex p Brady* [2000] 8 Lloyd's Rep Med 355, 367. See generally J Keown, *Euthanasia, Ethics and Public Policy* (Cambridge University Press, 2002) Ch 19; J Keown, "The case of Ms B: suicide's slippery slope?" (2002) 28 Journal of Medical Ethics 238; Ch 1. III.E.

lead to death.[84] If so, he conflates intention and foresight. A patient may refuse life-prolonging treatment not to hasten death but because the treatment is too burdensome. Similarly, McGee implies that the importance I attach to intention commits me to allowing only competent refusals which are not suicidal for "otherwise, a doctor would be assisting suicide ...."[85] However, the fact that a doctor knows that a patient's refusal is suicidal does not mean that the doctor intends to assist the patient's suicide. Finally, it does not follow, as McGee seems to think,[86] that denying legal validity to suicidal refusals would require doctors to investigate all refusals to ensure that they were not suicidal, any more than the law against intentional killing requires the investigation of all cases of life-shortening palliative care to ensure that they are not murderous. Nor does it follow, as he also claims,[87] that the law would have to allow doctors to force-treat suicidal patients. (The significance of the intention/foresight distinction in medical law has been underlined by section 4(5) of the Mental Incapacity Act 2005, which provides that a determination of whether life-sustaining treatment is in the best interests of an incompetent patient "must not ... be motivated by a desire to bring about his death."[88]

McGee's third ground concerns my understanding of futility. He claims that I hold that: "Whether the patient will live or die is an immaterial consideration in the judgement of whether treatment is futile."[89] On the contrary, I hold that the fact that a patient (like baby Bertha) is dying can be highly relevant in determining whether a proposed intervention offers a reasonable hope of restoring the patient to health. It is one thing to resuscitate a child who has choked on a coin, quite another to resuscitate a moribund nonagenarian. McGee continues that a relevant consideration is whether the treatment would allow the patient to continue living. With this it is difficult to disagree. He goes on:

Consider, for instance, the case of those who require kidney dialysis machines to continue living. Assume, for the sake of argument, that a kidney transplant is unavailable to them during their lifetime, and no cure will be discovered to improve their condition. In such a case, medical treatment as Keown understands it is certainly futile—nothing further can be done for them to *improve* their condition.[90]

---

[84] McGee (n 61) 376–7.
[85] Ibid 377.
[86] Ibid 378.
[87] Ibid.
[88] See Ch 1, text at n 34.
[89] McGee (n 61) 379.
[90] Ibid 379 (emphasis in original).

McGee clearly misunderstands the concept of futility as understood by the IOL. Treatments do not need to be curative to be beneficial. Some treatments cure; others prevent deterioration; still others palliate symptoms.[91] Dialysis clearly benefits kidney patients by maintaining their health and functioning even though it cannot cure their underlying condition. McGee adds that: "quality of life considerations necessarily and inescapably enter into the judgement of whether to continue or withdraw treatment, and therefore of whether treatment *really is* futile."[92] If by "quality of life" McGee means what chapter 1 referred to as "quality of life benefits" then of course such considerations should enter into such a judgment. If, by contrast, he means "beneficial Quality of life," I beg to differ. The question whether, say, dialysis will maintain Mrs Jones' health can (and should) be answered without any attempt to judge whether Mrs Jones' life is "worth living."

McGee's fourth ground seems to echo his second: that my approach has not been endorsed by court decisions since *Bland.* Judicial doubts have, however, been expressed about the propriety of withdrawing treatment on the basis of judgment that the patient's life is not "worth living"[93] and, as we saw above, about whether the right to refuse treatment extends to a right to commit suicide.[94] We may also recall section 4(5) of the Mental Incapacity Act 2005. In any event, it is the reasoning in *Bland* which is in question, not the extent to which that reasoning has been followed. The question of the extent to which the courts have or have not restored the IOL is different from the question whether they should have done so. McGee cites the decision of Butler-Sloss P in *NHS Trust A v M; NHS Trust B v H* that stopping tube-feeding of PVS patients with intent to kill does not amount to the intentional deprivation of life contrary to Article 2 of the European Convention of Human Rights.[95] But why one cannot be intentionally deprived of life by omission the judgment in that case failed to explain. The judgment, rather than reinforcing *Bland,* serves only to confirm the incoherence of the distinction *Bland* drew between intentional killing by injection and intentional killing by dehydration. Further

---

[91] See Ch 11, text at nn 22–3.

[92] McGee (n 61) 379 (emphasis in original).

[93] "Given the international conventions protecting 'the right to life', to which I will return later, I conclude that it is impermissible to deny that every life has an equal inherent value. Life is worthwhile in itself whatever the diminution in one's capacity to enjoy it and however gravely impaired some of one's vital functions of speech, deliberation and choice may be.": *Re A* [2001] Fam 147, 187–8, per Ward LJ.

[94] *R v Collins and Ashworth Hospital Authority, ex p Brady* [2000] 8 Lloyd's Rep Med 355, 367.

[95] *NHS Trust A v M; NHS Trust B v H* [2001] Fam 348.

lessening the authority of *Bland* and its progeny is the fact that the courts have not had the benefit of proper argument on the IOL.

Dr McGee concludes his paper with a defense of *Bland*. He argues that the lawfulness of withholding/withdrawing treatment "resides exclusively with issues of causation" and not with intention.[96] He argues that with euthanasia, unlike lawful withdrawal of treatment, we "wrest from nature control of our ultimate fate."[97] This approach is not free from difficulty. First, if with euthanasia "we decide when and how we should die, and we ensure thereby that *we* have the last word,"[98] and "we anticipate nature and override it by bringing about the patient's death before its time,"[99] and if the IOL should be understood as "not intentionally taking ultimate control of life and death,"[100] why is it not euthanasia intentionally to kill patients in PVS by removing their feeding tube? "Nature" will allow patients in PVS to live for years if we provide them with food and fluids and to die of dehydration if we do not. Nature is not a moral agent: we are. It is up to us to make a moral decision as to what course nature should take. To categorize intentionally ending life by lethal injection as "interfering with nature" and intentionally ending life by dehydration as "letting nature take its course" smacks more of semantics than ethics. As Lord Mustill observed in *Bland*: "Emollient expressions such as 'letting nature take its course' and 'easing the passing' may have their uses, but they are out of place here, for they conceal both the ethical and the legal issues.[101] Second, Lord Mustill also commented that it does not perhaps follow that if the doctor's withdrawal of tube-feeding is lawful it is not also a cause of death. He continued:

but this is of no interest since if the conduct is lawful the doctors have nothing to worry about. If on the other hand the proposed conduct is unlawful, then it is in the same case as active euthanasia or any other unlawful act by doctors or laymen. In common sense they must all be causative or none; and it must be all, for otherwise euthanasia would never be murder.[102]

Further, as Lord Browne-Wilkinson noted, the doctor who withdraws tube-feeding does not commit the *actus reus* of murder if he or she is under no duty to continue tube-feeding.[103] Is it not therefore the absence of a

---

[96] McGee (n 61) 384.
[97] Ibid 382.
[98] Ibid (emphasis in original).
[99] Ibid 383.
[100] Ibid 384.
[101] *Bland* 886–7.
[102] Ibid 895–6.
[103] Ibid 883–4.

duty which establishes the lack of causation (if it establishes even that)? In short, McGee's argument from causation seems circular if not irrelevant.

Dr McGee's paper is a welcome contribution to the surprisingly sparse medico-legal literature generated by one of the most important cases in English law. Sadly, his paper is not free from misunderstanding and obscurity. He seems sometimes to mistake my critique of the law for an account of the law. Moreover, his analysis of concepts basic to the IOL, particularly intention and futility, is fragile . His bold attempt to square *Bland*'s ethical circle is unlikely to convince those (whether adherents or opponents of the IOL) who agree that the law bequeathed by that case was indeed "morally and intellectually misshapen."

VII CONCLUSIONS

First, the IOL has long offered a coherent middle way between the extremes of "vitalism" on the one hand and "Quality of life" on the other. *Bland* represented a swerve toward the Quality of life extreme, accepting that life in PVS is of no benefit and may lawfully be intentionally terminated by omission. Second, *Bland* left the law in a "morally and intellectually misshapen" state, prohibiting active, intentional killing but permitting (if not requiring) intentional killing by omission, even by those under a duty to care for the patient. The significance of the decision was profound: although the Walton Committee reaffirmed that active killing, even on request, should not be made lawful, the Law Lords decided that intentional killing by dehydration even without request, was.[104] The making of such a fundamental change to the law seems, moreover, difficult to reconcile with the guidelines for judicial development of the law laid down by the House of Lords in *C v DPP*.[105] Third, to the extent that the Law Lords have embraced the Quality of life principle, and effectively delegated the judgment of which lives are of no benefit to medical opinion, there is little reason to expect that judgment to be confined to patients in PVS. Fourth, the Law Lords' rejection of the IOL appears to have been based on a misunderstanding of that principle. Lord Mustill, surely

---

[104] On the question of tube-feeding patients in PVS, the Committee was divided between those who regarded it as basic care which should be provided and those who regarded it as medical treatment which could properly be withdrawn. Nevertheless, the Committee was unanimous that the question need not, indeed should not, usually arise since it was proper to withdraw medical treatment, including antibiotics, from such patients. However, by confining itself to considering active killing and ignoring intentional killing by omission the Committee did not resolve the inconsistency in the law created by *Bland*.

[105] [1996] 1 AC 1, 28. See also *Bland* 865 (Lord Goff); ibid 880 (Lord Browne-Wilkinson); ibid 890 (Lord Mustill).

rightly, observed[106] that it was a great pity that the Attorney-General had not appeared to represent the interests of the state in maintaining citizens' lives. It is to be hoped that the Attorney will appear in an appropriate future case to represent, articulate, and defend the traditional ethic. Fifth, the decision whether to withdraw treatment and tube-feeding from a patient in PVS should be based on an evaluation of the worth-whileness of the treatment, not the supposed worthwhileness of the patient. While there appears to be a broad consensus that it is proper to withdraw treatment in such a case, there is a good argument that tube-feeding constitutes basic care and that it should, at least presumptively, be provided. Even if it were the better view that it may be withdrawn, this should be because it, and not the patient, is judged futile. Finally, the law's shape may well have been restored by section 4(5) of the Mental Capacity Act 2005, but it remains to be seen how that provision is interpreted by the courts.

POSTSCRIPT

In late September 2011 the first application to withdraw tube-feeding from a patient diagnosed to be in a "minimally conscious state" (MCS) was decided by Baker J.[107] In 2003 the patient, M, then aged 43, was struck down by viral encephalitis which caused extensive and irreparable brain damage. Since then she had been totally dependent on others for her care and had been fed via a gastrostomy tube. She was initially diagnosed as being in PVS and in 2007 members of her family, with the support of her doctors, applied to the High Court for a declaration that the doctors might lawfully discontinue her tube-feeding. It was then discovered that M was not in PVS but was in MCS and was aware to some extent of herself and her environment. The family nevertheless decided to proceed with the application, which came before Baker J in 2011 in the new Court of Protection, to which the jurisdiction to hear such applications had been transferred by the Mental Capacity Act 2005.[108]

M's family argued that withdrawal of the tube-feeding was in M's best interests as it would accord with M's past and present wishes and feelings. M's sister, B, and M's partner, S, testified that M had previously made statements indicating that she would not want to be kept alive in her

---

[106] *Bland* 889.
[107] *W (by her litigation friend B) and M (by her litigation friend, the Official Solicitor) and S and A NHS Primary Care Trust* [2011] EWHC 2443 (Fam) ("*W*").
[108] Ibid paras 1–3.

present condition.[109] The Official Solicitor on behalf of M submitted that where a person was in an MCS and was otherwise clinically stable it could never be in that person's interests to withhold or withdraw life-sustaining treatment, including tube-feeding. Just as PVS cases did not involve a "balance sheet" analysis of best interests, neither did MCS cases where the patient was clinically stable.[110] The Official Solicitor submitted that, even if a "balance sheet" approach were applicable, it came down clearly in favor of continuing tube-feeding.[111] The Primary Care Trust did not support the application to withdraw tube-feeding. The staff caring for M reported that she could express emotion and appeared at times to experience pleasure. It did not appear to the Trust that her life had no positive aspects to weigh against the discomforts she might at times experience. In the absence of a very clear and unambiguous statement of the patient's wishes in anticipation of the situation which had arisen, the Trust could not take the family's views of M's wishes as a direction of how it should proceed.[112]

Baker J helpfully set out the relevant authorities, in particular *Bland*. He quoted extensively from what he said was generally accepted as the principal speech in the House of Lords in that case, that of Lord Goff.[113] Baker J stated that the key principles to be drawn from that speech were:

(1) the principle of the sanctity of life is fundamental; (2) that principle is not, however, absolute and may yield in certain circumstances, for example to the principle of self-determination; (3) a decision whether ANH (artificial nutrition and hydration) treatment should be initiated or withdrawn must be determined by what is in the best interests of the patient; (4) in the great majority of cases the best interests of the patient were likely to require that the treatment should be given; (5) there was a category of case in which the decision whether to withhold treatment would be made by weighing up relevant and competing considerations, but (6) such an approach was inappropriate in the case of Anthony Bland as the treatment had no therapeutic purpose and was "futile" because he was unconscious and had no prospects of recovery.[114]

Baker J noted that the authorities also established that the burden of establishing that withdrawal of treatment was in a person's best interests was always on those asserting it: there was a very strong presumption in favor of taking all steps which would prolong life and, in cases of doubt,

---

[109] Ibid paras 5–6.
[110] Ibid para 36.
[111] Ibid para 37.
[112] Ibid para 39.
[113] Ibid paras 62–64.
[114] Ibid para 65.

that doubt fell to be resolved in favor of life.[115] Moreover, in determining the best interests of an incapacitated adult, the courts had developed a "balance sheet" approach, noting benefits and disbenefits to the patient and making some estimate of the possibility that the gains and losses might accrue. Only if the account was in "relatively significant credit" would a judge conclude that the application was likely to advance the best interests of the incompetent person.[116] And in drawing up the balance sheet, the court was concerned not only with medical but with other factors bearing on the welfare of the individual.[117] Further, the suggestion that in the case of patients other than those in PVS the test was whether the circumstances were "intolerable" to the patient, had been disapproved in the Court of Appeal as a potentially contentious gloss on the best interests test.[118]

Baker J then turned to the Mental Capacity Act 2005. Under section 1(4) the cardinal principle was that a decision made for or on behalf of an incapacitated person under the Act must be made in that person's best interests.[119] Section 4 set out the steps to be taken to determine what was in a person's best interests, including considering the person's past and present wishes and feelings and the beliefs and values that would be likely to influence his or her decision if he or she had capacity, as well as the views of anyone engaged in caring for the person or interested in his or her welfare.[120] The Code of Practice to the Act offered guidance at paragraphs 5.29 to 5.36 as to how to ascertain best interests when deciding about life-sustaining treatment. Paragraph 5.31 noted that all reasonable steps which were in the person's best interests should be taken to prolong life and that the decision-maker must not be motivated by a desire to bring about death for whatever reason, even compassion.[121] Baker J emphasized that while any decision-maker was bound to consider the person's wishes and feelings, and the beliefs, values, and other factors he or she would have taken into account if he or she had capacity, the decision must be based on the person's best interests, not on what the person would have decided if he or she had capacity. That "best interests" was not "substituted judgment" was confirmed by paragraph 5.38 of the Code of Practice which made it clear that

---

[115] Ibid para 73.
[116] Ibid para 74.
[117] Ibid para 75.
[118] Ibid para 76.
[119] Ibid para 79.
[120] Ibid.
[121] Ibid para 80.

the person's wishes and feelings would not necessarily determine his or her best interests.[122] Baker J then turned to the European Convention on Human Rights. He noted that Butler-Sloss P had held in *NHS Trust A v M*[123] that *Bland* was consistent with the Convention. In Baker J's judgment, a best interests assessment, properly conducted under English law in accordance with established principles, was fully compliant with the Convention.[124]

The judge continued that although there was little dispute between the parties about the above principles, there was one area of disagreement: whether the court should adopt a "balance sheet" approach in respect of a patient in MCS.[125] The Official Solicitor submitted that it should not be adopted where the MCS patient was, as in M's case, clinically stable, but the applicant and the Primary Care Trust submitted that it should be adopted.[126] Baker J ruled that there was no reason for extending the approach adopted in *Bland* in respect of patients in PVS to patients in MCS. Lord Goff in *Bland* had specifically distinguished between cases where it may not be in a patient's best interests in all the circumstances to continue treatment, and cases in which a patient was permanently insensate and thus unable to benefit at all from the treatment. There was, Baker J added, no justification for introducing a requirement of clinical instability before embarking on a balance sheet analysis in MCS cases. To do so would not only introduce an impermissible gloss on the best interests test laid down in section 4 of the Mental Capacity Act 2005 but would also provoke lengthy satellite arguments on the meaning of "clinical stability".[127] Clinical stability was, however, an important factor to be taken into account in the balance sheet analysis itself.[128]

Baker J reviewed the evidence, including the evidence of M's relatives and partner; the care home staff who looked after M; an expert in brain injury assessment who had conducted two SMART (Sensory Modality Assessment and Rehabilitation Technique) assessments of M; and two experts in rehabilitation medicine.[129] The judge then engaged in a "best interests" analysis, which encompassed several important factors: the preservation of life; M's wishes and feelings; her experience of pain; her enjoyment of life; her prospects of recovery; her dignity; and the wishes

---

[122] Ibid para 81.
[123] [2001] Fam 348.
[124] *W* para 96.
[125] Ibid para 98.
[126] Ibid paras 100–101.
[127] Ibid para 102.
[128] Ibid para 103.
[129] Ibid paras 104–218.

and feelings of family members and carers.[130] Drawing up a "balance sheet", the judge then listed the advantages and disadvantages of withdrawing M's tube-feeding.[131] While he accepted the previous statements made by M as recounted by B and S, those statements had not been directed to the question which had subsequently arisen—whether to withdraw tube-feeding from M in a minimally conscious state—nor did those statements provide a clear indication some eight years from the onset of her illness as to what M would now want to happen. While the judge took M's previous statements into account, he did not attach significant weight to them.[132] The principle of the right to life was "of the most profound importance" which "carries great weight in any balancing exercise".[133] Although M did experience pain and discomfort, and her disability severely restricted what she could do, she did have positive experiences and, importantly, there was a reasonable prospect that those experiences could be extended by a planned programme of increased stimulation.[134] In the light of all the evidence, the judge arrived at the "clear conclusion" that it was not in M's best interests for her tube-feeding to be withdrawn and he therefore refused the application.[135]

Baker J's refusal of the application, and his ruling that the factor of substantial weight in the case was the preservation of life, is significant and welcome. No less welcome is his ruling that in determining the best interests of an incapacitated adult under section 4 of the Mental Capacity Act 2005, the adult's previously expressed wishes are not decisive and that the criterion is "best interests" not "substituted judgment". As we noted in Chapter 1, section 4 is phrased in controversially subjective terms.[136] Baker J properly reaffirmed that best interests is an essentially objective concept.[137] It would have been all too easy for him to have ruled that life in MCS is no better, if not worse, than life in PVS, and to have held that the patient's previously expressed wishes, and those of her family and partner, sufficed to establish that continued tube-feeding was not in her best interests.

---

[130]   Ibid paras 220–242.
[131]   Ibid paras 247–248.
[132]   Ibid paras 6, 250.
[133]   Ibid para 222.
[134]   Ibid paras 8, 251.
[135]   Ibid paras 252, 9.
[136]   Chapter 1, Part III.D.2.
[137]   It is surprising that the judge did not invoke s 4(5) of the Act. The evidence from B and S about M's wishes suggested that M would rather have been dead than in MCS and that the withdrawal of tube-feeding was being sought as a way of bringing about her death. B testified: "It's not a life, it's an existence and I know she wouldn't want it": *W* para 112. S said: "She wouldn't want to continue with this burdensome life with a lack of dignity": ibid para 119.

The law after this case remains, however, unsatisfactory. First, as the judge pointed out, had M made an "advance decision" in compliance with the Mental Capacity Act 2005 that she would not want to be tube-fed were she ever in MCS, that decision would have been binding.[138] Second, the key authority invoked by the judge was *Bland*, and we noted earlier in this chapter some serious objections to the reasoning in that case. True, the judge cited the speech in *Bland* which was the least offensive to the inviolability of life, that of Lord Goff, but even Lord Goff misunderstood the principle by claiming that it is not absolute as by yielding to the principle of self-determination, a misunderstanding repeated by Baker J. As noted in Chapter 1, the principle of the inviolability of life, though not vitalistic, is indeed absolute.[139] Baker J rightly emphasized that the principle was of "the most profound importance" and "carries great weight in any balancing exercise".[140] But in drawing up the "balance sheet" listing the advantages and disadvantages of withdrawing M's tube-feeding, he listed as advantages: that she would be freed from "the indignities of her current circumstances"; that it would accord with comments she made prior to her illness, with what her family members believed she would have wanted, and with what they wanted, and that she would be spared further years of life in MCS.[141] These "advantages" are difficult to reconcile with the inviolability of life which holds that, whatever *undignified circumstances* a patient may find him or herself in (such as the double incontinence which affected M), and whatever the patient or others may think about the worth of the patient's life, the patient always retains his or her *inherent and ineliminable dignity* as a human being. The "balance sheet" approach was held to favor M's continued life, but it is not difficult to see how the calculation could have gone the other way. And what if M had not been receiving the high quality of care provided by her impressive team of carers? What if, like so many unfortunate, vulnerable patients, the quality of her care had been inadequate? Moreover, Baker J cited *NHS Trust A v M a*s authority that *Bland* is consistent with the European Convention. But, as we noted in our discussion of that case, Butler-Sloss P failed to explain *why* intentionally ending a patient's life by deliberately withdrawing tube-feeding does not breach Article 2. Further, at one point, Baker J commented that a patient in MCS is "recognisably alive" in a way that a patient in PVS is not.[142] Patients in MCS or in PVS are, however, living

---

[138]   *W* para 6.
[139]   Chapter 1, Part III.D.1.
[140]   Ibid paras 7; 249.
[141]   Ibid para 247.
[142]   *W* para 221.

human beings who, although profoundly disabled, enjoy an equality in dignity with those who are not disabled. And M's case illustrated that the borderline between MCS and PVS is far from bright. As Baker J pointed out, "a very significant proportion" of patients who were diagnosed as being in PVS prior to the development of assessment tools such as SMART have later been diagnosed as being in MCS.[143] How many patients have been misdiagnosed as being in PVS, have had their tube-feeding removed, and have been aware as they have suffered a slow death from dehydration?

---

[143] Ibid para 56.

BIBLIOGRAPHY

"About Derek Humphry" <http://www.finalexit.org/dhumphry>.

'Adviser sparks infanticide debate' BBC News Channel, 26 January 2004 <http://news.bbc.co.uk/1/hi/health/3429269.stm>

"Ageing Europe confronts demographic time bomb", *The Times*, 23 June 2007.

Alexander, L, "Medical Science under Dictatorship" (1949) 241 New England Journal of Medicine 39.

Alghrani, A, et al., "Healthcare scandals in the NHS: crime and punishment" (2011) 37 Journal of Medical Ethics 230.

Alleyne, R and M Beckford, "Patients in 'vegetative' state can think and communicate", *Daily Telegraph*, 3 February 2010.

Ambrose, *Concerning Virgins*.

Amundsen, DW, "Suicide and Early Christian Values" in BA Brody (ed), *Suicide and Euthanasia* (Kluwer Academic Publishers, 1989) 77.

Andrews, K (1995) 311 BMJ 1437, Letters.

——et al., "Misdiagnosis of the Vegetative State: Retrospective Study in a Rehabilitation Unit" (1996) 313 BMJ 13.

Annas, GJ, "A French Homunculus in a Tennessee Court" (1989) 19 Hastings Center Report 20.

Annual Register . . . for the Year 1812 (1813).

Anscombe, GEM, "Glanville Williams' *The Sanctity of Life and the Criminal Law: A Review*" in M Geach and L Gormally (eds), *Human Life, Action and Ethics: Essays by GEM Anscombe* (Imprint Academic, 2005) 243.

Archbold: Criminal Pleading, Evidence and Practice (43rd edn, Sweet & Maxwell, 1988) vol 2.

Asterley Jones, P and RIE Card (eds), *Cross and Jones' Introduction to Criminal Law* (10th edn, Butterworths Law, 1984).

Appleby, T, "Suicide law falls short, activist says", *Globe & Mail*, 7 December 1994, A10.

Aquinas, *Summa Theologiae*.

Association of Lawyers for the Defence of the Unborn, Newsletter (1979) no 1.

Atkinson, SB, "Life, Birth and Live-Birth" (1904) 20 LQR 134.

Augustine, *Questions on Exodus.*

Augustine, *The City of God.*

Babylonian Talmud Sanhedrin.

Bartley, OW, *A Treatise on Forensic Medicine* (Barry and Son, 1815).

Basil, *Letters.*

Battin, MP, et al., "Legal Physician-assisted dying in Oregon and the Netherlands: evidence concerning the impact on patients in 'vulnerable' groups" (2007) 33 Journal of Medical Ethics 591.

Beauchamp, TL and JF Childress, *Principles of Biomedical Ethics* (6th edn, Oxford University Press, 2008).

Beck, TR, *Elements of Medical Jurisprudence* (2nd edn, John Anderson, 1825).

Beckford, M, "Elderly suffer poor care in half of NHS hospitals", *Daily Telegraph,* 13 October 2011.

Black, E, *War Against the Weak* (FourWallsEightWindows, 2003).

Blackstone, W, *Commentaries on the Laws of England* (Clarendon Press, Oxford, 1765–1769) vol 1.

Boggan, S, "Reborn", *Guardian,* 11 September 2006.

Bowles, TGA and MNM Bell, "Abortion—A Clarification" (1979) 129 NLJ 944.

Boyle, J, "A Case for Sometimes Tube-Feeding Patients in Persistent Vegetative State" in J Keown (ed), *Euthanasia Examined* (Cambridge University Press, 1995).

Bradley, G, "Life's Dominion: A Review Essay" (1993) 69(2) Notre Dame Law Review 329.

—— "Academic Integrity Betrayed", First Things (August/September 1990) 10.

Brazier, M, *Medicine, Patients and the Law* (Penguin, 1992).

—— and J Miola, "Bye Bye Bolam: a Medical Litigation Revolution?" (2000) 8 Med L Rev 85.

Brennan, F, et al., "Pain Management: A Fundamental Human Right" (2007) 105 Anaesthesia and Analgesia 205.

——"Palliative Care as an International Human Right" (2007) 33(5) Journal of Pain and Symptom Management 494.

British Medical Association, "Annual Report of Council: Protection of Unborn Children" [1928] 1 BMJ Supp 137.

—— "Euthanasia and Physician-Assisted Suicide: Do the Moral Arguments Differ?" in Physician-Assisted Suicide Debating Pack PAS4 (2000).

Burleigh, M, *Death and Deliverance: "Euthanasia" in Nazi Germany c.1900–1935* (Cambridge University Press, 1995).

Burns, J, *The Principles of Midwifery* (3rd edn, Longman, Rees, Orme, Brown, Green & Longman, 1814).

Butterworth's Medical Dictionary (2nd edn, Butterworths, 1978, reprinted 1990).

Byrn, RM, "An American Tragedy: The Supreme Court on Abortion" (1973) 41 Fordham Law Review 807.

Caldwell, S, "Now the Dutch turn against legalised mercy killing", *Daily Mail*, 9 December 2009.

Callahan, D, "Organized Obfuscation: Advocacy for Physician-Assisted Suicide" (2008) 38(5) Hastings Center Report (2008) 30.

Campbell, Baroness et al., "Open Letter from Leaders of Disabled People's Movement in UK and USA" <http://www.carenotkilling.org.uk/?show = 775>.

Campbell, W and AD Campbell, *Introduction to the Study and Practice of Midwifery* (2nd edn, Longman, Rees, Orme, Brown, Green & Longman, 1843).

Catholic Bishops' Conference, "Intervention of the Catholic Bishops' Conference of England and Wales pursuant to Art 36 § 2 of the Convention" (available online using this search parameter).

Capron, AM, "Legalizing Physician-Aided Death" (1996) 5(1) Cambridge Quarterly of Healthcare Ethics 10.

Carter, G, "The Legal Definition of Live Birth" [1926] 2 BMJ 385.

Chin, AE et al., "Legalized Physician-Assisted Suicide in Oregon—the First Year's Experience" (1999) 340 New England Journal of Medicine 577.

Chrysostom, J, *Commentary On Galatians.*

Church Assembly Board for Social Responsibility, *Decisions about Life and Death* (1965).

Churchill's Illustrated Medical Dictionary (ed R Koenigsberg, Churchill Livingstone, 1989).

Clement Of Alexandria, *Stromata.*

Cohen-Almagor, R, *Euthanasia in the Netherlands* (Springer, 2004).

Coke, E, *Institutes* (1641) vol 3.

Coope, CM, *Worth and Welfare in the Controversy over Abortion* (Palgrave Macmillan, 2006).

Cronin, DA, *Ordinary and Extraordinary Means* (St Augustine's Press, 2009).

Curran, WJ, (1958) 71 Harvard Law Review 585.

Daly, CB, *Morals, Law and Life* (Scepter, 1966).

Davies, DS, "Child-Killing in English Law" (1937) 1 MLR 203.

Degler, C, *At Odds: Women and the Family in America from the Revolution to the Present* (Oxford University Press, 1980).

Dellapenna, JW, "Brief of the American Academy of Medical Ethics" *Planned Parenthood of Southeastern Pennsylvania v Casey*, 492 US 490 (1992).

—— *Dispelling the Myths of Abortion History* (Carolina Academic Press, 2006).

Destro, RA, "Abortion and the Constitution: The Need for a Life-Protective Amendment" (1975) 63 California Law Review 1250.

Devlin, P, *Easing the Passing: the Trial of Dr John Bodkin Adams* (The Bodley Head, 1985).

Dickens, BM, *Abortion and the Law* (MacGibbon & Kee, 1966).

—— *Medico-Legal Aspects of Family Law* (Butterworths, 1979).

—— and RJ Cook, "The legal status of in vitro embryos" (2010) 111 International Journal of Gynacology and Obstetrics 91.

Dictionary of Medical and Surgical Knowledge (RK Philp ed, Houlston and Wright 1864).

Didache Dictionary of Medicine (R Quain ed, Longman Green, 1882) vol II.

Donaldson James, S, "Death Drugs Cause Uproar in Oregon", ABC News, 6 August 2008.

Donnelly, RC, (1958) 67 Yale Law Journal 753.

Dorland's Illustrated Medical Dictionary (29th edn, Saunders, 2000).

Dowbiggin, I, *A Merciful End: the Euthanasia Movement in Modern America* (Oxford University Press, 2003).

—— *A Concise History of Euthanasia: Life, Death, God and Medicine* (Rowman & Littlefield Publishers, 2007).

Drife, JO, *The Times*, 5 May 1983, Letters.

Dworkin, R, "The Great Abortion Debate" (1989) 36(11) New York Review of Books.

—— *Life's Dominion. An Argument about Abortion and Euthanasia* (Harper Collins Publishers, 1993).

Edwards, JL (1958) Crim LR 413.

Edwards, RG, *Conception in the Human Female* (Academic Press, 1980).

Edwards, R and P Steptoe, *A Matter of Life* (Sphere Books, 1981).

Ekins, R, "*Yemshaw* and the constitutionality of updating statutes" (unpublished paper delivered at a meeting of the Statute Law Society, London, 9 May 2011).

Emanuel, EJ, "Euthanasia: Where the Netherlands Leads Will the World Follow?" (2001) 322 BMJ 1376.

—— "The History of Euthanasia Debates in the United States and Britain" (1994) 121(10) Annals of Internal Medicine 793.

Evans, M, "One in seven nursing homes breaking the law on feeding patients", *Daily Telegraph*, 16 October 2011.

Exodus.

Falconer, C, "A Right to Die—and a right to clarity in the law", *The Times*, 31 July 2009.

Fenigsen, R, "Dutch Euthanasia: the new government ordered survey" (2004) 20 Issues in Law and Medicine 73.

Finlay, IG and R George, "Legal physician-assisted suicide in Oregon and The Netherlands: evidence concerning the impact on patients in vulnerable groups—another perspective on Oregon's data" (2011) 37 Journal of Medical Ethics 171.

Finnis, J, "Abortion and Legal Rationality" (1970) 3 Adelaide Law Review 431.

—— *The Times*, 5 April 1983, Letters.

—— *Fundamentals of Ethics* (Oxford University Press, 1983).

—— "The Possibility of Criminal Proceedings in respect of Human Embryos Conceived In Vitro and Deliberately not Transferred to the Womb" (unpublished memorandum, 1984).

—— "Intention and Side-Effects" in RG Frey and CW Morris (eds), *Liability and Responsibility* (Cambridge University Press, 1991).

—— "*Bland*: Crossing the Rubicon?" (1993) 109 LQR 329.

—— "'Shameless Acts' in Colorado: Abuse of Scholarship in Constitutional Cases" (1994) 7(4) Academic Questions 10.

—— "We warned them, they mocked us, now we've been proved right", *Sunday Telegraph*, 7 December 2003.

—— "The Mental Capacity Act 2005: some ethical and legal issues" in H Watt (ed), *Incapacity and Care* (The Linacre Centre, 2009) 95.

—— *Intention and Identity* (Oxford University Press, 2011).

—— "Invoking the Principle of Legality against the Rule of Law" in R Ekins (ed), *Modern Challenges to the Rule of Law* (LexisNexis, 2011).

—— *Natural Law and Natural Rights* (2nd edn, Clarendon Press, 2011).

—— J Boyle and G Grisez, *Nuclear Deterrence, Morality and Realism* (Clarendon Press, 1988).

Fisher, A, *Catholic Bioethics for a New Millennium* (Cambridge University Press, 2011).

Fitzpatrick, FJ, *Ethics in Nursing Practice* (The Linacre Centre, 1988).

Foley, K and H Hendin, "The Oregon Report: Don't Ask, Don't Tell" (1999) 29(3) Hastings Center Report 37.

—— "The Oregon Experiment" in K Foley and H Hendin (eds), *The Case Against Assisted Suicide: For the Right to End-of-Life Care* (The Johns Hopkins University Press, 2002) 144.

Forsythe, CD, "Homicide of the Unborn Child: The Born Alive Rule and other Legal Anachronisms" (1987) 21 Valparaiso Law Review 563.

Foster, C, *Choosing Life, Choosing Death: The Tyranny of Autonomy in Medical Ethics and Law* (Hart Publishing, 2009).

Freedman, EB, "Historical Interpretation and Legal Advocacy: Rethinking the Webster Amicus Brief" (1990) 12(3) Public Historian 27.

Freeman, M, "Denying Death its Dominion: Thoughts on the Dianne Pretty Case" (2002) 10 MLR 245.

Friedson, E, "Review Essay: Kennedy's Masked Future" (1982) 4 Sociology of Health and Illness (1982) 95.

Ganzini, L et al., "Prevalence of Depression and Anxiety in Patients Requesting Physicians' Aid in Dying: Cross-Sectional Survey" (2008) 337 BMJ 1682.

Garrow, DJ, *Liberty and Sexuality: The Right to Privacy and the Making of Roe v Wade* (University of California Press, 1994).

Gearty, C, "Too much for a single law officer?", *The Tablet*, 8 August 2009.

George, K, "A Woman's Choice? The Gendered Risks of Voluntary Euthanasia and Physician-Assisted Suicide" (2007) 15 Med L Rev 1.

George, RP and P Lee, *Body-Self Dualism in Contemporary Ethics and Politics* (Cambridge University Press, 2007).

—— and C Tollefsen, *Embryo: A Defense of Human Life* (2nd edn, The Witherspoon Institute, 2011).

Gillon, R, "Foresight is not necessarily the same as intending" (1999) 318 BMJ 1431.

Glover, J, *Causing Death and Saving Lives* (Penguin, 1990).

Goff, R, "The Mental Element in the Crime of Murder" 104 LQR (1988) 30.

Gomez, C, *Regulating Death: Euthanasia and the Case of the Netherlands* (The Free Press, 1991).

Gómez-Lobo, A, *Morality and the Human Goods* (Georgetown University Press, 2002).

Good, JM, *The Study of Medicine* (Baldwin, Cradock, and Joy, 1822) vol IV.

Goodhart, CB, "Abortion Freedom" <http://www.galtoninstitute.org.uk/Newsletters/GINL9406/abortion_freedom.htm>

Gormally, L, "Reflections on Horan and Boyle" in L Gormally (ed), *The Dependent Elderly* (Cambridge University Press, 1992).

—— "Definitions of Personhood: Implications for the Care of PVS Patients" (1993) 9(3) Ethics and Medicine.

—— (ed), *Euthanasia, Clinical Practice and the Law* (St Augustine Press, 1994).

—— "Walton, Davies, Boyd and the Legalization of Euthanasia" in J Keown (ed), *Euthanasia Examined: Ethical, Clinical and Legal Perspectives* (Cambridge University Press, 1995) 113.

—— "Terminal sedation and the doctrine of the sanctity of life" in Torbjörn Tännsjö (ed), *Terminal Sedation: Euthanasia in Disguise?* (Springer, 2004) 81.

—— "The Good of Health and the Ends of Medicine" in H Zaborowski (ed), *Natural Moral Law in Contemporary Society* (The Catholic University of America Press, 2010).

Gorsuch, NM, *The Future of Assisted Suicide and Euthanasia* (Princeton University Press, 2006).

Gostin, LO, "Dedicatory Essay: Honoring Ian McColl Kennedy" (1997–8) 14(1) Journal of Contemporary Health Law and Policy v.

Griffiths, J et al., *Euthanasia and Law in Europe* (Hart Publishing, 2008).

—— *Euthanasia and Law in the Netherlands* (Amsterdam University Press, 1998).

Grisez, GG, *Abortion: The Myths, the Realities, and the Arguments* (Corpus Books, 1970).

—— and J Boyle, *Life and Death with Liberty and Justice* (University of Notre Dame Press, 1979).

Groenewoud, JH et al., "Clinical Problems with the Performance of Euthanasia and Physician-Assisted Suicide in the Netherlands" (2000) 342 New England Journal of Medicine 551.

Grossberg, M, *Governing the Hearth: Law and the Family in Nineteenth-Century America* (University of North Carolina Press, 1985).

—— "The Webster Brief: History as Advocacy, or Would You Sign It?" (1990) 12(3) Public Historian 45.

Grubb, A, "Glanville Williams: A Personal Appreciation" (1998) 6(2) Med L Rev 133.

—— "The legal status of the frozen human embryo" in A Grubb (ed), *Challenges in Medical Care* (John Wiley & Sons, 1992).

—— (ed), *Medical Law: Text with Materials* (3rd edn, Butterworths, 2000).

Gwyther, L et al., "Advancing Palliative Care as a Human Right" (2009) 38(5) Journal of Pain and Symptom Management 767.

Hamilton, NG, "Oregon's culture of silence" in K Foley and H Hendin (eds), *The Case against Assisted Suicide: For the Right to End-of-Life Care* (The Johns Hopkins University Press, 2002) 175.

Hammelmann, HA (1959) 22 MLR 343.

Harris, J, *The Value of Life* (Routledge & Kegan Paul, 1985).

Hawkes, R, *Daily Telegraph*, 26 February 2010, Letters.

Hawkins, W, *A Treatise of the Pleas of the Crown* (1716).

Hendin, H, *Seduced by Death: Doctors: Patients and Assisted Suicide* (WW Norton, 1998).

—— and K Foley, "Physician-Assisted Suicide in Oregon: A Medical Perspective" (2008) 106 Michigan Law Review 1613.

Hoche, A and K Binding, *Die Freigabe der Vernichtung Lebensunwertem Lebens* (Felix Meiner Verlag, 1920).

Hooper, R, *Lexicon Medicum: or Medical Dictionary* (7th edn, by K Grant, Longman, Hurst, Rees, Orme, and Co, 1839).

Horan, DJ, CD Forsythe, and ER Grant, "Two Ships Passing in the Night: An Interpretavist Review of the White-Stevens Colloquy on *Roe v Wade*" (1987) 6 St Louis University Law Review 229.

Hough, A, "'Disastrous' £11.4 bn NHS IT programme to be abandoned", *Daily Telegraph*, 21 September 2011.

Hughes-Hallett, T et al., *Palliative Care Funding Review* (<http://www.palliativecarefunding.org>, 2011).

Human Rights Watch, *Global State of Pain Treatment* (2011).

Humphry, D, "Oregon's Assisted Suicide Law Gives No Sure Comfort in Dying", *New York Times*, 3 December 1994, Letters.

International Association for the Study of Pain, *The Declaration of Montreal* (2010).

International Dictionary of Medicine and Biology (ed SI Landau et al., Churchill Livingstone, 1986).

Jackson, E, *Medical Law: Text, Cases and Materials* (Oxford University Press, 2006).

—— "Secularism, Sanctity and the Wrongness of Killing" (2008) 3 Biosocieties 125.

—— "Whose Death is it Anyway?" (2004) 57(1) Current Legal Problems 415.

—— and J Keown, *Debating Euthanasia* (Hart Publishing, 2012).

Jerome, *Letters*.

Jochemsen, H, "Dutch Court Decisions on Nonvoluntary Euthanasia Critically Reviewed" (1998) 13(4) Issues in Law & Medicine 447.

Jones, DA, *The Soul of the Embryo* (Continuum, 2004).

—— "Is there a Logical Slippery Slope from Voluntary to Nonvoluntary Euthanasia?" (2011) 21(4) Journal of the Kennedy Institute of Ethics 379.

Josephus, *Against Apion*.

Kaczor, C, *The Ethics of Abortion: Women's Rights, Human Life and the Question of Justice* (Routledge, 2010).

Kamisar, Y, "Physician-assisted suicide: the last bridge to active voluntary euthanasia" in J Keown (ed), *Euthanasia Examined* (Cambridge University Press, 1995) 225.

—— "Some Non-Religious Views Against Proposed 'Mercy-Killing' Legislation" (1958) 42 Minnesota Law Review 969.

Kaveny, C, "Peaceful and Private", Commonweal, 12 March 2010.

Kennedy, I, *The Unmasking of Medicine* (George Allen & Unwin, 1981).

—— "The Legal and Ethical Implications of Postcoital Birth Control" in *Postcoital Contraception* (Pregnancy Advisory Service, 1982).

—— *Treat Me Right: Essays in Medical Law and Ethics* (Clarendon Press, 1988).

—— "The Quality of Mercy: Doctors, Patients and Dying" (The Upjohn Lecture, 1994).

—— and A Grubb (eds), *Medical Law: Text and Materials* (1st edn, Lexis Law Publishing, 1989).

—— (eds), *Medical Law: Text with Materials* (2nd edn, Lexis Law Publishing, 1994).

Keown, D, *Buddhism and Bioethics* (Macmillan/St Martins Press, 1995).

Keown, IJ, "'Miscarriage': A Medico-Legal Analysis" (1984) Crim LR 604.

—— "Applying *Bland*" (1994) 53 CLJ 456.

—— "Life and Death in Dublin" (1996) 55 CLJ 6.

—— *Abortion, Doctors and the Law* (Cambridge University Press, 1988).

—— "The Law and Practice of Euthanasia in the Netherlands" (1992) 108 LQR 51.

—— (ed), *Euthanasia Examined: Ethical, Clinical and Legal Perspectives* (Cambridge University Press, 1995).

—— "Review of I Kennedy and A Grubb, *Medical Law: Text with Materials* (2nd edn, 1994)" (1995) 54(1) CLJ 190.

—— "Restoring moral and intellectual shape to the law after *Bland*" (1997) 113 LQR 481.

—— "Beyond *Bland*: a critique of the BMA Guidance on withholding and withdrawing treatment" (2000) 20 Legal Studies 66.

—— "The case of Ms B: suicide's slippery slope?" (2002) 28 Journal of Medical Ethics 238.

—— *Euthanasia, Ethics and Public Policy: An Argument against Legalisation* (Cambridge University Press, 2002).

—— "Mr Marty's Muddle: A Superficial and Selective Case for Euthanasia in Europe" (2006) 32 Journal of Medical Ethics 29.

—— "In Need of Assistance?" (2009) 159 NLJ 1340.

—— 'Five Flawed Arguments for Decriminalising Euthanasia' in A Alghrani et al. (eds), *The Criminal Law and Bioethical Conflict: Walking the Tightrope* (Cambridge University Press, forthcoming).

—— "A New Father for Medical Law" in RP George and J Keown (eds), *Reason, Morality and Law: The Philosophy of John Finnis* (Oxford University Press, forthcoming).

—— and Gormally, L, "Human Dignity, Autonomy and Mentally Incapacitated Patients: A Critique of *Who Decides?*" (1999) 4 Journal of Current Legal Issues XX. <http://webjcli.ncl.ac.uk/1999/issue4/rtf/keown4.rtf>.

—— and E Jackson, *Debating Euthanasia* (Hart Publishing, 2011).

Kevles, DJ, *In the Name of Eugenics* (Harvard University Press, 1995).

Keyserlingk, EW, *The Unborn Child's Right to Prenatal Care* (Quebec Research Centre of Private and Comparative Law, 1984).

Kimsma, GK, "Euthanasia Drugs in the Netherlands" in DC Thomasma et al. (eds), *Asking to Die: Inside the Dutch Debate about Euthanasia* (Springer, 1998) 135.

KNMG, *Op zoek naar normen voor het handelen van artsen bij vragen om hulp bij levensbeëindiging in geval van lijden aan het leven: verslag van de werkzaamheden van een commissie onder voorzitterschap van prof. J Dijkhaus* (2004).

—— *The role of the physician in the voluntary termination of life* (2011).

Kuhl, S, *The Nazi Connection: Eugenics, American Racism, and German National Socialism* (Oxford University Press, 1994).

Lactantius, *Divine Institutes*.

"More abortionists" [1861] 1 Lancet 295, Editorial.

Larson, JE and C Spillenger, "That's Not History: The Boundaries of Advocacy and Scholarship" (1990) 12(3) Public Historian 33.

Law, SA, "Conversations Between Historians and the Constitution" (1990) 12(3) Public Historian 11.

Lecky, WEH, *History of European Morals from Augustus to Charlemagne* (Longmans, Green, and Co, 1869).

Lee, P, *Abortion and Unborn Human Life* (2nd edn, Catholic University of America Press, 2010).

Leroi, AM, *Mutants: On the Form, Varieties and Errors of the Human Body* (Harper Perennial, 2005).

Linton, PB, "*Planned Parenthood v Casey*: The Flight from Reason in the Supreme Court" (1993) 13(1) St Louis University Law Review 15.

Macadam, J, "A Duty to Die?", *Life and Work* (October 2008) 23.

Mann, JD, *Forensic Medicine and Toxicology* (P Blackinston's Sons & Co, 1893).

Mann, PS, "Meanings of Death" in M Battin et al. (eds), *Physician-Assisted Suicide: Expanding the Debate* (Routledge, 1998) 11.

Marker, RL, "Assisted Suicide: The Continuing Debate" <http://www.patient-srightscouncil.org/site/assisted-suicide-the-continuing-debate/>.

Marston, C et al., "Impact on contraceptive practice of making emergency hormonal contraception available over the counter in Great Britain: repeated cross sectional surveys" (2005) 331 BMJ 271.

Martyr Justin, *Apology*.

Mason, JK, *Medico-Legal Aspects of Reproduction and Parenthood* (Ashgate, 1998).

—— and GT Laurie, "The Management of the Persistent Vegetative State in the British Isles" (1996) 4 Juridical Review 263.

—— and RA McCall Smith, *Law and Medical Ethics* (2nd edn, Oxford University Press, 1987).

—— and RA McCall Smith, *Law and Medical Ethics* (4th edn, Oxford University Press, 1994).

McCall Smith, A, "Beyond Autonomy" (1997) 14 Journal of Contemporary Health Law and Policy 23.

McCullagh, P, "Thirst in relation to the withdrawal of hydration" (1996) 46(3) Catholic Medical Quarterly 3.

McGee, A, "Finding a Way through the Ethical and Legal Maze: Withdrawal of Medical Treatment and Euthanasia" (2005) 13 Med L Rev 357.

McLaren, A, *Reproductive Rituals* (Methuen, 1984).

Means Jr, CC, "The Law of New York Concerning Abortion and the Status of the Foetus, 1664–1968: A Case of Cessation of Constitutionality" (1968) 14 New York Law Forum 411.

—— "The Phoenix of Abortional Freedom: Is a Penumbral or Ninth Amendment Right About to Arise from the Nineteenth-Century Legislative Ashes of a Fourteenth-Century Common-Law Liberty?" (1971) 17 New York Law Forum 335.

Megarry, RE (1959) 75 LQR 111.

Meier, DE et al., "A National Survey of Physician-Assisted Suicide and Euthanasia in the United States" (1998) 338 New England Journal of Medicine 1193.

Melloni's Illustrated Dictionary of Obstetrics and Gynaecology (ed IG Dox et al., Informa Healthcare, 2000).

Mohr, JC, *Abortion in America. The Origins and Evolution of National Policy* (Oxford University Press, 1978).

—— "Historically Based Legal Briefs: Observations of a Participant in the *Webster* Process" (1990) 12(3) Public Historian 19.

Monti, MM et al., "The Vegetative State" (2010) 341 BMJ c3765.

More, Thomas, *Utopia.*

Morgan, W and AG Macpherson, *The Indian Penal Code* (GC Hay & Co, 1861).

Morton, JD (1959) 37 Canadian Bar Review 241.

Moses, O St J, *Manual of Obstetrics* (1920).

New York State Task Force on Life and the Law, *When Death is Sought: Assisted Suicide and Euthanasia in the Medical Context* (The New York State Task Force, 1994).

Nursing Times, 10 February 1993, 7.

"Obituary: Huibert Drion" (2004) 328 BMJ 1204.

Oderberg, DS and JA Laing (eds), *Human Lives: Critical Essays on Consequentialist Bioethics* (St Martin's Press, 1997).

O'Neill, O, *Autonomy and Trust in Bioethics* (Cambridge University Press, 2002).

Onwuteaka-Philipsen, B et al., *Evaluatie Wet toetsing levensbeeindiging op verzoek en hulp bij zelfdoding* (ZonMW, 2007).

O'Rahilly, R and F Muller, *Human Embryology and Teratology* (3rd edn, Wiley-Liss, 2001).

Oregon Health Authority, "Death with Dignity Act, Current Annual Reports" <http://public.health.oregon.gov/ProviderPartnerResources/Evaluationre-search/deathwithdignityact/Pages/index.aspx>.

Oregon Public Health Division, "Characteristics and end-of-life care of 525 DWDA patients who died after ingesting a lethal dose of medication as of January 7, 2011, by year, Oregon, 1998–2010", Table 1.

Oxford English Dictionary (2nd edn, 1989) vol II; vol III.

Parry, LA, *Criminal Abortion* (John Bale, Sons, and Danielsson Ltd, 1932).

Percival, T, *Medical Ethics* (1803).

Philo, *Special Laws.*

Ponnuru, R, "Aborting History", *National Review,* 23 October 1995.

Pope Pius XII, (1959) 49 *Acta Apostolicae Sedis* 1027.

President's Council on Bioethics, *Human Cloning and Human Dignity: An Ethical Inquiry* (2002).

Price, D, "Fairly Bland: an alternative view of a supposed new 'Death Ethic' and the BMA guidelines" (2001) 21 Legal Studies 618.

—— "What Shape to the Law After *Bland?* Historical, Contemporary and Futuristic Paradigms" (2009) 125 LQR 142.

"Quality of death", *The Economist,* 14 July 2010.

Rafferty, PA, *Roe v Wade: The Birth of a Constitutional Right* (University Microfilm International Dissertation Information Service, Ann Arbor, MI 1993).

Raymond, E et al., "Population Effect of Increased Access to Emergency Contraceptive Pills" (2007) 109 Obstetrics & Gynecology 181.

Reproductive Medicine: from A to Z (HE Reiss, ed, Oxford University Press, 1998).

Rigby, E, *A System of Midwifery* (Lea & Blanchard, 1841).

Robertson, JA, "In the Beginning: the Legal Status of Early Embryos" (1990) 76 Virginia Law Review 437.

Roscoe, L et al., "Dr. Jack Kevorkian and Cases of Euthanasia in Oakland County, Michigan, 1990–1998" (2000) 343 New England Journal of Medicine 1735.

"Roundtable: Historians and the Webster Case" (1990) 12(3) Public Historian 9.

Russell, B (1958) 10 Stanford Law Review 382.

Ryan, M, *A Manual of Medical Jurisprudence and State Medicine* (2nd edn, Sherwood, Gilbert and Piper, 1836).

Seale, C, "End-of-Life Decisions in the UK Involving Medical Practitioners" (2009) 23 Palliative Medicine 198.

Severn, C, *First Lines on the Practice of Midwifery* (S Highley, 1831).

Sheldon, T, "Dutch GP found guilty of murder faces no penalty" (2001) 322 BMJ 509.

—— "Court upholds murder verdict on doctor who ended woman's life" (2003) 326 BMJ 1351.

—— (2004) 329 BMJ 1206.

—— "Dutch doctors adopt guidelines on mercy killing of newborns" (2005) 331 BMJ 126.

Silver, L, *Remaking Eden: Cloning and Beyond in a Brave New World* (William Morrow, 1997).

Simms, M and K Owen, *Abortion Law Reformed* (Peter Owen, 1971).

Singer, P, *Rethinking Life and Death: The Collapse of our Traditional Ethics* (St Martin's Griffin, 1996).

Skegg, PDG, *Law, Ethics and Medicine: Studies in Medical Law* (revised edn, Clarendon Press, 1988).

—— "Criminal Prosecutions of Negligent Health Professionals: The New Zealand Experience" (1998) 6 Med L Rev 220.

—— "Medical Acts Hastening Death" in PDG Skegg et al. (eds), *Medical Law in New Zealand* (Thomson Brookers, 2006) 505.

Smith, ATH (1998) 6(2) Med L Rev 262.

Smith, JC and B Hogan, *Criminal Law* (6th edn, Oxford University Press, 1988).

Smith, JG, *The Principles of Forensic Medicine* (T & G Underwood, 1821).

Somerville, M, *Death Talk* (McGill-Queen's University Press, 2001).

Spencer, JR, "Glanville Williams", *Oxford Dictionary of National Biography* <http://www.oxforddnb.com/view/article/66017>.

Starmer, K, "'Mercy killing' is not the same as assisted suicide", *The Times*, 25 February 2010.

"Statement from the Royal College of Psychiatrists on Physician Assisted Suicide" (2006).

Stedman's Medical Dictionary (27th edn, Lippincott, Williams & Wilkins, 2000).

Tanner, TH, *On the Signs and Diseases of Pregnancy* (Henry Renshaw, 1860).

Tännsjö, T (ed), *Terminal Sedation: Euthanasia in Disguise?* (Springer, 2004).

Taylor, AS, *A Manual of Medical Jurisprudence* (J & A Churchill, 1844).

—— *The Principles and Practice of Medical Jurisprudence* (2nd edn, J & A Churchill, 1873) vol 2.

—— *Taylor's Principles and Practice of Medical Jurisprudence* (ed AK Mant, 13th edn, Churchill Livingstone, 1984).

Temel, JS et al., "Early Palliative Care for Patients with Metastatic Non-Small-Cell Lung Cancer" (2010) 363 New England Journal of Medicine 733.

The Pregnancy Book <http://www.doh.govuk/pregnancybook>.

Tidy, CM, *Legal Medicine* (Smith, Elder, and Co, 1882) vol 2.

Toner, PJ, "Limbo" in *The Catholic Encyclopedia* (Encyclopedia Press, 1913) vol 9.

Tunkel, V, "Modern Anti-Pregnancy Techniques and the Criminal Law" [1974] Crim LR 461.

—— "Late Abortions and the Crime of Child Destruction: (1) A Reply" [1985] Crim LR 133.

Twycross, RG, "Where there is hope, there is life: a view from the hospice" in J Keown (ed), *Euthanasia Examined: Ethical, Clinical and Legal Perspectives* (Cambridge University Press, 1995) 141.

van Delden, JJM et al., "The Remmelink Study: Two Years Later" (1993) 23(6) Hastings Center Report 24.

van der Maas, PJ et al., *Medische beslissingen rond het levenseinde. Het onderzoek voor de Commissie onderzoek medische praktijk inzake euthanasia* (SDU Uitgeverij Plantijnstraat, 1991).

—— and LL Emanuel, "Factual Findings" in LL Emanuel (ed), *Regulating How We Die* (Harvard University Press, 1998) 51.

van der Wal, G et al., *Euthanasie en andere medische beslissingen rond het levenseinde. De praktijk en de meldingsprocedure* (SDU Uitgevers, 1996).

—— *Medische besluitvorming aan het einde van het leven* (De Tijdstroom, 2003).

Verhagen, E and P Sauer, "The Groningen Protocol—Euthanasia in Severely Ill Newborns" (2005) 352 New England Journal of Medicine 959.

Ward, BJ and PA Tate, "Attitudes among NHS doctors to requests for euthanasia" (1994) 308 BMJ 1332.

Wasby, SL, "Amicus Brief" in KL Hall (ed), *The Oxford Companion to the Supreme Court of the United States* (2nd edn, Oxford University Press, 2005).

Watt, H, *Life and Death in Healthcare Ethics: A Short Introduction* (Routledge, 2000).

Westchester Institute, "Emergency Contraceptives and Catholic Healthcare: A New Look at the Science and the Moral Question" (2011).

Westermarck, E, *The Origin and Development of Moral Ideas* (Macmillan, 1906).

Wicks, E, *The Right to Life and Conflicting Interests* (Oxford University Press, 2010).

Widdershoven, G, "Commentary: Euthanasia in Europe: a critique of the Marty report" (2006) 32 Journal of Medical Ethics 34.

Williams, GL (ed), *Salmond on Jurisprudence* (11th edn, Sweet & Maxwell, 1957).

—— "'Mercy-Killing' Legislation—A Rejoinder" (1958) 43 Minnesota Law Review 1.

—— *The Sanctity of Life and the Criminal Law* (revised edn, Faber and Faber, 1958).

—— *Textbook of Criminal Law* (1st edn, Steven & Sons, 1978).

—— *Textbook of Criminal Law* (2nd edn, Steven & Sons, 1983).

—— *The Times*, 13 April 1985, Letters.

—— "Controlling the Repetitive Dangerous Offender" (1993) 1 Med L Rev 1.

Winfield, PH, "The Unborn Child" (1942) 8 CLJ 76.

Witherspoon, JS, "Reexamining *Roe*: Nineteenth-Century Abortion Statutes and the Fourteenth Amendment" (1985) 17(1) St Mary's Law Journal 29.

World Health Organization, "Definition of Palliative Care" <http://www.who.int/cancer/palliative/definition/en/>.

Wright, AH, *A Text-Book of Obstetrics* (D Appleton and Co, 1905).

Wright, G, "Capable of Being Born Alive?" (1981) 131 NLJ 188.

—— "The Legality of Abortion by Prostaglandin" [1984] Crim LR 347.

—— "Late Abortions and the Crime of Child Destruction: (2) A Rejoinder" [1985] Crim LR 140.

Wright, WE, "Permitting the Destruction of Unworthy Life' (1992) 8 Issues in Law & Medicine 231.

Yeung et al. and Austriaco (colloquy) in (2008) 8(2) National Catholic Bioethics Quarterly 217.

OFFICIAL PUBLICATIONS

Constitution, Federalism and Property Rights Subcommittee of the Senate Judiciary Committee, Hearing on the 25th Anniversary of the Supreme Court's Decision in *Roe v Wade*, 105th Congress 13, 21 January 1998, 1998 WL 27127, Federal Document Clearing House.

Council of Europe, "Assistance to patients at end of life", *Report of the Social, Health and Family Affairs Committee*, December 10455, 9 February 2005.

—— Euthanasia, *An Opinion by the Committee on Legal Affairs and Human Rights* Doc 9923, 23 September 2003.

—— "Euthanasia," *Report of the Social, Health and Family Affairs Committee of the Council of Europe* Doc 9898, 10 September 2003.

—— "Protection of the human rights and dignity of the terminally ill and the dying" Recommendation 1418 (1999).

Crown Prosecution Service (CPS), "Decision on Prosecution—The Death by Suicide of Daniel James", 9 December 2008.

—— "Assisted Suicide" (2010).

—— "Policy for Prosecutors in Respect of Cases of Encouraging or Assisting Suicide" (2010).

—— "A public consultation on the DPP's interim policy for prosecutors on assisted suicide" (Crown Prosecution Service, 2009).

Dutch Ministry of Justice, *Outlines* [sic] *Report Commission Inquiry into Medical Practice with Regard to Euthanasia* (The Hague, no date), a summary of *Medische beslissingen rond het levenseinde. Rapport van de Commissie onderzoek medische praktijk inzake euthanasie* (1991).

Medische beslissingen rond het levenseinde. Rapport van de Commissie onderzoek medische praktijk inzake euthanasie (1991).

First and Second reports from the Select Committee on Death Certification Parl Pap (1893–94) XI.

Law Commission Consultation Paper, "A New Homicide Act for England and Wales?", Law Com 177 (2006).

Report of the Committee of Inquiry into Human Fertilisation and Embryology (Cmnd 9314, 1984).

Report of the Committee on the Working of the Abortion Act (Cmnd 5579, 1974) vol 1.

Report of the Interdepartmental Committee on Abortion (1939).

Report of the Select Committee on Medical Ethics (HL Paper 21-I, 1993–4).

Report of the Select Committee on the Assisted Dying for the Terminally Ill Bill (HL Paper 86-I, 2005); Oral and written evidence (HL Paper 86-II); Selected individual submissions (HL Paper 86-III).

UK Department of Health, *End of Life Care Strategy* (2008).

—— *The Pregnancy Book* (2009).

UN Human Rights Committee, "Concluding Observations of the Human Rights Committee: Netherlands" (2001). CCPR/CO/72/NET.

—— "Consideration of Reports Submitted by States Parties Under Article 40 of the Covenant" (25 August 2009). CCPR/C/NLD/CO/4.

INDEX